Elgar Studies

Reflecting the growth of international interest in Elgar's music, this collection of essays brings together leading scholars from the UK and the USA, and covers the broadest range of analytical approaches to his music. It is perhaps in textual analysis and criticism that Elgar studies are showing their most remarkable growth. In this volume, analysts and theorists place Elgar at the centre of research into late tonal music theory – particularly Schenkerian and neo-Riemannian – and the continually burgeoning area of musical hermeneutics. Through study of published scores and recently discovered sketches, different contributions explore Elgar's musical language and treatment of symphonic form, and themes in his music such as empire, race, the pastoral and idyllic, mourning and loss. The essays cover the entire range of current thinking on Elgar's music, and have wide ramifications for future approaches to music of the early twentieth century.

J. P. E. HARPER-SCOTT is Lecturer in Music at Royal Holloway, University of London. He has scholarly interests in Elgar, twentieth-century British music, Schenkerian theory and the philosophy of Heidegger. He is the author of *Edward Elgar, Modernist* (Cambridge University Press, 2006), and a contributor to *The Cambridge Companion to Elgar* (2004). His essays on Elgar have been published in *19th-Century Music* and *Music Analysis*.

JULIAN RUSHTON taught at the universities of Cambridge and East Anglia, and was West Riding Professor of Music at the University of Leeds from 1981 until his recent retirement. He has published principally on Gluck, Mozart, Berlioz and Elgar. His recent books include *The Music of Berlioz* (2001); *The Cambridge Companion to Elgar* (co-edited with Daniel M. Grimley, 2004); *Mozart* (2006); and *Europe, Empire, and Spectacle* (co-edited with Rachel Cowgill, 2006). He is General Editor of the Cambridge Music Handbooks series, to which he has contributed volumes on Berlioz and Elgar, and is also Chairman of *Musica Britannica* and editor of the *Elgar Society Journal*.

ELGAR STUDIES

EDITED BY

J. P. E. Harper-Scott

and

Julian Rushton

CAMBRIDGE UNIVERSITY PRESS
Cambridge, New York, Melbourne, Madrid, Cape Town, Singapore, São Paulo, Delhi

Cambridge University Press
The Edinburgh Building, Cambridge CB2 8RU, UK

Published in the United States of America by Cambridge University Press, New York

www.cambridge.org
Information on this title: www.cambridge.org/9780521861991

First published 2007

Printed in the United Kingdom at the University Press, Cambridge

A catalogue record for this publication is available from the British Library

ISBN 978-0-521-86199-1 hardback

Contents

Contributors

Editors

J. P. E. HARPER-SCOTT, Lecturer in Music, Royal Holloway,
University of London

JULIAN RUSHTON, Emeritus Professor of Music, University of Leeds

Other contributors

DANIEL M. GRIMLEY, Senior Lecturer in Music, University of Nottingham

JAMES HEPOKOSKI, Professor of Music History, Yale University

CHRISTOPHER MARK, Senior Lecturer and Head of Music, Department
of Music and Sound Recording, University of Surrey

PATRICK MCCRELESS, Professor of Music Theory, and Chair, Music
Department, Yale University

CHARLES EDWARD MCGUIRE, Associate Professor of Musicology
at the Oberlin College Conservatory of Music

JOHN PICKARD, Senior Lecturer in Music, University of Bristol

MATTHEW RILEY, Lecturer in Music, University of Birmingham

AIDAN J. THOMSON, Lecturer in Music, Queen's University, Belfast

Preface

In general terms, Elgar studies have made remarkable progress in recent years, with substantial bibliographical and source studies, a revived attempt to publish a complete edition of his music, and a number of biographies (some of this material is included in the core literature for which abbreviations appear below). A number of collections of essays have appeared, including the *Cambridge Companion to Elgar* (2004),[1] that address analytical and critical questions in the context of Elgar's life and times as well as his music. Nevertheless, not much has been written that matches parallel work on some of his contemporaries, notably Debussy and Mahler, in depth of critical penetration and analytical complexity. This volume addresses this situation by gathering essays from a variety of contributors from both sides of the Atlantic.

This is not the first contribution to deep analytical and critical study of Elgar's music, and some of the best work that precedes this volume is by the authors whose more recent work is presented here. The editors were both involved in the *Companion*, as were Daniel M. Grimley (as joint editor and contributor), Christopher Mark, Aidan Thomson, and Charles Edward McGuire; and J. P. E. Harper-Scott has published major essays on the First Symphony and *Falstaff*.[2] A chapter on the symphonies contributed by James Hepokoski is frequently cited in more recent literature.[3] Articles by Aidan J. Thomson, Charles E. McGuire, and Matthew Riley have also appeared in the University of California periodical *19th-Century Music*.[4] Harper-Scott and Riley are also the authors of substantial monographs on the composer.[5]

---

[1] Daniel M. Grimley and Julian Rushton (eds.), *The Cambridge Companion to Elgar* (Cambridge: Cambridge University Press, 2004).

[2] J. P. E. Harper-Scott, '"A nice sub-acid feeling": Schenker, Heidegger, and Elgar's First Symphony', *Music Analysis*, 24 (2005), pp. 349–82; 'Elgar's Invention of the Human: *Falstaff*, Op. 68', *19CM*, 28 (2005), pp. 230–53.

[3] James A. Hepokoski, 'Elgar', in D. Kern Holoman (ed.), *The Nineteenth-Century Symphony* (New York and London: Schirmer, 1997), pp. 327–44.

[4] Aidan J. Thomson, 'Elgar and Chivalry', *19CM*, 28 (2005), pp. 254–75; Charles M. McGuire, 'Elgar, Judas, and the Theology of Betrayal', *19CM*, 23 (2000), pp. 236–72; Matthew Riley, 'Rustling Reeds and Lofty Pines: Elgar and the Music of Nature', *19CM*, 26 (2002), pp. 155–77.

[5] J. P. E. Harper-Scott, *Edward Elgar, Modernist* (Cambridge: Cambridge University Press, 2006); Matthew Riley, *Edward Elgar and the Nostalgic Imagination* (Cambridge: Cambridge University Press, 2007).

As with most composers whose output covers a variety of genres, knowledge of Elgar's music is uneven. Focus on the works of his most glorious years, the two decades from 1899, beginning with the *Variations* ('Enigma'), is natural; and within that, most attention is paid to orchestral and choral music. The symphonic repertory is represented in this collection by the Second Symphony (Harper-Scott), the Cello Concerto (John Pickard, General Editor of the Elgar Society Edition), and the *Introduction and Allegro* for strings (Hepokoski). The choral repertory is represented by works sacred (*The Apostles*: Mark), secular (*The Music Makers*: Thomson), and, lying somewhere in between sacred and secular, *The Spirit of England* (Grimley). Charles Edward McGuire has previously published an important study of the oratorios,[6] and now presents original research on the origins and significance of the major work that immediately preceded the *Variations*, the dramatic cantata *Caractacus*, with particular attention to the librettist and his sources. His essay makes a powerful case for the serious contextual study of Elgar and Empire without theoretical bias, and of the significance of the texts of the choral works, too readily neglected, apologised for, or dismissed as fustian. Julian Rushton's essay on a short cycle of songs should also emphasise, as do Thomson's and Grimley's essays, the important role of literature in Elgar's output; not necessarily of the highest quality, the words of these authors – Acworth, Parker, O'Shaughnessy, and Binyon – are an integral part of some of Elgar's finest works. These authors demonstrate how, through this interaction with literature of love, idealism, and war, Elgar represents the very archetype of a Romantic artist, making universal feelings originating in the most intimate sensations – frustrated affections, private mourning, and grief.

The volume is framed by two essays that study aspects of Elgar's musical language from different perspectives. It is with particular pleasure that the editors welcome the first Elgar essay by Patrick McCreless, whose work has previously concentrated mainly on Wagner, a vitally important figure in Elgar's formation. His study of the taxonomy of Elgar's chromatic procedures is balanced by Matthew Riley's classification – making a virtue of a close focus to draw out far-ranging implications – of an aspect of Elgar's no less characteristic diatonic idiom.

The editors wish to express their gratitude to all the authors for their kindness in working to a deadline despite many calls on their time and energy, and for responding in a positive spirit to our few editorial suggestions. At Cambridge University Press they are grateful to Penny Souster and

---

[6] Charles E. McGuire, *Elgar's Oratorios: The Creation of an Epic Narrative* (Aldershot: Ashgate, 2002).

Victoria Cooper for supporting them in their conception of the project; and to Rebecca Jones and Elizabeth Davey for their help in the editorial process, and to Jonathan De Souza for producing the index. We are also grateful to Novello and the Elgar Will Trust for permission to reproduce score and manuscript materials.

J. P. E. HARPER-SCOTT
Royal Holloway, University of London

JULIAN RUSHTON
University of Leeds

Abbreviations

19CM	*19th-Century Music*
Anderson, *Elgar*	Robert Anderson, *Elgar* (London: Dent, 1993)
Anderson, *Manuscript*	Robert Anderson, *Elgar in Manuscript* (London: British Library, and Portland, OR: Amadeus Press, 1990)
Companion	Daniel M. Grimley and Julian Rushton (eds.), *The Cambridge Companion to Elgar* (Cambridge: Cambridge University Press, 2004)
EB	Elgar Birthplace Museum
ECE	Elgar Complete Edition (London: Novello, 1981–); continued as Elgar Society Edition (London: Elgar Society, 2002–)
ESJ	*Elgar Society Journal*
Future	Edward Elgar, 'A Future For English Music' and Other Lectures, ed. Percy M. Young (London: D. Dobson, 1968)
JAMS	*Journal of the American Musicological Society*
Kennedy, *Portrait*	Michael Kennedy, *Portrait of Elgar*, 3rd edition (Oxford: Clarendon Press, 1987)
Kent, *Guide*	Christopher Kent, *Edward Elgar: A Guide to Research* (New York: Garland, 1993)
Lifetime	*Edward Elgar: Letters of a Lifetime*, ed. Jerrold Northrop Moore (Oxford: Clarendon Press, 1990)
McVeagh, *Elgar*	Diana McVeagh, *Edward Elgar, his Life and Music* (London: Dent, 1955)
Monk, *Literature*	Raymond Monk (ed.), *Edward Elgar, Music and Literature* (Aldershot: Scolar Press, 1993)
Monk, *Studies*	Raymond Monk (ed.), *Elgar Studies* (Aldershot: Scolar Press, 1990)
Moore, *Elgar*	Jerrold Northrop Moore, *Edward Elgar, a Creative Life* (Oxford: Oxford University Press, 1984)
MT	*The Musical Times*
New Grove 2	The New Grove Dictionary of Music, 2nd edition, ed. Stanley Sadie (London: Macmillan, 2001)

Publishers	*Elgar and his Publishers: Letters of a Creative Life*, 2 vols., ed. Jerrold Northrop Moore (Oxford: Clarendon Press, 1987)
Redwood, *Companion*	Christopher Redwood, (ed.), *An Elgar Companion* (Ashbourne: Sequoia, 1982)
Windflower	*The Windflower Letters: Correspondence with Alice Caroline Stuart Wortley and Her Family*, ed. Jerrold Northrop Moore (Oxford: Clarendon Press, 1989)
Young, *Elgar*	Percy M. Young, *Elgar O.M.: A Study of a Musician*, 2nd edition (London: Purnell Book Services, 1973)

Rehearsal figures throughout the book are given in the form a:b, where 'a' is the rehearsal number in the score, and 'b' the number of bars after it.

1 Elgar and theories of chromaticism

Patrick McCreless

Of the various meta-narratives about the history of Western tonal music, two are especially familiar: in the realm of culture, the story of the development of the German canon to a position of ascendancy in Europe by the late nineteenth century; and in the realm of musical language, the story of the chromaticization of this music from the time of Corelli, Handel, and Bach, to that of Haydn, Mozart, and Beethoven, to that of Liszt and Wagner, and finally to that of Strauss, Debussy, Schoenberg – and Elgar. Even if we tend to grant less authority to such meta-narratives than we used to, the place of Elgar in the European constellation of art music is nevertheless clear. He is an English composer of the turn of the twentieth century, his music steeped in both the diatonicism of Handel and the chromatic harmony of Wagner and Strauss. Culturally, he is a post-Wagnerian tonal composer, one whose principal concert works were written with the explicit intent of gaining the power and prestige – both for himself and for England – of admission into what James Hepokoski has called 'the now reified, culturally politicized, and largely Germanic canon'.[1] Musically, he is, to be sure, an English composer, and thus somewhat removed from the centres of power; but he is one who understood that a central feature – possibly *the* central feature – of the advanced, German music of his time was chromaticism. That his music was championed by the likes of Richard Strauss and Hans Richter early in the twentieth century, not to mention that it so deeply moves us to this day, is in no small part due to his extraordinary capacity for making chromatic writing his own. His chromatic usage is technically as adept as that of his German peers, and it is expressive and communicative in a way that is uniquely his. He was a composer who, like his immediate Germanic models, had an uncanny knack for making the most sturdy diatonicism and the most daring chromaticism work together beautifully in the same piece.

But how did he do it? Why is his use of chromatic harmony and chromatic tonal relations so powerful? There is a way, of course, in which we have known for years how chromaticism works for Elgar. For him, and for many

[1] James Hepokoski, 'Elgar', in D. Kern Holoman (ed.), *The Nineteenth-Century Symphony* (New York and London: Schirmer, 1997), pp. 327–44, at p. 327.

Elgarians, the chromatic is simply that which is marked against, and thus that which is opposed expressively to, the diatonic. When Jerrold Northrop Moore writes, in an interpretation of *The Black Knight*, that 'The contrast of diatonic and chromatic was to be used throughout Edward's creative life as a paradigm of good and evil, hope and doubt', or, in his description of some of the music in Part II of *The Dream of Gerontius*, that 'In the middle of this chromatic intensity the Angel of the Agony found a moment of diatonic comfort', we know instinctively what he means, and we know that he is right.[2] This is precisely the way that the music works. The same could be said, in many respects, of *Parsifal*.

But wait. Byron Adams, quoting some critical writing on *Gerontius* by W. J. Turner, warns us against 'a reductive binary opposition between diatonic and chromatic that reflected the received opinion of many male British musicians and critics in the late nineteenth and early twentieth centuries': that diatonicism is upright, healthy, Protestant, and masculine, whereas chromaticism is decadent, morbid, Catholic, and effeminate.[3] Of Elgar's working and composing in a culture in which such a gendering of diatonic and chromatic operated only slightly below the surface – and indeed operated in his own emotional make-up – there can be little doubt. So there was a problem with his composing when he did, and in England. Consider the wild emotional and creative contradiction that such gendering of musical styles must have set up for him. In order to gain something that he deeply desired in the core of his being – admission into the highest international circle of (male) composers, and public recognition of the value and originality of his art – he had to write music with the sort of chromaticism that could most compromise his own masculinity and the respect that he could hope to command in his own country.

This inner conflict plays itself out in absorbing ways over the course of his creative career. And one way in which it makes itself manifest is that, instead of reserving chromaticism for representation of evil, doubt, fear, and terror, he at times foregrounds it in some of his most upright, optimistic, masculine, proud music, thereby cutting directly against the grain of the reductive binary opposition noted by Adams. Consider, for example, the following passage from *Pomp and Circumstance* March no. 1, a work that has indubitably earned its stripes, at least in the culture in which he composed, as energetic, masculine, and patriotic (Ex. 1.1). Or consider his setting of 'To give unto them that mourn a garland for ashes' in the Prologue to *The Apostles* (Ex. 1.2). This music is nothing if not righteous, healthy, and

[2] Moore, *Elgar*, pp. 163 and 312.
[3] Byron Adams, 'Elgar's Late Oratorios: Roman Catholicism, Decadence, and the Wagnerian Dialectic of Shame and Grace', in *Companion*, pp. 81–105, at p. 88.

Ex. 1.1 March, *Pomp and Circumstance* no. 1, bb. 26–34

Ex. 1.2 *The Apostles*, Prologue, from fig. 5

uplifting. And so it is not just the simple diatonic/chromatic opposition that enables us to understand and interpret these passages; if it were, we would be compelled to link them with darkness, fear, and doubt. It is rather the diatonic/chromatic opposition coupled intimately with many other essential aspects of the music: mode, tempo, instrumentation, dynamics, melodic contour and character, harmonic underpinnings, and much more. Understanding the import of these critical features of the music helps us to realize that the chromatic lines and harmonic progressions in *Pomp and Circumstance* No. 1 make its swaggering pride even more pronounced, and that the chromatic undercurrent in the passage from *The Apostles* affords it a soothing quality that a purely diatonic version of the same music would not have.

Yet again, how did he do it? But this time, how did he do it, in a musical, technical, compositional way? It is here that another meta-narrative becomes relevant, one less well known, even at times arcane: that of the history of the theory of chromaticism in tonal music. The *history* of music *theory*: how can *that* help us to understand the music of Elgar? It can help us because, on the one hand, so much of the expressive force of his music is tied up with chromaticism, and on the other, because music theory has, since around the time that Elgar began his compositional career, developed a number of effective tools for analysing chromatic music. Of course, a central task of harmonic theory, going back however far in time one wants to go – back to Riemann, back to Rameau, back to times when harmonic theory wasn't even called harmonic theory (Vicentino, or even further) – has been to deal with chromaticism. To tell the history of the theory of chromaticism would entail telling of the entire history of Western harmonic theory. But the various theories of chromaticism, as they have developed in the past 125 years or so, can illuminate Elgar's music in ways that we can ill afford to ignore.

A quick overview of our situation clarifies the problem. The modern project of chromatic theory properly begins in the United States, with two works of the late 1970s: Robert Bailey's essay 'The Structure of the *Ring* and Its Evolution' in 1977, and Gregory Proctor's dissertation, 'Technical Bases of Nineteenth-Century Tonality' in 1978.[4] These two works, both fostered by a desire to understand under-explicated aspects of chromaticism in nineteenth-century music, opened the gates to a flood of studies, on topics ranging from Schenker's treatment of chromaticism, to neo-Lorenzian formal and tonal analysis, to studies of music employing the octatonic and hexatonic collections, to neo-Riemannian theory, transformational theory, the notion of tonal pitch space, and in general to all sorts of analytical and interpretive work on chromatic music from the late eighteenth to the early twentieth century. As it turns out, though, most of this recent Anglo-American chromatic theory is deeply indebted to the work of four German theorists, working from roughly 1880 to 1935: Hugo Riemann (1849–1919), Heinrich Schenker (1868–1935), Ernst Kurth (1886–1946), and Alfred Lorenz (1868–1939).[5] Virtually all the central ideas of the modern theories appear, at least *in nuce*, in the work of these earlier German writers. The net result of all this work, both older German and newer Anglo-American, has been a deeper musical and hermeneutic understanding of the music of a number of composers, with whose music the theoretical work has inter-sected: Wagner, to be sure, but also Schubert, Liszt, Bruckner, Wolf, Mahler,

[4] Robert Bailey, 'The Structure of the *Ring* and its Evolution', *19CM*, 1 (1977), pp. 48–61; Gregory Proctor, 'Technical Bases of Nineteenth-Century Chromatic Tonality', Ph.D. diss. (Princeton University, 1978).
[5] The literature by and about these four theorists would fill volumes. For present purposes, the primary sources are: Hugo Riemann, *Skizze einer neuen Methode der Harmonielehre* (Leipzig: Breitkopf und Härtel, 1880) and *Harmony Simplified* [*Vereinfachte Harmonie, oder die Lehre von der tonalen Funktionen der Akkorde*, 1893], trans. anonymous (London: Augener, 1896); Heinrich Schenker, *Harmony* [*Harmonielehre*, 1906], trans. Elizabeth Borgese, ed. Oswald Jonas (Chicago: University of Chicago Press, 1954), *The Masterwork in Music: A Yearbook* [*Das Meisterwerk in der Musik: Ein Jahrbuch*, 3 vols., 1925, 1926, 1930], ed. William Drabkin, trans. Ian Bent *et al.*, 3 vols. (Cambridge: Cambridge University Press, 1994–7), and *Free Composition* [*Der freie Satz*, 1935], ed. and trans. Ernst Oster (New York: Longman, 1979); Ernst Kurth, *Romantische Harmonik und ihre Krise in Wagners 'Tristan'* (Bern: Haupt, 1920; reprint Hildesheim: Olms, 1975); and Alfred Lorenz, *Das Geheimnis der Form bei Richard Wagner*, 4 vols. (1924–33; reprint Tutzing: Schneider, 1966).

Strauss, and Franck, to name a few. But one composer with whose music the work has not intersected is Elgar: the name Elgar is not so much as mentioned in any of my sources on the theory of chromaticism.

The task, then, is clear: to bring these rich resources into contact with a music whose tonal language shares remarkably much with that of the Wagnerian and post-Wagnerian Germanic lingua franca of the turn of the twentieth century. My strategy will be to distil available analytical approaches to chromaticism into six techniques, each employing the insights of a particular theorist or theorists. To illustrate each one, rather than citing the theorists' examples from the canonical, mostly German repertoire, I will adduce examples from Elgar's music, which employs precisely the same techniques. The first three techniques involve Elgar's usage of chromaticism at the foreground and middleground levels – that is, from individual harmonies to passages of a few dozen bars. For each I will take a single, core idea from a relevant theoretical work or works, and show how it is central to Elgar's expressive use of chromaticism. Technique 1 is simply the usage of the *Tristan*, or half-diminished seventh chord, which Ernst Kurth ably demonstrated to be crucial to Wagner's musical language in *Tristan*, and which is ubiquitous in the music of Elgar. Technique 2 is the usage of line to render chromaticism comprehensible – especially the notion, promulgated famously by Schenker, but also to a degree by Kurth, that a unidirectional chromatic line in the melodic or bass voice can hold together a passage that is harmonically adventurous.[6] Technique 3 involves the symmetrical division of the octave – especially with respect to exact, rather than diatonically adjusted sequences: a feature of chromatic music pointed out early on by Kurth,[7] but also central to much recent work (Proctor's 'transposition operation'; Bailey's 'expressive tonality'; work of Arthur Berger, Richard Taruskin, and many others on the octatonic scale; and that of Richard Cohn and neo-Riemannian theorists on hexatonic spaces).[8] Examples of these techniques will be drawn from a wide spectrum of Elgar's music.

---

[6] The idea that linear forces generate chromaticism is present in all of Schenker's later work, beginning especially in 1925, with the publication of the first volume of *The Masterwork in Music*. For Kurth's view on this topic, see *Romantische Harmonik*, p. 353.

[7] Kurth, *Romantische Harmonik*, pp. 333–53.

[8] Proctor, 'Technical Bases', pp. 149–250; Bailey, 'The Structure of the *Ring*', p. 51; Arthur Berger, 'Problems of Pitch Organization in Stravinsky', *Perspectives of New Music* 2 (1963), pp. 11–42; Richard Taruskin, 'Chernomor to Kashchei: Harmonic Sorcery, or, Stravinsky's "Angle"', *JAMS*, 38

(1985), pp. 72–142, revised and reprinted as Chapter 4 of Taruskin, *Stravinsky and the Russian Traditions: A Biography of the Works Through 'Mavra'* (Berkeley and Los Angeles: University of California Press, 1996), vol. I, pp. 255–306; Richard Cohn, 'Maximally Smooth Cycles, Hexatonic Systems, and the Analysis of Late-Romantic Triadic Progressions', *Music Analysis*, 15 (1996), pp. 9–40 and 'Introduction to Neo-Riemannian Theory: a Survey and Historical Perspective', in 'Special issue: Neo-Riemannian Theory', *Journal of Music Theory*, 42 (1998), pp. 167–80.

The second set of three techniques deals with chromaticism at more global levels. Here I will draw examples exclusively from *The Apostles*, the largest compositional project of Elgar's career. Technique 4 is Schenkerian analysis of large-scale dramatic and instrumental works – a level of analysis that goes far beyond the relatively local lines noted in Technique 2, to include whole operas, or entire multi-movement instrumental works.[9] Inasmuch as a Schenkerian analysis of *The Apostles* would necessarily address many more aspects of the work than its chromatic tonal relations, I will only offer a few remarks about some of the published work in this area, and speculate on its possible relevance to the oratorio. Technique 5 is that of associative and cross-referential tonal relationships, posited first in Wagner's music dramas by Kurth and Lorenz in the 1920s, and explicated much further by Robert Bailey, with his notion of 'associative tonality', and many other writers on opera and dramatic music in the past thirty years or so. I will also argue that it is a global concern for key relations – especially a concern for tonal association and cross-reference – that underlies the tonal coherence (but *not* coherence in the Schenkerian sense) of many large-scale instrumental works from Beethoven on. This is a concern that is only implicit, but yet of towering importance, in the analytical work of writers as different as Charles Rosen and Milton Babbitt,[10] and it constitutes a hitherto unarticulated connection of Wagner and post-Wagnerian composers to the canonic symphonic tradition. Technique 6 involves the control of global tonal structure by means of various patternings of keys, often in a manner that interprets keys as players in a tonal narrative. Analytical work of this sort almost always combines associative keys with clear long-range tonal patterning; examples include Lorenz's volumes on Wagner's music dramas, Bailey's work on the *Ring*, David Lewin's and Fred Lerdahl's on *Parsifal*, and Hepokoski's on a scene from Verdi's *Falstaff* and on Elgar's First Symphony.[11]

Three final observations are necessary before we begin to bring chromatic theory and Elgar's music into creative contact. First, my references to

[9]Warren Darcy, *Wagner's* Das Rheingold (Oxford: Clarendon Press, 1993); Timothy L. Jackson, *Tchaikovsky: Symphony No. 6 (Pathétique)* (Cambridge: Cambridge University Press, 1999); J. P. E. Harper-Scott, '"A Nice Sub-Acid Feeling": Schenker, Heidegger, and Elgar's First Symphony', *Music Analysis*, 24 (2005), pp. 349–82, and 'Elgar's Deconstruction of the *belle époque*: Interlace Structures and the Second Symphony', this volume, Chapter 6.
[10]Charles Rosen, *The Classical Style: Haydn, Mozart, Beethoven*, 2nd ed. (New York: Norton, 1997; original ed. 1971); Milton

Babbitt, 'The Structure and Function of Music Theory', in Benjamin Boretz and Edward T. Cone (eds.), *Perspectives on Contemporary Music Theory* (New York: Norton, 1972), pp. 11–12.
[11]David Lewin, 'Amfortas's Prayer to Titurel and the Role of D in *Parsifal*: the Tonal Spaces of the Drama and the Enharmonic C♭/B', *19CM*, 7 (1984), pp. 336–49; Fred Lerdahl, *Tonal Pitch Space* (New York: Oxford University Press, 2002), pp. 119–38, 298–302; Hepokoski, *Giuseppe Verdi: Falstaff* (Cambridge: Cambridge University Press, 1983), pp. 91–109, and 'Elgar', 329–36.

'chromatic theory' by no means suggest that there exists, either now or at any time in the past, any single, monolithic theory of chromaticism in tonal music. The analytical approaches represented by the six techniques noted here developed rather haphazardly and independently of one another, over a hundred years or more. Some of them, such as those of Schenker and Rosen, were not conceived with the massive dramatic and instrumental works of the later nineteenth and early twentieth centuries in mind. Others, such as Schenkerian and neo-Riemannian theory, at times make incompatible claims about the music to which they are applied. And so forth: 'chromatic theory', as invoked here with respect to Elgar's music, constitutes less a unified theory than a useful arsenal of tools to approach chromatic tonal music. Nevertheless, we *can* use the theories and analytical approaches described here productively in concert with one another; I shall attempt to do so myself, at the end of the first half of this essay, with respect to a critical passage from the final movement of Elgar's First Symphony, and in the second half, with respect to *The Apostles*.

Second, chromatic theory continues to develop, in all sorts of ways, and in all sorts of directions: it is arguably the most lively of music-theoretical pursuits early in the twenty-first century. Accordingly, I necessarily leave much out of my account. I deal in only a peripheral way with neo-Riemannian theory (as it relates to tonal symmetry, in Technique 3), and I do not directly engage the work of Charles Smith, Daniel Harrison, or David Kopp – to name just three theorists whose work is original, influential, and current.[12] Nor do I cover in any thorough way harmonic progression, for example, or enharmonicism, in Elgar's music – topics clearly ripe for analysis and interpretation. Here limits of time and space make it essential to be selective. Perhaps more importantly, I have sought to use theoretical work that is as accessible as possible, as opposed to work that would require extensive and detailed exposition before I could make it relevant to Elgar's music.

Third, and finally, I want to emphasize the fluid relationship between analytical approach and compositional craft. Each analytical technique that I posit is also, in a sense, a compositional technique: for example, a clear, unidirectional melodic or bass line tying together a complex chromatic passage is both a means of explanation (to point out the line is to offer a theory of coherence) and a creative ploy (such lines, employed consciously or unconsciously by the composer, make difficult chromatic passages more

---

[12] Charles Smith, 'The Functional Extravagance of Chromatic Chords', *Music Theory Spectrum*, 8 (1986), pp. 94–139; Daniel Harrison, *Harmonic Function in Chromatic Music: A Renewed Dualist Theory and an Account of Its Precedents* (Chicago: University of Chicago Press, 1994) and 'Nonconformist Notions of Nineteenth-Century Enharmonicism', *Music Analysis*, 21 (2002), pp. 115–60; and David Kopp, *Chromatic Transformations in Nineteenth-Century Music* (Cambridge: Cambridge University Press, 2003).

audible, and more palatable, for the listener). Discovering and describing such techniques sheds light on Elgar's compositional craft, of course, but it also opens the door to interpretation and hermeneutics, for which the music ceaselessly cries out.

I Chromaticism at the surface, and slightly deeper

Of all the insights that our theorists have to offer regarding surface harmony in chromatic tonal music – chord quality, harmonic progression, local modulation – I shall choose but one: Ernst Kurth's observation, in *Romantische Harmonik und ihre Krise in Wagners 'Tristan'*, that the *Tristan* chord, the half-diminished seventh, is central to Wagner's opera in partic-ular, and to what Kurth called the 'intensive alteration style' in general.[13] Alfred Lorenz tagged the same chord as a focal harmonic and symbolic entity, the *mystische Akkord*, in *Parsifal*, and it is a small leap to the music of Elgar, which is replete with occurrences of the chord.[14] Kurth's approach to the chord, and to all Romantic harmony, is dictated by his view that music is not merely an acoustical phenomenon, but a dynamic, psychological one, a play of unconscious, psychic energies that press forward in melodies and contrapuntal lines, and that sometimes coalesce into chords. For Kurth, the members of a chord are not inherently stable, but bristling with potential energy. In Romantic harmony, as he conceives it, even ostensibly stable major and minor triads are invested with linear-melodic tensions, and are thus not really stable at all. The site in the nineteenth-century repertoire at which this principle reaches its apogee is, not surprisingly, the *Tristan* chord, of which, at least in the form in which it first occurs in the *Tristan* Prelude, the individual members are each charged with a powerful urge for specifically melodic resolution. Kurth devotes over forty pages at the beginning of *Romantische Harmonik* to the *Tristan* chord, differentiating carefully between what he calls 'energetic' instantiations (in which the chord spelling contains contradictory urges for melodic resolution and thus cannot be analysed as a functional chord spelled in diatonic stacked thirds in some key) and 'sensuous' instantiations (in which the chord spelling *is* that of a diatonic seventh, and in which, therefore, the urges toward resolution in the

[13] Kurth, *Romantische Harmonik*, pp. 44–87. For a recent view of the half-diminished seventh chord, influenced by neo-Riemannian theory, see Richard Bass, 'Half-Diminished Functions and Transformations in Late Romantic Music', *Music Theory Spectrum*, 23 (2001), pp. 41–60.

[14] Lorenz, *Das Geheimnis der Form*, vol. IV, pp. 29–45. Lorenz laboriously tracks appearances of the chord throughout the music drama.

individual notes tend toward a single chord).[15] The very first statement of the chord in *Tristan* is of course of the energetic type, while the occurrence at the climax in bb. 81–2 of the Prelude is of the sensuous type – although it changes, before our very eyes, as it were, into an energetic type again at b. 83. An inherent tension in Kurth's understanding of the *Tristan* chord is in fact that, even though he considers its sensuous versions to be more stable than energetic versions, his idea that even triads are full of linear energy suggests that *any* half-diminished seventh is surging with potential energy. That energy is surely, according to Kurth, a primary source of the wistful, yearning quality and the symbolic power that accrue to the chord, whether sensuous or energetic, throughout Wagner's music dramas.

Describing Wagner's use of the chord in the *Tristan* Prelude, Kurth writes: 'Its dominating position not only is implied by frequent occurrence, which discharges its basic permeating character over the entire symphonic music of the piece, but also it represents the decisive point in the Prelude's architectural design.'[16] Frequency, permeation, rhetorical emphasis, occurrence at important nodes of musical design: these are precisely my reasons for choosing the half-diminished seventh, in and of itself, as the first crucial locus in bringing about an intersection of chromatic theory and Elgar's chromatic writing. To be sure, he uses the chord hundreds of times in purely diatonic contexts, a few examples of which appear below. But it demands attention especially in chromatic usages – usages that resonate with *Tristan*, *Götterdämmerung*, and *Parsifal*, and that import into Elgar's music a weighty history from those works. The two composers use the chord differently, of course. The energetic/sensuous distinction is considerably less relevant to Elgar's music than to Wagner's: 'energetic' examples occur frequently in Wagner, at least from *Tristan* on, but more rarely in Elgar. Elgar's way of intensifying the chord was not so much to use non-diatonic versions of it, as Wagner did in the opening bars of *Tristan*, but to use a number of *Tristan* chords in succession – something that Wagner rarely did. Elgar's usage may seem conservative in comparison to Wagner's, but the chord permeates his work at least as much as it does his predecessor's, and his skill at using it to maximum expressive effect shows that he learned his lesson well.

An early and characteristic example of Elgar's use of half-diminished sevenths occurs in the opening of the first movement of the Organ Sonata (Ex. 1.3). Here there are three such chords: a 'sensuous' diatonic one built on F♯ (occurring twice, in two different inversions, bb. 6–7 and 8), and two

---

[15] See Rothfarb's useful exposition of Kurth's sensuous/energetic distinction in *Ernst Kurth as Theorist and Analyst* (Philadelphia: University of Pennsylvania Press, 1988), pp. 113–15, 132–3, and 152–89.

[16] Kurth, *Romantische Harmonik*, p. 63; translation from Robert Bailey, *Richard Wagner: Prelude and Transfiguration from 'Tristan und Isolde'* (New York: Norton, 1985), p. 193.

Ex. 1.3 Organ Sonata, first movement, opening

others (one sensuous, one energetic) involving chromatic notes – one on C♯ (b. 5), and one on A (spelt enharmonically as A–C–D♯–G, b. 6). Elgar achieves maximum melodic tension by placing the seventh in the top voice in three of four cases, always resolving it by step downward. Both diatonic half-diminished sevenths resolve to I^6, instantiating his tendency to resolve vii^{7}s conventionally to the tonic in the major mode. (In the minor mode, where the half-diminished seventh is common as ii^7, he frequently makes the resolution to some form of I, rather than to V – as in the theme of the *Variations* Op. 36, bb. 2, 3, 4, and 6.) Of the chromatic half-diminished sevenths in the Organ Sonata, the vii^7/V (b. 5) resolves to V^7/V before resolving to V, and the 'energetic' chord on the second beat of b. 6, surely the most poignant of them all, resolves to a diminished seventh, thereby rendering the half-diminished seventh more dissonant than its resolution. These chords, taken together, lend a particularly Elgarian cast to the passage – a quality rendered all the more touching when we feel Kurth's Tristanesque energy flowing through them.[17]

Given the linear-harmonic tensions embodied in each *Tristan* chord, Elgar sometimes achieves a remarkable effect by lining them up in succession, without resolution. The simplest progression of this sort is exemplified by the third and fourth bars of the opening movement of the Second Symphony (Ex. 1.4 (a)). Here the vii$^4_3$/V in E♭ major progresses not to the expected I^6, but to another half-diminished seventh, which soon leads to a brief toniciza-tion of the subdominant. Crucial to the effect is the behaviour of the leading tone in the vii$^4_3$, which slides down to D♭ rather than resolving up to E♭. This

[17] See also Matthew Riley's discussion of Elgar's use of diatonic tritones, this volume, ch. 10.

Ex. 1.4 Symphony no. 2, first movement, bb. 3–4

move, of course, has a history: it dates back to the descending, chromatic lament bass of the seventeenth century, $\hat{8}-\hat{7}-\flat\hat{7}-\hat{6}-\flat\hat{6}-\hat{5}$. Surely some of the expressive resonance of this move, both in the seventeenth century and four hundred years later, arises from the fact that the leading note, instead of following its natural inclination and resolving up, presses immediately down to the $\flat\hat{7}$. In the passage from the Second Symphony, this motion occurs not in the bass, but in an inner voice (Ex. 1.4 (b)). Ex. 1.4 (c) illustrates how this explanation works, in the 'tenor' voice, in the symphony. Robert Hatten has called attention to the $\sharp\hat{7}-\flat\hat{7}-\hat{6}$ effect in the music of Beethoven, dubbing the move from $\sharp\hat{7}$ to $\flat\hat{7}$ the 'yielding' effect; the locus classicus is the bass F♯–F♮–E in the opening phrase of the second movement of his Piano Sonata in E♭ Major, Op. 7, where the harmonies are $V_5^6/V - V_2^4 - I^6$.[18] What makes this inner-voice 'yielding' progression so Elgarian in the Second Symphony is precisely the move from one half-diminished seventh, which presses strongly toward I^6, to another, which frustrates this desired motion, while at the same time retaining the tensile, half-diminished sound. We can gain a sense of what the second half-diminished chord accomplishes expressively simply by imagining the harmony on the downbeat of b. 4 to be a tonic in first inversion. (Indeed, the passage soon modulates to A♭ major, to which the music of b. 3 is transposed in b. 6, but the first beat of the following bar is not a half-diminished seventh, as in b. 4, but the expected I^6 in A♭.)

Elgar achieves a stunning, related effect at the massive structural cadence at the end of the final movement of the Violin Concerto. Here he hammers home eight of these half-diminished sevenths successively, with each of the first three pairs producing precisely the same progression as noted above in the Second Symphony (Ex. 1.5, see especially 114:3–4). The $\sharp\hat{7}-\flat\hat{7}$ motion is now in the bass, with the former occurring regularly on strong beats. The entire cadential passage, of which this extraordinary moment is but a part, invites hermeneutic interpretation. There are three points to remark on here:

(1) The violent 'hammering' in the orchestra actually begins at 114:1, two bars before the half-diminished seventh passage; it establishes the duple

[18] Robert Hatten, *Musical Meaning in Beethoven: Markedness, Correlation, and* *Interpretation* (Bloomington: Indiana University Press, 1994), pp. 56–63.

Ex. 1.5 Violin Concerto, third movement, two bb. before fig. 114–fig. 116

high-low melodic contour for each pair of beats, the descending (almost complete) chromatic scale in the bass, and the predilection for half-diminished sevenths (the chords on the first and last beats of 114:1–2).

(2) What initially sounds like the structural melodic resolution, $\hat{5}-\hat{4}-\hat{3}-\hat{2}-\hat{1}$, occurs *not* in a melodic part over a supporting functional bass, as happens in thousands of other tonal pieces. Rather, picking up the downward energy of the preceding four bars, a diatonic, descending scale-wise line, from the F♯ of 115:2, blasts out in tripled, even quadrupled octaves in the strings, moving $\hat{5}-\hat{4}-\hat{3}-\hat{2}$, to the C♯ at 115:5–6, whereupon the changing harmonies and a more active bass line deny the expected resolution to B, and a more conventional cadence ensues at fig. 116.

(3) Even here, the cadential preparatory chord at 115:9–10 projects more the half-diminished vii^7 (A♯–C♯–E–G♯) as cadential dominant than V^7, which enters only at the last moment. Note also that this chord is already present in the two bars (just before fig. 114) that lead into the long cadential progression, so the entire passage is book-ended by the A♯ half-diminished seventh chord.

What does all this mean? Surely, given recent discoveries of biographical evidence, it has something to do with Alice Stuart Wortley (to whom Elgar dedicated the concerto, and to whom he consistently referred to it as 'our concerto') – with Elgar's intense feelings for her, and the utter impossibility of their ever consummating this love.[19] The half-diminished seventh, with its Kurthian urgings and incompleteness, is itself emblematic of this impossibility. It prepares the passage, and begins it, *strepitoso*, at fig. 114. Its descending hammer-blows, one right after the other, seem to nail any hope of consummation into the ground. But the sudden C♯ timpani roll at fig. 115 clears the air, and what emerges is pure B major diatonicism, both in the *Nobilmente* solo violin part, and in the powerful, low-register parallel-octave descent. That the whole orchestra is engaged in the half-diminished seventh hammer-blows (at fig. 114), but that the music, after being stopped in its tracks for a moment at fig. 115, then 'splits' into the solo violin's triple stops and the descending parallel octaves (also a kind of nailing into the ground, but maybe a less negative one) is surely significant: might the split signify a joint acceptance of the situation, in two different voices, even a rejoicing in that acceptance? And note that the F♯, octave-doubled head-tone of 115:2 picks up at exactly where the descending chromatic scale of the previous bars left off – at G (see fig. 114:4). (Indeed, the bass's scalewise $\overset{\wedge}{5}$ to $\overset{\wedge}{1}$ motion continues and completes a descending scale that started diatonically back at fig. 113 (not shown), turned chromatic just before fig. 114, and now is diatonic again.) Perhaps the loveliest touch of all is the solo violin line (at 115:2–10), the top voice of whose double stops also traces the descending *Urlinie* from $\overset{\wedge}{5}$, but wonderfully out of phase with the bass, and with a three-note melodic figure (up a step, then up a third, on each note of the descending *Urlinie*; see brackets in the example) that embroiders and comments on the resolution. The bass of the orchestra joins in for the last two of these melodic figures, accompanying the violin's line a tenth lower, the melody and bass reaching the cadence together at fig. 116 – a joint acceptance of the reality in which 'our concerto' was written? (Or, conversely, failing to achieve that joint acceptance because the melody does not cadence on the tonic?)

---

[19] See, for example. Michael Kennedy, 'The Soul Enshrined: Elgar and his Violin Concerto', in Monk, *Literature*, pp. 72–82. Kennedy offers a valuable, up-to-date summary in *Portrait*, pp. 116–24.

Ex. 1.6 *The Apostles*, Part I, two bars before fig. 20 ('Christ's Loneliness')

The Apostles offers another instance of successive iterations of the half-diminished seventh chord. Here the successive chords simply slide down chromatically by semitones, with slight rhythmic adjustments, and with an adjustment of the harmony to a fully diminished seventh at the end (Ex. 1.6). Occurring early in *The Apostles*, the figure was dubbed by Elgar's friend, August Jaeger, in his published analysis of the oratorio, as 'Christ's Loneliness'. Jaeger has come in for heavy criticism in the last few years, but although this leitmotivic designation may be characteristically limiting and over-specific, and expressed in poetic language, it does capture the musical essence of a distinctive moment: the first event in the drama, Christ's praying all night on the mountain. Jaeger's description of how the chords function, along with the implication of their inherent tension, suggests that he was finely tuned to their resonance: 'This is the symbol of CHRIST'S LONELINESS, a sequence of wailing chromatics, the two lower parts moving in diminished fifths. It is scored for viole and violoncelli, a conception well able to express acutest feeling – "tears from the depth of some divine despair".'[20]

The figure of half-diminished sevenths descending by semitone has strong intertextual resonances, both within Elgar's music and beyond. If we start here in *The Apostles* (1903), with the descending succession of half-diminished sevenths representing suffering and, in this case, 'divine' despair, and cast our net seven years into Elgar's future, we encompass the passage, discussed above, in the Violin Concerto. This later passage embodies the same chromatically descending bass line as 'Christ's Loneliness', with the circle-of-fifths root motion in the concerto (i.e. the movement of the roots of each chord, not the actual bass line: C♯–F♯–B–E–A–D–G at 114:3–4) replacing the descending-semitone root motion in the oratorio. (Note the striking effect whereby the upper melodic voice in the concerto leaps about, a tenth higher than the circle-of-fifths root motion, as though it were a bass line, while the melody of

---

[20] A. J. Jaeger, 'The Apostles', *by Edward Elgar, Op. 49: Book of Words, with Analytical and Descriptive Notes by A. J. Jaeger* (London: Novello, 1903), p. 10. Christopher Grogan sharply critiques Jaeger's analyses – especially his obsession with the naming of themes – in '"My Dear Analyst": Some Observations on Elgar's Correspondence with A. J. Jaeger Regarding the "Apostles" Project', *Music and Letters*, 72 (1991), pp. 48–60. Charles Edward McGuire, in turn, critiques Grogan's work in *Elgar's Oratorios: The Creation of an Epic Narrative* (Aldershot: Ashgate, 2002), pp. 188–91.

Ex. 1.7 Wagner, *Parsifal*, Act I, fig. 110

'Christ's Loneliness' descends in parallel sevenths with the bass.) Yet the two passages seem worlds apart. The passage in the Violin Concerto has none of the dark piety of the oratorio, and none of the quality of decadence (in spite of the religious subject) that Byron Adams perceives in both *The Dream of Gerontius* and *The Apostles*. If there is despair, it is purely human despair, bespeaking Elgar's often noted turn away from religion over the course of the first decade of the twentieth century, from oratorios to symphonies and concertos.

If we cast our net beyond Elgar – backwards twenty years or so to *Parsifal* (premiered 1882) and forward exactly thirty years to Alfred Lorenz's celebrated analysis of that work in 1933 – we encounter what is perhaps an even more telling intertextual reference. The theme or motive that Lorenz (and before him Hans von Wolzogen) designated as the 'Heilandsklage' was surely Elgar's model for the similar progression in *The Apostles* (Ex. 1.7).[21] The 'Heilandsklage' – a locution tantalizingly close to Jaeger's 'divine despair' – places the circle-of-fifths root progression in the bass, so that the second chord of each pair is *not* a half-diminished seventh, as in both Elgar examples, but a dominant seventh. Wagner also rhythmically displaces the upper voices and doubles the pace of the bass in the third bar, such that, even though we can ultimately understand that the motive is a straightforward sequence, with the bass moving by fifths and articulating a half-diminished seventh sonority on alternate chords, this regularity is obscured even in the initial bar. The parallels of harmonic technique and expressive import in the three passages place Elgar firmly in the orbit of the Wagnerian and post-Wagnerian musical worlds.

The locus classicus of the half-diminished seventh in Western music, for Kurth certainly, and for most of the rest of us since, is the *Tristan* chord – in Wagner's whole opera in general, and in its first-act Prelude in particular. At a

[21] Lorenz, *Das Geheimnis*, vol. IV, pp. 67–71; Lorenz takes the term 'Heilandsklage' from Hans von Wolzogen, *Thematischer Leitfaden durch die Musik des* *Parsifal* (Leipzig: Gebrüder Senf, 1882). In *Parsifal* the initial chord is sometimes a half-diminished seventh, and other times simply a minor triad.

Ex. 1.8 Symphony no. 2, third movement, figs. 121:9–122:6

critical moment in the third movement of the Second Symphony, Elgar
explicitly quotes a moment near the end of the *Tristan* Prelude. After the
shattering climax of the movement at 121:1–5, the music quickly disintegrates.
Beginning at 121:6, a sliding chromatic descent, with major thirds in the upper
voices, combines with an out-of-phase bass in such a way as to produce
alternate augmented and major 6/4 triads (see Ex. 1.8, which shows the end
of this motion starting at 121:9). At 121:10 the progression stalls, the bass
reaching as low as F♯, but the alternating F♯ and G, as the dynamic level recedes
to *ppp*. At fig. 122, the bass reaches its lowest point, F♮, and, at the entrance of
the two horns, reaches a moment of total stasis. The chord here, of course, is
the *Tristan* chord, at its original pitch level from both the beginning and end of
Wagner's Prelude. Indeed, the passage here almost exactly duplicates b. 102 of
the *Tristan* Prelude, with two bassoons holding F and B (one octave lower than
Wagner's bassoons) below, while two wind instruments above (two horns
here, oboe and English horn in Wagner) hold A♭ and E♭ (in the Elgar as a fifth
instead of a fourth, as in the opera). In the next bar, exactly as in the Prelude,
the timpani (accompanied by the double basses in the Symphony) enter with a
rolled G, while the melodic E♭ moves down to a D. A further intriguing *Tristan*
reference is the similarity of the symphony's ensuing C minor theme at 122:3
to the opening notes of the Sailor's Song in the opera. Whereas in the Sailor's
Song, the melody quickly reaches a cadence in E♭ major, the symphony
doggedly presses forward in C minor. What does this disturbing passage
mean? Given its rhetorical emphasis – the whirlwind movement virtually
comes to a halt, for the one and only time, to call attention to it – it is
unquestionably a critical locus of meaning, at least in the movement, and
probably in the symphony as a whole.[22]

---

[22] Inasmuch as an interpretation would
entail a reading of the symphony, I defer to
J. P. E. Harper-Scott, who, in another essay
in this book, takes account specifically of this
passage, including the reference to *Tristan*.
See ch. 6.

Ex. 1.9 *The Dream of Gerontius*, (a) sketch; (b), Part II, two bars before fig. 106; (c) Part I, two bars before fig. 63; (d) Part II, fig. 113:5–7

(a)

(b)

(c)

(d)

Finally, two examples give an intriguing biographical twist to Elgar's use of the half-diminished seventh. Jerrold Northrop Moore notes that, while composing *The Dream of Gerontius*, the composer wrote down, on a scrap of paper, a chord that he dubbed an 'appalling chord' – used in the oratorio to introduce the Angel of the Agony (Ex. 1.9 (a) and (b)). Months later, he wrote to Jaeger that he only realized 'long after it was in print' that this 'appalling chord' is precisely the same chord that he had used in Part I with the text 'In Thine own agony' (Ex. 1.9 (c), Part I, 62:6), and another that he used at the end of the Angel of the Agony's music (Ex. 1.9 (d), Part II, 113:4–6).[23] In the context of our discussion here, it is noteworthy that the 'appalling chord' – surely this is Elgar's most dramatic surviving reference to a particular chord in his music – is in fact a half-diminished seventh, but with a melodic appoggiatura a whole step higher. Note also that, with the

[23] Moore, *Elgar*, pp. 311–12. It is in this letter, the well-known comment: 'I really do it and with respect to this chord, that Elgar made without thought – intuitively, I mean.'

exception of Ex. 1.9 (b), all the half-diminished sevenths to which the 'appal-ling' chords resolve are 'energetic', not 'sensuous'. From all the above, we might surmise that Elgar had an intuition of the importance of the half-diminished seventh in his work, and that the specific features that make these particular chords appalling are (1) the appoggiatura, and (2) the 'energetic', enharmonic spelling.

Our last example comes from the end of *The Music Makers* (1912), Elgar's valedictory, autobiographical work – the work which, with the Violin Concerto and the Second Symphony, he described to Alice Stuart Wortley as those in which 'I have written out my soul ... I have *shewn* myself'.[24] Seven bars from the end of the F minor work, the music comes to a dead halt in E minor, a semitone below the tonic. After a poignant silence, we hear a single, haunting, *fppp*, accented half-diminished seventh on G, which at an instant turns the music back to F minor, in which we hear the chorus intone again the first line of the poem, 'We are the music makers, And we are the dreamers of dreams' – with the starkest possible orchestral accompaniment, and one last reminder of the same chord, *a cappella*, just before the final cadence.[25]

Thus the encounter of Elgar's music with (a tiny bit of) Kurth's theoretical explication of later nineteenth-century chromatic tonal music. But what of Schenker? What might an intersection of Elgar's music and Schenker's ideas about chromaticism produce? Obviously, the potential for Schenkerian theorising and for analysis in the Elgar oeuvre is vast, and Harper-Scott has already published interpretive essays on the First and Second Symphonies, as well as *Falstaff*.[26] I will not address his work, since my concern here is entirely with brief passages of music, and since large-scale Schenkerian analysis is beyond the purview of this essay. Schenker's theory, of course, is ultimately diatonic, and chromaticism is a feature of foreground and middleground structural levels, that must eventually be reconciled to a more background diatonic context.

Schenker's usual practice, in passages of the scope that concerns us here, is to show that surface chromaticism – often strings of parallel ascending or descending sixths or tenths, sometimes producing parallel major or minor triads – prolongs a particular harmonic scale degree, such that the strange-ness of harmonic distance of the individual chords is justified and rational-ized by the harmonic pillars at either end of the progression. Examples include his analyses, in *Free Composition*, of a passage from the second movement of Haydn's Symphony No. 104 (Ex. 1.10 (a)), where descending chromatic parallel tenths serve a prolongation of V in G major; and of

[24] *Windflower*, p. 107, quoted in Kennedy, *The Life of Elgar*, p. 4.
[25] See also Aidan J. Thomson's essay on *The Music Makers*, this volume, ch. 4.
[26] See note 9, above. Also, 'Elgar's Invention of the Human: *Falstaff*, Op. 68', *19CM*, 28 (2005), pp. 230–3.

Ex. 1.10 Schenker, *Der freie Satz*, (a) Ex. 106.3(a) (Haydn, Symphony no. 104, second movement); (b) Ex. 62.3 (Beethoven, Symphony no. 3, 'Eroica', first movement)

(a)

(b)

Ex. 1.11 *The Dream of Gerontius*, Part I, Prelude, figs 5:7–6:4

the development of the first movement of Beethoven's Symphony No. 3 (Ex. 1.10 (b)), where the famous E minor episode is shown as arising from a series of middleground parallel chromatic tenths.[27] Elgar's music offers many similar situations. A straightforward, entirely foreground one occurs early in *The Dream of Gerontius*: here a progression of descending parallel major tenths serves to prolong the D major sonority, or VI in F♯ minor (Ex. 1.11). A more extensive, and tonally far more adventurous passage is the entire middle section of *Carissima* (bb. 15–52; example not shown), which moves from the tonic G major, twice through the sequence B minor–F♯ minor–B minor–F♯ major–F major, and again back to G, the whole traversing a spectacular four-octave, mostly chromatic descent in the bass, and moving frequently in thinly veiled, descending parallel sixths (e.g., bb. 15–17 and 23–6, and their repetitions later).

---

[27] Schenker, *The Masterwork in Music*, vol. I, pp. 82–5; *Free Composition*, p. 85, and fig. 106/3a in Examples volume; also p. 64, and fig. 62/3. Schenker provides a vastly more detailed sketch, with extensive discussion, in his analysis of the *Eroica* Symphony in *The Masterwork in Music*, vol. III.

Ex. 1.12 *The Dream of Gerontius*, Part II, from fig. 114

The relation between Elgar's music and Schenker's theory becomes more perilous when a passage does not prolong a single harmonic unit or key, but moves from one to another. Since our concern here is still with relatively surface levels, we do not have to consider the massive deep-middleground and background questions with which many Schenkerian analysts of late nineteenth-century music have had to struggle. But how can Schenker's theory illuminate even relatively short spans of Elgar's music, when the conventional tonal and harmonic pillars are lacking? What it can do, at the very least, is to sensitize us to Elgar's penchant for tying together harmonically wayward passages with clear scalewise motion. *Carissima* shows such a line in the bass. An even more extraordinary passage, in which the connecting line is in the melodic voice, occurs in the music leading up to the climax (at Part II, fig. 120) near the end of *The Dream of Gerontius* – music that includes the very passage that August Jaeger prevailed upon Elgar to add to his original version, which did not, in Jaeger's view, attain a sufficient level of intensity.[28] The analytical graph given in Ex. 1.12 shows clearly a guiding line that spans across a wash of unrelated keys: the Db major (from a few bars before fig. 114) that anchors the end of the music of the Angel of the Agony; the E major of the supplications of the small chorus that follows; the A minor of the (other) Angel's brief song of praise and 'Alleluia'; and finally the F♯ minor that arrives with the Soul's climactic 'Take me away!' The graph shows that, at the deepest level represented here, the F (3̂ of Db major) connects by semitone to the E of the E major cadence at fig. 116, *and* that that E is the chief melodic tone of the Angel's music from fig. 116 to fig. 118, as 5̂ of A minor. Closer to the surface, in the whole passage from fig. 114, the line simply moves up, via a minor-third figure that is sequenced exactly, from F to Ab and then Cb; then the Cb is transformed enharmonically to B, as 5̂ of E major, and the line

[28] See Moore, *Elgar*, pp. 316–21, for a detailed account of this correspondence in June 1900; and *Publishers*, pp. 200–9.

descends diatonically in E. When the larger-scale climb to the climax begins, with the Judgement motive at fig. 118, we may well suspect that the melodic line will rise from the $f\flat^1/e^1$, on which it begins, to e^2, given the immediate prominence of E and the solid A pedal in the bass. But as the melodic line ascends, it becomes chromatically blurred, and as it approaches e^2, the bass is also chromaticized (note the mainly semitonal descent from A to F♯), with the result that, in the bars leading up to the crashing chord at fig. 120, the ascent reaches past e^2 all the way to the climactic a^2. In order to sort out what is happening tonally here, we might have to combine conventional tonal theory (surely there is a V–I connection between the D♭ major at the beginning of the passage and the F♯ minor at the end, despite the unrelated keys that are asserted in the interim) with neo-Riemannian theory (what is the significance of the hexatonic-polar relationship between the opening D♭ major and the A minor of 116:1–118:1? – regarding the hexatonic poles, see below, pp. 25–9). However, there can be no doubt that the directed linear motion in the melodic voice binds the whole passage together.

How well my analysis of the *Gerontius* passage accords with Schenker's theory, strictly interpreted, is, of course, open to question. To what extent is the notion that seemingly coherent, unidirectional lines can bind together anomalous harmonies Schenkerian at all? Would Schenker himself ever have countenanced music the likes of *Carissima* and *Gerontius*, or analysis that posits the linear-harmonic relations that I have pointed out therein? And wasn't Kurth, a contemporary theorist despised by Schenker, well-known for finding what we could now call 'Schenkerian' lines in Bach's solo violin and cello works, and – particularly relevant here – in some of Wagner's most richly chromatic progressions, such as the Prelude to Act III of *Tristan*?[29] And isn't a central problem of Kurth's observation of such lines the very fact that he, unlike Schenker, was unable to tie them to a broader superstructure that puts them into context? These are questions, of course, that take us away from Elgar into the history of music theory. However we choose to answer them, I would still maintain that it is primarily Schenker's work, with its sensitivity to linear motion at different structural levels, that inspires us to hear such connections at all.

Schenkerian readings of chromatic tonal music of necessity entail an anchoring of chromatic passages in a background diatonic framework – a framework that, with its predominant/dominant/tonic harmonic functions, depends crucially on the asymmetry of the diatonic scale. But, as is now common knowledge, a central feature of nineteenth-century tonal practice is the growing use of the symmetrical features of the twelve-note scale. In

[29] For Kurth's analyses of Bach, see his *Grundlagen des linearen Kontrapunkts: Bachs melodische Polyphonie* (Bern: Drechsel, 1917). Rothfarb translates the passages most relevant to linear analysis in *Ernst Kurth: Selected Writings*, pp. 75–95.

contemporary Anglo-American theory, it was Gregory Proctor's 1978 dissertation that first called attention to symmetrical divisions of the octave in nineteenth-century music – that is, repetitions of musical material that preserve the exact intervallic structure of the original, rather than adjusting the intervals diatonically to stay within a single diatonic system. Proctor designated such sequences and similarly exactly transposed repetitions as instances of the 'transposition operation', and he posited a 'second practice' of nineteenth-century tonality, characterized by such procedures, to succeed the diatonic, Schenkerian 'first practice'. Proctor's work was the first of many to point out symmetrical divisions of the octave in nineteenth- and early twentieth-century music. Indeed, a whole cottage industry has sprung up around the notion – though, curiously, in many cases the authors (some who consider themselves theorists, and some who consider themselves music historians) are either unaware of each other's work, or did not realize that they were all dealing with the same fundamental principles of symmetry in the seven-in-twelve-note tonal universe. Robert Bailey's seminal article, already cited, introduced the idea of the 'expressive' use of tonality in Wagner's music: the technique of building tonal intensity by tonicizing keys that are successive half- or whole-steps higher than the original, often over vast spans of musical and dramatic time, and usually with the repetition of thematic material at each successive step. In 1985 Richard Taruskin traced the octatonic scale (so named in Arthur Berger's famous 1963 article on Stravinsky), back to Rimsky-Korsakov and Musorgsky, and thence back to Glinka, Liszt, and even Schubert, showing the nineteenth-century roots of a practice that derives from the symmetricality of the twelve-note scale. Many scholars have published work noting small- and large-scale equal-octave divisions in the work of particular composers.[30] Robert Morgan, with his well-known essay on 'dissonant prolongation' (usually of symmetrical sonorities), and Richard Cohn, with his work on hexatonic systems and on neo-Riemannian theory in general, have contributed major

---

[30] For example Eitan Agmon, 'Equal Divisions of the Octave in a Scarlatti Sonata', *In Theory Only*, 11/5 (1990), pp. 1–8; Martin Chusid, 'A Suggested Reading for Schubert's Piano Sonata in E-flat, Op. 122', in Otto Bussotti (ed.), *Schubert-Kongress Wien 1978* (Graz: Akademische Druck- und Verlaganstalt, 1979), pp. 37–44; Michael C. Tusa, 'When did Schubert Revise his Op. 122?', *Music Review*, 45 (1984), pp. 208–19; Friedhelm Krummacher, 'Schubert als Konstrukteur: Finale und Zyklus im G-Dur-Quartett D.887', *Archiv für Musikwissenschaft*, 51 (1994), pp. 26–50; R. Larry Todd, 'Franz Liszt, Carl Friedrich Weitzmann, and the Augmented Triad', in William Kinderman and Harald Krebs (eds.), *The Second Practice of Nineteenth-Century Tonality* (Lincoln: University of Nebraska Press, 1996), pp. 153–77; Howard Cinnamon, 'Tonic Arpeggiation and Successive Equal Third Relations as Elements of Tonal Evolution in the Music of Franz Liszt', *Music Theory Spectrum*, 8 (1986), pp. 1–24; Deborah Stein, *Hugo Wolf's 'Lieder' and Extensions of Tonality* (Ann Arbor: UMI Research Press, 1985). The essays edited by Kinderman and Krebs address in the title Proctor's notion of a 'second practice', and the book as a whole is a tribute to Bailey.

music-theoretical studies.[31] Finally, the recognition of the theoretical possibilities and compositional uses of equal-octave divisions is not limited to late twentieth-century theorists and historians. Even in the 1850s Karl Weitzmann, an associate of Liszt, recognized the compositional usefulness of equal-third cycles (the diminished seventh and augmented triad); Hugo Riemann's mature harmonic theory recognizes the inherent symmetry of the tonal system; Schenker, though he never discusses the notion explicitly, nevertheless shows, in graphs in *Free Composition*, equal-octave divisions in works of Beethoven and Wolf; and Kurth ranks the *aussertonale Sequenz* – the equivalent of Proctor's transposition operation – high in his list of features of Romantic harmony that threaten the stability of tonality.[32]

This quick rehearsal of so much theory about equal-octave divisions in an essay on Elgar dramatizes the fact that, on the one hand, the transposition operation (or whatever one wants to call it) is absolutely crucial to the canonic Germanic harmonic practice of his time, and to Elgar's practice as well, since he emulated it and incorporated it brilliantly into his music; nevertheless, virtually none of the theory, from Riemann, Schenker, Kurth, and Lorenz, to Proctor, Bailey, and beyond, has intersected at all with Elgar's music. A single essay, needless to say, cannot rectify this imbalance. But it can at least point out some examples and demonstrate that Elgar's music belongs securely in the repertoire that the theories were developed to illuminate. Passages that involve equal-octave division are easy to find in Elgar, and they generously repay detailed analytical and interpretive consideration. The examples adduced here are of three types: first, a general category that involves the tracing of equal-interval cycles at, or at least very close to, the musical surface; second, a category that occurs only infrequently – literal statements of whole-tone and octatonic scales; and third, a more specialized type that involves a particular kind of symmetry – hexatonic spaces.

Of the first category it will be deemed sufficient to show one example each of equal octave divisions by the major second, minor third, and major third. For the major second, a passage from an early cantata, *Scenes from the Saga of King Olaf*, offers a simple sequence whereby a figure centring on a minor triad descends by major seconds through an entire octave, outlining a whole-tone scale in the process (Ex. 1.13).

[31] Robert Morgan, 'Dissonant Prolongation: Theoretical and Compositional Precedents', *Journal of Music Theory*, 20 (1976), pp. 49–91.
[32] Carl Friedrich Weitzmann, *Der übermässige Dreiklang* (Berlin: Guttentag, 1853) and *Der verminderte Septimen-Akkord* (Berlin: Peters, 1854). Schenker shows equal-third octave divisions in his analysis of the first movement of Beethoven's Piano Sonata, Op. 57, in *Free Composition*, p. 92, and fig. 114/8 in the Examples volume; and in his analysis of Wolf's 'Das Ständchen' (*Eichendorff-Lieder*), p. 82, and fig. 100/6c. Kurth discusses the *aussertonale Sequenz* in *Romantische Harmonik*, p. 353.

Ex. 1.13 *King Olaf*, no. 3 ('King Olaf's Return'), four bars after F to two after G

For the minor third, a passage from the last movement of the Second Symphony offers a compelling example, and one at a somewhat deeper structural level. Here a four-bar musical unit (see Ex. 1.14) is stated in B minor, then transposed up a minor third to D minor. Before continuing, it turns back to B minor again, then D minor again, before proceeding to new statements in F minor and Ab minor. The increasing intensity of these last two statements is underscored by the crescendo and the foreshortening of the figure to two, rather than four, bars. When the cycle returns to B minor, there is another hypermetric adjustment, this time to units of three bars each of B minor and D minor, before the pattern is finally broken. Finally, for the major third, we return to *King Olaf*, and to a descending sequence again, which cycles four times through the triadic succession G minor, Eb minor, B minor (Ex. 1.15).

The second category, that of literal statements of whole-tone and octatonic scales, is so rare as to be virtually non-existent in Elgar's music. Unsullied, unambiguous occurrences of these pitch-class collections are far less frequent than they are even in the music of Liszt, much less in the music of Russian tonal composers from Musorgsky to Rimsky-Korsakov, and turn-of-the-century

Ex. 1.14 Symphony no. 2, fourth movement, figs. 152–155:2

French music by composers such as Fauré, Debussy, and Ravel. There are occasional examples – the two whole-tone scales occur in succession at fig. 114 of Part II of *The Dream of Gerontius*, and a striking whole-tone figure, in descending parallel major thirds, occurs in *The Music Makers* at 25:1–6, 30:8–9, and 83:2–84:3.[33] As to the octatonic scale, a virtually unique occurrence is in the bass part (played by a number of instruments) in the third movement of the Second Symphony, from 105:14 (second quaver) to 105:18.

The third category turns on a symmetrical feature central to the neo-Riemannian theory that has assumed such importance in Anglo-American theory since the mid-1990s. What Richard Cohn has dubbed a 'hexatonic system' derives from a six-note pattern within the octave, expressible as two augmented triads a semitone apart, or the pitch-class set (0, 1, 4, 5, 8, 9) (Ex. 1.16 (a) and (b)). Any hexatonic system contains six consonant triads – three major and three minor – which can be generated by starting with any triad in the system and successively applying two (neo-)Riemannian operations: L (or 'Leittonwechsel' – that is, the root of a major triad moves to its leading note, or the fifth of a minor triad moves up a semitone to the sixth); and P (or 'Parallele' – that is, the third changes from minor to major, or vice versa), one note at a time (thus producing 'parsimonious' voice-leading). In Ex. 1.16 (c), the six triads are the major and minor triads on A♭, C, and E. Note that after three operations (LPL), none of the original notes is left; A♭ major is replaced by E minor. This relation of a consonant triad in a

---

[33] I am grateful to Julian Rushton for drawing my attention to the *Music Makers* reference.

Ex. 1.15 *King Olaf,* no. 9 ('The Wrath of Odin'), from B to two bars before C

hexatonic system to the triad in the same system that preserves none of its original pitch-classes is called the hexatonic pole.

There are four such hexatonic groups in the twelve-note equal-tempered system; these four designated by Cohn as Northern (the system of Ex. 1.16),

Ex. 1.16 The hexatone system, after Richard Cohn

Ex. 1.17 Richard Cohn's diagram of hexatone groups, reproduced by kind permission of Blackwell Publishing

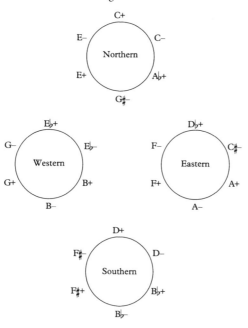

Western, Southern, and Eastern (Ex. 1.17).[34] Unadulterated occurrences of hexatonic passages are as rare at the surface of Elgar's music as those of whole-tone and octatonic scales; I know of no other example than the development of the First Symphony, 24:6 (beat 3)–24:12 (beat 2), where eight-crotchet units of the Southern system alternate with eight-crotchet units of the Northern system (the passage begins with six crotchet beats of lurching in the Southern system from 24:5, beat 1). More intriguing are structurally deeper instances of hexatonic spaces, which can occur when governing triads are a major third apart. A splendid example is the part song, 'There is Sweet Music', Op. 53, No. 1, which famously interweaves a male chorus singing in G major with a female chorus singing in A♭ major. Although these principal G and A♭ major triads are not in a single hexatonic

[34] The diagram in Example 1.17 is from Cohn, 'Maximally Smooth Cycles', p. 17.

Ex. 1.18 'Sweet Music', op. 53, no. 1

Ex. 1.19 *The Dream of Gerontius*, Part I, outline from Prelude to fig. 70

system, the major and minor triads on A♭, C, and E are, as is the augmented triad comprising these three pitch-classes. As the song progresses, it moves through various of these triads at critical points in the harmonic fabric, as shown in Ex. 1.18.

An example governing a much longer time span occurs in Part I of *The Dream of Gerontius* (see Ex. 1.19).[35] Here the Prelude begins in D minor, then moves via P (the parallel operation) briefly to D major at 1:7 and 2:1, which, after a densely chromatic passage leads to music that seems to be in D major because it continually returns to a D pedal, but which is actually in F♯ minor – the D pedal representing a deceptive cadence in F♯, with a single definitive cadence coming at fig. 7. In neo-Riemannian terms, D major produces F♯ minor via the L ('Leittonwechsel') operation. Eventually the tonic D minor returns (by L + P) at fig. 20, then makes a P move to D major at fig. 21, before proceeding via L + P to B♭ major at fig. 22, where we hear the first words of Gerontius. The two choruses that follow, in E♭ major (fig. 29) and A♭ major (fig. 35), clearly proceed in descending diatonic circle-of-fifths space rather than hexatonic space, but it is significant that Gerontius's next section, 'Sanctus fortis' (fig. 40), begins in B♭ minor (produced by the P operation from the B♭ major of fig. 20) and in fact alternates between B♭ minor and major throughout. Although the succeeding choruses depart to non-hexatonically related keys, plunging further down the circle of fifths, again from E♭ (now minor, at fig. 63), now to A♭ minor (fig. 64), and even C♯ minor (fig. 65), the D major Prelude material

---

[35] This example from *Gerontius* will be the only example in which any of our first three chromatic techniques are used to address a whole large-scale unit of a composition. I will be concerned only with examples from *The Apostles* in my exposition of the three remaining techniques, and I will not discuss hexatonic spaces there.

returns at fig. 67, preparing the Priest's B♭ major 'Proficiscere' at fig. 68. Note the hexatonic polar relation between the B♭ minor of fig. 40 and the D major of fig. 67. At fig. 68, the harmony descends, now by whole step, twice, from B♭ major to A♭ major to G♭ major, and then, near the end of the Priest's music, trenchantly juxtaposes G♭ major on the word 'world' (69:6) to D major just before the word 'God' (70:1), the latter introducing the final chorus in this key. (The chorus, it should be noted, twice reiterates this B♭–A♭–G♭ motion, at 72:3ff. and 74:2ff.) The music of Part I thereby tracks through all six consonant triads of the Southern system. Furthermore, once we step back and look at the tonal pattern of all of Part I, we note that the descending circle-of-fifths motion, which progresses from B♭ to E♭ to A♭ beginning at fig. 29, picks up E♭ again at fig. 63 and proceeds to A♭ (fig. 64) and C♯ (= D♭, 65:2), and might be said to 'feed into' the prevailing hexatonic structure with the arrival of G♭ major at figs. 68 and 69.

A final, relatively large-scale example from the First Symphony (so large that the music is not reproduced here) illustrates how Elgar can bind these seemingly independent elements – the half-diminished seventh chord, a guiding line that binds together disparate and chromatically related harmonic entities, and symmetrical aspects of the tonal system – into a stunningly effective musical statement. The passage in question is the music that leads up to the return of the A♭ major 'Ideal Call' theme in the final movement of the symphony. As is well known, in the First Symphony a structural frame in A♭ major (the utterly diatonic Ideal Call), occurs only at the very beginning and end of the first movement and the very end of the last. The first movement, after the Ideal Call, consists of a full-blown sonata in D minor; the second movement is a scherzo in F♯ minor; the third is an Adagio in D major; and the Finale a Lento–Allegro, of which the Allegro is a deformation of a sonata structure – in James Hepokoski's terms, a sonata with a 'nonresolving recapitulation'.[36] What fails to resolve is the D minor sonata that constitutes most of the Finale: after off-key recapitulations of the primary and secondary themes, the music powerfully swerves toward the global tonic of A♭ major, never returning to the D minor of the exposition.

The music that will concern us here is the forty-three-bar passage that leads into the arrival of the Ideal Call, in the tonic, 'Grandioso (poco largamente)' at fig. 146. It begins with a straightforward equal-interval cycle. The theme that begins at fig. 141 is the exposition's third theme, which (unusually) appeared in the tonic D minor there (fig. 118), and then

[36] Hepokoski, 'Elgar', pp. 330–6; for the concept in general, see his 'Back and Forth from *Egmont*: Beethoven, Mozart, and the Nonresolving Recapitulation', *19CM*, 25 (2001), pp. 127–54.

was repeated sequentially in F minor and A♭ minor. Here it begins a minor third higher, in F minor, then gains energy quickly through statements in A♭ major and B minor. The B minor statement does not lead to another in D minor, as might be expected in order to complete the cycle – is a statement on D obliterated here, or is D the one place to which the music *cannot* go? Rather, it leads to a bizarre *forte* statement on a diminished triad – one that prepares the *fff* return of the theme (now in a foreshortened group of three rather than four bars) in the original F minor.

At fig. 143 everything changes. Gone is the theme, with its sequential, intensifying repetitions. Now the melodic material is more generic – a series of desperate sweeps up to a high register in the first violins, from 143:1 to 144:7, followed by an equally frantic succession of falling gestures, which leap over one another in a rush to the climactic ab^3 of 145:8. And much of the actual musical motion in this latter passage is given over to an absolutely consistent and unidirectional, mostly chromatic descending line in the bass, connecting from f at fig. 143:1 to d♮ just before fig. 146: continuity via descending bass supplants continuity via ascending equal-minor-third cycle. The crowning, fraught-with-anxiety Elgarian touch is the sudden appearance of taut half-diminished sevenths in the harmonic mix beginning around fig. 143: pairs of these tense chords occur at 143:4, 143:8, and 144:4, in ascending fifths, as is clear from the bass in these bars – D♮, A♮, E♮ (this regular, ascending-fifth motion is not apparent in the upper registers). But within each pair, the root movement of the successive chords is down by fifth – exactly the same relation that Elgar would use later at the beginning of the Second Symphony (see Ex. 1.4(a) above), such that the (raised) root of the first chord moves down by semitone rather than up. This descending chromatic motion is worked smoothly into the long descending bass line, with d♮–d♭ at 143:4, A♮–A♭ at 143:8, and E♮–E♭ at 144:4. More half-diminished sevenths are heard at 145:2–4, but the *coup de grace* is saved for the end: the last, cataclysmic chord before the arrival on A♭ at fig. 146 is a half-diminished seventh on D♮. Its fifth is the violins' and flutes' stratospheric ab^3, the upper registral goal of all the music since fig. 144, while its D♮ root is the goal of the more-than-two-octave descent of the entire passage. More tellingly, this last harmony before the global return to A♭ is of neither dominant nor subdominant function, but rather a half-diminished seventh, a tritone from the tonic, that thus at the last moment juxtaposes the D, the enclosed key of the larger structure, with A♭, the enclosing one. Techniques that Elgar uses so effectively on the musical surface – expressive half-diminished seventh chords, unidirectional lines to span across challenging harmonic territory, and equal divisions of the octave – serve here, near the end of the symphony, to articulate its climactic structural and expressive moment.

II Large-scale chromaticism

Our hearing of chromatic techniques in the First Symphony suggests the possibility of taking chromatic theory to a higher power, to see what it has to offer on the large scale rather than the small. For Elgar, of course, there is no larger scale than that of *The Apostles*, his longest work. Ultimately the work is tonal, like Wagner's dramatic works; I entirely concur with Charles McGuire's claim that it is in E♭ major, with an off-tonic, subdominant opening chorus.[37] But many of the sections, large and small, within the oratorio are in keys chromatically related to E♭, so our questions must be: how do theories of tonality, or theories of chromatic function within large-scale tonal pieces such as symphonies and operas, shed light on the large-scale tonal structure of *The Apostles*, and how does this structure lead us toward a hermeneutic interpretation?

Despite the considerable rewards that Schenkerian theory might offer on the deeper middleground and background scale, I shall not pursue it here. Nevertheless I still posit it as the first of my three proposed theories for explaining large-scale chromaticism. For although Schenker's theory is fundamentally not a chromatic theory at all, but a diatonic one, it claims to be able to contextualize the most complex chromatic events and give them meaning in a broadly diatonic context. But Schenker limited himself strictly to single monotonal works or movements: he heard tonal pieces as the coming to life in real time of a single tonic triad. His outer boundary was the individual *Ursatz*, and he *never* extended the claims of his later theory across movements of multi-movement works, much less across a whole dramatic work, or even an act of a dramatic work. So, to say the very least, there is no model from Schenker himself as to how his theories might apply to whole Wagner music dramas or Mahler symphonies. A number of theorists have refused to accept Schenker's own limitations of scale, and we now have some impressive precedents for Schenkerian readings of late nineteenth- and early twentieth-century multi-movement and dramatic works.[38] Closest to our concerns here, J. P. E. Harper-Scott, as we have seen, relies centrally on Schenker for his interpretations of both the Elgar symphonies. Much of this work is compelling, and I find his Schenkerian

[37] Charles Edward McGuire, 'Elgar, Judas, and the Theology of Betrayal', *19CM*, 23 (2000), p. 258.
[38] Darcy, *Wagner's 'Das Rheingold'*; '*Die Zeit ist da*: rotational form and hexatonic magic in Act II, Scene 1 of *Parsifal*', in William Kinderman and Katherine Syer (eds.), *A Companion to Wagner's 'Parsifal'* (Rochester: Camden House, 2005); and 'Rotational Form, Teleological Genesis, and Fantasy-Projection in the Slow Movement of Mahler's Sixth Symphony', *19CM*, 25 (2001), pp. 49–74. Timothy L. Jackson, 'The Finale of Bruckner's Seventh Symphony and Tragic Reversed Sonata Form', in Paul Hawkshaw and Timothy L. Jackson (eds.), *Bruckner Studies* (Cambridge: Cambridge University Press, 1997); and *Tchaikovsky: Symphony No. 6*.

reading of the First Symphony quite persuasive – a reading in which he hears the work projecting a unifying *Kopfton* of C, as $\hat{3}$ of A♭ major, throughout, even across movements in F♯ minor and D major, to the final cadence of the work (where, despite all that, it doesn't resolve).[39]

I could offer a Schenkerian reading of an excerpt of a section of the oratorio, rather as I did for a passage in *The Dream of Gerontius*, but it would add little to what I have already said, and to present an analysis of *The Apostles*, with a Schenkerian background rationalizing and explaining its many chromaticisms on all levels, is more than I can undertake here. Schenkerian hearings of huge swathes of Wagner, Mahler, and Elgar are costly, not only in terms of the investment of analytical time and graphic space, but also in terms of the theoretical undergirding and rhetorical prose required to make one's analysis credible and convincing. In particular, even if one's Schenkerian bass line for a dramatic work (as in Darcy's analysis of *Das Rheingold*) traces out a comprehensible and meaningful pattern, there remains the problem of upper-voice counterpoint and the *Urlinie*. It is here that the cost exceeds my willingness to invest; to claim that a large-scale tonal orientation governs a symphonic or dramatic work over an expanse of time is one thing; to claim that tonal orientation is controlled by an outer-voice counterpoint that progresses to a clinching scalewise descent to the tonic at the end of an hour, or much more, of music, is a much stronger assertion, and one that I am not willing to make for *The Apostles*. I certainly do not foreclose the possibility that someone may be able to offer a convincing Schenkerian reading. And I *am* willing to make a (purely diatonic) Schenkerian point, which might eventually be useful. That is, given that the oratorio is in E♭ major, one cannot help but notice that the opening chorus, 'The Spirit of the Lord', *almost* has an *Urlinie* resolving cadence at the end of its section in E♭: a♭^{1}–g^1–f^1 over a strongly supporting bass line at 8:12–9:1; but the upper voice refuses to close, moving from the f^1 back up to g^1. The same melody, still in E♭, recurs in precisely the same way in 'The Lord hath chosen them to stand' (figs. 52 to 53), and in the Introduction to Part II (figs. 142 to 143), both times cadencing on $\hat{3}$ rather than $\hat{1}$. Then, near the end of the work, Jesus's final lines replicate the last few bars of this same music (figs. 214 to 215), with an even stronger bass line, and this time the melody does indeed resolve to the tonic. One could conceivably hang a Schenkerian reading on this (diatonic) observation – one that would sweep up the masses of chromatic relations in the work into a convincing linear-harmonic narrative, with the *Ursatz* closing precisely at fig. 215.

---

[39] Harper-Scott, '"A nice sub-acid feeling"' and ch. 6 of this volume.

My hearing of the work, though, is more harmonic than linear, and it has music-theoretical forebears other than Schenker. What do we need, music-theoretically speaking, to make large-scale tonal sense out of a two-hour, harmonically ambitious, post-Wagnerian turn-of-the-century dramatic work? We need harmonic theories that can deal with extensive chromaticism, and we especially need harmonic principles that can govern the tonal relations of triads across wide spans of musical-dramatic time. By the early twentieth century, harmonic theories of chromaticism had developed sufficiently to have much to say about harmony in the works of Wagner and his contemporaries, and of composers of the following generation. Rameau, hardly a theorist of chromaticism, recognized the enharmonic capabilities of diminished-seventh and similarly unstable chords, as did later eighteenth- and early nineteenth-century theorists such as Kirnberger and Reicha. Vogler reified such capabilities in his concept of *Mehrdeutigkeit*, and his student Gottfried Weber put them to productive, if obsessive, use in his famous analysis of the slow introduction to Mozart's Quartet in C major, K. 465. Weber also contributed the first exhaustive tabular chart of key relations – relations that had been theoretically possible since Heinichen's circle of fifths in 1711, but in Weber's time were beginning to be worked out in real pieces. Weber's was the first of many such maps of tonal relations conceived as a spatial network; the *Tonnetze* of Oettingen and Riemann, Schoenberg's 'Chart of the Regions', and David Lewin's and Fred Lerdahl's more recent maps of tonal space all hearken back to Weber. In the mid-nineteenth century Carl Weitzmann published treatises on the symmetrical diminished seventh and augmented sixth chords, in an attempt to come to grips with the harmonic practice of Liszt; and the essentially unknown Heinrich Joseph Vincent argued for the replacement of diatonic fundamental-bass theory (like that of Sechter) with a legitimately chromatic theory. Picking up threads from both Weber and Oettingen, Riemann developed theories of harmonic function and harmonic transformation that were fully chromatic, explaining the relation between any two major and/or minor triads.[40] Yet, although his theories could have coped with the chromaticism of Wagner's post-*Tristan* music, he himself limited his analyses to the music of Bach and Beethoven. And finally, as we saw above, Ernst Kurth, in the early twentieth century, fashioned his harmonic analyses primarily on principles that he derived from the Wagnerian *Tristan* style.

[40] I am indebted in this paragraph to David Bernstein's useful summary of the historical development of harmonic theory in the nineteenth century, in 'Nineteenth-Century Harmonic Theory: the Austro-German Legacy', in Thomas Christensen (ed.), *The* *Cambridge History of Western Music Theory* (Cambridge: Cambridge University Press, 2002), pp. 778–811. See also Robert Wason, 'Progressive Harmonic Theory in the Mid-Nineteenth Century', *Journal of Musicological Research*, 8 (1988), pp. 55–90.

But of these later writers, whose theories could, in one sense or another, handle the chromaticism featured in the music of their time, virtually none paid any attention to large-scale tonal relations – not even in Beethoven, much less in Wagner or his successors. Kurth's *Romantische Harmonik*, as I have shown elsewhere, comes close. He recognizes the dramatic association of pitch-specific chords (such as the Samiel chord in Carl Maria von Weber's *Der Freischütz*), as well as the tendency of acts in Wagner's music dramas to move by thirds – often chromatic thirds.[41] It was left to Alfred Lorenz, whose monumental *Das Geheimnis der Form bei Richard Wagner* began to appear in 1924, to conceive of dramatic works on the scale of whole operas or music dramas as a tonally coherent whole. It was once fashionable to dismiss and ridicule Lorenz; after all, he was a member of the National Socialist Party in the 1930s, and his obsession with 'Bar' form, and with leitmotivs, in the manner of Hans von Wolzogen, makes his sometimes eccentric and easily refutable analyses an easy target. But after David Lewin reprimanded Lorenz's critics and proceeded to make insightful use of his work in his magisterial analysis of the entirety of *Parsifal*, and especially after Stephen McClatchie's even-handed study of the theorist and his work, his ideas now are common currency.[42] Whatever his faults, he unquestionably pinpointed precisely the last two of the six chromatic-tonal techniques identified here in my study of Elgar: technique 5, what Bailey, fifty years later, dubbed associative tonality; and technique 6, the critical notion that the works of Wagner and of many composers in the succeeding generation make large-scale *tonal sense* – a sense that derives usually from a combination of the dramatic association of keys and the abstract planning of keys on a massive scale. For example, he noticed that Scenes 2–4 of *Das Rheingold* form a ternary structure in the pattern tonic/relative minor/tonic (D♭/B♭ minor/D♭), that the E♭ major of Scene 1 prepares the larger, D♭ major ternary as the dominant of the dominant, and that all these keys are associated with a dramatic symbol – E♭ major for the Rhine, D♭ major for Valhalla, and B♭ minor for Nibelheim. Similarly, he claimed that the governing tonality of *Tristan und Isolde* is a modally indeterminate E, the fulcrum between the opening of the opera in A minor and its conclusion in B major.[43] And on a slightly smaller scale he frequently demonstrated all sorts of relations of more chromatic keys, applying for the first time Riemann's powerful and flexible functions and transformations to forge a way through a massive tonal work containing

---

[41] See my 'Ernst Kurth and the Analysis of the Chromatic Music of the Late Nineteenth Century', *Music Theory Spectrum*, 5 (1983), pp. 56–75.
[42] Lewin, 'Amfortas's Prayer'; Stephen McClatchie, *Analysing Wagner's Operas:* *Alfred Lorenz and German Nationalist Ideology* (Rochester: University of Rochester Press, 1998).
[43] Lorenz, *Das Geheimnis der Form*, vol. I, pp. 23–7; vol. II, pp. 173–80.

many keys. Hardly anyone now would accept this tonal view of *Tristan*, but at a single stroke he advanced Wagner analysis by a number of decades. Before him, Wagner analysis, such as it was, was concentrated in leitmotiv-hunting; it was Lorenz who made it abundantly clear that the tonal structure, including especially its associative key relations, is at least as important an aspect of these works as the motivic structure – that keys, like motives, span coherently across dramatic time. Without Lorenz, or at least without someone to come to the same sorts of conclusions about tonal structure in large-scale turn-of-the-century tonal works, much of the theory and analysis, from Bailey and Proctor to Lewin and Lerdahl, on which the present study relies, would not have been possible.

The notion of associative tonality (technique 5), or more generally, tonal cross-reference, is worth a brief detour before our discussion of *The Apostles*. Bailey and others use the term 'associative tonality' to refer specifically to tonal associations in dramatic works. So far, so good; this is clearly a tool that we need for Wagner's music, and for Elgar's. But there is an interesting history here, both in the history of composition and in the history of theory. Take, for example, the familiar opening chords of *Götterdämmerung*. It is common knowledge that these four triads resonate back and forth to the very beginning and very ending of the *Ring*. The opening E♭, now modally coloured minor, is the key of the Rhine, and of the beginning of the cycle. The second chord, C♭ (now major), is the enharmonic equivalent of B, the (minor) key of the Curse, as asserted by Alberich in Scene 4 of *Das Rheingold*. After a return to E♭ minor, the fourth triad, D♭ minor, modally colours the associative key of Valhalla, and of the end of the music drama and *Ring* cycle. These triads/keys all have associations with elements of the drama. But suppose they didn't. Suppose that the drama – the characters, the story, and so forth – were somehow subtracted from the *Ring*, and what was left was the sixteen hours or so of its music. Then would not these four chords cross-reference (purely) musical triads and keys, as well as their associated motives? Such a supposition, of course, raises the spectre of 'absolute music', plays easily into charges of formalism, and comes close to suggesting the idea of 'Wagnerian music drama as symphony', an idea blasted almost (but not quite) into oblivion by Carolyn Abbate fifteen years ago.[44]

I would argue, though, that Wagner here *is* appropriating a symphonic model – or at least a model of tonal coherence derived from German instrumental music from the time of Beethoven, and even before. Consider, for example, pieces or movements that introduce a single chromatic pitch early

---

[44] Carolyn Abbate, 'Opera as Symphony, a Wagnerian Myth', in Carolyn Abbate and Roger Parker (eds.), *Analysing Opera: Verdi and Wagner* (Berkeley and Los Angeles: University of California Press, 1989), pp. 92–124.

on in a tonal work, then develop it in richer and richer detail as the piece progresses. The tonal repertoire is swimming with such works, of which we all have our favourite examples – what happens, over musical time, to the famous C♯ in the opening bars of Beethoven's *Eroica* Symphony, or the bizarre C♯ in the Finale of the Eighth (Wagner's favourite Beethoven symphony, by the way)? Of dozens of analytical treatments of pieces of this sort, there is Edward T. Cone's 'Promissory' F♭/E in Schubert's *Moment Musical* No. 6, and Charles Rosen's massive analysis of the adventures of B♮ and F♯ in the *Hammerklavier* Sonata.[45] But where did this idea originate? Modern writers, such as Rosen or Milton Babbitt, seem to take it for granted, as though it has always been with us. For example, it is tonal cross-referential logic – assumed rather than theorized – that Rosen plays as a trump on behalf of Haydn against C. P. E. Bach. And Babbitt summarily casts an earlier analyst's work into the flames because of a failure to realize that the move to C♭ in the middle of the slow movement of Mozart's G minor Symphony is, apparently, an inevitable outgrowth of the C♭ in the cellos and basses in the opening bars; the foolish analyst called it 'a surprise'.[46] The unstated principle that underlies Babbitt's airy dismissal is that chromatic pitch-classes can, in a tonal context, cross-refer to one another, as seeds for growth, and indeed develop into some sort of tonal plot. Schenker seems a logical suspect as the originator of this idea, until we realize that his cross-referential elements are not pitch-classes at all, but voice-leading paradigms. This is no place for research into the origins of what some theorists now call 'pitch-class motives' in tonal music, but I want to emphasize as strongly as possible (a) that such tonal-chromatic narratives occur in (especially Germanic) instrumental music from at least Beethoven on; (b) that one of the most important techniques that Wagner took from Beethoven (even though the many writings in which he claims to pick up Beethoven's mantle do not refer to such tonal narratives but more generally to the symphony and symphonic expression) was precisely tonal-chromatic cross-reference, imported into a texted genre from an untexted one; and (c) that we should not be surprised to encounter the technique in Elgar's music, just as we do in the music of Bruckner, Mahler, and Strauss.

Of what I am calling tonal-narrative patterning (technique 6) there are many examples in Lorenz, of course, and also in more recent work by many writers noted above. Wagner frequently manages to make a number of tonal-chromatic techniques work simultaneously. Act I of *Siegfried* progresses from B♭ minor in Scene 1 to C in Scene 2 and D in Scene 3. These keys are cross-referential, since B♭ minor is the key of Nibelheim, C of Wotan's plan for

---

[45] Edward T. Cone, 'Schubert's Promissory Note: An Essay in Musical Hermeneutics', *19CM*, 5 (1982), pp. 233–41; Rosen, *The Classical Style*, pp. 409–34.

[46] Rosen, *The Classical Style*, pp. 11–17; Babbitt, 'The Structure and Function of Music Theory', pp. 11–12.

the redeeming of the world, and D of the reforging of the Sword. At the same time, they trace part of an equal division of the octave (three loci in an ascending whole-tone scale), and instantiate, over an hour or so of dramatic time, the chromatic third relation of Bb minor and D major – a relation easily describable by Riemannian harmonic theory, and now identifiable as a relation of hexatonic poles. Warren Darcy's analysis of *Das Rheingold* goes one step further: *every* key that he shows is associated with a dramatic element, there are numerous cross-referential relationships, the tonal structure exhibits a clear patterning at both background ([Eb]–Db–Bb–Db) and middleground (filling in of thirds, and so forth) levels, *and* the whole music drama plays out a Schenkerian *Ursatz*.[47]

What then, having declined to offer a Schenkerian reading, but having introduced the notion of tonal-chromatic cross-reference and patterning, can I do with *The Apostles*? In brief, what I hope to show is that the oratorio, which, needless to say, traverses many keys chromatically related to the global tonic of Eb major, relies for its large-scale structure on associative and cross-referential tonal relationships, and on the abstract, but dramatically motivated patterning of keys. Indeed, I would like to do for *The Apostles* something like what Lorenz and Bailey did for the *Ring* and Wagner's other music dramas: to show that there is far more to this music than leitmotivs, and that the tonal cross-references are at least as crucial to the dramatic and musical plan as the motives, sometimes even more so. This is not to denigrate the work of von Wolzogen and Jaeger, who made necessary and critical contributions to Wagner and Elgar analysis, respectively. If they both pursued motive-naming in ways less sophisticated than the music deserves, they nevertheless had a lot to say, and their observations are central to our modern understanding of the works. But there can be no doubt that Wagner lavished the greatest care on tonal structure in his works, even though he virtually never wrote about it, and I will argue here that Elgar did the same in composing *The Apostles*.

We begin with the fundamental key of the oratorio – Eb major, the key to which all the others must ultimately relate. Eb major is without question the global key of the whole, just as D major/minor is the key of *The Dream of Gerontius*, and Eb major of *The Kingdom*.[48] Eb, as we have seen, makes a crucial appearance even within the opening chorus in Ab major. More importantly, it is the key in which the choosing of the apostles is confirmed and made

---

[47] See McCreless, *Wagner's 'Siegfried': Its Drama. History, and Music* (Ann Arbor: UMI Research Press, 1982), pp. 100–1; Darcy, *Wagner's 'Das Rheingold'*, pp. 216–19.
[48] J. P. E. Harper-Scott offers some broad insights about tonal usage in *The Dream of Gerontius*, including a persuasive claim that it makes use of associative tonality. See *Edward Elgar, Modernist*, p. 14. In addition, in 'Elgar and the Invention of the Human', he argues for associative tonality in *Falstaff*.

manifest, in the chorus, 'The Lord hath chosen them to stand'. And, of course, it is the key of Jesus's final commandment, 'Go ye therefore and teach all nations', his parting words immediately before his ascension, and the final chorus of affirmation. E♭ major anchors the work of Jesus and the work of the apostles; it is the key of the beginning of the Church.

A few Elgar scholars have given attention to tonal structure in *The Apostles*. Jerrold Northrop Moore's contribution to the discussion involves less his observations about the tonal structure of individual works, which tend to be as broad and general as possible, than his tracking of keys through Elgar's compositional life. Thus G major and minor dominate the works of the 1890s; the D minor and major of *Gerontius* briefly interrupts the tendency toward flat keys that begins with the E♭ major of *Caractacus*; the A♭ major opening chorus of *The Apostles* is Elgar's 'furthest journey into a tonic of flats for a major work'; 'There is Sweet Music' (1907) juxtaposes the 'old G major' with the A♭ of the Symphony to come; and so forth.[49] There is, as it were, a 'tonal structure' stretching across Elgar's work as a whole, often combining conventional key associations with the resonances that emerged and grew as his compositional career proceeded. Within *The Apostles* itself, he notes the principal keys that are used, and he points out that Part I unfolds from the opening A♭ major to the tritone-related D major. More importantly, he identifies D minor with Judas in Part II, and ties *The Apostles* closely to the First Symphony, which would follow a few years later:

> So Edward's Symphony embodied again the central theme of *The Apostles* – an ideal set in the diatonic music of an older world, and then put to the extreme test of a chromatic future . . . And the tonal territory of *The Apostles* also lay between the A flat major Prologue and the D minor uprising of Judas – precisely the tritone of the Symphony. Only the Symphony's D minor 'Judas' now rose up directly on the heels of its master. The challenge not finally met in *The Apostles* stood at the head of the Symphony with peremptory insistence.[50]

Charles McGuire offers much more in his study of the character of Judas. On the broadest level he, like Moore, points out a large-scale tritone relation: not A♭/D, but the global E♭ major of the whole oratorio (representing Jesus, the Church, and the goal of the apostles' spreading the gospel) and the A minor (*not* D minor, *pace* Moore; Judas's scene has a D minor section, but revolves clearly around A minor) of much of Judas's music in Part II. Especially perceptive is his more detailed reading of the dramatic and musical function of E♭ major in the work. In Part I, and particularly in the chorus 'The Lord hath chosen them to stand', E♭ major has a tendency to swerve toward G minor, the purity of Christ's actions contaminated by the inability of the very human apostles to understand his purpose (see, for

---

[49] Moore, *Elgar*, pp. 162–3, 189–94, 387, and 524.   [50] Moore, *Elgar*, pp. 397 and 521.

example, the move to G minor at 43:5ff.).[51] In Part II, his analysis addresses a troubling paradox: why, if E♭ major represents the purity of Christ and the church, is much of the music portraying his betrayal in this key (see, for example, fig. 153)? Because this action concerns Christ himself and what is happening to him (McGuire notes, though, that this E♭ music, like that in Part I, dissolves into G minor at 153:8ff); when the drama turns toward Judas's experience, it establishes A minor. McGuire's recounting of the tortuous relation of E♭ major and A minor in the scene climaxes with his description of the very middle of Judas's monologue, where he is suddenly moved by his memory of Jesus ('Never man spake like this man; He satisfied the longing soul', 176:3). Not only does the music turn to the Beatitude leitmotiv from 'By the Wayside' (as pointed out by Jaeger a century ago) but it – incongruously, in the A minor context here – brings back Christ's key of E♭ major.[52] The poignancy of this touching moment resides as much in Elgar's calculated disposition of keys across time as in his dispersal of themes across time.

But there is much more in this moment. To understand what that is will require that we return to Part I and consider more closely the tonal portrayal of Jesus. To be sure, his first appearance, naturally, is in the E♭ major triumphant chorus of the anointing of the apostles (fig. 55, 'Behold, I send you forth'). When Jesus begins his ministry immediately after this chorus, with the Beatitudes, his music is in F major (fig. 60), diverging only occasionally to other keys. He next appears in order to reassure the disciples in the violence of the storm (fig. 100). Although the storm is centred on C minor, at Jesus's appearance the music turns, suddenly, to F♯ major. (Might we hear a *Tristan* reference in the three bars (99:5–7) that connect the C minor music to the F♯ major music? The passage sounds remarkably like bb. 83–4 of the Prelude.) The warmth of F♯ major surrounds the scene, the soft tonic triad undergirding Jesus's first word, and (especially) his self-identification: 'It is I.' Thus, his first three appearances involve a stepwise ascent of keys, each one referencing an element of the drama, in the manner of *Siegfried*, Act I: E♭, Jesus himself and his mission; F, the Beatitudes; F♯, Jesus's self-identification. Jesus's remaining music in Part I is more diverse tonally, touching upon E♭, A♭, and D♭ major, with respect to the establishment of the church (figs. 113–16), and D major for the passage in which he offers forgiveness to Mary Magdalene.

In Part II, Jesus's only pre-Crucifixion appearance occurs at the moment when, after Judas's betrayal, the soldiers come to take him away. This

[51] McGuire, 'Judas', p. 258.
[52] McGuire, 'Judas', pp. 268–70. McGuire rightly points out a love/power dialectic taking place in this scene and in *The Apostles* as a whole – a dialectic reminiscent of Wagner's *Ring*.

passage, from 157:1 to 159:4, constitutes some of the densest, richest, most powerful music in the oratorio; coming together here are impressively many leitmotivic and tonal cross-references, resonating with moments ranging from the very beginning to the very end of the drama. It is in every sense what we might call, recollecting the music dramas of the late Wagner, a 'node': a musico-dramatic ganglion in which the most critical dramatic themes of the work come miraculously together, and whose thematic and tonal connections extend throughout the drama: Tristan and Isolde drink the love potion in Act I of *Tristan*; Brünnhilde sees a horrific and unrecognizable Siegfried emerge from the fire near the end of Act I of *Götterdämmerung*. To attempt to untangle all the threads here would deflect us from our task of tracing Jesus's 'expressive' (as Bailey would call it) ascent of keys, so I will not dwell on it here. But even to show only how this music incorporates a step on that ascent will give a sense of how this short passage constitutes a dramatic crux in the oratorio.

When Judas and the men arrive at Gethsemane, Judas speaks first, hailing Jesus. The first word of his greeting, 'Hail', is set to an F♯ minor triad (157:4), suggesting a recall of Jesus's self-identification in Part I, and a picking up of the scalewise ascent of associative keys. The following music does much to strengthen this suspicion. The F♯ minor progression in this and the following bar brings back the leitmotiv of the Beatitudes, and the descending scale of the progression arrives, at fig. 158, at an F♯ major triad, which enharmonically changes to G♭ major as Jesus begins to sing 'Whom seek ye?' (The bare thirds in the accompaniment also derive from 'By the Wayside'.) The soldiers shout Jesus's name on g♭, and the musical upbeat to his answer consists of a G♭ major triad (158:3). The same triad occurs on the second beat of the bar in which Jesus sings the words, 'therefore ye seek Me'. Both the F♯ and G♭ major triads clearly function as musical symbols to refer to who Jesus is.

Jesus is present once more before the Crucifixion – not physically, but in the imagination of Judas. The passage occurs as a sort of flashback: Judas, tormented by his betrayal of Jesus, and never free from the unforgiving A minor Psalm 94 in the background, is struck by a phrase from the psalm ('Rest from thy days of adversity'), which sparks in him a distant memory of Jesus. From Charles McGuire we have already learned that this moment – the moment at which Judas begins, 'Never man spake like this man' (176:3) – juxtaposes Jesus's key of E♭ major against the local A minor of the psalm and of Judas. To this insight we can now add the observation that the image of Jesus invokes not only E♭ major and the Beatitudes theme, but also his self-identifying F♯ major, to the words 'And filled the hungry soul', with music (in both vocal melody and accompaniment, 176:7) from the opening chorus of the oratorio (fig. 5) – the real Jesus, whom Judas could never see. But, of course, as McGuire points out, the memory of Jesus dissolves quickly, by 177:2, Judas comes back to his misery and guilt, and the stern, A minor psalm, which was briefly interrupted for his vision, returns in all its grimness. We thus have a powerful instance of associative keys (E♭ major, F♯ major, A minor) ascending through a partial equal-interval cycle of minor thirds – at a critical moment in the drama.

After the Crucifixion Jesus appears one last time, and his ascent of keys progresses by one last step. His first words, 'Peace be unto you' (fig. 209) are set in G major, leading to his first instruction to his disciples ('Behold, I send the promise of my Father upon you'), to the accompaniment of a full-fledged return of the opening music of the oratorio, now a semitone lower than in its original appearance. The long-range ascent goes no further than G, however, and by the time Jesus comes to his final commission ('Go ye therefore and teach all nations', fig. 213), the music is back solidly in his home key of E♭ major, in which key he made his first appearance in the oratorio (fig. 55), and in which key he proceeds to his final words, 'I am with you always, even unto the end of the world', and thus to his majestic cadence in E♭, already noted, at fig. 215.

But between these two moments – his initial 'Peace be unto you' and the final cadence – there is one last, telling reference to F♯/G♭ major. At the critical words '[baptizing them in the name of the] Father, and of the Son, [and of the Holy Ghost]' (213:4–5), Jesus sings f♯–g♯–a♯, as the orchestra (at 213:5) articulates a short progression moving from a G♭ first-inversion chord to the dominant seventh of E♭ major – the two principal keys associated with Jesus throughout the work (the vocal part is spelled in sharps, the orchestra in flats). In his analysis Jaeger points out the confluence of associative themes here: using his names, 'Father' is set to his Lord's Prayer theme, 'Son' to what he calls the Christ theme, and 'Holy Ghost' to his 'Spirit of the Lord' theme.[53] But the tonal reference is compelling as well: F♯/G♭ major has accumulated a considerable referential charge, in association with Jesus, over the course of the oratorio, and it is fitting, and meaningful, that it make one last appearance here, just prior to Jesus's Ascension.

We will soon see that the F♯/G♭ reference resonates through the work to an even greater depth than I have shown thus far. But before pursuing that issue, I want to pause a moment to consider Elgar's dramatic characterization of Jesus, because here the cross-referential chromatic key relations begin to intersect significantly with my hermeneutic reading. Charles McGuire has pointed out that *The Apostles* is a drama of *character*; we, and Elgar's audience, all know how the plot goes before we hear the first notes, so the drama turns on the composer's musical characterization of the protagonists.[54] The first musical notation for *The Apostles* – subsequently used in *Gerontius* – was

[53] Jaeger, *The Apostles*, pp. 57–8.   [54] McGuire, 'Judas', p. 237.

associated with Judas,[55] and modern criticism has strongly claimed that Mary Magdalene and Judas – especially the latter – are the central characters of the oratorio, not Jesus. Particularly persuasive is Byron Adams, who writes of 'Elgar's oddly hesitant treatment of the Saviour', who is 'reduced to a mere bystander at the drama of the apostles unfolding around him'. For him, 'Elgar is clearly more interested in the human sufferings and doubts of the apostles than in the supernal travails of their Master'.[56] McGuire's description of Christ's music lends musical credence to Adams's claim: 'During all of His speeches in *The Apostles*, Christ sings in a very formulaic manner, with a small vocal compass, and a static orchestration. His melodic speech patterns are either themes recalled from the Prologue, used for dramatic pronouncements, or what Elgar termed 'Quasi Recit.' passages for teaching the apostles.'[57] By contrast, the far richer vocal parts of Mary Magdalene and Judas are positively operatic in character, and even Peter, John, and Mary have more interesting melodic lines than Jesus.

All these perfectly correct observations cut sharply against the grain of the conventionally Christian view of a critic like Jaeger, who takes *The Apostles* at face value, seeing in it 'the old, yet ever-new and ever-welcome message brought to a stressful, materialistic world by this great contribution to sacred art – the good tidings of Peace, of God's goodness and the love of Christ'. The Elgar who produced *this* oratorio is a 'master whose [artistic] contributions ... make a powerful appeal to our noblest emotions ... and leave us the better for having come under his exalting influence'.[58] Against Jaeger we can contrast McGuire's revisionist, but still Christian view, that sees Mary Magdalene and Judas as the central characters in a didactic drama, in which Judas is 'Christ's betrayer, unrepentant sinner, and ... eternal outsider'.[59] McGuire takes a somewhat darker view of the work, and an entirely darker view of its composer: 'The mixture of subterfuge and revelation surrounding Judas resonates with Elgar's own ambivalence in the face of ... conflicts [between science and religion] and hints of the difficulties of living in a rapidly changing and dehumanizing world.'[60] Adams then takes a still darker view of the work, and a stark and disturbing view of its composer, whose libretto for *The Apostles* 'reflect[s] how deeply *fin-de-siècle* aestheticism pervaded [his] imagination', and who 'subverted, perhaps inadvertently, the original meaning of his biblical sources in order to realise his own artistic vision' – a vision of 'habitual despair', 'repress[ion]', and 'self-betrayal'.[61]

[55] Moore, *Elgar*, pp. 294–5.
[56] Adams, 'Elgar's Late Oratorios', p. 96.
[57] McGuire, *Elgar's Oratorios*, p. 213.
[58] Jaeger, *The Apostles*, p. 63.
[59] McGuire, 'Judas', p. 270.
[60] McGuire, 'Judas', p. 271.
[61] Adams, 'Elgar's Later Oratorios', pp. 96–7, 98, and 99.

It goes without saying that Jaeger's interpretation of the drama comes off as a bit naive and unsophisticated, even for its day, not to mention for us, a hundred years later. So I will not argue here for a wholesale critical revival of his earnest, hopeful, turn-of-the-(twentieth)-century Christianity. But I *will* argue that a *tonal*, as opposed to a vocal, reading of Jesus's music in the oratorio yields a far stronger picture of 'the Saviour' than is suggested by McGuire and Adams. The extent to which such a reading might serve as a gauge of the state of Elgar's religious faith in 1903 – whether it was steadfast or fading – I leave open to question; but I do claim that, at the very least, Elgar was fully engaged in his representation of Christ, and a careful hearing of the oratorio's tonal plan hews closer to a traditional view than the blandness of his vocal parts might lead us to suspect.

The music of Jesus, in a word, constitutes the central nervous system of *The Apostles*, and his own appearances – plus the exposition of his mission and purpose in the Prologue and 'The Lord hath chosen them', and Judas's vision of him in Scene 4 – serve as the nodes and ganglia of that system. In terms of leitmotivs, one of McGuire's insights about the oratorio in his monograph lays the foundation for such a claim: that the piece contains both 'local' and 'work-spanning' themes, and the latter are almost exclusively concerned with Christ and his mission.[62] Many of these originate in the Prologue (in which Jesus himself is essentially present, since it is he who reads the words of Isaiah in the passage from Luke imported into the libretto), and a few others appear first in 'In the Mountain – Night' (14:1–24:8), in which he is at prayer. The Wagnerian parallel here is completely transparent, of course: motives such as Jaeger's 'Spirit of the Lord', 'Christ the Man of Sorrows', and 'Christ's Prayer' are analogous to, say, 'the Ring', 'the Curse', and 'the Sword' in the *Ring*; while most of the music of the two chief human characters, Mary Magdalene and Judas, is analogous to, say, Siegmund's 'Winterstürme' in Act I of *Die Walküre*, and Mime's 'Starling Song' in Act I of *Siegfried*. Even Jesus's early, brief appearances bring back previous leitmotivs, and his betrayal scene and scene before the Ascension are perhaps the most concentrated thematic nodes of the drama.

A strength of Jaeger's analysis is that he, like his model, von Wolzogen, knew well what a node was – what it was like for reminiscence themes to enter, one right after another, or even at the same time as others, delivering powerful juxtapositions of meaning that the listener must work to absorb. His description of part of the chorus, 'The Lord hath chosen them', is characteristic: 'Thence . . . we pass into a perfect maze of leitmotives [*sic*], of highly ingenious combinations of different rhythms, and very Elgaresque spinning of long melody-threads out of the filaments distributed broadcast over

---

[62] McGuire, *Elgar's Oratorios*, pp. 229 and 235–8.

voices and instruments. With consummate art the different themes are dovetailed, linked together, and combined, and the whole complex movement is made to run its stately course to a most impressive close.'[63] To recognize and internalize the concentration and intensity of such musico-dramatic nodes is, in some deep sense, to know one's Wagner – and also to know one's Elgar. And Jaeger knew both. What is more, he goes further than von Wolzogen – he is, in my view, the more perceptive analyst – and offers the occasional, but usually insightful, observation about harmony.

It is here that we can begin a more nuanced critique of Jesus and his musical portrayal. Significantly, given our task here, even though the flat-side, major-mode character that so dominates the music depicting Christ's mission and the establishment of the Church (E♭ as the global key, A♭ for the Prologue, D♭ for the building of the Church (15ff.)) is predominantly diatonic, some of his music has strongly chromatic elements. Until now we have followed the E♭/F♯(G♭) tonal argument (itself a relation of a chromatic third) over long spans of time; but now we can see the concentrated moment in which it is introduced in the first place. Jaeger points to the end of the very first vocal phrase in the work (2:6–7), noting that:

> The concluding notes, G♭, A♭, and B♭, embody in their progression of whole-tones a leitmotive [*sic*] of the utmost significance. Yet it is as mere soulless clay without its life-giving harmony. The unfathomable power of genius, however, is 'Dead things with inbreathed sense able to pierce', and thus we have three bare notes transformed by the magic of a master's harmony into the most solemn motive in the work – suggesting CHRIST, THE MAN OF SORROWS ... The one touch to work this wonder is the 'passing-note' B♭♭, the resultant dissonance giving to the progression of chords that suggestion of mystery, of sorrow and suffering which the circumstances demand.[64]

Jaeger's instinct is absolutely on target: analysis of the piece offers ample justification for designating this motive as one of 'utmost significance', and I, for one, would second his claim that it is 'the most solemn motive in the work'.

We can begin to see why. First, the progression moves from a G♭[6] chord, through a dissonant passing chord, to a root-position dominant seventh on B♭: that is, it directly juxtaposes, at the end of the first vocal sentence of the piece, G♭ major and E♭ major (implied by its dominant seventh), the two keys or triads that we have already seen to be so central to Jesus's tonal path through the oratorio. Second, and even more pointedly, the text on the three melodic notes of the ascending whole-tones – g♭[1], a♭[1], b♭[1] – is 'anointed me'. The 'me' thus anointed is none other than Christ himself, since it is at this

[63] Jaeger, *The Apostles*, p. 18. Jaeger's metaphor   [64] Jaeger, *The Apostles*, p. 5.
of threads and filaments fits nicely with my
nodes and ganglia.

moment that he stands up to read Isaiah 61 in the synagogue, at the beginning of his ministry. Thus arises the association not only of this motive, but of these three melodic notes, with Christ. Clinching this association are the f♯–g♯–a♯ melody in his passage just before the Ascension (213:4–6), and two melodic fragments in the scene where he is accosted by the soldiers in Gethsemane (fig. 157ff.). When he asks them, 'Whom seek ye?' they reply, 'Jesus of Nazareth', on the notes G♭–B♭–A♮ (158:2–3; the dramatic context here clearly calls for A♮, rather than A♭). In his response, 'I am He; if ye seek me', these last three words are on the G♭–A♭–B♭ figure, over the harmonic motive in the orchestra (158:5).

There is much more to say about this motive, but to do so requires that we focus briefly on Jaeger's observation regarding the B♭♭ passing note in the 'tenor' voice. As in his characterization of the parallel half-diminished seventh chords in 'Christ's Desire', his language here, however flowery, is perfect: it *is* the passing B♭♭ that imbues the progression with the wrenching (suffering?) quality that it exudes. It is also the passing B♭♭ that makes the short progression, so far as I know, absolutely original; we can usually, if we look hard enough, find at least one or two other instances in the turn-of-the-century repertoire of virtually any progression that we encounter, but this one seems unique. Elgar makes powerful use of this aspect of the progression; it is an essential component of much of the harmonic and melodic expression of suffering in the oratorio. Consider, for example, the agonizing chord at the climax of the searing orchestral statement (just before fig. 193), 'Eli, Eli, lama sabachthani?' at the very beginning of Scene 5, immediately after Christ's death: it is the same chord as the dissonant passing chord of 'Christ, Man of Sorrows', (B♭♭–C–E♭–A♭), transposed down a semitone.

The 'Man of Sorrows' progression ramifies in other directions if we consider its top (G♭–A♭–B♭) and tenor voices (B♭–B♭♭–A♭), moving in contrary motion. The two lines together comprise the pitch set (G♭–A♭–B♭♭–B♭), or the pitch-class set (0, 2, 3, 4) (not in prime form). If we posit that the soldiers' line, 'Jesus of Nazareth', from the Gethsemane scene is an untransposed reference to the motive G♭–B♭–A♮, or more generally, to the inversionally related sets (0, 1, 4) and (0, 3, 4), we can quickly extrapolate other related instances, all implying, in my hearing, sorrow. For example, in 'Golgotha' (figs. 193–9) the closing notes of Mary's mournful refrain are B♮–G–B♭–A♭–G (194:2–4, 195:3–5, and 198:2–4),[65] the B♮–G–B♭ seemingly doing the piercing (cf. Jaeger's 'inbreathed sense able to pierce'). (See also John's 'and they shall mourn for him', on A♭–C–B♮, a transposition of the soldiers' line up a whole-tone (196:3).) We might then hear the A♭–E♮–F that accompanies the words 'The Spirit of the

---

[65] In 196:4–6 the motive opens with an A♭ instead of B♮.

Lord' at the first vocal entry of the Prologue, and then becomes its own motive, at the same pitch level, at 4:3, a few bars later, to be an inversion of the soldiers' tune. And finally, Christ's very first words in the oratorio, 'Behold, I send you', on [B♭]–C–B♮–E♭, represent a retrograde inversion of the same melodic pattern (55:2–3). Jaeger, of course, made none of these connections, and he surely considered the last two (the motives in the Prologue and Christ's opening words) entirely benign. In contradistinction, I prefer to suggest that his instinct that the 'Christ, Man of Sorrows' motive holds in its brief span the seeds of much of the representation of suffering in *The Apostles*, is precisely right. I further suggest that indeed the A♭–E♮–F in the orchestra at the first entrance of the choir (2:2) already hints at Christ's inevitable suffering, though perhaps not so tellingly as the crucial progression that follows but a few bars later (2:6–7). (Thus I disagree with Jaeger's label 'Preachers'.)

Our detailed focus on 'Christ, Man of Sorrows' has shown its progression to spawn a melodic figure that spans much of the work, and our study of this figure has in turn led us back to the beginning of the Prologue. Let us now take the A♭–E♮–F figure that we just noted there, and focus, not on the three-note melodic motive, but only on the single chromatic note within it, E♮. This note, like the 'Man of Sorrows' motive, is work-spanning; it has an important story to tell – a story that will take us through the most wrenching part of *The Apostles*, but which will also ultimately link up with the 'Man of Sorrows' motive to bring the work to an extraordinary conclusion. Consider Judas's entire monologue, in 'The Temple' and 'Without the Temple' (167:1–192:6), including the chorus's brutal chanting of Psalm 94, and then its transforming itself into the mob that brings about Jesus's Crucifixion. What single note pierces our consciousness throughout the scene? Surely that note is E. Although the monologue is unquestionably in A minor, it is the structural melodic tone, e^1, that holds our attention in the opening verses of the psalm (167:1–169:5). Judas's line immediately thereafter ranges from e to e^1, and after two more bars the orchestra establishes a massive, hostile, low E pedal (170:3) that will, with little respite, take us all the way to Judas's vision of Jesus at 176:3. Who, having heard this passage, can forget the octave and unison shrieks on E with the word 'Selah!' (fig. 171). Or who, despite the A minor tonic, will remember A minor triads here rather than the hideous c♯^{6} chord at 170:3, grounded by the low-E bass? And who, after Judas's vision of Jesus, and after a contrasting turn to D minor rather than A minor (178:1–186:4), will not cringe at the sinister c♯^{6} chord's return on Judas's words 'A sudden fear' (186:5), immediately after the chorus's first 'Crucify Him!'. Elgar portrays the moment of Crucifixion neither with the pitch-class E, nor with A minor, but with a bitterly ironic return to E♭ major, the key of the betrayal, and the whole chorus singing on g^1 (187:1–4). But the grisly bass E returns to introduce the end of the scene (fig. 189). It is the goal of the gruff, chromatic bass ascents at 190:4–9 and 191:1–6, and it pierces our very being as the bass of the last c♯^{6} chord at 191:4, and as the last, howling note after Judas's final words (191:6), leading into a brief echo of the psalm, again with e^1 as the melodic fifth scale degree, which never resolves. Leaving the scene of the Crucifixion, what remains in our ears is E.

It remains now only to tie together the two central chromatic/harmonic ideas of the oratorio – the 'Christ, Man of Sorrows' motive and the pitch-class E – to show how the tonal structure turns on the play of chromaticism in a globally diatonic context. In *The Apostles*, E, in the context of E♭ major, is a 'pitch-class motive' par excellence. E♮ is the first chromatic note in the drama, just before fig. 1. Spelled as F♭, it slides in as a passing note at 1:4, in preparation for its already discussed role once the choir enters. Its relation to 'Christ, Man of Sorrows' already begins to be made manifest in the Prologue. The first time the choir sings the text 'The Spirit of the Lord . . . hath anointed me', E♮ is not in the picture, except for the A♭–E♮–F motive in the orchestra at 2:2; as we have seen, the words 'anointed me' bring the 'Man of Sorrows' motive, juxtaposing G♭ and V^7/E♭, with the melodic notes d♭^{2}–g♭^{1}–a♭^{1}–b♭^{1} (2:6–7). But when the choir sings the same words to the same tune at the end of the Prologue (10:5), no longer do we hear the G♭/E♭ juxtaposition; now we hear the motive on F♭ (C♭–F♭–G♭–A♭), accompanied by the first F♭/E♮ triad in the work. Even before Christ's ministry begins, with the calling of his apostles, the seeds of his betrayal and death are planted. We learn this, not through some random planting of E♮s and F♭s early in the piece, but from the specific use of this pitch-class as its very first chromatic element, and especially the unmistakably clear juxtaposition of Christ's keys of E♭ and G♭ in the first statement of 'anointed me' in the Prologue, and of the threatening F♭/E♮ at exactly the same place in the last statement.

In the tradition of Beethoven and Wagner, these chromatic elements must be reconciled to the ultimate tonal centre at the end. Elgar is more than up to the task. Almost at the end of the final, triumphant, E♭ major chorus, the chromatic elements make their stunning, final appearance. At 235:5 we hear 'Christ, Man of Sorrows', now transposed up a fourth, so that it starts on a C♭^{6} chord – a transposition that means that the third chord of the progression is no longer V/E♭, but E♭^{7} (presumably V^7/A♭), and that the descending chromatic motion below is E♭–D♮–D♭. The contrary motion that is of the essence of the figure is now allowed to continue scalewise in opposite directions, so that, as the music approaches fig. 236, we reach the same motive at the same pitch level, but now registrally dispersed over a number of octaves. Elgar makes two critical changes here. First, in 235:9 he alters the expected F♮ to F♭; this F♭ resolves then down to E♭, after which it never appears again; the global E♭ is purified of E♮/F♭. Simultaneously, for the first time in the oratorio, the descending figure in the tenor of the motive does *not* move by semitone, but by whole-tone – E♭–D♭–C♭, and then one step further, to B♭. Thus, for the first time ever, the second chord is not acutely dissonant, and the 'resolving' chord is not an unstable dominant seventh, but a pure E♭ major triad – albeit with a brief suspended A♭. The pitch-class motivic and leitmotivic chromaticisms are worked out of the piece at exactly the same time, and the final 'Alleluias!' conclude the drama in a purely diatonic E♭.

The musical drama that is *The Apostles* is Wagnerian in the sense that it is not only a drama of themes, but a drama of tonal structure – not one so complex, say, as that of *Götterdämmerung* or *Parsifal*, but unquestionably one that shows that Elgar had learned his Wagnerian lessons well. *The Apostles*, of course, is his largest work, the one that he started as the beginning of a sacred trilogy, adopting the conscious model of the *Ring*. Whatever its relation to Wagner – and it is pointless to claim that it, as opposed to *Gerontius* or *The Kingdom*, is the most Wagnerian – one thing is certain: here, as in Wagner, pitch counts, and it counts at all levels, from the single E♮, to surface harmonic progression, to the tonal organization of scenes, to the tonal structure of the entire oratorio. In tracking this structure, I unashamedly reveal my structuralist, music-theoretical, modernist bias – though not without subjecting that bias to constant interrogation. Neither my tonal analysis of *The Apostles* nor my essay as a whole is for those who have 'transcended' structural listening.[66] But I would argue that it is important to do this work. The harmonic and tonal relations that I have shown are demonstrably present in the music, and they raise all sorts of intriguing questions. Most crucial, in my view, for *The Apostles*, is this: my analysis suggests that Elgar structured the oratorio tonally around the figure of Christ. How does this analysis square with the interpretations of the many Elgar scholars who find Mary Magdalene and Judas to be stronger and more dramatically and musically successful characters? Does this situation indeed suggest that surface trumps structure? More generally, can my structuralist, pitch-based analysis co-exist fruitfully with interpretations that valorize sonic presence, physicality, and social context – that seek to correct 'the damage wrought by half a century of structural listening'?[67]

I recognize and respect this point of view, and I am indeed more than happy to acknowledge that the seemingly organic, stable masterwork that appears to be under my control slips outside that control with the slightest probing. For example, if the pitch-class E, as embodied in the melody of the solemn Psalm 94 and the extensive pedals of Judas's monologue, is about the

[66] See the essays in Andrew dell'Antonio (ed.), *Beyond Structural Listening: Postmodern Modes of Hearing* (Berkeley and Los Angeles: University of California Press, 2004), especially dell'Antonio's introductory essay, 'Introduction: Beyond Structural Listening?', pp. 1–12.

[67] dell'Antonio, 'Beyond Structural Listening?', p. 4.

ultimate betrayal of Christ, why is his Ascension ('He was taken up; and a cloud received Him out of their sight', fig. 216) on precisely the same pedal, only five bars after his massive, Schenkerian-structure-defining cadence in E♭ major (fig. 215)? If the tendency of E♭ to dissolve into G (minor) suggests the human limitations of the apostles, who cannot fully understand Christ's mission, why is the large-scale tonal motion of Christ himself from E♭ to G (albeit major)? And what could a quotation of the *Tristan* Prelude mean, inserted at the point of the apostles' greatest moment of terror as Jesus walks on the water toward them in the storm (99:5–7)? Finally, let us look one last time at Jesus's cadence at fig. 215. At the moment of Jesus's melodic resolution to E♭, the orchestra, eliding with the cadence in *echt* Wagnerian style, begins the 'Spirit of the Lord' motive, on the E♭-major triad, but now with a more daring harmonic progression than the diatonic melody itself always has: E♭ major to D major to C major. We have, of course, heard this before, with even more dramatic harmony: essentially the same progression emerges from the E♭ major cadence of the 'Spirit of the Lord' near the end of the Prologue (9:1–4). Here we had a series of descending major triads on E♭, D, C, B♭, and A♭ – after the initial semitone descent, these chords fall through a whole-tone scale to B♭. And in the Introduction to Part II, the same progression goes one step further, all the way to G♭ major (143:1–3). So we are now used to the feeling of hearing the succession: cadence in E♭ major, elision, and magical descent of major triads.

But have we not heard this before, in another way? – somewhere else entirely, on a different stage, and in a different context? Does this cadence and continuation not remind us of the moment, at the end of *Die Walküre*, where Wotan kisses the godhead from Brünnhilde (Act III, bb. 1615–17)? – a critical, defining moment at the end of a musical drama, featuring the central male character; a melodic cadence on the tonic; a long–short–long melodic rhythm; the orchestral elision, bringing in a major triad with the third in the melody (in the opera, of course, the eliding chord enters on ♭VI of the tonic, C, whereas in the oratorio the eliding chord is on the tonic itself); the slow, majestic, homophonic texture and rhythm of the entering orchestra, proceeding from major triad to major triad, with an initial descending semitone in the melody? Why, at the moment that an at-least-partially mortal man finally establishes his divinity and departs from the human world, with his $\hat{3}-\hat{2}-\hat{1}$ cadence in E♭, do we hear a reminiscence of a defining moment in a spectacularly non-Christian secular work, where a divine figure kisses away the divinity of a previously immortal figure – and a woman, at that? In the words of the current vernacular, I haven't a clue. But the juxtaposition of the divine and the mortal, the sacred and the secular, the diatonic and the chromatic, suggests that I have but scratched the surface of a work that richly repays concentrated listening and study.

2 Elgar and Acworth's *Caractacus*: the Druids, race, and the individual hero[1]

Charles Edward McGuire

The second scene of Harry Arbuthnot Acworth and Edward Elgar's *Caractacus* begins with a vivid description of a pagan rite, led by a number of Druids. This texted rite contains all of the accoutrements we have come to expect from grisly nineteenth- and twentieth-century tales of ancient magic and lore: a series of symbols, including a 'mystic circle', a 'Sacred Oak', and mistletoe; dishevelled participants, here in the guise of the Druid Maidens, who complete the ritual only through letting their hair down and baring their breasts ('Loose your locks, your bosoms bare'); two explicitly gory allusions to human sacrifice ('Where the stones are wet and red / With the blood of victims dead' and 'Thrice the sacrificial knife / Reddens with a victim's life'); an invocation to Taranis, who will grant soothsaying abilities; and, of course, a haunted location to host the ritual ('Bear your torches through the gloom / Quench them on the Hero's tomb'). The effect, even when one takes into account the tripling metre and rhyme of the poetry, is chilling, not unlike incantations of witches and warlocks in so many B-movies of the last forty years:

ARCH-DRUID AND DRUIDS:
Tread the mystic circle round,
Measure off the holy ground,
Through the fire and through the smoke,
Girdle slow the sacred oak,
Tree of eld, whose branches show,
Brightest in the winter snow,
The pearl-fruited mistletoe,
Bear your torches through the gloom,
Quench them on the hero's tomb,
Where the stones are wet and red
With the blood of victims dead.

[1] This paper was originally given at the New Directions in Elgar Research Conference in 2002, at the University of Surrey. Given the reputation of *Caractacus*, it should come as no surprise that other scholars are currently working on aspects of this cantata. I am grateful to Timothy Barringer, Matthew Riley, and Laura Upperton for showing me drafts of their work, cited below. I wish also to thank Sam Smiles and David Coppen for their help in securing the illustrations for this chapter; and Fiona Aiken, Carla Myers, Malavika Kasturi, T. A. Subramanian, and Meena Subramanian for their aid in untangling some of the biographical details of Acworth's life and civil service in India.

DRUID MAIDENS:
Thread the measure left and right,
Druid maidens, clad in white,
Loose your locks, your bosoms bare,
Breathe the godhead brooding there,
Hov'ring round your floating hair,
Breathe the power – hearken well
For the coming of the spell.

ARCH-DRUID AND CHORUS:
Lord of dread, and lord of pow'r,
This is thine, the fateful hour,
When beneath the sacred oak
Thrice the mighty charm is spoke,
Thrice the sacrificial knife
Reddens with a victim's life,
Thrice the mystic dance is led
Round the altar where they bled,
Taranis, descend to aid,
Let the future fate be said.

In the hands of a typical pictorially inclined composer of the nineteenth century, such as a Berlioz or a Liszt, this Invocation would be the moment for an amazing blaze of dark, chromatic action, including the presentation of an out-of-control infernal dance, with references to familiar songs and chants of the dead, and orchestral effects that would convincingly imitate the screams and moans of the victims.

But Elgar approached this scene of Druidic description and invocation in a different manner. The beginning of the Invocation, sung by the chorus and a bass soloist representing the Arch-Druid (Ex. 2.1), includes some colouring of specific words with chromatic or dissonant sounds to give them more rhetorical weight. For instance, Elgar sets the phrase 'Thrice the sacrificial knife' with repetitions of the word 'Thrice' emphasized both by heavy accented quavers (fig. 9, bb. 2–3), and by the word 'knife' landing on a chord that takes a moment to resolve into a simple C minor (fig. 9, b. 3), the sound of the entire passage is not gloomy or even mysterious in the slightest. Rather, it is celebratory, even reverential, as shown by the use of the organ to emphasize important words (including the very beginning and the self-same 'knife', mentioned above). It is as if Elgar has turned this potentially chilling moment into an ordinary nineteenth-century church service: dramatic perhaps, but ultimately comforting – despite his own comments to August Jaeger that the effect of the Invocation was 'curdling'.[2]

---

[2] '[T]hat *Invocation* has made me ill! Oh! the effect is curdling'. Letter to Jaeger, 12 July 1898; *Publishers*, p. 79.

Ex. 2.1 *Caractacus*, scene ii, figs. 8–10

Why would Elgar treat the Druids with such reverence, especially considering that later in the cantata, they betray Caractacus, causing the capture of both himself and his family at the hands of the Romans? Answering this requires one to question one of the tacit assumptions about the cantata: that the composer dominated the design and execution of the work. Indeed, the discussion as it exists within Elgar literature has heretofore centred on Elgar alone, with the explicit supposition that the composer was ultimately responsible for the plot of *Caractacus*. The two pieces of evidence most often presented to support this view are the subject of the cantata itself, supposedly originated by Ann Elgar, the composer's mother – though she suggested only

Ex. 2.1 (cont.)

'some tale' about the Malvern Hills[3] – and Elgar's now infamous letters which defend the aggressively patriotic final chorus in the face of Jaeger's concern.[4] We might counter this with specific evidence of Acworth's own

[3] Young, *Elgar*, pp. 80–1 and Moore, *Elgar*, p. 225. Moore takes his quotation from Young, who drew it from a letter of Ann Elgar to Polly Grafton.

[4] See the letters of Elgar to Jaeger of 21 June and 12 July 1898, in *Publishers*, pp. 76–7 and 79, and also Moore, *Elgar*, p. 239.

Ex. 2.1 (cont.)

promotion of his role in *Caractacus*. First, as Elgar states, Acworth was 'anxious to put "written for music" on the title'.[5] Second, the vocal score includes both a long preparatory 'Argument' as well as a libretto complete with several lengthy passages that Elgar did not set to music, presented in square brackets – and with no explanation as to why they are included in that manner.[6] The Argument describes the location, gives the action of the plot in some detail, and in the last paragraph adds a lengthy explanation as to the particulars of the libretto's construction:

> The general lines of history – or, failing history, of tradition – have been followed. The British Camp on the Malvern Hills is locally attributed to Caractacus. It is doubtless a British work, and is of such an extent as infers occupation by very large numbers. The scene of Caractacus's last disastrous battle is much disputed; but it was almost certainly in the line of the Severn (Habren), and may probably have been at Caer Caradoc, in Shropshire. The unusual circumstance of mistletoe growing on the oak may still be observed in the woods below the Herefordshire Beacon. Caractacus's appearance before Claudius in Rome, his bold defence, and the pardon of himself and his daughter are historical. Orbin is an imaginary character.[7]

This paragraph clearly establishes the story as one based on history, with potential liberties taken as to characterization and setting, attempting to justify this through the folklorist's 'tradition' and external evidence. The

[5] Letter to Jaeger, 21 June 1898, in *Publishers*, pp. 75–6. Elgar responded to Acworth's request in a stereotypical way by deflecting it into his own concerns. 'I can't see how we are to word my small part in the matter – I hate COMPOSED.'

[6] They are also included in the *Caractacus . . . Book of Words with Analytical Notes by Herbert Thompson* (London: Novello, [1898]).
[7] Elgar and Acworth, *Caractacus* (vocal score, London: Novello, 1898), [v] ('Argument'); *Caractacus . . . Book of Words*, p. 3.

longer bracketed passages differ from the shorter stage and scene directions, also bracketed within the libretto pages, and include passages in the voices of Caractacus, Eigen, the Maidens, and Claudius which clarified aspects of the action. Both of these inclusions indicate that Acworth was actively engaged in the libretto's design, and that Elgar either considered the words to be important or did not wish to challenge Acworth actively on this issue.

We may never know the exact nature of the working relationship between Elgar and Acworth. When they conceived and executed *Caractacus*, they both lived in the Malvern area, negating any need for significant and revealing correspondence. The veritable horde of memoir-writing acquaintances, such as Dora Penny, who described Elgar's libretto production while working on *The Apostles* and *The Kingdom*, had not yet formed. This does not mean the task is impossible, however. By closely examining Acworth's life and career, we can come to a deeper and more nuanced understanding of the cantata. For Acworth, as a product of the Indian Civil Service, tinged his libretto with references to contemporary debates on race, the Celtic revival, and religion. Through an investigation of Acworth's beliefs on these subjects, we discover that *Caractacus* is not merely a simple paean to Empire or nationalistic celebration of Ancient Britain, as has been commonly thought,[8] but a dramatic celebration of the individual. The Druids and their rituals presented within the cantata are the key to this reading, as Acworth presents characters with different alliances and abilities to emphasize the perceived worth of the noble individual over the corrupt community. This corrupt community relies on deceitful artefacts, while the noble individual is always grounded in the land and the pastoral premise.

Acworth's role in the creation of *Caractacus* has received scant attention in the Elgar literature. Like most of Elgar's vocal works of the 1890s, little is known about the context surrounding its composition, other than items reflected in the Novello correspondence.[9] The background to the libretto is a case in point.

---

[8] See, for instance, Jeffrey Richards, *Imperialism and Music: Britain 1876–1953* (Manchester: Manchester University Press, 2001), especially pp. 49–51. In the past few years, the subject of Elgar and imperialism has garnered even more attention than it did in the revisionist era of the 1960s, when Michael Kennedy, among others, used Cecil Gray's 'two Elgars' construction to posit an 'imperialist' Elgar (compositions such as *Caractacus*, the *Coronation Ode* and the marches) versus the 'real' Elgar (mostly instrumental compositions), with the rule understood that 'imperial' Elgar did not produce a masterpiece while the 'real' Elgar did. Currently, there are several opposing

camps arguing various aspects of this topic, as described by Harper-Scott in this volume, ch. 6, and in my 'Functional Music: Imperialism, the Great War, and Elgar as Popular Composer' in *Companion*, pp. 214–24, at p. 215. Given the unresolved conflicting views, the subject could sustain a monograph-length study, considering both the cantata's history and the historiography of its criticism.

[9] Shorter biographies such as McVegh, *Elgar* (p. 114) and Anderson, *Elgar* (p. 37) mention Acworth in passing; Michael De-la-Noy's *Elgar the Man* (London: Allen Lane, 1983) does not mention him at all.

Jerrold Northrop Moore, Robert Anderson, Percy Young and other biographers note that *Caractacus* is based on classical sources such as Tacitus and Dio Cassius, and that it may have had additional background drawn from a volume of Malvern local history by James McKay entitled *The British Camp on the Herefordshire Beacon*, but none of them gives any details as to the contents of these sources.[10] As Acworth was a somewhat fleeting figure in the lives of the Elgar family, information about him in the Elgar biographies is even less complete. At his retirement, Acworth was the Municipal Commissioner to the City of Bombay (Mumbai), having been, in Percy Young's phrase, 'a regular Pooh-Bah'.[11] In his retirement he lived in Malvern Wells, and became, as Rosa Burley put it, 'a rather pompous friend' of the family.[12] Before writing the libretto for *Caractacus*, he had contributed additional material for Elgar's 1896 cantata, *Scenes from the Saga of King Olaf*, and in 1894 he had published *Ballads of the Marathas Rendered into English Verse*, a number of songs and poems translated into English.[13] Acworth was paid a fee of ten guineas for his libretto. Acworth's daughter Rosamund (later Rosamund Champion) was a long-time friend of Carice Elgar; and Elgar may have been in contact with Acworth in 1902 concerning a further collaboration; and finally, Elgar wrote to Acworth in late 1904 about the possibility of turning *Caractacus* into an opera.

Unfortunately, the biographies provide no consistent account of Acworth's arrival in Malvern, nor any agreement as to the facts of his career.[14] This situation means that specialized analytical articles like Michael Pope's on *King Olaf* could not draw upon any stable or reliable secondary sources concerning Acworth, and so even within this otherwise excellent study, Acworth is only mentioned in passing.[15] While acknowledging that scholars

[10] Moore, *Elgar*, p. 230, n. 161; and in Elgar, *Caractacus* (*ECE* vol. V), [v]. The accounts of Caractacus in Tacitus are found in *Histories*, III, p. 45 and *Annals*, XII, pp. 33–6, 38, 40; Dio Cassius's discussions of Caractacus occur in *History*, LX, p. 20 and *Epitome* of LXI, p. 33. The book by James McKay (*The British Camp on the Herefordshire Beacon. Fifteen Short Essays on Scenes and Incidents in the Lives of the Ancient Britons* (Malvern: the 'Advertiser' Office, 1875)) draws some aspects from these sources, but appears to focus more on popular myths of Caractacus.

[11] Percy M. Young, *Alice Elgar: Enigma of a Victorian Lady* (London: Dennis Dobson, 1978), p. 138, n. 2.

[12] Rosa Burley and Frank C. Carruthers, *Edward Elgar: the Record of a Friendship* (London: Barrie and Jenkins, 1972), p. 88.

[13] Harry Arbuthnot Acworth, *Ballads of the Marathas Rendered into English Verse from the Marathi originals* (London: Longmans, Green, 1894).

[14] Young reports that Acworth left Malvern 'after 13 years in various offices, in 1901', implying that he had been there since 1888 (*Alice Elgar*, p. 138, n. 2). He unfortunately conflates Acworth with another of Elgar's acquaintances, Henry Dyke Acland. Moore and Anderson in the preface to *ECE* vol. V report that Acworth had a 'distinguished career' in the Indian civil service, and that he settled in Malvern Wells in 1896 (*ECE* vol. V, [v]). This differs from Moore's statement that Alice Elgar had tea with the Acworths in 1895, and that in November of that year, Acworth offered to help Elgar with the libretto of *King Olaf* (Moore, *Elgar*, pp. 185 and 202).

[15] Michael Pope, 'King Olaf and the English Choral Tradition', in Monk, *Studies*, pp. 46–80.

cannot always illuminate every figure within a composer's circle, we note that Acworth was an important individual during Elgar's life in the late 1890s. His biographical context informs a much-needed deeper consideration of *Caractacus*, if for no other reason than the cantata's subject, wholly entwined as it is in myth and history, folklore, and even amateur archaeology. Acworth was well placed to provide Elgar with this sort of cultural support. A brief glance at his *Ballads of the Marathas* identifies him as 'President, Bombay Anthropological Society'. The volume further contains Acworth's thirty-three-page scholarly and detailed introduction to Maratha culture, tradition, and grammar.[16]

What experiences gave Acworth these cultural boons? Appendix 2.1 is a chronology of various events from his life. From these we may surmise that Acworth was a rather typical product of the India Civil Service (hereafter ICS): well educated, interested in folklore, and quite willing to use his official position to aid local philanthropy.

Acworth was born in Worcestershire in 1849. Typically for a member of the ICS, he came from an upper middle-class professional family that valued education: his father had a career in the British East India Company, and his mother was the daughter of a cathedral dean. He attended Brighton College and Worcester College, Oxford, passed the exam for the ICS, completed a few additional studies for service in India, and was called to the bar.[17] Appointed to the Bombay Presidency, he served in a variety of junior positions over the next two decades before being named the Municipal Commissioner for the City of Bombay in 1890.[18] His last years of Civil Service, from 1890 to 1895, were busy indeed, for he established the Matunga Leper Asylum, and as already mentioned he published a book of folklore about the Marathas and their ballads.[19] He was President of the Bombay Archaeological Society, and was named Companion of the Most Eminent Order of the Indian Empire.[20] To this we can add that Acworth was a civilian expert on leprosy and sanitation, who

[16] Acworth, *Ballads of the Marathas*, pp. [i] and [v]–xxxviii.
[17] *Who Was Who*, vol. II, 1929–1941; Joseph Foster, *Alumni Oxonienses*, vol. I, p. 5 (for full citations, see Appendix 2.1).
[18] Between 1870 and 1879, Acworth was an Assistant Collector, and *Hart's Army List* of 1873 notes that he held in 1873 the relatively minor position of a Sixth Class Post serving as Third Assistant Collector and Magistrate of Ahmednuggur (a town to the east of Bombay). He rose steadily through the ranks of the ICS, serving variously as Under-Secretary to the Bombay Presidency's Finance and Revenue departments from 1879 to 1881; Collector and

Magistrate, Collector of Salt Revenue, and Deputy Municipal Commissioner of Bombay.
[19] According to the Leprosy History website (http://tinyurl.com/bgltk, accessed 2 August 2005), the hospital was established in Bombay (now Mumbai), in November 1890 as the 'Homeless Leper Asylum'. Later in the 1890s it became known as the Mantunga (or Matoonga) Leper Asylum. Renamed the 'Acworth Leper Asylum' in 1904 in his honour, it still exists today as the Acworth Leprosy Hospital and Museum.
[20] Much of this information was drawn from *Who Was Who*, and Acworth's obituary in *The Times*, 30 May 1933. See Appendix 2.1.

wrote and spoke publicly on these subjects.[21] He retired after twenty-five years in the ICS in 1895, possibly because that was the minimum service necessary to enjoy a £1,000 per annum pension,[22] or possibly for political reasons.[23] Acworth was specially commended by the Indian Government for services during a riot in 1893, and his interest in religion in general and the Church of England in particular was marked enough to be noted in his *Times* obituary.

Thus far, the only attempt to insert any of the biographical material into a consideration of *Caractacus* occurred in a short centenary article in the *Elgar Society Journal* by Patrick Little, who interpreted the closing chorus of the cantata as an allegory for the British Empire's rule of India.[24] Little's linchpin is the Arch-Druid's deliberate falsification of the augury to Caractacus, which causes the warrior to enter a battle that he cannot win. Little argues that the prediction given by the Arch-Druid is not false; it is just mistimed, for it is not Ancient Britain's Caractacus who will win the day, but the British of the nineteenth-century Empire – attaching *Caractacus* to a trope about the links between the British and Roman Empires that was first detailed by Raymond Betts in 1971.[25] Jeffrey Richards develops Little's thesis in his recent study, *Imperialism and Music*.[26] But however provocative they may be, these claims do not go nearly far enough.

To achieve an appropriate reading of *Caractacus*, we must untangle a knot of questions: what would Acworth have known about Druidism, what were

---

[21] For details see Appendix 2.1 (1898, 1899, 1900). As a sanitation expert, Acworth was quoted in Alfred Russell Wallace's *The Wonderful Century: Its Successes and Its Failures* (New York: Dodd, Mead and Company, 1899), pp. 340–4. Wallace's assessments of Acworth's claims as to the sanitary conditions of Bombay are incredulous, if not negative.

[22] Anthony Kirk-Greene, *Britain's Imperial Administrators, 1858–1966* (Houndmills: Macmillan Press Ltd; New York: St Martin's Press, 2000), p. 109.

[23] Terms for high-ranking posts, such as Municipal Commissioner, lasted only five years, and as a member of the middle class, he could not hope for an appointment to the higher echelons of service (such as Viceroy) that were reserved for the nobility. See P. J. Cain and A. G. Hopkins, *British Imperialism, 1688–2000*, 2nd edn (Harlow: Longman, 2001), p. 295; Kirk-Greene, *Britain's Imperial Administrators*, p. 98. Another reason might have been the controversy that flared up around the operation of the policies of the Leper Asylum, which segregated lepers (fearing spread of the disease through contagion) from the rest of the population – an act that the contemporary

Leprosy Commission believed to be illegal (Acworth, 'Leprosy in India', p. 425).

[24] Patrick Little, 'A Reading of Caractacus', in *ESJ*, 10/4 (March 1998), pp. 158–67.

[25] Raymond Betts, 'The Allusion to Rome in British Imperialist Thought of the Late Nineteenth and Early Twentieth Centuries', *Victorian Studies*, 15/2 (December 1971), pp. 149–59.

[26] Richards, *Imperialism and Music*, pp. 48–51. Richards and Little both put the onus of empire on Elgar only, and do not discuss Acworth in any level of detail at all. Timothy Barringer came to these conclusions separately in a paper entitled 'Music and Vision: Landscape, History and Empire in Elgar's *Caractacus*', delivered at the Fifth Music in Nineteenth-Century Britain Conference, Nottingham, 2005. Barringer believes that the Roman/British Empire links go further within the work, as the 'Processional Music' at the beginning of Scene vi of *Caractacus* matches 'the blustering dynamism of the modern imperial city' – London – in Elgar's *Cockaigne*. For additional context on the trope likening the Roman and British empires, see Norman Vance's *The Victorians and Ancient Rome* (Oxford: Blackwell, 1997).

Acworth's feelings regarding patriotism and the complex problem of race, and why do there seem to be ambiguities within *Caractacus*'s characters and their view and experience of religion? The first of these questions is somewhat easily answered. From his Brighton College and Oxford education, we can surmise that Acworth was well versed in the classics. Indeed, he may have even read them at university, since this was a popular subject of study for the budding civil servant.[27] The classical sources include a great deal of reported information about Druidism in Ancient Gaul and Britain.[28] Besides the history of Caractacus himself found in Tacitus and Dio Cassius, information regarding the Druids and their rites appears in the writings of Caesar, Cicero, Diodorus, Strabo, Suetonius, Pomponius Mela, Lucan, and Pliny, and a number of others.[29] Even if Acworth did not remember these details from his youthful studies, as an accomplished folklorist who had worked closely with original sources in his ballad publications, and as an amateur archaeologist, he would arguably have returned to these sources when compiling the *Caractacus* libretto. Indeed, Acworth's reliance on these sources is obvious from the ritual nature of the Druidic scenes, as will be seen shortly.

Of course, by the end of the nineteenth century, such classical reports were no longer wholly trusted, nor were they the only basis for an interpretation of the Druids. As the genteel eighteenth-century hobby of antiquarianism spread into the nineteenth-century academic study of archaeology, scholars and amateurs began to appropriate all of the ancient Britons – Druids, bards, and others – within new ideas of national identity. The ancient Britons gave the English a sense of history they would otherwise have lacked when compared to continental countries, such as Greece or Italy. As scholars like Stuart Piggott and Sam Smiles identified in the late 1960s and the mid-1990s respectively, the Celtic Revival that ensued from the eighteenth to the nineteenth centuries throughout Great Britain transformed the ancient Britons and Druids into sophisticated theologians (proto-Christians to some, and even one

[27] Kirk-Greene, *Britain's Imperial Administrators*, p. 97.

[28] Acworth would most likely have known of classical sources about Druidism beyond Lucan, the only source named by Little ('A Reading of *Caractacus*', p. 163). This is particularly evident in how he structures the two Druidic auguries within the libretto: both include three ritual motions that closely follow the classical sources. In the first, for example, mistletoe is cut with a sickle – a description drawn most likely from Pliny's *Natural History*, XVI, p. 249.

[29] These include: Caesar, *De Bello Gallico*; Cicero, *De Divinatione*; Diodorus Siculus, *Histories*; Strabo, *Geographica*; Suetonius, *Claudius*; Pomponius Mela, *De Situ Orbis*; Lucan, *Pharsalia*; Pliny, *Natural History*. English translations of relevant passages may be found in T. D. Kendrick, *The Druids* (London: Methuen & Co., Ltd, 1927; reprint: London: Senate, 1996), especially pp. 73–103. These accounts, of course, are all written from the viewpoint of the victors. Aside from a few credulous tales of the soothsaying abilities of the Druids, most classical reports focus on negative aspects: their human sacrifices, the absolute power they held over the rest of Gallic and British society, and their perceived barbarism. See, for instance, the report by Diodorus Siculus, in his *Histories*, V, pp. 28, 6. An English translation may be found in Kendrick, *The Druids*, pp. 82–3.

of the lost tribes of Israel to others), great astronomers and mathematicians who taught the ancient Greeks philosophy, and lovers of freedom and individual liberty.[30] These 'Druids-as-wished-for'[31] were explicitly compared to other eighteenth- and nineteenth-century so-called 'noble savages', including Native Americans and Tahitians. By the middle of the nineteenth century Ancient Britons were fully ensconced within the nationalist imagination of Great Britain. Bardic poetry and fragments of their literature were published; heroes like Caractacus and Boadicea were enshrined in paintings and public sculpture to celebrate nation and empire; and unified histories of the island, such as that by Charles Isaac Elton, included long descriptions of Druidic rites pulled from a combination of classical authors, amateur antiquarians, and emerging archaeologists.[32] Eighteenth- and nineteenth-century Druid enthusiasts were ultimately responsible for perhaps the best-known myth of the ancient Britons, that they were the builders of such megalithic monuments as Stonehenge and Avebury.[33] All of these threads came together in the popular Covent Garden productions of Vincenzo Bellini's *Norma*, staged by Edward Corbould in the late 1840s with what Smiles fittingly describes as 'the full panoply of the by now standard Druidic imagery in the British artistic tradition' – a megalithic circle, as well as a classically dressed Druid with a sickle and a garland of oak leaves in her hair (Fig. 2.1).[34]

Such a positive, untroubled view of the Celts is developed by James McKay in his aforementioned *The British Camp on the Herefordshire Beacon*, a volume typically cited as a possible source for Acworth's libretto.[35]

---

[30] See Stuart Piggott, *The Druids* (New York: Thames and Hudson, 1985 (reprint of editions from 1968 and 1975)), especially Chapter 4, and Sam Smiles, *The Image of Antiquity: Ancient Britain and the Romantic Imagination* (New Haven and London: Yale University Press, 1994).

[31] Piggott borrows this terminology (to great effect) from R. G. Collingwood. See Piggott, *The Druids*, p. 11.

[32] See, for instance, the descriptions of Druids and Druidic rites in Charles Isaac Elton's *Origins of English History*, 2nd edn (London: Quaritch, 1890), especially pp. 252–3, 256 and 258. The descriptions closely track the scenes set by Acworth, including the white robes of the ritual participants, the sacrifice, and the Druidic maidens' loose hair.

[33] Piggott traces the myth from its seventeenth- and eighteenth-century origins in the writings of such figures as John Aubrey and William Stukeley (the first of whom might have been responding to Inigo Jones's 1655 claim that Stonehenge was a Roman monument; see Piggott, *The Druids*, especially

pp. 133–51); Smiles traces the progression of megalithic monuments in the background of paintings depicting the ancient Druids (*The Image of Antiquity*, especially Chapter 8).

[34] Smiles, *The Image of Antiquity*, pp. 108–9.

[35] These essays were originally published as columns in the *Malvern Advertiser*, so their dissemination was probably regional. See McKay, *The British Camp*, p. [vi]. Acworth arrived in Malvern long after the publication of the columns or the book, and there must remain some uncertainty about the connection. Anderson and Moore state 'Acworth probably found detail for the libretto in a book about the British Camp on the Herefordshire Beacon by James McKay' (*ECE* V, p. [v]), however, and Moore points to a personal connection: 'One source for the Caractacus libretto was probably James McKay's *The British Camp* . . . The volume was dedicated to the Revd. W. S. Symonds of Pendock, near Redmarley, who had taught local geology to Alice Roberts and Minnie Baker' (Moore, *Elgar*, p. 230, n. 161).

6   NOTICE SUR NORMA.

riers, et, au milieu de tous, s'avance lentement Orovèse. Les pâles rayons de l'astre nocturne éclairent déjà la cime des arbres séculaires, et la multitude fanatique abritée sous leur ombre, prévenant l'arrêt que va dicter l'oracle de son dieu, salue cette aurore mystique par un chant de guerre et de carnage. Mais tout à coup paraît Norma entourée de ses prêtresses. — Norma, c'est Julia Grisi, et jamais, à coup sûr, Irmensul n'eut prêtresse plus belle et mieux inspirée. Elle va au delà de l'idéal. Quand elle entre, droite et fière dans les plis de sa tunique, la faucille d'or à la main, la couronne de verveine sur la tête, avec son masque de marbre pâle, ses sourcils noirs et ses yeux d'un bleu verdissant comme celui de la mer, c'est dans toute la salle un cri involontaire d'admiration; quelles épaules et quels bras! ce sont ceux que la Vénus de Milo a perdus!

Norma est le triomphe de Julia Grisi. Quiconque ne l'a pas vue dans ce rôle, ne peut pas dire qu'il la connaît; elle

Fig. 2.1 Edward Corbould, scene from staging of Bellini's *Norma*

McKay's essays are unabashedly pro-Celtic within their presentation, and fantastic within their orientation. They virtually ignore the wider context of Welsh, Scottish, and Irish nationalism for a rather parochial regionalism, within which McKay connects all of the Malvern Hills' geographical, linguistic, and botanical features to Druidism and climactic British history. For instance, McKay claims that the contemporary Malvern practice of singing 'Derry down, derry down, ho!', a peasant refrain during May Festivals, was a corrupted Celtic saying, 'Let us dance round the oak! Let us dance round the oak!' He further intuits that the valley between the Herefordshire and Worcester Beacons 'used to be covered with trees' including an oak's trunk splotched with white, 'round which superstitions still lingered, which were unquestionably of Druidical origin'. McKay notes the presence of mistletoe on oak trees in Malvern, which leads to the conclusion that 'then we have one more reason for the high favour in which, according to the evidence, the heights of Malvern were held by our long-removed Celtic progenitors'. Opening epigrams for the book and its individual chapters link the Druids to both Stonehenge and individual freedom and liberty.[36] McKay's suppositions, based heavily on local amateur antiquarian clubs,[37] go so far as to posit that a stone circle once existed on the Malvern Hills – a circle that degenerated much more quickly that those at Stonehenge or Avebury, because, as he states, 'Malvern stone is likely to moulder away in a remarkable manner'.[38]

Similar enthusiasm for projected Worcestershire Celtic history may be found in a second local source, William Salt Brassington's *Historic Worcestershire: Worcestershire Historical, Biographical, Traditional, Legendary and Romantic*. This book was a more likely source for aspects of the libretto, being a privately published history that included Elgar among the subscribers.[39] In his history, Brassington does not dwell on the context of Caractacus, just the landscape in Worcestershire and Gloucestershire that might have witnessed his battle with the Romans, thus giving credence to Acworth's 'Argument'. Using a combination of contemporary archaeological evidence and Roman sources, Brassington includes long descriptions of Celtic settlement and use around the Malvern Hills, and discusses each location Acworth later mentions: the British Camp, the line of the Severn, and Caer Caradoc in Shropshire. Like Acworth, and unlike McKay, Brassington is careful to note that his projection of Caractacus onto this landscape is only speculation, even if that speculation becomes at times quite enthusiastic:

> When Caractacus was arranging the defences of the eastern border of his territory overlooking the wide valley of the Severn and the Roman outposts, he would

---

[36] See McKay, *The British Camp*, pp. 31; 38–9; 12–13; 68–9, and 8.

[37] For details concerning the amateur works cited, see, for instance, the reference on p. 5 to 'an address delivered by Mr. H. H. Lines, of Worcester'.

[38] McKay, *The British Camp*, pp. 8 and 32–3. McKay made his supposition long before it became known that Stonehenge had more ancient, and pre-Druidic, origins (see the 'History' section of the National Heritage website, http://www.english-heritage.org.uk/server/show/nav.881 – accessed 16 August 2005).

[39] William Salt Brassington, *Historic Worcestershire: Worcestershire Historical, Biographical, Traditional, Legendary and Romantic* (Birmingham, Leicester, and Leamington: The Midland Educational Company, Limited; London: Simpkin, Marshall, Hamilton, Kent, and Co., Limited., [1895]), p. iv.; the chapter of most interest is entitled 'A British Hero', pp. 31–41. None of the standard Elgar biographies mentions this source. Timothy Barringer uncovered this book and discussed it at length in his paper, 'Music and Vision'.

probably consider the Midsummer Hill encampment insufficient to protect that side of Siluria, and would make stronger works upon the more commanding heights of the Herefordshire Beacon, one mile further north. To the west upon Wall Hills near Ledbury, are the remains of other camps and an extensive British settlement, while on the eastern side was, it is said, the old town at Gadbury. The wings of the two Malvern camps are large enough to hold many thousand people and large herds of cattle. Caractacus, or whoever fortified the beacon camp, expected the attack to come from the east, and on that side he made the works the strongest, but when the enemy appeared they came from the west along the valley of the Wye.[40]

To Brassington, the fact that the British Camp in the Malvern Hills was attacked gave credence to the claim that Caractacus used it. Yet the vivid account does include the caveat 'Caractacus, or whoever fortified the beacon camp', showing a degree of historical distance (however slight) not present within McKay's work.

While McKay and Brassington eagerly described their Worcestershire Celtic cultures in the 1890s, they did not do so at the vanguard of an historic movement. Had Elgar and Acworth completed *Caractacus* in the middle of the nineteenth century, rather than at the end of it, the Celtic Revival history just described would have been sufficient to support Richards's and Little's reading of the cantata as manifesting British imperial destiny. However, during the last few decades of the century, the Celtic Revival became embroiled in race politics, and McKay's and Brassington's enthusiastic Celtic parochialism was certainly outmoded by the time Acworth wrote the libretto for *Caractacus*. Indeed, as Matthew Riley notes, 'The Victorian period had witnessed the gradual eclipse of "Celtic" Britain as a source of national myth and a growing preference for peoples who seemed less easily vanquished, such as the Saxons and the Vikings', leading him to classify Elgar and Acworth's presentation of *Caractacus* as a new revival of Celtic culture rather than a continuation of the mid-century one.[41] Signs of this manifestation are easily visible in the growing Welsh and Scottish nationalist movements. It was widely believed throughout the entire period of this revival that the last vestiges of the Celtic race could be found in Wales, Scotland, and Ireland. Scotland and Wales both claimed Caractacus as their own; public and semi-public painting and sculpture celebrated a venerable ancient British past for both of these countries, and the perceived superior musicality of the Welsh was directly and explicitly linked to ancient bardic traditions, reinvented into the nineteenth-century Eisteddfod.[42] Ireland used the

[40] Brassington, *Historic Worcestershire*, p. 39.
[41] Matthew Riley, *Edward Elgar and the Nostalgic Imagination* (Cambridge: Cambridge University Press, 2007), Chapter 6.

[42] The literature on the use of the Celtic revival to promote nationalism in Scotland and Ireland is vast. Some general introductions, besides those already cited, include *English Romanticism and the Celtic World* (ed. Gerard

enthusiasm drawn from the Celtic Revival to reinforce its own national traditions and political aspirations.[43]

Drawing on the rhetoric of evolution, the English responded forcefully to these threats of other nationalisms by reasserting the imagined supremacy of the Anglo-Saxons, who were ostensibly superior because they had conquered the Celts throughout England.[44] This strain of argument, which relied predominantly on the assumption that the Celts fled those locations taken over by the Anglo-Saxons rather then mixing in with the new population, found its eventual expression in the so-called 'Apes and Angels' depictions of the Irish.[45] In these, Anglo-Saxon English caricaturists drew the Celtic Irish in political cartoons as brutish, simian creatures, while depicting Anglo-Saxons as beautiful, symmetrical humans.[46] Artistic representations like those by William Holman Hunt portrayed this tension through casting Druids as bloodthirsty, corrupt individuals bent on murdering the peaceful Christian priests who evangelized ancient Britain.[47] Such paintings contrasted a perceived ancient and barbaric Celtic paganism with the modern, eventually triumphant Anglo-Saxon Christianity.

Carruthers and Alan Rawes, Cambridge: Cambridge University Press, 2003); Gregory Castle, *Modernism and the Celtic Revival* (Cambridge: Cambridge University Press, 2001); James Simon, *The Atlantic Celts: Ancient People or Modern Invention?* (Madison: University of Wisconsin Press, 1999); and T. J. Edelstein (ed.), *Imagining an Irish Past: The Celtic Revival, 1840–1940* (Chicago: The David and Alfred Sand Museum of Art; University of Chicago Press, 1992). A second-generation essay that draws on some of this vast literature to good effect is Trevor Herbert, 'Popular Nationalism: Griffith Rhys Jones ("Caradog") and the Welsh Choral Tradition', in Christina Bashford and Leanne Langley (eds.), *Music and British Culture, 1785–1914: Essays in Honour of Cyril Ehrlich* (Oxford: Oxford University Press, 2000), pp. 255–74.

[43] Such arguments may be found in Edelstein (ed.), *Imagining an Irish Past*.

[44] The writings of Charles Kingsley and Anthony Froude, especially the latter's *Oceana* (London: Longman, 1886) exemplify this.

[45] A middle-of-the road interpretation was also present: Matthew Arnold's *The Study of Celtic Literature* (London: Smith, Elder and Co., 1905), p. 104, described the English as successful because they were a mixture of the best qualities of Celts (melancholy and sentimental attitudes) combined with the

'steadying' Saxon temperament. This granted the English a middle place between the extremes of the Germans and the Welsh.

[46] See L. Perry Curtis, Jr., *Apes and Angels: The Irishman in Victorian Caricature* (Washington, DC: Smithsonian Institution Press, 1971) and *Anglo-Saxons and Celts: A Study of Anti-Irish Prejudice in Victorian England* (Bridgeport: Conference on British Studies, 1968). Some of the conclusions of this early study have been challenged by S. Gilley in 'English Attitudes to the Irish in England, 1780–1900', in Colin Holmes (ed.), *Immigrants and Minorities in British Society* (London and Boston: Allen & Unwin, 1978), especially pp. 81–110, and D. G. Paz in *Popular Catholicism in Mid-Victorian England* (Stanford: Stanford University Press, 1992). Many of Curtis's points still remain valid. Smiles discusses the aspect of race as it developed from the late eighteenth century well into the nineteenth (Smiles, *The Image of Antiquity*, especially pp. 118–28). See also Paul B. Rich, *Race and Empire in British Politics* (Cambridge: Cambridge University Press, 1986), p. 15 and Curtis's 'Comment: The Return of Revisionism', in the *Journal of British Studies*, 44 (2005), pp. 134–45.

[47] See, for instance, Hunt's *A Converted British Family Sheltering a Christian Priest from the Persecution of the Druids* (Oxford: The Ashmolean Museum, 1850).

As an amateur archaeologist and published folklorist, Acworth was certainly aware of these larger racial debates. While his published writings do not directly address the Celtic Revival, they do discuss race at length, as a typical contemporary marker of British and European superiority over the population of India; as a sign of the progress of a particular Indian racial group against another; and as an element of identification of mixed-race ancestry for the English and Scotch, among others.[48] Within these passages, a clear sense of hierarchy is present: Acworth does identify (as was unfortunately typical for his time) white Britons and Europeans as superior to members of other racial groups, but allows great latitude for the admiration of individuals from Hindu subgroups like the Marathas – especially when compared to Indian Muslims. He carried these taxonomies of individual admiration well into his libretto for *Caractacus*.

This relatively sophisticated view of race contrasts sharply with the simplistic one promoted in McKay's book. McKay's Celts are near-perfect. He presents Druidism first as a religion based on freedom and liberty, and the Celts as satisfied with this until they are given the chance to convert to Christianity. This is the largest point of difference between McKay and Acworth, and the character Eigen, Caractacus's daughter, exemplifies the competing ideologies.[49] Within Acworth's libretto, Eigen and Orbin (a character Acworth describes in his Argument as 'imaginary') are betrothed to each other; they are allowed to marry once they arrive in Rome and are pardoned by Claudius, and they are Acworth's vessels for promoting the individual above the community. McKay's contrasting version of the events is an attempt explicitly to link the Celts with the Christian conversion of Britain. McKay relates that once in Rome, Eigen converted to Christianity (changing her name to Claudia as she did so, in honour of the Emperor). Most of the last third of McKay's book attempts to show that Eigen/Claudia partially inspired the Christian conversion of Celtic Britain, which McKay centres in Malvern.[50] By forcing such Christian proclivities onto the Celts, McKay positions his Malvern heroes in an extremely positivistic historical process: they sacrifice their own deeply held beliefs for a larger community that will eventually become a mighty and Christian Great Britain. In other words, McKay feels the need to make his Malvern Celts the instigators of the

[48] Acworth, *Ballads of the Marathas*, pp. [v]–vi; xviii–xix; and vi–vii, respectively.

[49] There are a few similarities within Acworth's and McKay's accounts. Both spend a good deal of time discussing Caractacus's meeting with the Druids and the Soldiers the night before the climactic battle; the battle itself and defeat of Caractacus at the hands of the Romans; as well as the gaudy and circus-like procession of the captive Celts into Rome.

[50] McKay's overwrought enthusiasm for Malvern in all aspects of Ancient Briton history is acute; he even ropes Caractacus into the evangelical evolution: 'Whether Caractacus himself was ever brought to the faith of Christ we cannot say; but there can be little real doubt that, even if we utterly reject, as pure legends, the story of the conversion of his father and daughter, he did hear the love of the Saviour of men proclaimed.' McKay, p. 175.

religion, contemporaneously perceived as superior, that powered the nineteenth-century British Empire. They could not remain nobly savage individuals believing in Druidism, but had to become a Christian community.

Acworth's Druids have much more distinction; he informs his presentation of religion and its import with a greater grasp of historical and cultural possibilities, and Elgar emphasized these within the music of *Caractacus*. The librettist and composer together present two opposing visions of religion within the cantata, one based on the corrupt community, and one based on the honourable individual. Elgar and Acworth represent the corrupt community through the large Druidic ritual in Scene ii, where the Arch-Druid deliberately lies about the auguries. Here (as was discussed above) are signs of the potential mystical savagery of the Druids: human sacrifice (with typical threefold Druidic motions of the knife into the victim), destructive fire, and unnatural artefacts (a procession to an altar made of stone, and the fact that the future is read by magical divination within a shield). Note, however, that the Arch-Druid does not make the prediction; this task is left to Orbin, described within the libretto as one of 'the half-priestly order of minstrels' – something Acworth modelled perhaps on his own description of the Gondhalis, a subgroup of the Marathas who were both 'bards and priests'. Membership of this group suggests on the one hand a bard (one of the three types of Briton described by the classical sources and recycled continuously by the nationalists – though none but Acworth gave the power over omens to this class), and on the other a device to create the necessary conflict between these two groups: the corrupt druids and the noble individuals.[51]

The second scene is perhaps the most important of the entire cantata, for within this scene, Acworth presents the only visible direct conflict. The two other conflicts in the cantata – Scenes iv and vi – pale by comparison.[52] Scene iv is a vivid description of the battle between the Britons and Romans: the

---

[51] Acworth, *Ballads of the Marathas*, pp. xxxii–xxxiii. This is not the only part of the *Ballads of the Marathas* that Acworth recycles in *Caractacus*. The final chorus's subject of freedom, its rhythmic scansion, and its first two lines are clearly modelled after the end of 'The Death of Abudulkhan', one of the ballads Acworth translates (p. 13): 'The noise of war is over, / The songs of victory sound, / The lady Jeeja calls the chiefs, / The loyal chiefs, around; / They throng the halls of Jowli, / The minstrels sing and play, / And, master of all melodies, / Agrindas gains the day. / With the sweet Kadaka rhythm / A village rich he won, / For ever free from tax or fee / From father unto son; / Two golden bracelets deck'd him, / Gifts from the goodly king. /

Hearken, Maratha princes, / His glorious state I sing.'

[52] The only conflict in Scene iii is Orbin's short self-narration to Eigen (via vivid description) of his conflict with the Druids: 'Last night beneath the sacred oak, / The dreaded rite was ta'en, / Last night the mystic word I spoke / That told of Britain's bane; / Then came the King, and false as hell, / A blessèd bode the Druids tell, / Alone my voice was raised to sing / A warning to our glorious King; / Silenc'd, and curs'd, and driv'n to flight, / I tore my bardic robes of white – / A warrior now, for Britain's weal / I change my golden harp for steel.' The monologue serves to make clear his transformation from bard to warrior, as well as emphasize that the Druids were being duplicitous.

soldiers narrate their loss of the battle immediately after the fact. Scene vi, the trial of Caractacus, Eigen, and Orbin by Claudius in Rome, is much shorter; the conflict evaporates after each character makes one monologic statement. In Scene ii, the conflict is presented in the best dramatic form: introduced slowly, given reasons for its occurrence, and finally manifesting itself as a microcosm of the conflict within the entire piece: the corrupt community of the Druids (including the Arch-Druid and Druid maidens) against the noble individual Orbin. This is also the only scene that includes all of the major characters of the cantata with the exception of Claudius.

Scene ii is designed to include increasing levels of character interaction to effect the drama. After the introduction, the Arch-Druid and chorus continue with an invocation by the maidens (discussed above). Each section is ritualistic in its presentation, and includes only declarations. Orbin then makes his prediction: 'I see an eagle flying / With beak and talons red, / I see a warrior lying / On the green earth dead'. The prediction is indeed dire: the eagle symbolizes the victory of Rome over the Britons, who symbolically lie dead within a pastoral setting. The drama is increased not just by the prediction, but in how Acworth reveals it – as a dialogue between the Arch-Druid and Orbin. Further, it seems that each needs the other in order to read the fortune of Caractacus and the Britons. Orbin cannot read the shield until the Arch-Druid banishes the shadows away from it. Once this dialogue is completed, the Arch-Druid considers Orbin's prediction in an echo effect, stating his thoughts, immediately answered by the Druids. Elgar increases the dramatic intensity here by having the maidens return to singing their circular dance around the sacred oak (Ex. 2.2). Within this intensified monologue, the Arch-Druid decides that he and the other Druids will lie about the prediction. When Caractacus enters a moment later, the Arch-Druid gives him a long and false augury, predicting a victory in the battle with the Romans, entreating him to 'Go forth, O King, to conquer ... In thunder on the foe' (fig. 23, echoed homophonically by the chorus), before describing the ruin of the Roman army via a powerful Druidic spell. Caractacus follows suit: he adopts the model of the Arch-Druid, singing joyfully about the forthcoming battle, echoed by his soldiers at the ends of lines (28:11–29:3). In his enthusiasm, he even calls upon Orbin for a song to 'Sing till the fiery echoes roll / To every free-born warrior's soul'. Orbin uses this opportunity to warn Caractacus and the soldiers that the spells of the Druids will not work and trust instead their own swords (Ex. 2.3).

> Shall we greet them?
> Shall we meet them?
> And with mighty spell defeat them?
> Meet them with our war cry ringing,

Ex. 2.2 *Caractacus*, scene ii, fig. 17.7–14

Meet them [with] songs of triumph singing!
In thy hand thou bear'st the omen,
Trust to that against the foemen;
Spell and charm will fail thee ever,
But thy sword deceive thee never.

Ex. 2.3 *Caractacus*, scene ii, fig. 36.1–9

In a short dialogic recitative section, the Arch-Druid and Orbin spar verbally with each other. The Arch-Druid entreats Orbin to stay with the Druids and their message; Orbin once again begs Caractacus and the soldiers not to listen to the Arch-Druid's prediction. At this climactic moment, the Druids curse Orbin; Caractacus and the soldiers exult in the forthcoming battle; and Orbin leaves the sacrificial space to become a warrior. The final words of the scene, 'Taranis, descend to aid', are the same ones heard at the beginning of the invocation.

This long description was necessary to describe all of the action Acworth presented in Scene ii. The scene is complicated because of the shifting allegiances and sheer number of characters present. It is the only scene in

Ex. 2.3 (cont.)

the cantata (save the extremely short Scene v) which does not feature any cuts or transpositions of Acworth's words. Yet Elgar shows a steady dramatic hand throughout the entire scene; a great deal of his success results from judicious use of typical musical iconography. A few motives and textures return throughout the scene to link it together. Elgar even uses some typical 'spooky' orchestrations, such as a lone contrabassoon to accompany the Arch-Druid's words 'The dark and dreadful spell' at 26:3–8; the sections of the prediction themselves are also much more motivically fragmented than those of the opening dance and invocation.

But Elgar also twists some of these musical icons in ways we would not expect: as was mentioned at the beginning of the essay, the opening and closing vocal textures invoke a grand idea of religion, not unlike a ritual processional instead of a macabre dance. Indeed Elgar, until fig. 8, always presents a steady, loping rhythm, and stasis is achieved through typical devices such as long pedal notes (such as the F from the beginning of the scene to fig. 2) or repetitive motives (including the two patterns that cover figs. 3 and 4). Perhaps most important, though, both because it is dramatically significant and also because it shows Elgar pulling ever so slightly away from Acworth's libretto, is Orbin's entreaty to Caractacus and the soldiers (starting at fig. 35). Elgar foreshadows Orbin's difficult and revelatory speech by moving from the F major cadence not to an expected strong elision (such as the dominant), but to C minor. But through the use of symmetry, not present within the libretto itself, he makes Orbin's pronouncement almost manic. Whereas in Acworth's words, the echoing of the Arch-Druid and Caractacus, by the Druids and soldiers respectively, is spelled out in the directions, Elgar offers Orbin his own chorus answering him: both Caractacus and the soldiers echo his words, focusing especially on his words of battle and war (Example 2.3, drawn from 36:1–6). Each time Orbin calls for a warlike, rather than a magical response, Caractacus and the soldiers unify behind him, in either a homophonic or near-homophonic texture. This is especially effective because it casts into relief a typical Elgarian trick used in the next part of the scene: when the Druid chorus responds to Orbin (starting at fig. 45), it takes them some time to come to a temporary unified response (just before fig. 48) and a more permanent, settled one (the deliberate reinvocation of Taranis at fig. 56 – not to help predict, but to cast suffering onto Orbin).

In this first moment of real drama in the cantata, Acworth shows how the community of Druids becomes corrupt. The community, initially staid and static, becomes active and vengeful when its attempt to hide the true meaning of the prediction is challenged by the individual Orbin. In this scene, they triumph, and Orbin leaves the order. Yet elsewhere in *Caractacus*, Druids represent honour – but only when they are individuals, evoking shamanistic, rather than mystical, worship. Acworth places these 'good' Druids within pastoral scenes. In the first scene, Eigen and Orbin describe to Caractacus the divinations of 'a fair Druid Maiden':

> EIGEN:
> At eve to the greenwood we wander'd away,
> To hear the birds singing, as happy as they.
> When we came to the oak where the mistletoe grows,
> Before us a fair Druid maiden arose.
> [With ivy and oakleaf her brow was entwined,
> Her dark hair unhooded was stirr'd with the wind;
> On her bosom a glittering jewel she wore,]
> In her hand a weird emblem, a sickle, she bore,
> She raised it, and thrice reap'd a twig from the oak,
> And the songs of the forest were hush'd as she spoke:[53]

In direct contrast with the awesome but ponderous ritual of organized religion, this Druid maiden gives her prediction alone within the forest, and at the most sacred point: an oak with mistletoe growing upon it – an act, unlike the one of the larger Druid community, that was described explicitly in classical sources such as Pliny.[54] The Druid Maiden's ritual is gentle: rather than kill, she reaps (though with the same tripartite motion as the Arch-Druid used to kill his sacrifice); and when she utters her

---

[53] The brackets indicate text Elgar did not set. Note that this text emphasizes the naturalistic aspects of the Druid maiden: plants suffusing her brow and wind stirring her hair.

[54] Pliny, *Natural History*, XVI, p. 249.

predictions, the entire forest – one with her – grows silent. The text of her prediction itself has a much more naturalistic bent (compare her descriptions of the land, where no artefact is mentioned save the sickle, to those of the Arch-Druid, Druids, and Druid Maidens, which are full of swords and 'dark and dreadful spells'). The second report of the Druid Maiden is much the same. Eigen finds the Maiden again by an oak tree; her countenance now is dark, and she continues to speak in natural images, using the language of artefacts (swords and cords) to warn Eigen that if her father strays from the pastoral world, he will fall in battle and be taken prisoner. Elgar sets the Druid Maiden's second omen within a B♭ major/G minor region, using the first pastoral image to move towards the dominant of E♭ major – the primary key of the entire cantata – but turning away from it for the Druid Maiden's words.[55] Elgar does not return to the B♭ major/E♭ major region until the end of the cantata itself, after the personal nobility and explicit attachment to the land are once again reinforced by Caractacus, Eigen, and Orbin.

The Druid Maiden's dour prediction turns out to have been true, of course, setting the stage for the final scene of the cantata in Rome. Once again, Acworth presents a dichotomy between a corrupt community and a noble individual. The Romans are corrupt, heady from the potential to use power irresponsibly. When confronted with the captured Celts Caractacus, Eigen, and Orbin, they cry with one voice for their death. The Emperor Claudius, a Roman, but one of Acworth's noble individuals, spares the Britons – but only after he hears of their attachment to the land. All three of Acworth's characters describe their explicit pastoral fixation: Eigen describes the hills and rills; Orbin wishes to see Eigen on the 'wooded glade' or 'tripping on the lea'; and Caractacus states 'We dwelt among our woodlands, and were blessed' – a line Elgar explicitly and famously described to Jaeger as important: 'I made old Caractacus stop as if broken down on p. 168 & choke & say "woodlands" again because I'm so madly devoted to my woods.'[56] In a final gesture of pastoral solidarity, E♭ major is finally fully re-established at the end of the cantata, when the final commentary chorus proclaims Acworth's last natural metaphor ('The Oak has Grown').

Thus the pastoral is associated with the good characters, who are all heroic individuals set in opposition to the corrupt, artefact-obsessed communitarian Druids and the bloodthirsty Roman citizens. These Celts are not a mere simplistically triumphant race; rather, Acworth's characters inhabit a subtler world, which includes treachery. And, when linked by Acworth to love of the

---

[55] G minor is the key that all the 'power figures' (the Arch-Druid, Orbin, and the Druid Maiden) come to eventually.

[56] Moore *Elgar*, p. 238; full letter in *Publishers*, vol. I, p. 86.

land, race becomes a signifier of personal nobility. Thus the pastoral is part of the key; as Jan Marsh noted in *Back to the Land: The Pastoral Impulse in England from 1880 to 1914*, the nineteenth-century shift in Britain's economy from predominantly agrarian to industrial and commercial brought with it an intense, almost pathological nostalgia for the countryside. As poverty and crime became more visible in the larger, densely populated urban areas, the British began to construct rural areas as arcadias, the home of a 'real England', untainted by vice, poverty, or crime.[57]

Elgar's love for the country is well documented, and needs little further explanation.[58] But what of Acworth's? Acworth, of course, upon his retirement, followed the vigorous pursuits of the country gentleman just as Elgar did. Young informs us that he was 'Captain and Treasurer of the Golf Club and Swimming Club, and President of the ... Naturalists Club in Malvern at various times'.[59] Acworth also retired directly to Malvern and the natural beauty it offered when he left the ICS, rather than to London or one of the other industrial centres. To this we can add that the typical member of the nineteenth-century ICS was expected to be not only mentally and spiritually fit, but also physically able and willing to play outdoor games. As far as the worth of the individual is concerned, we have to look no further than the generally accepted model of the Indian civil servant, forced to be an individual because of the rather small colonial bureaucracy. Between the years 1869 and 1900, a period that roughly corresponds to Acworth's career, the service grew from 883 members to 1,021 – a small number to administer the entire subcontinent.[60] With such limited human resources, by necessity the civil servant had to be a powerful, resourceful, but ultimately a lone figure. As Clive Dewey noted, Indian civil servants

> above all ... were intellectuals. Yet they pretended to be men of action, to escape the stigma attached to cleverness by the late-Victorian middle class ... They quelled riots with a glare, silenced subordinates with a word, played games with manic determination. But the harder they tried, the less plausible their pose became. Whether they like it or not, they were competition-wallahs chosen for their intellectual ability: mandarins unable to escape their condition.[61]

[57] Jan Marsh, *Back to the Land: The Pastoral Impulse in England from 1880 to 1914* (London, Melbourne and New York: Quartet Books, 1982), pp. 1–2. In her investigations, Marsh presents these rural arcadias as mostly utopian, socialist ideals that were a 'pantheistic substitute for religion' (see especially p. 4).
[58] Elgar's love of the country is a well-worn trope often exaggerated in an attempt to identify his music with England in general, as was the case with Ken Russell's famous BBC documentary film *Elgar* (re-released on DVD; London: BFI Video, 1996). See Matthew Riley, 'Rustling Reeds and Lofty Pines: Elgar and the Music of Nature', *19CM*, 26 (2002), pp. 155–77, for the problems of this iconic identification.
[59] Young, *Alice Elgar*, p. 138, n. 2.
[60] Kirk-Greene, *Britain's Imperial Administrators*, p. 91.
[61] C. Dewey, *Anglo-Indian Attitudes: The Mind of the Indian Civil Service* (London and Rio Grande, Ohio: The Hambledon Press, 1993), pp. 5–6.

Thus the great focus on the individual and the pastoral within *Caractacus* cannot be viewed as merely a sign of Elgar's predilections, but of Acworth's own temperament as well. And through Acworth's centring of 'good' Druids on such noble pastoralism opposed to the 'bad' Druids and their mystical artefacts, the great strength of the individual Celt triumphs in the end over the Druidic community (corrupt through treachery) and the Roman community (corrupt through enervating entertainment).[62]

This information about Acworth, his character, and the impact of his character on the libretto of *Caractacus* takes a necessary first step to a larger study of this cantata and its place within Elgar's work and British music history. While Elgar biographers mention Acworth, his contribution to *Caractacus* is continually minimized within the literature. Issues of imperialism, characterization, and patriotism, whether objectionable to our later mores or not, are laid solely at the feet of Elgar. This is unfortunate, because it renders a great disservice to history: scholars and enthusiasts both continually try to remove Elgar from aspects of the wider world around him. Within the biographies these limitations of context not only deny Acworth his due, but also greatly simplify Elgar's role and the role of music in the web of late Romantic culture. For instance: the final scene of this cantata is often cited as one of Elgar's 'imperial' moments, because of the final chorus 'The clang of arms is over'. While Elgar was obviously responsible for setting the words and defending them to Jaeger (he could ultimately have refused to do either), he was not responsible for casting them in such an imperial light. That task was primarily Acworth's; his enthusiasm for the British empire might have been ultimately greater than Elgar's because of his years of successful service on its behalf. After all, Acworth's honorary title (Commander of the Indian Empire) is given on the title page of the vocal score. As was mentioned above, Acworth was particular about having the description 'The Words Written for Music by' above his name; we can assume that he was also particular about how Novello presented his name, identifying him with the British empire. Yet Acworth's own history has not been brought to bear on this final chorus. We shall only escape such errors of omission when we begin successfully to locate Elgar and his compositions within this larger world, instead of relying solely on his personal biography to provide all of the answers.

Race, religion, and the pastoral are merely three tools that we can use to help locate Elgar and Acworth's *Caractacus* within this larger world. They show us that *Caractacus* is a thematically complex work, displaying many of the ambivalences and ambiguities of Victorian culture: the destiny of

---

[62] To this could be added a discussion of the place of the character Orbin, for he seems most like the stereotypical civil servant. When unthinking political bureaucracy pushes him aside, he becomes a man of action, even though he knows it will be a doomed fight.

empires, the role of the individual in society, and what sort of religion best suits both. Merely deriding the text of this work and dismissing the cantata as a whole as outmoded, jingoistic Empire celebration misses the point. *Caractacus* and its authors, when queried deeply and properly, reveal much about this Victorian world we as scholars all celebrate.

Appendix 2.1

Harry Arbuthnot Acworth   A Chronology of His Life
A bibliography of sources cited within this list (other than standard abbreviations used elsewhere in this volume) is found below.

1849: born in Worcestershire, son of N. B. Acworth of Northaw, Herts., retired from the British East India Company (*Times*; *Brighton*; *WWW*)

c.1860–7: education at Brighton College (*WWW*; Hart 1873; *Brighton*)

1867–70: attends Worcester College, Oxford

1879, 30 April: called to the bar; enters Civil Service (*WWW 29–40*; *AO*)

1870–79: serves as Assistant Collector (*Brighton*)

1872, 16 October: matriculates from Worcester College, Oxford (*AO*)

1873: holds a Sixth Class Post in the Presidency of Bombay (under four years' standing); Third Assistant Collector and Magistrate of Ahmednuggur; he had a sick furlough (Hart 1873)

1878: thanked by Government of India for his services during the famine of the previous two years (*Times*)

1879–81: Under-Secretary to the Finance and Revenue Departments, appointed by Richard Temple (*Brighton*; *Times*)

1880: marries Anna Jenkins, Daughter of Gen. C. V. Jenkins; they have two daughters including Rosamund, a friend of Carice Elgar, and two sons (*Times*)

1881: begins serving as Deputy Collector of Salt Revenue (*Brighton*)

1885: appointed Deputy Municipal Commissioner for City of Bombay (*Brighton*)

1890: appointed Municipal Commissioner for City of Bombay (*WWW*)

1890: establishes Matunga Leper Asylum (*WWW*; *JSA*)

1893, August: takes a 'leading part' in suppressing the Hindu–Muslim riots (*Times*, misdated 1892; Michael 1902, 456–7)

1893: visits the Madras Leper Hospital mentioned in William Tebb's *Leprosy and Vaccination* (London, 1893; Chapter 2)

1894: publishes a collection of Marathi ballads and songs translated into English; identifies himself as president of the Bombay Anthropological Society (Acworth, 1894, [i])

1895: made CIE (Companion of the Eminent Order of the Indian Empire; *WWW*); retires from Civil Service (*Brighton*); ? moves to Malvern Wells.

1895, November: Alice Elgar has tea with the Acworths; Acworth offers to help Elgar with the *King Olaf* libretto (Moore, *Elgar*, 202)

1896, 31 October: letter from Acworth to Elgar, congratulating him on the success of *King Olaf* at Hanley (Moore, *Elgar*, 217–18; *Publishers*, 39)

1897, 11 November: Elgar meets with Henry Embleton of the Leeds Festival; *Caractacus* is discussed as a novelty (Moore, *Elgar*, 229)

1897, 10 December: A. J. Jaeger informs Elgar that another composer, Joseph Read, set the Caractacus story earlier (*Publishers*, 60)

1898: Acworth delivers a paper to the Imperial Institute entitled 'Leprosy in India'; this paper is called 'the ablest statement of the case ... ever heard from a non-medical man' (*Times*)

1898, 24 January: Elgar confirms financial arrangements with Novello for *Caractacus* (*Publishers*, 65)

1898, 20 June: letter from Elgar to Jaeger, mentioning that 'Acworth has made most of the cuts in the libretto' (*Publishers*, 75)

1898, c. 20 June: letter from Elgar to Jaeger, discussing Acworth's desire to have 'written for music' on the title page of *Caractacus* (*Publishers*, 75–6)

1898, 21 June: letter from Elgar to Jaeger discussing the 'patriotism' of the last chorus (Moore, *Elgar*, 239 (selection); *Publishers*, 76–77)

1898, 12 July: letter from Elgar to Jaeger: 'I knew you would laugh at my librettist's patriotism (& mine) – never mind: England for the English is all I say – hands off ! there's nothing apologetic about me.' (Moore, *Elgar*, 239; *Publishers*, 79)

1898, 5 October: *Caractacus* premiere

1898, October: Acworth's Druids called 'Unmitigated Bores' by a music reviewer from *The Globe* (Anderson, *Elgar*, 39)

1898, 17 November: letter from Elgar to Littleton, discussing Acworth's fee of ten guineas (*Publishers*, 97–8)

1898, 11 December: Ann Elgar's anecdote about the suggestion of *Caractacus* published: 'When I was staying at Colwall E[lgar] and Alice came to see me – on going out we stood at the door looking along the back of the Hills – the Beacon in full view – I said Oh! Ed. Look at the lovely old Hill. Can't we write some *tale* about it. I quite long to have something worked up about it; so full of interest and so much historical interest. I said to write some *tale*, and you *can* "do it yourself Mother" He held my hand with a firm grip "do" he said – No I can't my day is gone by if ever I could and so we parted ... ' (Moore, *Elgar*, 225; also Young, *Elgar*, 80–1)

1899, 9 March: Acworth delivers a paper entitled 'Leprosy in India' to the Society of Arts; it is published on 31 March, along with the discussion, in the *Journal of the Society of Arts* (*JSA*)

1900: publishes 'The Matoonga Asylum in Bombay' in *Bib. Int. Lep.* 1900: 1 (3) 151

1901: ? leaves Malvern Wells (Young, *Elgar*, 138 – uncertain)

1902, 18 April: letter from Boosey to Elgar, discussing the possibility of a further collaboration with Acworth (*Publishers*, 348–9)

1904: Mantunga Leper Asylum in Bombay/Mumbai renamed the Acworth Leper Asylum

1904, 14 November: letter from Elgar to Acworth regarding turning *Caractacus* into an opera (*Lifetime*, 158–9)

1906: Carice Elgar stays with the Acworths (Moore, *Elgar*, 485)

1933, 19 May: Acworth dies in Malvern (*WWW*; *Times*), with estate at death £12,519 (net personalty £9,652 – published on 10 July)

Sources for Appendix 2.1 (other than those listed on pp. x–xi):

Acworth 1894: Harry Arbuthnot Acworth, *Ballads of the Marathas Rendered into English Verse* (London and New York: Longmans, Green, 1894).

AO: Joseph Foster, *Alumni Oxonienses: the Members of the University of Oxford, 1715–1886: Their Parentage, Birthplace, and Year of Birth, with a Record of Their Degrees; Being the Matriculation Register of the University, Alphabetically Arranged, Revised and Annotated* (Oxford and London: Parker, 1888). Additional information may be found in Joseph Foster, *Men at the Bar: a Biographical Hand-list of the Members of the Various Inns of Court, Including Her Majesty's Judges, etc.* (London: Reeves and Turner, 1885).

Brighton: Brighton College Register of Pupils

Hart 1873: *Hart's Army List of 1873* http://members.ozemail.com.au/~clday/hartsICS.htm

JSA: Harry Arbuthnot Acworth, 'Leprosy in India', in *Journal of the Society of the Arts* 47, no. 2,419 (31 March 1899), 415–41; a report on this paper appeared in the *Journal of Tropical Medicine*, March 1899, 219–20.

Michael 1902: L. W. Michael, *The History of the Municipal Corporation of the City of Bombay* (Bombay: Union Press, 1902)

Times: Obituary of Acworth, *The Times*, 30 May 1933

WWW: *Who Was Who*, vol. III: 1929–1940 (London: Adam and Charles Black; New York: Macmillan, 1941)

Neither the *Dictionary of National Biography* nor *Who Was Who in British India* contains entries on Acworth.

3 Elgar and the idyllic: 'By the Wayside' and other perspectives

Christopher Mark

'Idyll' is defined by Merriam Webster's Online Dictionary as 'a simple descriptive work in poetry or prose that deals with rustic life or pastoral scenes or suggests a mood of peace and contentment'.[1] Representations of the idyllic have long been part of music's symbolic and expressive territory. Geoffrey Chew notes that

> in its long history, the pastoral tradition has served a variety of audiences and artistic purposes ... It has proved vital and flexible, not only as a self-contained genre, but (as in German Romantic music) occasionally in its ability to colour a variety of music not necessarily considered pastoral either by its composers or by critics. Arcadia or its equivalent can be an eschatological religious symbol, where the wolf lies down with the kid or where Christ is the Good Shepherd (as in Bach's cantata no. 104). Or it may be a symbol of Nature whose response to the sacred, or to art, is immediate and authentic (as in the Orpheus legend and in the popular pastoral tradition where animals speak on Christmas Eve).[2]

Matthew Riley sees 'meanings and values surrounding "nature"' as including 'such concepts as immediacy, freshness, simplicity, spontaneity, and the imaginative vision of childhood, along with the implicit negation of the everyday world, social mores, mundane adulthood, and even modern civilization itself'.[3] But the idyllic is not concerned only with 'peace and contentment'. It may also, as Chew says, be 'a symbol of the ideal to which the artist vainly aspires'; while 'within the pastoral setting, disruptive events may occur, and they are not always negligible or accountable in terms of *double entendre*: the idealized surroundings may only heighten the sense of loss (as in Schubert's *Die schöne Müllerin*)'.[4] Riley, in a brief survey of *fin-de-siècle* treatments of the pastoral figure of Pan, observes that he 'haunted the imaginations of the late Victorians and Edwardians', symbolizing 'a desire to escape Progress and the commercial, industrial future', as well as promising 'spiritual relief from the Victorians' protracted religious controversies' and embodying 'favourite Edwardian pastimes such as sport, outdoor

---

[1] http://www.m-w.com/, accessed 7 March 2006.
[2] Geoffrey Chew, 'Pastoral', in *New Grove 2*, vol. XIX, p. 217.

[3] Matthew Riley, 'Rustling Reeds and Lofty Pines: Elgar and the Music of Nature', *19CM*, 26/2 (2002), p. 157.
[4] Chew, 'Pastoral', p. 217.

recreation, children's games and the Boy Scout movement'.[5] Much of the literature centred on him

> sounded a note of lament even as it invoked magic, freedom, or the rural idyll. After all, the pagan Pan was said by Plutarch to have died at the moment of Jesus' birth. (In Christian iconography he had later become the devil.) To call on Pan was often a fundamentally nostalgic act: an attempt to reconnect alienated, modern humanity with nature, to 're-enchant' the world and endow nature once again with personal significance, so that it seems to speak to us.[6]

As I hope to show, it is this nostalgic, melancholy construction of the idyllic – sometimes invoking pastoral imagery or, more usually, Schiller's notion of idyll as mode of perception 'in terms of its psychological and expressive value rather than its subject matter'[7] – that, generally speaking, appeals to Elgar. It is, I would suggest, central to his expressive persona: 'the sense of loss' apparent in so much of his music has been highlighted by most commentators. The example of German Romanticism – pre-eminently Schubert and Schumann[8] – is obviously of central importance in this construction, though a specifically English representation of the idyllic, associated with a particular treatment of diatonicism, also forms a significant part of the mixture.

Intersecting with Chew's 'disruptive events' and Riley's 'note[s] of lament' is Reinhold Brinkmann's notion of 'broken idyll', which he elaborates in his study of Brahms's Second Symphony.[9] He declares an 'interest in detecting the sombre undertones in this music and their conditioning factors, individual and historical', as well as a 'sympathy with a broken presentation of serenity, with an "interference" in the idyll'. The final phrase is particularly significant. Brinkmann hears Brahms's Second Symphony as embodying an ' "interference" in the idyll' within what he describes as the 'peculiar opening',[10] the first span up to the structural cadence at b. 44 (the very opening and the structural cadence are reproduced in Ex. 3.1 (a) and (b)). He describes the basic elements of what he calls the 'tone' of the music thus:

- the horn sound, using the natural notes of the instrument to begin with, harmoniously alternating with a bright woodwind passage, the two underlaid by the drone of the string basses;
- simple, clearly articulated melody, with arpeggiated triads and diatonic steps in the upper voices, thirds and sixths;

[5] Riley, 'Rustling Reeds', p. 159. For an extensive account of the late Victorian penchant for the idyll, see Shelagh Hunter, *Victorian Idyllic Fiction: Pastoral Strategies* (London: Macmillan, 1984).
[6] Riley, 'Rustling Reeds', p. 160.
[7] Chew, 'Pastoral', p. 217.
[8] For a recently published extended examination of the role of the idyllic in

Schumann, see Erika Reiman, *Schumann's Piano Cycles and the Novels of Jean Paul* (Rochester, NY: University of Rochester Press, 2004).
[9] Reinhold Brinkmann, *Late Idyll: The Second Symphony of Johannes Brahms*, trans. Peter Palmer (Cambridge, MA: Harvard University Press, 1995).
[10] Ibid., p. 75.

Ex. 3.1 (a) Brahms, Symphony no. 2, opening

- four-square periods with correspondences between the rhythmic motifs, a vibrant oscillating rhythmicality about the lightly agitated 3/4 beat;
- sound, repose, balance, manifestly a world without conflicts. The Romantic nature-topos is patent.[11]

Brinkmann recognizes that this description is superficial; that beneath the apparently effortless flow there is a structural conflict – a 'dislocated overlaying of phrases'[12] – with various consequences, so that while the opening is 'seemingly serene and confident, the symphony begins in a surprisingly unstable, ambiguous fashion'.[13] Furthermore, there is a certain framing of the apparent naturalness arising from Brahms's positioning of himself historically (a positioning that Brinkmann outlines in relation to Beethoven's *Eroica*); he suggests that '[The] relationship of the Brahms symphony to music history . . . makes it clear that the natural note at the beginning of the work has, in fact, only the semblance of spontaneity. Even the nature-idyll is determined reflectively; there is, in Brahms, no naive immediacy that has escaped from the idea and obligation of history.'[14] Meanwhile a rather more straightforward 'interference' in the idyll is to be heard in the entrance of the trombones in b. 33, instruments which, in contradistinction to their traditionally positive role, form (together with the timpani) 'the sombre antithesis to the idyllic nature-metaphor of the beginning, realizing more directly, eventually, what the structural configuration in that section was

[11] Ibid., pp. 53–4.
[12] Ibid., pp. 71–2.
[13] Ibid., p. 74.
[14] Ibid., p. 57.

Ex. 3.1 (b) Brahms, Symphony no. 2, first movement, bb. 32–46

surreptitiously hinting at: an emphatic questioning of the pastoral world, a firm denial of the possibility of pure serenity'[15] (they enter on a diminished seventh).

A crucial aspect of the effect of the idyllic as Brinkmann sees it is the separation from 'reality':

> The process of civilization defines the flight into nature as an idyll, at the same time relativizing and questioning the promise of happiness. It is true that the idyll presents the *form* in which the 'dream of the great unity' is perceived, and where 'social harmony and nature's immediate presence' might come together in a higher synthesis – in a nutshell, the imagined promise of a harmony between man and life, prefigured in the work of art. 'But it will prove to be the case that this idyllic fulfilment can only be achieved at the cost of a separation: one must turn one's back on cities and city-dwellers' [Jean Starobinski, *Die Erfindung der Freiheit* (Geneva: Skirta, 1964), pp. 159–60]. At the onset of the modern age the compensatory dream of the idyll is seen through as such; the idyllic and utopian plan, on the one hand, and the thought of its unreality, on the other, will together generate that 'melancholy enthusiasm' that blends idyll and elegy. 'So the mind gives itself up to contemplating an asset which it lacks, which exists no longer or does not exist as yet. It gives itself up to the passion of absence, to thinking continually about a desire that will no longer find a commensurate object' (Starobinski 160) . . . The late idyll of the nineteenth and early twentieth century is always purchased through an act of renunciation with regard to the totality of life, as Renate Böschenstein-Schäfer has shown in poems by Mörike and Trakl. The crucial point is 'that the idyllic state is one which has been battled for, where the banished demons can still be traced' [Renate Böschenstein-Schäfer, *Idylle* (Stuttgart: Metzler, 1967), 94].[16]

This is a valuable starting point for a discussion of Elgar's own rich interaction with the idyllic. It is a varied interaction, so I shall be referring to a number of works and contexts. My main focus, though, is on 'By the Wayside' from *The Apostles* (1903), which seems to me to present a particularly sophisticated and intriguing case.

For the *locus classicus* of the broken idyll in Elgar's music, one might well turn to *Dream Children* (1902; originally for piano, orchestrated that year), in spite of its modest dimensions and ambitions. Diana McVeagh describes the two movements, of only twenty-four and 141 bars, as being 'almost entirely composed of sequences, modified just enough to sustain attention'.[17] The work can be argued to be central in the development of a characteristically Elgarian form of expression; Christopher Grogan has described it as 'perhaps the earliest manifestation of a vein of nostalgia which was to become an

---

[15] Ibid., p. 79.
[16] Ibid., p. 142.

[17] Diana McVeagh, 'The Shorter Instrumental Works', in *Companion*, p. 58.

essential part of his idiom'.[18] As is well known, the work is prefaced by a quotation from *Dream Children; a Reverie* by Charles Lamb:

> . . . And while I stood gazing, both the children gradually grew fainter to my view, receding, and still receding till nothing at last but two mournful features were seen in the uttermost distance, which, without speech, strangely impressed upon me the effects of speech: 'We are not of Alice, nor of thee, nor are we children at all . . . We are nothing; less than nothing, and dreams. *We are only what might have been'* . . .

The work's origins would appear to have been in Elgar's own childhood: Michael Kennedy states that it is based on 'music he had written for the play he and his siblings had performed when they were children', while McVeagh refers to the work being 'worked up' from 'old sketches'.[19] As she notes, *Dream Children* was composed in a historical period that idealized child-hood.[20] There is no doubt that, whatever the provenance of the material, the viewpoint is that of the melancholic adult. This is most clear in the ending to the second movement, in which the dance-like music that forms its main material recedes (finishing on the tonic chord in 6/3 position) and the opening section of the first movement returns, slightly varied – the opening eight bars are recalled minus bb. 4–5 and 7 (Ex. 3.2: the truncated reminis-cence as index of nostalgia is a well-known Elgarian fingerprint). Not that the rest of the second movement is devoid of nostalgic leanings; the thematic material might be dance-like and for the most part 'innocently' diatonic, but the stock chromaticism in bb. 1 and 3 (V/V), coupled with the chord's 4/2 position, are sufficiently sophisticated to indicate a longing for what is past rather than living in the present. The same is true of the contrasting section from b. 54, expressed through the languorous yearning of the 9–8 appoggiaturas in the initial presentation of the theme, which is sub-sequently heightened by those of the antiphonal inner part in the third iteration from b. 70.

In the first movement the symbolism is decidedly pastoral (prompted perhaps by the country setting for the Lamb story), with its 12/8 metre and lilting parallel thirds. McVeagh has written that it 'opens innocently, then deepens in feeling, becoming richer, more passionate'.[21] Certainly it is more 'knowing' in its more far-reaching harmonic excursions and the longing of the tierce de Picardie. But the tonal ambiguity leads one to doubt the

---

[18] Christopher Grogan, Forward to *ECE*, vol. XXV (*Dream Children, Wand of Youth*), p. vii.
[19] Kennedy, *Life of Elgar*, p. 107; McVeagh, 'The Shorter Instrumental Works', p. 58.
[20] Ibid. See also J. P. E. Harper-Scott, 'Elgar's Unwumbling: the Theatre Music',

Companion, pp. 177–8, regarding 'youth's precious and fantastic insouciance', which is 'celebrated in much Victorian and Edwardian art'.
[21] McVeagh, 'The Shorter Instrumental Works', p. 58.

Ex. 3.2 (a) *Dream Children*, no. 1

Ex. 3.2 (b) *Dream Children*, no. 2, ending

'innocence' of its opening: no sooner has the music begun solidly enough with a G minor triad than it is cadencing into B♭, only to revert to G minor in the next bar.

Writing about a later context, the 'Dream Interlude' in *Falstaff*, op. 68 (1913), in which the knight looks back to his time as page to the Duke of

Norfolk, J. P. E. Harper-Scott seems to be in no doubt about Elgar's view of childhood:

> In mature works that contain nostalgic passages or are concerned almost exclusively with retrospection, Elgar's opinion of the child's relation to the man could scarcely be further from the comfortable Victorian idealization of *Peter Pan* or Lewis Carroll's stories about Alice. Elgar certainly treats childhood with a fantastic fascination, seeing in it things that disgrace the state of adulthood as he perceived it, but he did not see much real hope in retrospection, since childhood itself is imperfect and no guide to the future.[22]

He adds that 'nostalgic feeling and diatonic language, both identifying marks of the "Dream Interlude", are rarely presented straightforwardly in Elgar, even when they do represent dreams: they are usually tools for shaping his profoundest musical cynicism'.[23] But in later stating that 'Elgar was neither Arcadian nor Utopian, for such persons need hope, either in a return to Eden or the promise of Heaven, and Elgar had little of that, as his many despairing letters bear witness', Harper-Scott perhaps goes too far: it is equally clear from Elgar's letters and from various biographical accounts that his moods were frequently changeable, and it is surely a negation of the expressive richness of both the Dream Interlude (which is discussed further below) and *Dream Children* – a richness born of a complex mixture of recalled experience and lament for the impossibility of a return to that state – to regard them as 'cynical'.

   If *Dream Children* is a relatively straightforward and compact case of 'melancholy enthusiasm', instances of the phenomenon in two ostensibly abstract instrumental works composed during the next eight years, the Violin Concerto, op. 61 (1910) and *Introduction and Allegro*, op. 47 (1905), operate on a rather broader scale, and are of a more complex order. It could be argued, for instance, that in the Violin Concerto the idyllic is the pivot around which this immensely rich work revolves.[24] As in several of Elgar's works, a dichotomy between public and private worlds of feeling, and public versus private utterance, is central. In the final movement's cadenza – which, I would argue, is crucial to the character of the work as a whole – Elgar inverts the usual function: while it still clearly requires virtuoso technique, it is not concerned with ostentatious public display, watched admiringly by a silently respectful orchestra and conductor. Rather it is, as Ernest Newman suggested, 'an interlude of serious and profound contemplation, as it were the soul retiring into itself and seeking its strength inwardly, in the midst of the

[22] J. P. E. Harper-Scott, 'Elgar's Invention of the Human: *Falstaff*, Opus 68', *19CM*, 28 (2005), pp. 230–53, at p. 245.
[23] Ibid.

[24] The following discussion of the Violin Concerto elaborates material presented in Christopher Mark, 'The Later Orchestral Music (1910–34)', *Companion*, pp. 154–70.

swirling life all around it'.[25] Elgar himself said that 'it sadly *thinks over* the 1st movement'.[26] However, this neglects the long stretches of optimistic B major between figs. 103:6 and 104, whose warmth is enhanced (rather than threatened) by the Neapolitan inflections – an idyll glimpsed, or even inhabited, before the shift to B minor at fig. 104 leads to the impassioned shift flatward at fig. 105.[27] The end of the cadenza sees the possibility of recapturing the idyllic: the soloist's trill on A from fig. 105:15 sets up expectations of a cadence into D major, while the underlying reminiscence of one of the main themes of the second movement – the location of the most sustained engagement with the idyllic, as we shall see – enhances the idyllic sensibility (see Ex. 3.3). A cadential 6/4 is set up in the bar before fig. 107, but the expected progression to the D major triad is thwarted by the return of the soloist's very first utterance, in B minor (as in the first movement, fig. 19). It is true that the work eventually closes in B major, the key of the idyllic ruminations between figs 103:6 and 104, but this is the closing gesture of the most public, display-conscious section of the work, very far from the promised intimate major-mode close of the cadenza. In the conclusion to his article Riley observes that

> if the musical gestures I have identified as signifiers of the natural testify to a recurrent desire to achieve musical 'freshness' or 'vitality', there must exist some 'mundane' framing context from which the freshness can emerge or to which it can be contrasted. Especially common is a sense that 'reality' – determined by the conventional frame and form of a movement – gives way, in a sudden moment of transformation, to a magical 'inner' world of pastoral simplicity, childlike innocence, or imaginative vision. Such transformative moments – or 'thresholds' (the word used by the guardian angel in *Gerontius*) – are usually the places where the imitation of natural sounds is heard.[28]

Clearly I am suggesting that the end of the cadenza effects the reverse of this, the inner world being brusquely dismissed by 'reality'. The beginning of the cadenza is not so much a sudden transformation but, rather like the beginning of the slow movement of the First Symphony, is carefully prepared and continuous with what precedes it.

Previous movements of the Violin Concerto are not devoid of the idyllic. In the first movement, for example, there is the *dolce* second subject in figs. 16–19, the main material of which returns in the cadenza to introduce the B major passage, and which also provides the model for the cadenza's attempt to end in D (though it is less momentous at fig. 19 because it is not so

---

[25] Ernest Newman, 'Elgar's Violin Concerto', *MT*, 51 (1910), p. 634.
[26] Letter to Frank Schuster, 29 June 1910; *Lifetime*, p. 221.
[27] As Riley notes, 'the Aeolian harp effect' that underpins the cadenza from fig. 102 is

'unmistakable' (Riley, 'Rustling Reeds', p. 175), and is one of Elgar's most direct invocations of the pastoral, as are the bird-like decorated arpeggios and trills of figs. 103:6–104.
[28] Ibid., p. 177.

Ex. 3.3 (a) Violin Concerto, first movement, figs. 106–108

Ex. 3.3 (b) Violin Concerto, first movement, from 3 bars before fig. 19

prepared – see Ex. 3.3). But, as suggested earlier, the idyllic is most sustained in the second movement, which exists on a separate plane from the rest of the work: it is B♭- rather than B-centred, and is therefore set apart from *Allegro/Allegro molto* hubbub. The idyllic is particularly apparent in the first stretch up to fig. 47. This is not entirely untroubled music: see, for example, the shift to the parallel minor at the *poco animato* passages as early as the fifth bar, and

Ex. 3.4 Violin Concerto, second movement from 3 bars after fig. 46

again from fig. 45:5, with greater urgency through the syncopation in the solo line as well as in the bass. But the basic material is remarkably loose-limbed harmonically, almost casual in its scalar and (modal) circle-of-fifths bass movement recycled in sequence, and its repetitive use of the ♫ ♩ figure. It is the latter that sets up the exquisite cadence onto G at fig. 46:7, when the ♫ ♩ figure is finally deflected (see Ex. 3.4). I suggest that this opening is the closest thing, in Elgar's post-*Gerontius* music, to the 'genuine' (i.e. unbroken) idyll at the beginning of Part II of that work. The soul's new environment is conveyed by music that is (mostly) restricted to the F major collection, but which floats freely within these confines, largely unencumbered by the duties and desires of conventional functional harmony. Thus the two alternative cadences onto D in b. 8 and fig. 3:4, and onto F in the bar before fig. 2, are entirely equal in weight and interchangeable. The gentle dissonances – many of which are born through maintaining the pastoral parallel sixths (see, for example, the first beat of b. 6, alto A against bass B♭) – enhance rather than threaten the effect. (The flatward excursion from fig. 2:7 sets up the B♭ version of the opening – in the violins, a literal repeat of fig. 1:5 with Es turned to E♭s, with inner part added, all underpinned by a B♭ pedal.)

While the formal strategies are handled differently in the *Introduction and Allegro*, the idyllic is no less central. It is embodied in the so-called Welsh Tune, whose first iteration is reproduced in Ex. 5.1. As Daniel M. Grimley has observed, the origins of the work are traceable to the sketchbook containing material for *The Apostles* and *The Kingdom*.[29] The Welsh tune seems to have been destined for the oratorio, 'possibly to illustrate Christ in the wilderness at the start of the first scene where Elgar provided a brief orchestral interlude

[29] Daniel M. Grimley, ' "A smiling with a sigh": the Chamber Music and Works for Strings', *Companion*, p. 124. There has been much discussion on the possible provenance of the 'Welsh tune': see, for example, James Hepokoski's discussion in this volume from p. 139.

Ex. 3.5 *Introduction and Allegro*, from b. 13

Solo viola from bar 16

for distantly heard reed instruments (two oboes and cor anglais)'.[30] It is assigned to the (traditionally pastoral) cor anglais in the sketch. The first iteration fulfils Riley's criterion of 'reality' giving way 'in a sudden moment of transformation, to a magical "inner" world of pastoral simplicity': it emerges at fig. 2:4 – prefiguring the *Allegro* material from fig. 2 – on the viola, with a basic accompaniment, the harmony shifting from E♭ to its relative minor and back. The lack of C minor's dominant lends an archaic, modal touch. The augmentation of the figure from the *Allegretto* reinforces the interiority (see Ex. 3.5). However, there is already some of the 'know-ingness' identified in *Dream Children*, when certain notes of the viola line are doubled (between fig. 2:10 and fig. 3 itself): these small instances of subtle reinforcement, for which Elgar is celebrated, are synecdochically representa-tive of the sophistication of Elgar's compositional technique. Meanwhile, when the second part of the tune, from fig. 3, adopts, with the arrival of the full quartet, a yearning, passionate tone (*molto espress.*), there is clarification that the idyll it simultaneously embodies is lost.

The second iteration of the Welsh tune (fig. 3:4–fig. 5: see Ex. 5.2) ends with an enigmatic move to D♭ followed by a diminished triad built on that pitch. If taken as vii/V in G (the D♭ treated enharmonically as C♯), the diminished triad would seem to effect a smooth enough progression to the I^6_4 that ushers in the return of the opening gesture at fig. 5. Yet, as Grimley observes, the abrupt change in rhetoric ensures this 'sounds very much like a brutal return to reality and the musical "present tense" of the home key', G minor.[31] It is highly significant that, as in this context, none of the later appearances of the Welsh tune manage to achieve closure. Thus the next iteration, which acts as codetta to the Introduction (from fig. 6), ends on ii^6_5, and the appearance at fig. 15:6 that marks the end of the exposition (before the famous 'devil of a fugue') ends on the same chord in a different posi-tion.[32] At the corresponding point in the recapitulation, fig. 30, the Welsh tune provides the work's apotheosis (see Ex. 5.6). There is no gradual

[30] Grimley, ' "A smiling with a sigh" ', *Companion*, p. 125.
[31] Ibid., p. 126. See also Hepokoski, this volume, p. 143.

[32] These are of course *Tristan* chords; see McCreless, this volume, ch. 1.

emergence here, but a tutti *ff* opening chord, moving to *con fuoco* at fig. 31. But again, there is no closure for this material: after the intense *fff* of fig. 31:7 there is a rapid *diminuendo* to *p* over a submediant chord during the last half bar of fig. 31:10, from which point the *Allegro* material takes over to fashion the final cadential flourishes. There is a sense in which the rhetorical presentation of the Welsh tune here is at odds with its essential nature, which lies in – or perhaps, as an ideal, behind – the first part of its initial presentation.[33]

In contrast, *Falstaff*'s 'Dream Interlude' (figs. 76–81) *does* achieve closure. It is essentially a slow neo-baroque gavotte, the solo violin tune supported by quasi-continuo bass punctuated by lute-like arpeggios on harp and viola, and it is through its very self-containedness that it achieves its central *Affekt*, stepping out of the narrative flow of the work into a nostalgic reverie as Falstaff recalls his time as page to the Duke of Norfolk. The interlude is set off rhetorically from the preceding and succeeding music: the gesture of fig. 75 creates expectations of a new event, but the key prepared by the imperfect cadence is the relative major, C; while fig. 81 is a clear return to the more 'public' character of the earlier music – indeed, to 'what will turn out to be the recapitulation'.[34] Thus there is *some* sense of an ordered succession of events into and out of the Interlude, but not of a seamless progression.[35]

While A minor is the central territory (with a momentary – though not insignificant – deflection towards F major at fig. 80:4), C major turns out to have a role after all: on the second beat of the bar in which the Interlude gets properly under way (fig. 77), C's dominant seventh is introduced (it is difficult to regard the bass G♮ merely as an Aeolian inflection here: the octave displacement gives it too much weight and it takes on the quality of a root), while fig. 77:4 provides strong preparation for a C major cadence (see Ex. 3.6). In fact C major maintains a presence almost to the very end, and the possibility of closure onto it is sustained up until the final cadence point (see Ex. 3.7). When A minor is chosen, C major is clarified as the embodiment of Falstaff's hopes, now clearly abandoned.[36] As in *Dream Children* and

---

[33] Because of this, *Introduction and Allegro* seems to anticipate the First Symphony, at the end of which the so-called motto theme provides, according to some views, a similarly overblown apotheosis to the whole work. James Hepokoski suggests that 'the sheer stress and trembling of the A♭ "resolution" can leave us with lingering questions about how affirmative this symphony actually is' ('Elgar', in D. Kern Holoman (ed.), *The Nineteenth-Century Symphony* (New York: Schirmer, 1997), p. 336).

[34] Harper-Scott, 'Elgar's Invention of the Human', p. 243.
[35] Harper-Scott notes that 'The sketches for *Falstaff* show that the Dream Interlude was pasted onto an earlier sketch that had lacked it altogether.... It is clear that Elgar simply troped the interlude into the work's structural dominant. In effect, then, the interlude is a parenthesis in the larger structure' (Ibid., p. 250).
[36] For further discussion of the role (or roles) of C in *Falstaff*, see Harper-Scott, 'Elgar's Invention of the Human'.

Ex. 3.6 *Falstaff*, 'Dream Interlude', from fig. 77

Introduction and Allegro, the idyllic is also distanced by the knowingness of the yearning (highly romantic) lines heard, for example, in the violas and solo cello at fig. 79, and in the clarinet from fig. 79:11. Though the main melodic line is quite mobile, the overall trajectory is downwards (which the

Ex. 3.7 *Falstaff*, from fig. 80

doubling by second violins and solo cello at cadence points at fig. 77:4–5 and
78ff. emphasizes).

In the cases examined above, the broken idyll is associated with that which is
unrecoverable or unattainable. They might therefore be seen to represent

instances of what Svetlana Boym terms 'reflective nostalgia', which 'does not pretend to rebuild the mythical place called home; it is "enamored of distance, not of the referent itself" '.[37] 'By the Wayside' – the first sketch of which is dated 13 October, just over a month after the first performance of the orchestral version of *Dream Children* on 4 September 1902 – would seem to be set apart, however, in that rather than reflecting on the past, the scene looks forward to the future; though it could be argued that, by looking forward to the coming of The Kingdom, Christ's followers were, in fact, longing for the restoration of a state that existed before the Fall, and are therefore genuinely nostalgic. In order for the idyllic future (the coming of the Kingdom) to be desired, it has to be envisioned, yet at the same time it obviously cannot be fully 'present'. As in the commentaries above, it is the technical means by which this effect is achieved that will form the basis of the discussion.

Evidently, much of the success of the scene hinges on the role of Jesus. It has often been remarked upon that, with the foregrounding of the characters of Mary Magdalene and Judas, the role of Jesus seems to be downplayed. As Byron Adams says,

> Prominent among the doctrinal anomalies that permeate both *The Apostles* and *The Kingdom* is Elgar's curiously hesitant treatment of the Saviour, who appears in the first two of the oratorios. While *The Apostles* is organized around specific incidents in the life of Christ, the narrative proceeds with a disconcerting obliquity: the Saviour is reduced to a mere bystander at the drama of the apostles unfolding around Him. Elgar is clearly more interested in the human suffering and doubts of the apostles rather than in the supernal travails of their Master.[38]

However, it is dangerous to equate 'importance' with 'stage time': Jesus and what he represents is central to the experience of *The Apostles*. 'By the Wayside' is the section in which Jesus has the most sustained 'stage time'. Alice Elgar described the music as 'quite new and different from everything else'.[39] Much of it is unassuming – appropriately enough for the Beatitudes, with their emphasis on the meek, the poor, and 'the pure of heart' – but in providing a vision of the Kingdom of Heaven (or, at least, a *glimpse* of it), it can be regarded as being at the heart of the work, if not the trilogy.

Christopher Grogan has demonstrated that, from the first, Elgar intended the second scene of *The Apostles* to have a pastoral setting.[40] Originally conceived as taking place in the public space of the cornfields, with Jesus

[37] Svetlana Boym, *The Future of Nostalgia* (New York: Basic Books, 2001), p. 50. The quotation is from Susan Stewart, *On Longing* (Baltimore: Johns Hopkins University Press, 1985), p. 145.
[38] Byron Adams, 'Elgar's Later Oratorios: Roman Catholicism, Decadence and the Wagnerian Dialectic of Shame and Grace', in *Companion*, p. 96.
[39] Kennedy, *Portrait*, p. 190.
[40] Christopher Grogan, 'A Study of Elgar's Creative Process in *The Apostles* (Op. 49) with Particular Reference to Sc. II "By the Wayside" ' (Ph.D. dissertation, University of London, 1989).

among children, this later developed into the more intimate delivery of the Beatitudes. As the title confirms, the scene remained pastoral, and Canon Gorton went so far as to associate it with some of the countryside Elgar most loved; he wrote: 'may not the sweep of the Malvern Hills, the Worcester plains and by-ways claim sacred association and aid in the interpretation of the scene "By the Wayside"? Here, then, we feel Nature's peace and joy.'[41]

The strongest projection of the pastoral is in the opening, with its lilting rhythm and lyrical tune paralleled (initially at least) at the sixth.[42] Though this introduction is replete with chromaticism, a basic diatonic structure underpins it. Despite the 'tranquillo' indication, the music is a little restless in (for example) the way that the head-motive is shifted to different levels in bb. 5 and 7. The more figuratively minded might see this as perambulatory, a seeking out of a tonal spot from where the Beatitudes can be delivered – a gradual homing in on the F triad as tonic. In 'By the Wayside' the play of tonalities – and not just tonal relationships, but differences in the character of the tonalities – is crucial in the evocation and ultimate breaking of the idyllic, and it is this that I will concentrate upon for the remainder of my commentary.

Table 3.1 is a summary of the succession of tonal centres with comments on the action. Formally, the scene is interpreted as a series of strophes with one episode at fig. 68 and a coda. This contrasts with Grogan's outline of the structure of the scene, reproduced as Fig. 3.1,[43] which marks Strophes 4 and 6 as distinct from the others (Grogan labels them 'B'), presumably because of the inversion of the initial melodic shape; he doesn't identify what I have labelled as Strophe 8, but sees this as a continuation of the 'Rejoice' section. There are also some minor differences in tonal interpretation. As with all outlines of this kind, the two presented here are inevitably crude, unable adequately to convey Elgar's mosaic technique at its most subtle, involving as it does a highly complex, fluid interweaving of repetitions, variations, extensions, and Elgar's characteristic splicing technique (for instance the mid-phrase return to earlier music, as at fig. 69:4–5, where music from fig. 63:6 is spliced in). I trust it will, however, suffice as a focus for the limited investigation I am able to offer here.

Elgar's use of what Charles McGuire terms a 'formula'[44] to introduce each Beatitude enables shifts of tonal centre and changes in harmonic stability to register all the more strongly. As Elgar's sketch tonal plan for the scene shows

[41] Charles Vincent Gorton, *'The Apostles': An Interpretation of the Libretto* (London: Novello, 1903), p. 145.

[42] There are parallels here with the opening of Scene iii in *Caractacus* ('The Forest near the Severn. Morning').

[43] Grogan, 'A Study of Elgar's Creative Process in *The Apostles*', p. 222.

[44] Charles Edward McGuire, *Elgar's Oratorios. The Creation of an Epic Narrative* (Aldershot: Ashgate, 2002), p. 213.

Table 3.1 'By the Wayside': Summary of tonal centres related to the action

Section		Tonal / Modal centre(s)	Comments
Intro		homing in on F	
Strophe 1 'Blessed are the poor in spirit'	Fig.60	F F—d	'Response' from Mary, Peter, John, and Judas. Judas takes music to d.
Strophe 2 'Blessed are they that mourn'	Fig.61	d—V of F C—a—F	'Response': truncated repeat of Intro, voices mostly following the original melodic line. NB order of singers: Jesus, Mary / John / Peter, 'the people'.
Strophe 3 'Blessed are the meek'	Fig.62	F—A (!) A—a	Variation of Strophe 1. Markedly sharpwards move to A major, effected by Jesus at the first cadence. Move back to the minor emphasizes that the time when the meek 'shall increase their joy' has not yet arrived (the people inhabit A major for only a short time).
Strophe 4 'Blessed are they which hunger…'	Fig.63	A Aeolian / a a—F / F Lydian	Jesus departs from his 'formula' (McGuire) for the first time. Judas sings with the others for the first time (homophony): shows that he, too, seeks after 'Mercy and truth' and 'peace and righteousness'.
Strophe 5 'Blessed are the merciful'	Fig.64	F / F Lydian F—d	Variation and extension of Strophe 1 (including the transposition of bb. 1–4 of the Intro to F).
Strophe 6 'Blessed are the pure in heart'	Fig.66	d—F F—E flat (!)	Introduction of motifs from Prologue. 'Response': phrases from Mary and John in partic. are much more expansive and impassioned. Development of material from Intro. Flattening to E flat (effected by the chorus, 'the people') is, again, a reminder that The Kingdom has not yet arrived.
Strophe 7 'Blessed are the peace makers'	Fig.67	E flat E flat—F	
Episode 'Rejoice and be exceeding glad'	Fig.68	A flat (!)	This takes the place of the normal 'response'. Draws on music from the Prologue, Fig. 5ff. Remote key again to emphasize the earthly unattainability of The Kingdom. Last utterance from Jesus in this number.
Strophe 8 'Blessed are they which have been sorrowful'	Fig.69	V^7 of d—a	**Climax.** Mary & Apostles and chorus only.
Coda	Fig.70	to C	Again, this takes the place of the normal 'response'. Starts with material from the 'development' in Strophe 6. Reaches the C triad only at the very end.

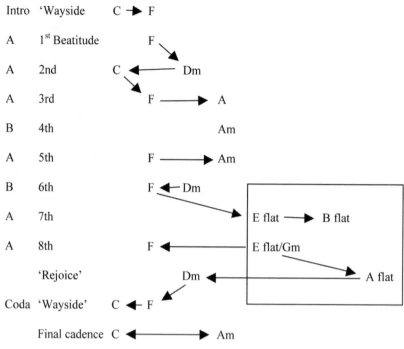

Fig. 3.1 'By the Wayside': Christopher Grogan's outline of tonal centres related to Beatitudes (see note 43)

(reproduced from Grogan as Fig. 3.2), a strong projection of F was always intended, and the reworking of the Introduction at pitch in the latter half of Strophe 2 ensures that F is indeed solid. The first strong move away from this (traditionally pastoral) territory is in Strophe 3, where Jesus effects a markedly sharpward move to A major (at 'they shall *inherit the earth*') – not, perhaps, a startling move in 1902, but nonetheless of some impact in this particular context. Having been led to A major, the chorus enters in the new key, but soon moves to the minor, making it clear that the time when the meek 'shall increase their joy' has not yet arrived.[45]

Grogan suggests that behind 'By the Wayside' lies the shadowy presence of sonata form.[46] It is doubtful whether he would want to take this very far, and neither do I, but it makes some sense to regard Strophe 6 (the point at which Elgar's sketched tonal plan leaves off) as the beginning of some kind of 'treatment', as distinct from 'statement', moving onto a different plane. Certainly, after the return to F in Strophe 5, Strophe 6 shows some typical

[45] I realize that my saying that *Jesus* effects the move, rather than Elgar, begs a number of questions concerning voice, narrative, etc., but to address them fully would necessitate a degree of theoretical detail that would be out of proportion with the main thrust of this essay. It is important for my overall argument, however, that the listener buys into the conceit that Jesus is fully in command of where his music leads.

[46] Grogan, 'A Study of Elgar's Creative Process in *The Apostles*', p. 223.

F—F   poor

d—F   mourn

F—A   meek

a—d   hunger

F—a   merciful

a—F   pure

Fig. 3.2 'By the Wayside': Elgar's sketch of tonalities for the Beatitudes

Ex. 3.8 'By the Wayside': return to F

developmental characteristics, including the reworking of melodic material from the Introduction. There is also a greater sense of urgency and expansiveness in the phrases sung by Mary and the Apostles, and the strophe contains *two* Beatitudes rather than the usual one (which is why my diagram departs a little from Grogan's). Most significantly, Strophe 6 also contains an excursion to E♭. This, the most remote region thus far, is initiated by the Apostles and solidified by the chorus. Quite what meaning one might attach to this I am not sure – I have suggested in Table 3.1 that its palpable remoteness is a further indication of the people's own remoteness from the Kingdom of Heaven.

The further flatward move at the beginning of the section I have labelled 'Episode' has a more certain effect, however. It comes after the move back to F outlined in Ex. 3.8. F's presence is secure enough, though not entirely stable: the tonic triad appears in the less stable 6/4 and 6/3 positions, and direct V–I progressions are avoided. The A♭ tonality is unprepared (I find it hard to hear the E♭ at the beginning of Strophe 7 as dominant preparation except in the most abstract way), though it is 'bound in' with what precedes it by stepwise voice-leading. The episode stands out in a number of ways: it is the first time Jesus genuinely *sings* (previously he has declaimed, in quasi-recitative fashion); the melodic lines (vocal and orchestral) are quite the most expansive in the scene; there is a degree of orchestral opulence unmatched elsewhere in the scene; and there is a genuine sense of harmonic momentum for the first time (a circle of fifths to the C minor triad of fig. 68:3). However, the music fairly quickly recedes back into McGuire's formula (suggesting perhaps that Jesus does not think his flock ready for too much of this sort of thing); and while the momentum picks up for the entrance of the quartet of soloists and chorus (who sing together for the first time), the music soon settles back into the reverential ecclesiastical tone of the rest of the scene. The Ab region is re-engaged during the final solidification of C major in the coda (71:3–4), but its role is now clearly an elaboration, like the chromaticism of the introduction that these final bars recall.

There is an undeniable serenity about the C major of the ending, yet it is the visionary Ab episode that lingers longest in the memory. The latter is not, perhaps, conventionally idyllic music: the introduction is rather more so. Yet in the relatively restrained surroundings its expansiveness, momentum, and opulence allow it to take on this role. I mentioned earlier that the chorus's music quickly returns to the ecclesiastical (for which read 'earthly') tone of utterance: this suggests, again, that 'the people' are unable fully to comprehend Jesus's words; indeed, Jesus's silence after the episode and the chorus's continuation with the Beatitude ritual emphasize the distance between them.

Although 'By the Wayside' is ostensibly optimistic (it has what one might call an exit trajectory of optimism, ending one notch higher in the circle of fifths from where it began), the overall effect is ultimately nostalgic and melancholic. Normally it is Elgar's instrumental works (works without texts) that one is drawn to reading biographically. But in the light of the compositional history of the trilogy – the difficulty Elgar had in finishing *The Kingdom* and the subsequent abandoning of the project as disillusion with religion set in – it is difficult not to hear 'By the Wayside', with its yearning for an 'other' place existing only in the imagination, in this way. No less than Brahms – indeed, rather more self-consciously so – Elgar's music reflects Starobinski's words quoted by Brinkmann about 'the mind [giving] itself up to contemplating an asset which it lacks, which exists no longer or [more to the point with regard to 'By the Wayside'] does not exist as yet'.

4   Unmaking *The Music Makers*

Aidan J. Thomson

Of all Elgar's mature, pre-war works, none – with the possible exception of *The Crown of India* – has received as much negative criticism as *The Music Makers*, a setting of the 'Ode' that begins Arthur O'Shaughnessy's 1874 anthology, *Music and Moonlight*. As a poet, O'Shaughnessy (1844–81) enjoyed only limited success during his life, and has received scant attention since: Elgar's work is arguably what keeps his name alive today.[1] It is worth noting, however, that the subject-matter of his poetry is often typical of the 'decadent' movement, and this may explain Elgar's familiarity with it.[2] As Byron Adams has argued, Elgar's sympathies for – and incorporation of the tropes of – the decadent movement are manifested in several earlier choral pieces, notably *The Dream of Gerontius* and *The Apostles*.[3] On the surface, at least, the 'Ode' itself is virtually free of decadent tropes. It is perhaps significant, however, that Elgar first considered setting it as early as March 1904, within six months of the premiere of *The Apostles*, and in the immediate aftermath of the three-concert Elgar Festival at Covent Garden, at which both *Gerontius* and *The Apostles* were performed.[4] But it was not until 1907, after the completion of *The Kingdom*,

---

[1] See, for instance, the somewhat partisan (Ellen) Louise Chandler Moulton, *Arthur O'Shaughnessy: His Life and his Work with Selections from his Poems* (London: Elkin Matthews & John Lane, 1894); *Poems of Arthur O'Shaughnessy*, selected and edited by William Alexander Percy (New Haven: Yale University Press, 1923); and W. D. Paden, 'Arthur O'Shaughnessy: the Ancestry of a Victorian Poet', *Bulletin of the John Rylands Library*, 46/2 (March 1964), pp. 429–47.

[2] Indeed, perhaps the most striking example of decadence in O'Shaughnessy's poetry is 'Music and Moonlight', the principal poem of the eponymous anthology. It tells the tale of Lady Eucharis, whose midnight piano-playing leads to her being spirited away into a metaphysical world by 'the lovely spirit even of him / Whom all her soul loved – Chopin'; here she encounters 'High gardens, where the freed souls of all flowers / Talked magically, and blue river bowers, / Where sirens slept and

moaned', and hears the intoxicating song of Phoenix to Aloe, but, as she ponders the opportunity to dwell forever in this ecstatic environment, she is brought back to earth by a 'snapt' piano string, and is found dead in the morning.

[3] See Byron Adams, 'The "Dark Saying" of the Enigma: Homoeroticism and the Elgarian Paradox', in *19CM*, 23 (2000), pp. 218–35; and the same author's 'Elgar's Later Oratorios: Roman Catholicism, Decadence and the Wagnerian Dialectic of Shame and Grace', in *Companion*, pp. 81–105.

[4] Interview with E. A. Baughan, *The Daily News*, 25 March 1904; see Moore, *Elgar*, p. 438. This festival also included the premiere of the overture *In the South*. Elgar fitted the second and fourth stanzas of Shelley's poem, 'To Jane: "The keen stars were twinkling"', to the melody of the 'canto popolare' of the overture; the fourth stanza, perhaps revealingly, includes the words 'Where music

---

that he sought permission (via O'Shaughnessy's publishers, Chatto and Windus) to set the 'Ode'; only in 1908 was permission granted by O'Shaughnessy's literary executor, his cousin Canon A. W. Newport Deacon; and only in May 1912 – after the completion of both Symphonies and the Violin Concerto – did he begin work on the vocal score.[5] *The Music Makers* (the title is taken from the opening line of the poem) received its premiere at the Birmingham Festival on 1 October 1912.

I shall return briefly to the decadent movement at the end of this essay. First, however, we must consider why critical reaction to the work has been so ambivalent. Undoubtedly the variable quality of O'Shaughnessy's poetry is one reason: the opening couplet of stanza 2, 'With wonderful deathless ditties / We build up the world's great cities', has invited scorn, while the Trinitarian-sounding pretensions of a quatrain later in that verse – 'One man with a dream, at pleasure, / Shall go forth and conquer a crown; / And three with a new song's measure / Can trample a kingdom down' – was dismissed, by the generally anti-Elgar critic Charles Maclean, as 'the verbal titillation of the Victorian minor poet'.[6] A more serious objection, however, has been the subject-matter of the poem: that artists, who 'remain a little apart' from the rest of society, are the driving agents of history, rather than kings or soldiers. Elgar's sympathies with this conceit have never been doubted. He commented to Ernest Newman that the 'Ode' was concerned above all with artistic 'continuity' and 'never-ceasing change'; that 'the duty of the artist to see that this inevitable change is progress' was a serious one; that this necessitated a degree of suffering as part of the creative process; and that, for this reason, 'the atmosphere of the music is mainly sad'.[7] Whether Elgar's audiences shared his idealism is doubtful. The socially regenerative tone of O'Shaughnessy's call for artists to 'renew the world as of yore' seems more appropriate to Bayreuth than to Birmingham: 'Did a single member of the chorus who sang these words . . . really believe them?' asked one critic of the premiere.[8] Maclean's endorsement of this 'common sense' aesthetic attitude, two months after the premiere, is revealing: 'The poem consists of a sustained boast that poets, and not the men of action, create the world's living and practical history; though it is generally supposed that exactly the opposite happens, and that the men of action act first and the poets sing afterwards.'[9] Art as a means towards moral improvement, or even art for art's

---

and moonlight and feeling / Are one'; see Brian Trowell, 'Elgar's Use of Literature', in Monk, *Literature*, pp. 243–4.
[5] Moore, *Elgar*, p. 518; *Publishers*, p. 692; *Lifetime*, p. 245; Paden, 'Arthur O'Shaughnessy', pp. 443–4.
[6] Moore, *Elgar*, p. 634; Charles Maclean, 'London Notes', *Zeitschrift der internationalen*

Musikgesellschaft, 14/3 (December 1912), p. 79.
[7] 'Introductory Note', sent to Newman on 14 August 1912, quoted in Moore, *Elgar*, pp. 631–2.
[8] Quoted in Moore, *Elgar*, p. 639.
[9] Maclean, 'London Notes', p. 79.

sake, was acceptable to English audiences; art as the harbinger of social and cultural renewal was a step too far.

But by far the most common criticism of *The Music Makers* has been Elgar's use of self-quotation from his earlier works. Most prominent among these are the 'Enigma' Variations: Elgar uses the 'Enigma' theme in the introduction and in stanzas 1 and 7 to portray the loneliness of the creative artist, and recalls the 'Nimrod' variation, movingly, as a tribute to August Jaeger in stanza 5 at the words 'But on one man's soul it hath broken'.[10] Other works quoted include *Gerontius*, *Sea Pictures*, *The Apostles*, both symphonies and the Violin Concerto (see Table 4.1); in addition to these Elgar also quotes 'Rule Britannia' and the 'Marseillaise' in stanza 2.[11] In a letter to Ernest Newman, who was preparing an analysis of the work for the *Musical Times* prior to the premiere, Elgar asked not to 'insist too much on the *extent* of the quotations which after all form a very small portion of the work', a request with which Newman complied.[12] Indeed, he seemed ambivalent about the quotations, stating that

> [I]f the original place of any one of these [quotations] is known to the hearer, he may feel the reason for its presence, appreciate the propriety and appositeness of its inclusion here. If these quoted passages are unknown, the music may be listened to simply as an expression of feelings called up by the poem, without regard to the quotations as such.[13]

Elgar's implication – that the quotations *can* be interpreted, yet *need* not be – might seem to be a case of having one's hermeneutic cake and eating it. But this apparent paradox is easily explained. As Christopher Reynolds has recently observed, the idea that a symbol might exist as both a signifier and as a *Ding an sich* separate from it has its roots in early Romanticism;[14] early-twentieth-century orchestral music, which often aimed at both structural coherence and the explication of programmatic or poetic content, might seem merely to be a post-Lisztian manifestation of this. Thus the intertextuality of *The Music Makers*, if we take Elgar at his word, is no different from the works of many of his contemporaries, a practice whereby the informed listener might make connections between the later work and its predecessors, and 'appreciate the . . . appositeness' of the quotation, but might equally

---

[10] 'Introductory Note', quoted in Moore, *Elgar*, pp. 633, 636.

[11] I do not discuss 'Rule Britannia' and the 'Marseillaise', partly because these were not Elgar's own compositions, and partly because his ironic reasons for quoting 'Rule Britannia', at least, are well known: 'under the present government "Rule Britannia" has been made the most foolish of national boasts' (letter to Ernest Newman, 14 August 1912, quoted in *Lifetime*, p. 249).

[12] *Lifetime*, p. 249. Newman included a footnote in his article that reads 'the reader must be warned against thinking that they form anything more than episodes in the work as a whole' (' "The Music Makers", by Edward Elgar', *MT*, 53 (1 September 1912), p. 569).

[13] Letter to Newman, quoted in *Lifetime*, p. 249.

[14] Christopher Reynolds, *Motives for Allusion* (Cambridge, MA: Harvard University Press, 2003), p. 7.

Table 4.1 Elgar's self-quotations in *The Music Makers*

Stanza	Figure	Source work	Part
Introduction	6, 7:5	Variations	Theme
1	10:4	*The Dream of Gerontius*	Judgment motif
	11:2	*Sea Pictures*	'Sea Slumber Song', opening
	11:4, 14	Variations	Theme
5	51	Variations	Variation IX ('Nimrod')
	53	Symphony no. 2	4th movement, fig. 143:6
7	75, 76:5	Variations	Theme
	76:4	Violin Concerto	1st movement, fig. 17
	77:2	Violin Concerto	2nd movement, fig. 53:6
	77:3	*The Apostles*	Part VI ('There shall ye see him')
8	79	Symphony no. 1	1st movement, motto
9	101, 102	*The Dream of Gerontius*	'Novissima hora est'

understand it to be part of a 'purely' musical argument intrinsic to the piece in question.

Nevertheless, critical reaction to the quotations has sometimes been hostile or, at the very least, perplexed. Maclean, for instance, complained about the 'long series of musical quotations in leit-motiv fashion' that Elgar had 'fashion[ed] from his previous works'; the whole work was 'a very strange revelation of the composer's intentions and thoughts [which] as music has found favour with few'.[15] A generation later, John F. Porte also felt that, as Elgar 'composed the themes in certain moods or as expressive of experiences and outlook', to quote them out of context was to 'drag [them] from the only associations which gave them spiritual life'.[16] Thomas Dunhill, writing a few years after Porte, was less dismissive, but nevertheless found Elgar's use of quotation 'carried to such lengths and used so persistently, disturbing'. 'It is difficult', he wrote, 'to find adequate reasons for invoking the memories which are so frequently brought to consciousness in the course of this ode'. Unlike Porte, however, he accepted that there might be such reasons: 'One finds oneself wondering, over and over again, if any special point has been missed, and, when some particularly Elgarian turn of phrase appears, it is

---

[15] Maclean, 'London Notes', pp. 79–80.

[16] John F. Porte, *Elgar and his Music: an Appreciative Study* (London: Pitman, 1933), pp. 48–9.

difficult to avoid searching for some allusion which may not really be there at all.'[17]

Had any special point been missed? Scholars who have attempted to provide the 'adequate reasons' that Dunhill found missing have seen the quotations as evidence that *The Music Makers* is a piece about music-making itself.[18] But this is surely too facile a hermeneutical response to a work that, although outwardly expressing sympathy with the idea of artistic progress and immortality, is at its most powerful when it is either consciously retrospective (such as Elgar's memorial to August Jaeger in stanza 5) or concerned with human mortality (the conclusion of stanza 9). The quotations are undoubtedly important. But no less important is Dunhill's last point: the 'allusion which may not really be there at all'. For alongside the quotations and (many) pieces of hitherto unused sketch material that Elgar assembled to make this piece, there are perhaps as many as six musical figures that in some way resemble earlier works by Elgar, without directly quoting them (see Table 4.2).

The status of these 'indirect quotations' is potentially problematic, for the very idea of musical 'allusions' – as distinct from quotations – is beset by controversy. As Reynolds has noted, many commentators dismiss it altogether in tonal music, on the grounds that the limitations of the diatonic scale make thematic (or at least motivic) resemblances inevitable. There also remains the question of whether one theme can be considered to allude to another only if there is some evidence to suggest that the composer of the allusion intended the reference, something of particular importance to critics, like Reynolds, who are concerned primarily with the process of composition rather than that of reception.[19] Whether this stipulation should apply to a composer renowned for covering his tracks is, however, another matter. It is hard to 'prove' that Elgar deliberately meant certain themes to allude to certain others, but this is as much as anything because of his

[17] Thomas F. Dunhill, *Sir Edward Elgar* (London: Blackie, 1938), pp. 119–20.
[18] Diana McVeagh, for example, claims that the quotations tell us more 'about the introspective process of creation than . . . its effects' (Diana McVeagh, 'Elgar's Musical Language: the Shorter Instrumental Works', in *Companion*, p. 61). Jerrold Northrop Moore sees the work as an attempt at reassurance on Elgar's part after the lukewarm reception of the Second Symphony, with the quotations hinting at a 'final synthesis' for his music, in keeping with the revelation promised in the poem (Moore, *Elgar*, pp. 631, 637). Frank Howes – writing in 1935 but anticipating by over thirty years Michael Kennedy's categorization of Elgar's works into

'public' and 'private' – sees O'Shaughnessy's 'Ode' as a poem with which 'Elgar A' (the composer of serious works) was in sympathy, but to which he could add nothing in his musical setting, which was instead spoiled by the 'obvious meretricious touches about "trampling a kingdom down" and so on' composed by 'Elgar B' (the miniaturist/populist). The self-quotations were, for Howes, proof of this: the 'second-hand music in *The Music Makers* is evidence not of simple vanity (as it might be in *Heldenleben*) but of a weak impulse to compose it' (Frank Howes, 'The Two Elgars', *Music and Letters*, 16 (1935), pp. 26–9, reprinted in Redwood, *Companion*, pp. 258–62).
[19] Reynolds, *Motives for Allusion*, pp. 5–6.

Table 4.2 Indirect allusions to earlier works by Elgar in *The Music Makers*

Stanza	Figure	Source work	Part
1	13:4	*Sea Pictures*	'Sea Slumber Song'
2	23	*Sea Pictures*	'Sea Slumber Song'
	25	*The Dream of Gerontius*	Part II, fig. 55:6, etc.
3	29:6, 30:6	*The Apostles*	Part III, 'In the Tower of Magdala', 'Fantasy', fig. 90
	30:8	*The Dream of Gerontius*	Part II, fig. 55:6, etc.
	35:8	Symphony no. 2	2nd movement, fig. 76
4	44:4, 44:9	*Sea Pictures*	'Sea Slumber Song'
	45, 46 etc.	*The Kingdom*	'New Faith' motif
6	55	*The Kingdom*	'Signs and Wonders' motif (rhythm only)
	65	*The Kingdom*	'New Faith' motif
8	80	*The Kingdom*	'New Faith' motif
	81:5	*Sea Pictures*	'Sea Slumber Song'
	83:2	*The Dream of Gerontius*	Part II, fig. 55:6, etc.
9	92:13	Symphony no. 2	2nd movement, fig. 76
	98	Symphony no. 2	2nd movement, fig. 76

tendency to deny or deflect obvious influences upon him (perhaps most famously his insistence that the idea of using melodic diminution to connote youth in *Cockaigne* came to him from Delibes' *Sylvia* rather than *Meistersinger*, his favourite Wagner music drama).[20] Admittedly, one can go too far in the opposite direction and see resemblances everywhere; for this reason I have resisted, for instance, interpreting every falling second as an allusion to the 'Judgment' motif of *Gerontius*.[21] Nevertheless, I would argue that the figures in Table 4.2 can be regarded not merely as examples of Elgarian *langue* but of Elgarian *parole* as well. They recall their antecedents

[20] Quoted in Moore, *Elgar*, p. 345. A denial of Wagnerian influence can also be detected in a comment he made in 1900 that his first acquaintanceship with 'representative-theme[s]' was in *Elijah* rather than in *The Ring* (Kennedy, *Portrait*, p. 76). His use of such motifs is, arguably, more Mendelssohnian than Wagnerian, and he certainly heard *Sylvia* before he heard *Meistersinger* (see Peter Dennison, 'Elgar's Musical Apprenticeship', in Monk, *Studies*, pp. 21, 28).

[21] That said, a rather intriguing case could be made for the falling seconds at the end of stanza 4 (figs. 47:5 to 48) having connections with the idea of 'judgment'. They appear in GB-Lbl Add. MS. 63154, fo. 49, and are followed by several folios of sketches for the final part of the 'Apostles' trilogy, *The Last Judgment*. Robert Anderson describes this sketch as 'playful' (the bass and soprano lines are labelled 'He' and 'She' respectively; see Anderson, *Manuscript*, p. 140), but the passage ends with the marking 'Asleep' and then, following a change of key, 'Fate', which hints that Elgar's original intentions for this theme might have been somewhat more eschatological.

in some way – motivically, harmonically, rhythmically, gesturally – without being exact quotations; indeed, it is *because* they undergo a transformation that they acquire their particular significance.

My task here is to examine how the quotations and allusions function within the internal musical processes of *The Music Makers*. Do the memories that they recall assist the formal and tonal development of the work, or do they disrupt it? In particular, do the reminiscences support or subvert Elgar's ideals of artistic progress, especially in the closing stanzas where they acquire particular focus in the poem? As a result, what might we conclude about Elgar's approach to narrative in this work? To answer these questions requires first answering another: in what form, if any, is *The Music Makers*?

Form: the problems

Most accounts of *The Music Makers* make no attempt to consider the frame within which Elgar's music (whether old or new) functions. Although few commentators would subscribe to Maclean's view that the piece 'indulges in quite extensive word-painting, to the detriment of the general jubilancy which is the tenour [*sic*] and purport of the poem', there appears to be a tacit assumption that, because the 'Ode' is a secular cantata, any structural desiderata are of minor importance.[22] Yet an inscription on the manuscript vocal score that reads '? Symphony / (for solo chorus & orchestra) / The Music Makers' hints that Elgar's conception of the work might have extended beyond local word painting to something formally more concrete but, in terms of meaning, more abstract.[23] Admittedly, this inscription is struck out, but there is still evidence to suggest that Elgar was thinking symphonically when composing the piece. For a start, there are the markings that Elgar made on his typescript copy of the poem: the phrase 'more space – short rall' appears after stanza 3; 'space as last – short rall' after stanza 4; and 'space as before – short rall' after stanzas 6 and 8. Also marked are 'Solo' passages for the first half of stanzas 5 and 9, with the second halves of both these stanzas being marked 'Solo and Chorus'.[24] The final version of the piece is different in certain respects: the solo contralto, for instance, features in stanza 6 as well as in stanzas 5 and 9, albeit not as a soloist. But the very

---

[22] Maclean, 'London Notes', p. 80.
[23] GB-Lbl Add. MS. 58036, quoted in *ECE*, vol. X (*The Music Makers* and *The Spirit of England*), p. xviii. The query is Elgar's, but cf. also GB-Lbl Add. MS. 63161, fo. 8ᵛ, which includes the barely legible inscription 'Sym. in slow four' above the ascending scale of fig. 32 (scored out), below which is added 'The Music

Makers'. It is worth noting that an earlier Elgar cantata, *The Black Knight*, was originally designated by Elgar as 'Symphony for Chorus and Orchestra founded upon Uhland's poem "Der schwarze Ritter" '; see Michael Pope, Sleeve note for *The Black Knight* (EMI recording CMS 5 65104 2, 1984), p. 4.
[24] GB-Lbl Add. MS. 47908, fos. 81–2.

idea of creating 'space' at the ends of stanzas has the effect of dividing the poem into five sections that, as we shall see, might share characteristics with parts of a symphonic movement.

That said, Elgar's conception of 'space' is far from clear. Do the fermatas on individual notes or chords at the end of stanzas 3 and 6, for instance, provide the same amount of 'space' as the general pauses after stanzas 4 and 8, let alone that after stanza 7, which is marked 'lunga'? For one critic, at least, the answer is 'no'. Percy Young divides *The Music Makers* into four sections: stanzas 1–4; stanza 5; stanzas 6–7; and stanzas 8–9 ('there are other possible divisions', he adds, 'but this appears to be the most convincing'). He does not elaborate on this arrangement, stating only that the repetition of the opening themes of the introduction throughout the work bind 'technically what is already imaginatively united by the allusions [i.e. quotations]', thus giving the work its 'symphonic quality'.[25] Young's instincts are sound, but a four-part division of the sort that he outlines (Fig. 4.1) is flawed in several respects. First, it is unclear to what he considers the four sections to be an analogy. The separation of stanza 5, marked 'Lento', from the faster stanzas that surround it, suggests a symphonic slow movement, albeit a rather brief one by Elgar's standards; on the other hand, the most logical justification for perceiving stanza 8 to be the start of the final section (besides the 'lunga' pause immediately before it) is the recapitulation-like return of the musical material of the opening stanza in the tonic key. The suggestion of both multi- and single-movement structures thus hints at 'double-function' sonata form: a single, quasi-sonata movement where the exposition and recapitulation are analogous to the first and last movements of a symphony, and where the development, which would include slow and fast sections, is analogous to the middle two movements.[26] In this arrangement, stanzas 1 to 4 fulfil the dual roles of first movement and exposition, and stanzas 8 and 9 those of finale and recapitulation.

Young's first subject-group is easy to identify: the F minor theme that sets 'We are the music makers' in stanza 1 (called the 'artist' theme by Elgar) and its livelier C minor melodic variant in stanza 2.[27] These are recapitulated, albeit fleetingly, at the beginning and end of stanza 8 (and again, in the case of the 'artist' theme, at the end of stanza 9), and in the same keys as in stanzas 1 and 2. The second subject-group, however, is harder to define. Of the musical material in stanza 3, the passage from figs. 27 to 32 does not appear in the recapitulation at all (and is thus marked in Fig. 4.1 as a transition), while that

[25] Young, *Elgar*, p. 305.
[26] As James Hepokoski has noted, 'double-function' sonata form was by no means uncommon in late nineteenth-century orchestral music; see 'Beethoven Reception: the Symphonic Tradition' in Jim Samson (ed.), *The Cambridge History of Nineteenth-Century Music* (Cambridge: Cambridge University Press, 2002), pp. 453–4.
[27] Letter to Newman, 14 August 1912; *Lifetime*, p. 248.

FIRST MOVEMENT/EXPOSITION

Section	Text	Key
Introduction	Introduction, **Ii, Iii**	F minor
First subject	Stanza 1: 'Artist' theme, **Ii** (includes 'Sea Slumber Song' and 'Judgment' quotations)	F minor
	Stanza 2: 'Artist' theme, altered	C minor to C major
Transition A	Stanza 3, lines 1–5	D minor
Second subject (I)	Stanza 3, lines 6–7	F major
Second subject (II)	Stanza 3, line 8; **Ii**/'Artist' theme	F major to F minor
Transition B	**Iii**; Stanza 4, lines 1–4	various
Third subject	Stanza 4, lines 5–8	to G major

SLOW MOVEMENT/INTERLUDE

Section	Text	Key
Recitative	Stanza 5, lines 1–4: **Iii**	G minor to
Aria / Chorus	Stanza 5, lines 5–8 ('Nimrod', 2nd symphony)	E♭ major to A♭ major

THIRD MOVEMENT/DEVELOPMENT

Section	Text		Key
Strophe and refrain (x2)	Stanza 6	Bar form: A	F minor to B♭ minor
		A'	A♭ minor to C minor (refrain is 'artist' theme)
Third subject	Stanza 6 (various lines)	B	E♭ major to B♭ major
Transition B (part)	**Ii**	coda	F minor to A♭ major
Second subject (I)	Stanza 7, lines 1–4		A♭ major
Strophe (part)	Stanza 7, lines 5–7		E♭ minor
Coda	Stanza 7, lines 7–8 ('Windflower', *Apostles*)		E♭ minor to F major

FOURTH MOVEMENT/RECAPITULATION

Section	Text	Key
First subject, including	Stanza 8: 'Artist' theme, lines 1–2	F minor
Third subject	Stanza 8, lines 3–4 (1st symphony motto)	B♭ major
First subject	Stanza 8, 'Artist' theme, altered, lines 5–8	B♭ minor to C minor
Transition B/strophe	Stanza 9, lines 1–2	C minor to A♭ major
Second subject (II)	**Iii**/Stanza 9, lines 3–6 and Stanza 7	A♭ major to C major
Second subject (II)	**Iii**/Stanza 9, lines 5–6, 3–4	A♭ major to D♭ major
	Stanza 7, lines 7–8/Stanza 8, lines 1–2	
Coda	**Ii**/Stanza 9, lines 7–8 ('Novissima hora est')	F♯ minor to E minor
	'Artist' theme	F minor

NB: Elgar's self-quotations (excluding the 'Enigma' theme) are included in parentheses in the sections when they occur.

Fig. 4.1 A possible four-part formal division of *The Music Makers*, based on Young's model

between figs. 32 and 35 reappears in stanza 7, which, in this model, is part of the 'scherzo/development'. The one figure that receives a more than cursory restatement is the passage at fig. 35, which *is* recapitulated in stanza 9, along with certain parts of stanza 4 (the so-called 'acrobatic-music' at fig. 42 and the setting of 'Unearthly, impossible seeming' at fig. 43).[28] But this raises questions about the role of the G major *grandioso* march at fig. 46, which brings Young's 'first movement/exposition' to an end. Its extensive treatment and relative tonal stability in a non-tonic key suggests the structural function of a second subject, rather than that of a coda; conversely, however, its recapitulation in stanza 8 is only as a four-bar counter-melody (to a quotation of the motto theme of the First Symphony). A possible solution might be to regard fig. 35 as the 'true' second subject, with the *grandioso* march as a third, closing subject of the exposition, but the fact that the march never appears in the tonic (it returns in B♭ major) is potentially problematic within an orthodox sonata-form model.

No less so is the third 'movement' in Young's model: stanzas 6 and 7. Beyond the reappearance of the 'to-day is thrilling' music (from fig. 55:5) at fig. 73, there is relatively little to connect the two stanzas. Stanza 6 is, essentially, in Bar form: the two *Stollen* are quasi-strophic settings of the full stanza that begin at figs. 55 and 61, and which conclude with *fff* statements of the 'artist'-theme refrain; and the *Abgesang* is the *maestoso* passage at fig. 65ff., which sets fragments of text from the stanza (particularly from the closing couplet), and then returns to the 'thrilling' music at fig. 67. By contrast, the form of stanza 7 is unclear: it begins by recapitulating part of stanza 3 (fig. 71), recalls the 'thrilling' music (73), returns again to the stanza 3 music (74), and then, after an echo of the 'Enigma' theme (75), quotes the two 'Windflower' themes from the Violin Concerto (fig. 76; see Ex. 4.5 below). Admittedly, one might argue that this free combination of previously heard themes fulfils the function of a development, but this raises questions about the purpose of stanza 6, which consists mostly of newly composed music. The impression we are left with, if we follow Young's schema, is of a section that tries to be two different things and succeeds in being neither.

Form: an alternative model

A further shortcoming of Young's model is that it takes no account of how the opening themes of the introduction are used elsewhere: a strange

---

[28] Elgar added the appellation 'acrobatic-music' to a sketch of this passage for string quartet, possibly part of the projected string quartet from 1907; see GB-Lbl Add. MS. 47908, fo. 71, and Anderson, *Manuscript*, p. 141.

Ex. 4.1(a) Ii: *The Music Makers*, introduction, bar 3

Ex. 4.1(b) Iii: *The Music Makers*, introduction, fig. 2

oversight, given his claim that they bind the piece together. These two themes, which I have labelled respectively 'Ii' (bar 3) and 'Iii' (fig. 2; see Ex. 4.1), assume the function of first and second subject in the introduction, but elsewhere in the piece their role is seemingly slighter.[29] Iii is used variously as a transition (stanza 4) and as a recitative introduction (stanza 5), and is developed fully only in stanza 9. Ii is used even more sparingly: as an introduction to the 'wonderful deathless ditties' music at the beginning of stanza 2 and the end of stanza 8, as a consequent to the 'Novissima hora est' quotation in the coda of stanza 9, and as a refrain at the end of stanzas 3 and 6. But this last use actually offers a key to how *The Music Makers* works formally. On both occasions, Ii coincides with a return to the tonic, F minor, thereby suggesting that the main sectional demarcations might fall at the ends of these stanzas, rather than those of stanzas 4 and 7.[30]

This hypothesis is supported by a division of the poem into three groups of three stanzas. Stanzas 1 to 3 are concerned with the music makers' view of themselves. The first-person narrative voice describes the music makers' apartness, their achievements in society, and then the nature of progress in their art: the relationship between progressives and overthrown reactionaries of a previous generation. Both the social and artistic changes brought about by the music makers are part of a historical process ('For each age is a dream that is dying, / Or one that is coming to birth'); consequently, these three

[29] Moore (*Elgar*, pp. 634–5) argues that the rising scale figures at the beginning (fig. 27) and the middle (fig. 32) of stanza 3 are variants of 'Iii'. They might indeed be heard this way, but their origins are very different: the passage at fig. 27 was originally intended for a 'Callicles' project, based on Matthew Arnold's *Empedocles on Etna* (GB-Lbl Add. MS. 63160, fo. 20ᵛ; Anderson, *Manuscript*, 140); and that at fig. 32 – or rather, its reprise at fig. 71 – was originally intended for a setting of 'And that a higher gift than grace' in *The Dream of Gerontius* (GB-Lbl Add. MS. 47902, fo. 215; Anderson, *Manuscript*, p. 139).

[30] Robert Anderson alludes to such a demarcation but does not develop the point; see Anderson, *Elgar*, pp. 198–9.

stanzas, although written mostly in the present tense, sometimes have a retrospective character. Stanzas 4 to 6, by contrast, are written mostly in the third person, and focus on the mundane recipients of the music makers' work: the soldier, king and peasant, who 'had no vision amazing'; and the multitudes of the present day 'enlisted / In the faith that their father resisted', incapable of understanding progressive movements in art until they had already become outmoded. The last three stanzas return to the 'we' of the music makers; they tell of the 'glorious futures' that the music makers see for their art – and the warning that 'ye of the past must die'.

The appearances of Ii at the ends of stanzas 3 and 6, therefore, play an important part in articulating both the poem and the structure of Elgar's setting of it. Consequently, a more appropriate double-function sonata form model for *The Music Makers* might be that in Fig. 4.2. There are several advantages to this arrangement compared with Young's. Firstly, with the exception of the Ii and Iii fragments, none of the music of the exposition reappears until the recapitulation; consequently, the development possesses an internal structure – a self-contained slow aria (stanza 5) framed by two faster stanzas that reach their apotheosis with the same *grandioso* march – that is far more cohesive than Young's third 'movement'. Secondly, because the march appears for the first time only in the development, it cannot be the second subject in the exposition. That role falls to the two F major themes of stanza 3: the fugal section between figs. 32 and 35 ('second subject (I)' in Fig. 4.2) and the 2/4 passage between figs. 35 and 37 ('second subject (II)'). Both these themes return in the last three stanzas, as does the first-subject material (the 'artist' theme and its stanza 2 variant), although in a different order from before: the second subject (I) appears in stanza 7, the first subject in stanza 8, and the second subject (II) in stanza 9. Indeed, the recapitulation incorporates elements of the development as well as the exposition – by no means an unusual procedure for a symphonic sonata-form movement of this era.[31] Thus in stanza 8 there is a return of the *grandioso* march alongside the recapitulation of the 'artist' theme, while in stanza 9 comes not only the reprise of the second subject (II) but the reappearance of the 'thrilling' music of stanza 6, the 'acrobatic-music' and 'Unearthly, impossible' music of stanza 4 (here labelled 'Transition B'), and Iii. Perhaps most importantly, the appearance of the 'thrilling' music in stanza 7 is regarded as an incursion of development material into the recapitulation of the second subject (I), not as a continuation of the development itself.

---

[31] For example, the use of developmental 'breakthrough' material in the recapitulations of Strauss's *Don Juan* and the first movement of Mahler's First Symphony (Hepokoski, 'Beethoven Reception', p. 450).

EXPOSITION

Section	Text	Key
Introduction	Introduction, **Ii, Iii**	F minor
First subject	Stanza 1: 'Artist' theme, **Ii** (includes 'Sea Slumber Song' and 'Judgment' quotations, and 'Dämmerung' allusion)	F minor
	Stanza 2: 'Artist' theme, altered ('Dämmerung' and whole-tone allusions)	C minor C major
Transition A	Stanza 3, lines 1–5 (whole-tone allusion)	D minor
Second subject (I)	Stanza 3, lines 6–7	F major
Second subject (II)	Stanza 3, line 8 (2nd symphony allusion)	F major
Codetta	**Ii**/Artist theme	F minor

DEVELOPMENT

Section	Text	Key
Transition B	**Iii**/Stanza 4, lines 1–4	various
Episode 1	Stanza 4, lines 5–8 ('Dämmerung' and 'New Faith' allusions)	to G major
Recitative	**Iii**/Stanza 5, lines 1–4	G minor to A♭ major
Aria (Quotation 1)	Stanza 5, lines 5–8 ('Nimrod', 2nd symphony)	E♭ major to A♭ major
Episode 2 (x2)	Stanza 6	F minor to B♭ minor; A♭ minor to C minor; (refrain is 'Artist' theme)
Episode 1 reprise major	Stanza 6, various lines ('New Faith' allusion)	E♭ major to B♭
Codetta	**Ii**	F minor to A♭ major

RECAPITULATION

Section	Text	Key
Second subject (I)	Stanza 7, lines 1–4	A♭ major
Episode 2 (part)	Stanza 7, lines 5–7	E♭ minor
Quotation 2	Stanza 7, lines 7–8 ('Windflower', *Apostles*)	E♭ minor to F major
First subject	Stanza 8, lines 1–2: 'Artist' theme	F minor
Episode 1	Stanza 8, lines 3–4 (1st symphony motto and 'New Faith' allusion)	B♭ major
First subject	Stanza 8, lines 5–8: 'Artist' theme, altered ('Dämmerung' and whole-tone allusions)	B♭ minor to C minor
Transition B/Episode 2	Stanza 9, lines 1–2	C minor to A♭ major
Second subject (II) (x2)	**Iii**/Stanza 9, lines 3–6/Stanza 7 (2nd symphony allusion)	A♭ major to C major
	Iii/Stanza 9, lines 5–6, 3–4/ Stanza 7, lines 7–8/Stanza 8, lines 1–2 (2nd symphony allusion)	A♭ major to D♭ major
Coda	**Ii**/Stanza 9, lines 7–8 ('Novissima hora est')	D♭ to F♯ minor to E minor
	'Artist' theme	F minor

NB: Elgar's self-quotations (excluding the 'Enigma' theme) and allusions are included in parentheses in the sections when they occur. Indentations in the recapitulation refer to passages that are heard first in the development.

Fig. 4.2 A possible three-part formal division of *The Music Makers*

Ex. **4.2** *The Music Makers*, middleground reduction of introduction and stanzas 1–3

The case for a threefold division of the piece is strengthened when we consider the movement to and from the different key centres of the piece. As Ex. 4.2 shows, the introduction and first three stanzas can be considered a prolongation of a fundamental i-V-i progression in F minor. Within this there are middleground prolongations that extend across individual stanzas: the introduction is a i-ii-V-i prolongation of the tonic, the first stanza a i-iv-V-i prolongation also of the tonic, and the second stanza a i-V-I prolongation in the dominant minor, via ♭vii and ♭vi at figs. 20 and 22 respectively, and ending in the dominant major at 25. The chromatically descending repetitions of the two-bar phrase at the beginning of stanza 3 lead to the D minor passage between figs. 28 and 32; befitting its formal role as 'Transition A', this passage is perhaps best understood as an upper neighbour-note prolongation of the structural dominant, C. The cadence at fig. 32 marks a return to the tonic major, which is itself prolonged, first by the cycle-of-fifths passage of the second subject (I) at 32ff, and then by the $V(^6_4-^5_3)$-I progression that underpins the second subject (II) at 35. Fig. 36:4 sees the reappearance of Ii and with it a $i(^6_4-^5_3)$ prolongation in F *minor*, which concludes at fig. 38.

The middle three stanzas can also be considered as a much prolonged tonal progression. Stanza 4 begins in F minor, but moves eventually to G major with the arrival of the *grandioso* march at fig. 46. As Ex. 4.3 shows, at a middleground level figs. 41–43 represent a prolonged V^7-I progression in A♭, which proceeds – via descending whole-tone steps at 43:2 (G♭) and 43:4 (E) – to a perfect cadence in G at fig. 46; consequently figs. 43 to 46 can be understood as a much prolonged (♭II-V-I)/II. Stanza 4 ends

Ex. 4.3 *The Music Makers*, middleground reduction of stanzas 4–6

with a modal shift from G major to G minor, and it is in this key that stanza 5 begins, before shifting, via E♭ (fig. 51), to A♭ major (52:2), where it remains for the rest of the verse.[32] The underlying harmonic

[32] The second half of the stanza is in E♭ (figs. 51–52:2) and A♭ (fig. 52ff.) in all the sketches, but Elgar considered opening the stanza in other keys. In GB-Lbl Add. MS. 63162, fos. 48^v-50, the vocal line begins a major third higher than in the final version, and the passage continues at this pitch level until the end of bar 50:10; consequently fig. 50 occupies the tonal space of A minor/C major rather than F minor/A♭ major, and the harmony of 50:10 is G^6 not E♭^{6}. Fig. 50:11, however, has the pitch level and harmony (F^6) of the final version, to ensure that the quotation of 'Nimrod' at fig. 51 appears in its original key of E♭. In GB-Lbl Add. MS. 47908, fos. 33–7, the stanza begins in G minor, but moves a major third higher at fig. 49:4 (the last crotchet of the bar is g^1, not e^1♭) and, again, remains at this pitch level until the end of 50:10. Both sketches have a one-sharp key signature, suggesting a continuation of the G major of stanza 4, and possibly that the move to G minor at fig. 49 was a relatively late idea. Certainly in Add. MS. 63162, fo. 37, Elgar sketched (but struck out) a C minor opening to stanza 5, with the vocal melody starting on e^2♭ – an indication, perhaps, that G major was meant to act as a local dominant. Elgar also considered ending stanza 4 with a 4/4 version of Ii (in G minor), with stanza 5 opening at the pitch level of the final version (Add. MS. 63162, fo. 48^r). I mention these sketches not to suggest that Elgar chose to open stanza 5 in G minor because of the tonal plan I outline above, but to illustrate that this choice was by no means inevitable.

progression of the stanza is thus (III/V-V-I)/III. The chromaticism of stanza 6 complicates the musical foreground somewhat, but as both *Stollen* end with tonally unambiguous statements of the 'artist' theme one can make a case at a middleground level for considering figs. 55–60 and 61–65 to be prolongations of $\sharp vi^{7}_{\flat 5}$-III^{6}_{4}-V^{6}-i progressions in B♭ minor and C minor respectively.[33] The C minor statement is followed immediately by the *Abgesang*, which begins in E♭, but reaches its climax, at fig. 66:2, in B♭ (i.e. IV of F minor). This gives way to a reprise of the *Stollen* music at fig. 67, which in turn is followed by the return of Ii at 68 above a pedal C. The return of F minor at fig. 69 reveals this C not only to be the root of the local dominant, but also that of the structural dominant of a progression in F minor (i-II-III-iv-IV-V-i) that spans the three middle stanzas.

The first two thirds of the piece would therefore seem to justify the use of a tripartite model, rather than the four-part one suggested by Young. Elgar's setting makes musical sense: an exposition about the deeds of the music makers prolongs one fundamental progression in F minor, and a development describing their worldly audiences' reactions prolongs another. But the tripartite model might appear to run into problems in the final third of the work, for the musical conjunction of exposition and development materials is diametrically opposed to the text that ends stanza 7: 'O men! it must ever be / That we dwell, in our dreaming and singing, / A little apart from ye.' The seemingly irreconcilable distance between the music makers and their audiences is, however, not the only source of tension in the closing stanzas. The music makers dream of world renewal, yet increasingly we begin to doubt their ability to fulfil these dreams. As we shall see shortly, this imposes increasing strain on the long-range tonal organization of the work, and particularly the music's ability to achieve tonal closure. But it is also manifested in Elgar's use of quotations and allusions in the final three stanzas: an indication that memories from the past, far from being a source of inspiration, have now become an obstruction. It is to these quotations that we shall now turn.

---

[33] The 'artist' theme does not appear in some of Elgar's sketches for this stanza. In GB-Lbl Add. MS. 47908, fo. 75, and BL Add. MS. 63158, fo. 25ʳ, bar 59:6 is followed by a half-diminished seventh on G (the chord that opened the stanza), not the B♭ minor statement of the 'artist' theme. (The latter sketch has 'p. 59' marked at fig. 60; this refers to fo. 26ᵛ, where Elgar sketched the passage at fig. 61.) Similarly in Add. MS. 47908, fo. 39 and Add. MS. 63158, fo. 25ᵛ, bar 64:7 (the second half of which is a tone lower than in the final version) cuts straight to the *Maestoso* at fig. 65. Sketches for the 'artist' theme at fig. 60, and, implicitly, six bars before fig. 65 (the sketch consists of five empty bars followed by the bar before fig. 65) appear in Add. MS. 63158, fo. 27ʳ; it is unclear, however, at what stage Elgar chose to include them in the final version.

Quotations and stanza 7

Unlike Strauss's self-quotations in *Ein Heldenleben*, which are confined to a single section of that work, 'Des Helden Friedenswerke', Elgar's occur at four different places in *The Music Makers*: stanza 1, stanza 5, stanzas 7–8 and stanza 9 (see Table 4.1). Moreover, whereas Strauss's citations are integrated with the musical material of *Heldenleben*, Elgar's are often set apart from the surrounding music. An exception to this is the group of quotations from stanza 1, where the 'Judgment' motif from *Gerontius*, the 'Sea Slumber Song' from *Sea Pictures*, and the 'Enigma' theme follow in close proximity as a counterpoint to the 'Artist' theme (Ex. 4.4). As Robert Anderson has aptly commented, 'if any test were needed for the unity of Elgar's creative imagination, it is here … The disparate ideas dovetail happily, and it is only their associations that conjure up thoughts of an enigmatic judgment by the sea.'[34] The unity of Elgar's creative imagination is at work again in stanza 5, when 'Nimrod' mutates seamlessly into a theme from the finale of the Second Symphony (fig. 53). But the context here is very different. As mentioned earlier, stanza 5 is essentially a self-contained slow movement within two thematically connected faster sections: a recitative and cavatina for contralto and chorus, preceded by the framing device of a general pause. There is some development of music from earlier in the piece in the recitative section (namely the third couplet of stanza 1, the 'Callicles' music that opens stanza 3, and Iii). But the cavatina itself consists solely (indeed, for this piece, uniquely) of the quotations from

Ex. 4.4 *The Music Makers*, stanza 1, opening

[34] Anderson, *Elgar*, p. 197.

Ex. 4.4 (cont.)

'Nimrod' and the Second Symphony. Unlike those in stanza 1, they are not a counterpoint to another theme (and thus an extra layer of thematic argument), but the themes themselves. Indeed, their thematic interest lies entirely in their relationship to each other, for they have not appeared in the piece hitherto, and nor will they do so subsequently.[35] This is not to deny the wider musical significance of this section: as we have already

[35] I assume here that 'Nimrod' has an identity separate from the 'Enigma' theme – a reasonable assumption, given that 'Nimrod' here is a conscious tribute to Jaeger, rather than a further development of the loneliness of the artist, which 'Enigma' signifies in this piece.

noted, the move to A♭ major at fig. 52 forms part of the directed tonal motion of the middle three stanzas. But the fact that these quotations – unaltered from their original forms, except in key – should appear at the heart of a piece extolling the 'never-ceasing change' of artistic progress is deeply ironic. Both discursively and semantically, then, stanza 5 functions episodically 'outside' the rest of the piece.

Let us return to stanza 7. The musical setting of the first five lines of the stanza is straightforward enough: having begun by recapitulating the second subject (I) in A♭ major (III of F minor), Elgar settles on a B♭ pedal (fig. 75) that prolongs a V($^{6-5}_{4-3}$) progression in E♭ minor; above this pedal, the chorus sings 'O men!' to the 'Enigma' theme, the signifier of artistic loneliness. But rather than cadencing in E♭ minor, this theme is supplanted by the 'Windflower' theme from the first movement of the Violin Concerto, beginning in D♭ major, and ending, four bars later, on a secondary dominant: V of F major (Ex. 4.5). The shift to D♭ is not as strange as it might seem – in the equivalent passage in the concerto, this opening harmony is ♭VII of the local tonic, its role here – but whereas, in the earlier work, the closing secondary dominant forms part of a larger progression that eventually returns to the tonic, here the cadence with which it is associated is instead prolonged over four bars by the 'Windflower' theme from the second movement of the Concerto.[36] The conflation of the two 'Windflower' themes thus resembles a musical stream-of-consciousness: one incomplete memory gives way to another, disrupting the harmonic logic of the original work in the process.

In some respects the quotations in stanza 7 resemble those in stanza 5. In both cases, the quotations are separated from the surrounding music by framing devices: a change in texture (the orchestra is silent) in the bar before the first 'Windflower' theme enters, and a general pause afterwards. Given the text here – 'That we dwell, in our dreaming and our singing, / A little apart from ye' – this sense of separation is most appropriate. But whereas the quotations in stanza 5 at least made some sense within the tonal context of the middle three stanzas, and as a complement to the recitative that preceded it, those in stanza 7 seem arbitrary, both tonally and thematically. It is as if the quotations *cannot* now engage with the other music, or even exist in the same musical space: the complementarity of quotations and newly composed music that we saw in stanza 1 now appears to be a thing of the past.

[36] Elgar considered a more extended quotation of the first-movement 'Windflower' theme; see GB-Lbl Add. MS. 47908, fo. 47, where he continues this theme for another five bars. The folio ends with a quotation of the motto theme of the First Symphony in its original key, A♭, not the B♭ in which it appears in stanza 8.

Ex. 4.5 *The Music Makers*, stanza 7, end

Ex. 4.5 (cont.)

Allusions and stanza 8

It is not only newly composed music with which the quotations cannot co-exist. At the beginning of stanza 8, Elgar sets the couplet 'And out of the infinite morning / Intrepid you hear us cry' to the motto theme of the First Symphony: in its original context an 'ideal call', 'noble & elevating'.[37] If

<hr />

[37] Letter to Ernest Newman, 4 November 1908, quoted in Anderson, *Elgar*, p. 321.

Ex. 4.5 (cont.)

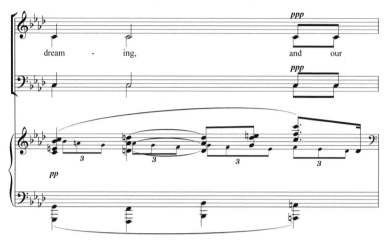

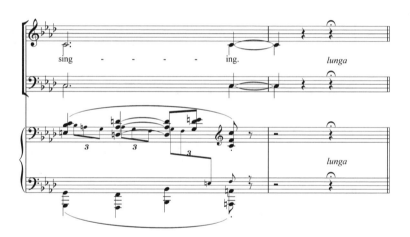

any theme might realize the music makers' dreams of world renewal, it would surely be this one. Yet it fails to do so. The antecedent of the motto is stated unaccompanied, but at fig. 80 it acquires a counterpoint: the *grandioso* march from stanza 4, which provides a link to the consequent of the phrase. The effect of this intrusion is immediate and almost completely destructive: the consequent is broken off, incomplete, at 81, and is replaced by the music set to the final couplet of stanza 1, and then, at 82, the opening of stanza 2. Within a few bars the 'infinite morning' has given way to something more apocalyptic: 'Once more God's future draws nigh, / And already goes forth the warning / That ye of the past must die.' The orchestra's response to this last word is to recall a descending whole-tone motif (fig. 83) first heard in stanza 2 (Ex. 4.6).

Ex. 4.6 *The Music Makers*, stanza 8, figs. 81–84 (first note omitted)

The particular significance of this passage lies in the fact that the *grandioso* march, the closing couplet of stanza 1 and the descending whole-tone figure are all examples of 'allusion' as I defined the term earlier; thus, there is an intertextual element to this passage that we must unravel. Indeed, in the case of the final couplet of stanza 1 this element goes beyond Elgar himself. The words 'shakers / Of the world', which form the climax to this stanza, are set to descending quavers that recall the second half of the opening bar of the 'Sea Slumber Song', which Elgar quoted directly in line 3. The intervals are slightly altered, but the melodic contour is virtually unchanged; more strikingly, however, the legato *p* arpeggio of line 3 has now become *fff* and accented, with the result that the sea breakers have been transformed into something approaching the 'Götterdämmerung' motif from Wagner's *Ring* (Ex. 4.7). Is this merely coincidence? O'Shaughnessy's poem certainly

Ex. 4.6 (cont.)

suggests that the 'renewal of the world' the music makers seek is the successful overthrow of an anachronistic, if not necessarily corrupt, old artistic
order; and this need for world transformation is also a feature of Elgar's
use of the 'Götterdämmerung' figure in both stanzas 2 (fig. 23: 'Shall go forth
and conquer a crown') and 4 (fig. 44:4–5 and 44:9–10: 'Are working together
in one'). In stanza 8, however, the motif recalls the destructive, not the
cathartic, aspect of *Götterdämmerung*, as it provides the transition from the
music makers' eternal hopes to their eternal fate.

    If the connection between this allusion and *Götterdämmerung* might seem
simply to be an aural fluke, that between the descending whole-tone figure
and its antecedent has the supporting evidence of Elgar's manuscripts. In *The
Music Makers* the whole-tone motif appears three times: in stanza 2, as an
accompaniment to 'Tramples a kingdom down' (fig. 25); in stanza 3, as an

Ex. 4.6 (cont.)

accompaniment to 'o'erthrew them [i.e. Nineveh and Babel] with their prophesying' (fig. 30:8); and, as we have just noted, in stanza 8, immediately after 'That ye of the past must die' (fig. 83:2). Elgar made several sketches of this figure, although quite why he took so much care over it is unclear.[38] One

---

[38] The passage appears more or less in full in GB-Lbl Add. MS. 47908, fos. 22–28 and GB-Lbl Add. MS. 63156, fo. 37ᵛ; for piano only in Add. MS. 47908, fo. 62 and GB-Lbl Add. MS. 63154, fo. 1; for melody only (above the C pedal of stanza 8) in Add. MS. 47908, fo. 79 and GB-Lbl Add. MS. 63158, fo. 28ᵛ; and for melody only (plus one bar of bass) in Add. MS. 63156, fo. 35ᵛ.

Ex. 4.6 (cont.)

Ex. 4.7(a) Wagner, *Das Rheingold*, scene iv, 'Götterdämmerung' motif

Ex. 4.7(b) *The Music Makers*, stanza 1, fig. 13:4: 'Götterdämmerung' allusion

possible explanation might be its importance as transitional material: among the sketches in the British Library, Additional Manuscript 63156, folio 35^{v}, for instance, suggests that Elgar considered ending stanza 8 with the whole-tone material leading into an F minor statement of Ii. But the reason is unlikely to have been the material of the theme itself, for it first appears in the sketches for Part II of *The Dream of Gerontius* alongside part of 'Praise to the Holiest'

(GB-Lbl Add. MS. 47902, fo. 251). In the end, it was not used in *Gerontius*, yet descending whole-tone scales play an important role in that work, where they are associated with the Soul's impending judgment and, in a broken form, with the chorus of Angelicals as they sing 'Praise to the Holiest'.[39] Whole tones therefore symbolize not only the awesomeness of divine judgement, but also the quasi-magical beauty and infinity of the hereafter. But there is no such eternal peace in *The Music Makers*. Instead, the whole-tone scale depicts only the destruction left in progress's wake: trampled kingdoms, o'erthrown cities – and, in stanza 8, superannuated artists. Christian hope has been ironically transformed into modernist insecurity.

The relationship between faith and modernity is also central to the Grandioso march. The distinctive ♩ ♩ 𝅘𝅥𝅮𝅘𝅥𝅮𝅘𝅥𝅮 rhythm of this march not only betrays 'Elgar's fondness for second beat accent and fourth beat triplet',[40] as Anderson notes, but explicitly recalls the 'New Faith' motif in *The Kingdom*, a work not traditionally associated with *The Music Makers* (Ex. 4.8). To be sure, the changes in tempo and harmonic rhythm between the two works obscure the resemblance. But it is surely no coincidence that the *Kingdom* 'New Faith' figure appears in several sketchbooks in close proximity to *Music Makers* sketches.[41] Moreover, the connection between the 'New Faith' motif and the *Music Makers* march is clarified when we note the words to which the march is set in the three stanzas in which it appears: 'till our dream shall become their present' (stanza 4, fig. 46); 'the multitudes are bringing to pass the dream that was scorned yesterday' (stanza 6, fig. 65); and 'out of the infinite morning / Intrepid you hear us cry' (stanza 8, fig. 80). The first two statements represent a secularization of the apostles' 'New Faith' in the form of the music makers' 'dreams', while the third sees the dream momentarily become reality in an aesthetic Pentecost, as the march appears in counterpoint with the First Symphony motto.[42] The First Symphony thus appears as the successor to the *Apostles* trilogy: sacred

---

[39] The associations of the scale with impending judgment are at fig. 55:6, when it accompanies the Soul's question 'shall I see / My dearest Master when I reach His throne?'; fig. 102, when the Angel sings 'Thy judgment now is near'; and fig. 114, when the Soul sings 'I go before my Judge'. The broken form of the motif supports the chorus of Angelicals at figs. 60 and 68, and also accompanies the Angel at fig. 73 ('And now the threshold, as we traverse it / Utters aloud its glad responsive chant') immediately prior to the full choral setting of 'Praise to the Holiest'. For a different reading of Elgar's use of whole-tone scales,

see Patrick McCreless in this volume, ch. 1, esp. pp. 23–5.
[40] Anderson, *Elgar*, p. 198.
[41] E.g. GB-Lbl Add. MS. 63159, fos. 23ᵛ-24, immediately prior to the opening of stanza 9 of *The Music Makers* (fos. 24ᵛ-25); and GB-Lbl Add. MS. 63160, fo. 22, immediately after a sketch of the final lines of stanza 3 (fo. 21ᵛ).
[42] The motto theme of the First Symphony is itself linked to that of *The Apostles*; both share a common ancestor in the *Liebesmahl* motif of *Parsifal*; see Aidan J. Thomson, 'Elgar and Chivalry', *19CM*, 28 (2005), pp. 259–65.

Ex. 4.8(a) *The Kingdom*, Prelude, fig. 6: 'New Faith' motif

Ex. 4.8(b) *The Music Makers*, stanza 4, fig. 46: 'New Faith' allusion

choral and secular instrumental combine to proclaim the historical tran-
scendence of Elgar's creations.

Or so it might seem at first. But *The Kingdom* brought the *Apostles* trilogy
to an end: not temporarily, as it turned out, but permanently. Various
reasons have been put forward for this: Elgar's ill-health during the composition of *The Kingdom*; his need to write a symphony; even simply the fact
that, as Jerrold Northrop Moore has commented, the *Apostles* project 'ended
by defeating his musical impulse'.[43] But most crucial, perhaps, was Elgar's

---

[43] Moore, *Elgar*, pp. 489–90, 506–7. Ernest
Newman felt that the 'general level of
inspiration' of the work was 'below that of
"Gerontius" or "The Apostles"' that a good
deal of the music was 'dull in itself'; and that
the scheme of the trilogy was 'unwieldy,

impossible': 'until that scheme is done with ...
the most sanguine of us cannot expect much
from him in the way of fresh or really vital
music' (*The Birmingham Daily Post*, 4 October
1906, 22 March 1907, quoted in ibid.,
pp. 505–6, 507).

gradual loss of religious faith, which began during the period he was completing *The Kingdom*.[44] Thus the 'New Faith' march in *The Music Makers*
might allude not to a permanent, transcendental value-system, but, ironically, to one that Elgar increasingly viewed as illusory; consequently, it calls
into question the legitimacy of the music makers' aesthetic transcendental-
ism. The immediate consequence of the combination with the First
Symphony in stanza 8 is, as we have seen, the destruction of the
'Götterdämmerung' motif and the whole-tone scale of *Gerontius*. Far from
depicting artistic immortality, the allusion seems instead to draw attention to
artistic transience.[45]

Thus Elgar's ideal, noble call is swallowed up by a succession of false
memories, leading to destruction, death and judgement. The implications
of this are profound. In the symbiotic relationship between the quotation
and the allusions, there is a metaphor for the modernist dilemma thrown up
by the closing words of stanza 7: the emerging gulf between the creative
artists of the poem, committed to progress but also aspiring to immortality
through their art; and their audiences, on whom the artists' posthumous
reputations depend, but who are increasingly unable to understand them.
This problematizes our interpretation of the quotations. On the one hand,
they represent in miniature the 'great' works that might transport Elgar to
O'Shaughnessy's 'infinite morning': they are the proof of the progress in art
that he has already achieved. But the recognition of this depended on these
works' conforming to, or entering into dialogue with, the laws of commonly
understood musical language and syntax. In *The Music Makers*, Elgar trans-
gresses these laws: the quotations disrupt the structure and tonal logic of the
work, and thereby question the coherence both of the quotations (now
removed from the contexts where they originally made sense) and of the
music surrounding them (whose thematic development is interrupted by the
isolated, non-developed memories). At one level, this disruption comes from
outside the boundaries of *The Music Makers* itself: Moore's comment that
Elgar's use of the First Symphony motto in stanza 8 'flash[es . . .] as spas-
modic inspiration' because it has 'no organic place' in the piece misses, in its
criticism, the point that it accidentally makes – namely that it is precisely
because that motto does not exist organically in *The Music Makers* that it can
critique, and be critiqued by, the other music in stanza 8.[46] But at a wider,

[44] Kennedy, *Portrait*, p. 200.
[45] Admittedly the First Symphony was
one of Elgar's greatest triumphs. But it is
worth noting that the reception for its
successor – premiered only sixteen months
before *The Music Makers* – was noticeably
lukewarm.
[46] Moore, *Elgar*, p. 637.

discursive level, the disruption still comes from within, because the musical language Elgar uses to disrupt *The Music Makers* is his own. Thus, by decontextualizing the quotations from their originals, Elgar reveals the limitations of his musical language, above all how it might *not* make musical sense. This seriously undermines any notion of the music's inherent greatness, let alone its ability to transcend its original circumstances: in its quest for the 'infinite morning', Elgar's musical language succeeds only in realizing O'Shaughnessy's statement that 'ye of the past must die'. (Ironically, the process of dying is illustrated by allusions whose very existence depends on an act of *mis*-remembering that thereby denies the immutable, transcendental nature of the original.) Moreover, if *The Music Makers* is concerned with the 'duty' of seeing that the 'inevitable change' in art was progress, as Elgar claimed, it raises the question of what 'progress' in music actually means. By betraying the 'mortality' of his musical language, Elgar provides his own somewhat nihilistic answer.

Elgar's last stanza

The combination of allusions and quotation in stanza 8 thus leaves a powerful imprint of artistic mortality. The 'correctly' remembered symphonic motto is successfully subverted by three false memories: a depiction of the sea that has turned apocalyptic; a vision of judgement divorced from any sense of hope; and a credo that is no longer believed. But there remains a final stanza, one that speaks of renewal and of new dreams, which might possibly overcome the pessimism of stanza 8. Moreover, it might provide the tonal closure that is surely a precondition for the fulfilment of the music makers' dreams. As we noted above, stanza 7 begins in A♭ (III of F minor), but ends in F major. Stanza 8 opens in F minor, but this is quickly revealed to be V of B♭ (IV of F minor), the key in which Elgar quotes the First Symphony motto. It is followed in turn by a perfect cadence in C minor (v of F minor) at fig. 82, thus creating tonal centres of III-IV-v across the two stanzas (Ex. 4.9). All that is needed now to confirm F as the tonic of the piece is a final, structural perfect cadence, and stanza 9, with its call to 'renew the world as of yore', would seem the obvious place for this to happen.

The key to stanza 9 lies in another allusion: the theme of the 'second subject (II)' that first appears at the end of stanza 3 (fig. 35). Its musical characteristics are a melodic line that ascends from c to a^1, immediately repeated an octave higher; a pedal C that underpins a prolonged V($^{6-5}_{4-3}$)-I cadence in F major; and, at the cadence itself (fig. 35:8), a ♪♪ ♩ rhythm that articulates the progressions I-ii^7-V^{13}-I^6 and (I-ii^7-I^6)/IV. This same rhythm articulates an F major climax in another, relatively recent piece: the funereal

Ex. 4.9 *The Music Makers*, middleground reduction of stanzas 7–8

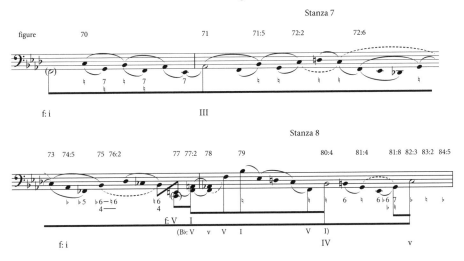

C minor *Larghetto* of the Second Symphony.[47] The F major climax comes roughly a third of the way into the movement, following a particularly dark passage based on sketches Elgar had made for 'City of Dreadful Night', an unfinished overture based on James Thomson's poetic vision of urban dystopia. Marked 'Nobilmente e semplice', this climax has many of the same characteristics as that in *The Music Makers*: a slow anapaestic rhythm on the trumpets, a *ff* dynamic, a pedal C, and $I({}^6_4)$-V^{13}-I^6 harmony. That the two themes were associated in Elgar's mind is surely confirmed by their appearance on the same line in sketch GB-Lbl Add. MS. 63160, fo. 21^v (Ex. 4.10).[48] And, once again, the meaning of the earlier work is transformed ironically in the latter. Whereas in the symphony, the F major climax is a rock of diatonic calm and hope amid a sea of chromaticism,[49] in *The Music Makers* it is associated more with unfulfilled expectations. In stanza 3 it

[47] Although conceding that the movement was 'elegiac', Elgar insisted that the *Larghetto* was not a funeral march; rather, it was essentially 'a "reflection"' suggested by Shelley's 'Song', 'Spirit of Delight', whose opening couplet appears at the top of the score (letter to Alfred Littleton, 13 April 1911, quoted in Moore, *Elgar*, p. 604). The *Larghetto* is often viewed as a tribute to the work's dedicatee, King Edward VII, who had died in May 1910, but if it was inspired by a death it is more likely to be that of Elgar's friend Alfred Rodewald, who died in 1903, a few months before Elgar made his first sketches for this movement (Kennedy, *Portrait*, p. 200).

[48] Ironically, in this sketch the 'coming' theme of *The Music Makers* has the ♩ ♩ ♩ note values of the Symphony, and the Symphony theme (here in its recapitulation key of E♭ major) has the ♫ ♩ note values of *The Music Makers*.

[49] Jerrold Northrop Moore has described the climax as a 'response of simple nobility' to the sorrow that surrounds it; see Moore, *Elgar*, p. 606.

Ex. 4.10 Sketches for *The Music Makers*, stanza 3, and Symphony no. 2, second movement (GB-Lbl Add. MS. 63160, fo. 21ᵛ)

sets part of a couplet – 'For each age is a dream that is dying / Or one that is coming to birth' – that focuses yet again on artistic transience, not permanence; and, as we shall see, this implicit instability is a key feature of the allusion's two reappearances in stanza 9.

Stanza 9 opens in C minor, but a combination of recapitulated themes from the development – the *Stollen* music from stanza 6, the 'acrobatic-music' and the setting of 'Unearthly, impossible seeming' from stanza 4 – moves the tonality flatwards; and it is in Db and Ab that the contralto intones the first six lines of the stanza, between figs. 88 and 90, to the music of Iii. Fig. 90 marks the beginning of a return to C major, and this key is confirmed at 92 with a change of key signature (to no sharps and flats) and the first recapitulation of the second subject (II), complete with C major cadence at 92:13. But if the music has now reached the structural dominant – which, given that 92:13 is the last perfect cadence in C major in the piece, this surely is – the text has gone backwards. Rather than set the closing couplet, with its uncomfortable reference to a 'dreamer who slumbers, / And a singer who sings no more', Elgar has returned to the more optimistic text of stanza 7; the contralto sings at figure 92 of 'The glory about you clinging / Of the glorious futures you see', and reaches a climax on 'Your souls with high music

Ex. 4.11   *The Music Makers*, middleground reduction of stanza 9

ringing'. The expectation is heightened by the return of these words, but increasingly we are left wondering when – if? – these glorious futures might actually appear. This apprehension is confirmed by a return to Iii, which, having effected the move from A♭ to C, now reverses the process: fig. 95 sees a return to four flats, and fig. 97 another statement of the second subject (II) in D♭ major, with a climactic cadence in that key at 98. Again, the text is drawn from earlier stanzas, and again it refers to unfulfilled aspirations, not to the realization of the music makers' dreams: the chorus sings the opening of stanza 8 ('For we are afar with the dawning'), while the contralto returns to stanza 9 ('And renew our world as of yore'). But more importantly, by moving from C major to D♭ the music is, if anything, *further* than before from the closure in F that might realize these dreams. Indeed, there *is* no return to C major. It is in D♭ that this climax subsides at fig. 99:7; and the passage that ensues following the restart at fig. 100 moves further away still: to F♯ minor at fig. 101, B minor at 101:5, and E minor at 102:5, after which the music, once again, fizzles out. Consequently, the return to F minor at fig. 103 feels disconnected, indeed shocking: an accented ii[7] chord provides a link to a final, tonic intonation of the 'artist' theme (see Ex. 4.11).

One might argue that, as the structural dominant, C, occurs at fig. 92:13, the return to F minor at fig. 103 is simply a long-delayed structural perfect cadence. Technically this is correct, but it is to miss the trees for the wood, as it were. Firstly, the D♭ major climax of the second subject (II) at 98 is rhetorically much grander than the C major climax earlier in the stanza: the contralto is supplemented by the chorus, and, in addition to the *poco allargando*, there is also a written *rallentando* because of the doubled note values. Secondly, there is the significance of the long-delayed final couplet, with its intimations of mortality. This is at last set at fig. 100, to the 'Unearthly, impossible seeming' music that, earlier in the stanza, had depicted a more optimistic-sounding 'dazzling unknown shore'. The contrast between the two passages is most poignant, but the poignancy results from the thematic repetition, not from any tonal factors. Lastly, there is the importance of the final quotation: 'Novissima hora est', the motif that appears at the moment of death in Part I of *Gerontius*. Unlike the quotations in stanzas 5 and 7 – but like those in stanzas 1 and, arguably, 8 – 'Novissima' is combined with peculiarly *Music Makers* music, rather than set apart from it: it is stated twice, at figs. 101 and 102, and on both occasions is succeeded, four bars later, by the final statements in the piece of Ii. This juxtaposition is highly significant. Musically, 'Novissima' is characterized above all by its inability to close. It forms a self-perpetuating four-bar progression which travels from I to IV – which then is itself tonicized, and travels, in turn, to IV/IV, and so on ad infinitum. The chain can be broken only by some sort of caesura: by another theme, or by rests or pauses (as in *Gerontius*). In *The Music Makers* Elgar does both: after the second statement of Ii, there is a *pausa lunga*, by which point we have reached a key – E minor – that is almost as far away from F minor as it is possible to be. Consequently the return to F minor after the pause feels utterly arbitrary: an ironic nod by Elgar to formal and tonal convention (though not to the extent of including a dominant chord) that is undermined by what immediately precedes it.[50] True closure has been denied; the music makers' dreams thus remain forever unrealized.

In short, the long-term structural cadence in stanza 9 is less important than the problematization of closure that exists in the musical foreground. Instead of a reaffirmed tonic, there is a sense of tonal dissolution. But this dissolution is not only local to stanza 9; rather, it has been going on since the beginning of the work. The themes of our exposition, far from being contrasted tonally, are centred on F: F minor in stanza 1 and F major in stanza 3. In the recapitulation, by contrast, they are in several different keys: A♭ in stanza 7, F minor (briefly) in stanza 8, and C major and D♭ major in stanza 9. It is as if we have begun with the recapitulation and ended with the exposition: not merely a 'sonata deformation', to use James Hepokoski's now celebrated term, but a 'sonata reversal' that fractures an initially unified tonality.[51] And this may provide the key to why Elgar's setting of what is

[50] Cf. also the ends of 'Twilight' (op. 59, no. 6; see ch. 9), *Falstaff*, and the Cello Concerto.
[51] 'Sonata deformation' is defined by Hepokoski as 'an individual work in dialogue primarily with sonata norms even though

certain central features of the sonata-concept have been reshaped, exaggerated, marginalized or overridden altogether. What is presented on the musical surface of a composition ... may not be a sonata in any "textbook" sense, and yet

often an optimistic text frequently sounds so pessimistic: the price of O'Shaughnessy's progress is disintegration.

Conclusion

The presence of the allusions alongside the quotations suggests that there is more than one narrative agent at work in *The Music Makers*. There is the narrative voice of the quotations: conscious of itself (insofar as the quotations are cited 'correctly') and of its value, it emphasizes the optimistic spirit of O'Shaughnessy's poem, and, to some extent, the laws of music that enable the quotations to function poetically (the long-range tonal goals, for instance). Above all, this is the voice of Romantic sincerity: the quotations mean what they meant before. But, as we have seen, this narrative voice appears more extrinsic to *The Music Makers* the longer the piece goes on: the quotations provide no material for development, and seem unable to co-exist with the newly composed music in the piece. (Revealingly, the one late exception to this – 'Novissima' – essentially depicts a composer falling on his sword.) In contrast to this conscious voice, however, is the subconscious narrative voice of the allusions. This voice is characterized by misremembering and distortions, and thus might be said to act as a counterpoint to the voice of the quotations. Initially, the voice of the allusions seems nothing more than local colour: the whole-tone writing at the end of stanza 2, for instance, provides an apt depiction of 'trampling a kingdom down' without our necessarily being aware of its origins in *Gerontius*. But that colour manages to ingratiate itself into the fabric of the work far more successfully than the quotations ever do, and almost invariably in pessimistic contexts that bespeak destruction or, at the very least, unfulfilled hopes. By the last two stanzas, this destructive narrative comes more and more to the fore: in dismissing the aesthetic pretensions of the First Symphony motto in stanza 8; in the manner that the tonal foreground and middleground stretch the fundamental structure to, or beyond, breaking point; and in the way that 'sonata reversal' denies any real sense of tonal resolution. The narrative voice of the quotations expresses the composer's hopes, that of the allusions his fears.

   To some extent, this polyphony of narrative voices was implicit in the poem from the start. Artistic progress, for O'Shaughnessy, meant that 'ye of

the work may still encourage, even demand, the application of one's knowledge of traditional sonata procedures as a rule for analysis and interpretation' (Hepokoski, 'Beethoven Reception', p. 447). Hepokoski mentions 'double-function' sonata forms as one type of deformation, but does not refer to any 'sonata reversals'.

the past must die'; and if it was on those artists' mortality that Elgar chose to dwell, rather than on a *Zukunftsmusik*, that perhaps reflects a realization on his part that his own reputation was beginning to fade. But the implications of narrative duality extend beyond the biographical to a dialectic of progress and loss that is quintessentially modernist. *The Music Makers* can be read positively as a harmonically goal-directed paean to the forward-looking vision of the Romantic artist-subject, yet within this celebration of progress are the seeds of its own destruction. The inverted formal model exposes the tonal planning as artificial and thus bereft of meaning, while the voice of the allusions, in revealing itself to be a more significant generator of thematic material than that of the quotations, deconstructs the very idea of the conscious, self-willed Romantic composer that the quotations embody. In view of Elgar's (and O'Shaughnessy's) aesthetic tastes, we might see this as a decadent interpretation of the piece, for 'decadence', as Byron Adams has noted (quoting Ellis Hanson), is synonymous with the idea that 'religion, sexuality, art, *even language itself*, had fallen at last into an inevitable decay'.[52] More intriguing still is a possible Freudian reading of the work, where the voices of the quotations and the allusions might be seen as analogous with, respectively, rational and irrational modes of thought. Under this model, the allusions would be viewed as repressed by the quotations, able to resurface only when they have been 'displaced' in some way. The fact that this resurfacing should take place in *The Music Makers* is particularly appropriate, for music-making, in O'Shaughnessy's 'Ode', is ultimately synonymous with dreaming dreams. That Elgar presents us with both his conscious and unconscious thoughts gives us, the analysts, the chance also to be the therapists.[53]

[52] Ellis Hanson, *Decadence and Catholicism* (Cambridge, MA: Harvard University Press, 1997), p. 2 (my italics), quoted in Adams, 'Elgar's Later Oratorios', 85.
[53] I am indebted to Daniel M. Grimley for raising the subject of Freud and Elgar after a version of this paper given at the Fifth International Conference on Music in Nineteenth-Century Britain, University of Nottingham, 10 July 2005, and to Byron Adams, Jan Smaczny, Helen Swift, and Katharine Thomson.

5   Gaudery, romance, and the 'Welsh tune': *Introduction and Allegro*, op. 47

James Hepokoski

1

When one confronts the works of Elgar it is difficult to keep analysis from merging into hermeneutics – explorations into broader systems of meaning. In this repertory of enigmas, embedded secrets, and allusive themes, merely technical analyses that steer clear of questions of larger interpretation can be unsatisfying, as if missing the point. Similarly, hermeneutic decodings that bypass close analysis can seem unmoored, insufficiently grounded in the actual workings of the music. But these two aspects are not separate domains in any repertory – and certainly not in Elgar's compositions. Under these circumstances, our goal should be to devise methods whereby analysis and hermeneutics become one and the same thing, different modalities of the same issue. This essay, like others in this volume, is an exercise in both analysis and interpretation.

Elgar composed *Introduction and Allegro for Strings* in January and early February 1905. The non-programmatic title and musical structure imply that it may be regarded generically as a single-movement abstract piece, something on the order of an overture scored for strings and string quartet.[1] One obvious string-orchestra precedent was the early, three-movement *Serenade for Strings* (1892), but within Elgar's mature output its only significant sonata-form-based, orchestral predecessors were the concert overtures *Froissart* (1890), *Cockaigne* (1901), and *In the South* (1904): the larger challenge, the First Symphony, was still a few years away. As is well known, the composer produced *Introduction and Allegro* for a concert devoted to his works to be presented by the London Symphony Orchestra – then less than a year old.[2] From the perspective of the orchestra, the audience, and the critics – the public face of the work – it was to be a celebratory piece affirming a new

---

[1] The very different *Introduction and Allegro* for harp, flute, clarinet, and string quartet by Ravel also dates from 1905. Compare the titles from Schumann: *Introduction and Allegro Appassionato* (Concertstück) op. 92; and *Introduction and Concert-Allegro* op. 134, both for piano and orchestra.

[2] A overview of the circumstances of this commission, along with other background information about *Introduction and Allegro*, may be found in several commentaries, including Moore, *Elgar*, pp. 450–4 (cf. the deeper, 'Welsh' background of the piece on pp. 352–3), and Kennedy, *Portrait*, pp. 219–20.

institution within English music. At the same time it was to solidify further
the growing prestige of Elgar as the strongest, most controversial English
early-modernist composer.[3]

From this perspective, the occasion of its London premiere on 8 March
1905 – marked as a significant cultural event and clustered with five other
works by Elgar – is a central, affirmational feature of the piece's social
meaning. This was a material-culture meaning, operating within a cultural
economy fuelled by publicity, nationalism, class, European musical change
and challenge, and English-elite artistic prestige. Just as Elgar, invited to
conduct, was to help confer aesthetic legitimacy on the new orchestra with
his presence, so too the orchestra, with its invitation, was to burnish the not
fully solidified reputation of the perpetually insecure Elgar. For both sides the
premiere may be read as a strong positioning – a calculated chess move –
within the institution of art music, itself competing for recognition within
the larger, sharply charged field of cultural production. One aspect of the
work's meaning inheres in the details of its historical situatedness. It resides
not in its notes alone but in the relations that the work sought to set up or
maintain with existing power networks generating the current state of
English art music – its quality as a mutually benefiting transaction within
the field.[4] To that publicly strategic, institutional meaning belong many
aspects of the piece's craft: its early-modernist treatment of form and harmony; its virtuosic string writing; the proclamatory grandness of its sonorities; the creative rethinking of the pseudo-concerto-grosso, perhaps Bachian
or Handelian texture of chamber group and larger orchestra – in which the
richness of the orchestral string tutti recedes periodically into more personalized individual voices; and its placement (along with the more unassuming
Serenade for Strings) within a growing European tradition of canonic works
for strings alone – by Grieg, Tchaikovsky, Dvořák, and others – and the

[3] Within Europe the 'early modernist'
composers were those born in the years
around 1860, 'the generation of the 1860s':
Strauss, Mahler, Wolf, Debussy, Puccini,
Sibelius, Elgar, Nielsen, Busoni, Glazunov,
and others. On the designation 'early
modernist' (as opposed to the misleading 'late
romantic' or 'post-romantic'), see Hepokoski,
'Beethoven Reception: the Symphonic
Tradition', in Jim Samson (ed.), *The
Cambridge History of Nineteenth-Century
Music* (Cambridge: Cambridge University
Press, 2001), pp. 424–59 (especially pp. 454–8
on the two generational waves of composers
after 1870); 'Elgar' and 'Sibelius', in D. Kern
Holoman (ed.), *The Nineteenth-Century
Symphony* (New York: G. Schirmer, 1997),
pp. 327–44 and 417–49; *Sibelius: Symphony*

No. 5 (Cambridge: Cambridge University
Press, 1993), especially pp. 1–9 ('Introduction:
Sibelius and the Problem of "Modernism" ').
[4] As many readers will recognize, several of
these concepts are resonant of the sociological
methodology found in Pierre Bourdieu. See,
for example, the general sociological model
provided in the essays included in Bourdieu,
*The Field of Cultural Production: Essays on Art
and Literature*, ed. Randal Johnson (New
York: Columbia University Press, 1993); and
The Rules of Art, trans. Susan Emanuel
(Stanford, CA: Stanford University Press,
1992). From this vantage-point one could
imagine a study that investigated this and
similar events further as one of several
effective – though often emotionally
strenuous – *prises des position*.

consequent alignment of Elgar as continuing in that tradition. As I shall suggest below (section 3), other features of 'the commission' and 'the event' proper may also be written, however tacitly, into the piece's structural substance.

But all works harbour multiple strata of potential meaning, none of which excludes the others. The institutional stance of *Introduction and Allegro* as a transaction of cultural prestige is only one of its aspects. Elgar also interwove strands of private significance into this music. Many may be irrecoverable, although the glimmers of evidence that we do have are suggestive. However one might regard the work as an individual statement, at its conceptual core is a single melody, appearing four times, that lights up the whole from within. As Elgar himself, shortly after completing work on the composition, described it to Frank Schuster on 13 February 1905, *Introduction and Allegro* was 'the string thing most brilliant with a real tune in it however'.[5] On the same day he wrote a slightly different characterization in a letter to Alfred Littleton: '[The work] is not for amateurs but I think as there are two good tunes in it, it may be boiled down for small String Orch.'[6]

Of the 'two good tunes' mentioned to Littleton, the 'real tune' singled out to Schuster, surely, was what several subsequent commentators have called the 'Welsh' theme. Decades later both Rosa Burley and William H. Reed also referred to it as the 'second subject' or 'second subject-tune' of the composition, although Elgar seems to have thought of it as something standing outside the sonata proper, a point to which I shall return.[7] As will emerge, Elgar set forth the tune in two closely related versions, referred to here as 'weaker' and 'stronger' – a distinction to be amplified in sections 2 and 3 below. For the present we need only note that we first encounter this 'folk-like' theme before the onset of the sonata-form Allegro, about one minute into the piece, shortly into the Moderato, G minor Introduction. Following a grandiloquent, declamatory opening, it emerges at fig. 2:6/b. 18 as a quiet voice in the shadows of G minor's submediant, Eb major, a memory – suffused with longing, melancholia – introduced tenderly by the solo viola, initially in two cycles through the brief melody. Ex. 5.1 shows the tune's immediate preparation from G minor (fig. 2:3–5/bb. 15–17) and its first, 'weaker' cycle on Eb major (fig. 2:6–3:4/bb. 18–29), along with the onset of what turns out to be its altered and 'strong' repetition, the second cycle (fig. 3:5–4:4/bb. 30–41, to be discussed in section 2 below). A fragmented adaptation of the 'stronger' version of the melody is also heard at the end of the G minor Introduction (fig. 6:1–7/bb. 52–8), and the Welsh Tune resurfaces

---

[5] Elgar to Schuster, 13 February 1905, quoted in Kennedy, *Portrait*, p. 219.
[6] Elgar to Littleton, 13 February 1905, in *Publishers*, p. 609.

[7] W. H. Reed, *Elgar as I Knew Him* (London: Gollancz, 1936), pp. 87 and 148 (see n. 19 below); Rosa Burley and Frank C. Carruthers, *Edward Elgar: The Record of a Friendship* (London: Barrie & Jenkins, 1972), p. 156.

twice more in the G major Allegro: the first time only partially, *con sordino*, [*sul*] *ponticello*, and *pianissimo*, the 'weaker' version, now in D major, just before the fugal developmental space (fig. 15:6–12/bb. 137–43; see Ex. 5.5); the final time climactically, the 'stronger' version, near the end, *fortissimo*, in G major (figs. 30:1–31:10/bb. 279–300; see Exx. 5.6 and 5.7).

In pursuit of its connotative richness, our task takes on two dimensions, *vertical* and *horizontal*. A musical idea's vertical meanings refer to what that idea, considered only as an isolated musical module, might seek to allude to beyond itself. Vertical meanings encompass the assigned or implied metaphorical connotations of the musical idea – a constellation of inner connotations considered apart from the idea's contextual placement. An idea's vertical meanings centre on the larger conceptual image or family type onto which we are invited to map it, perhaps in the manner of a leitmotiv or ad hoc musical sign or symbol. What a musical idea, qua idea, might signify in this dimension might be gleaned, as here, from external comments that Elgar and others made about it, as well as from its resonances with historical or generic topoi, intertextual allusions, and the like. From this perspective the 'extramusical' content or implications of an idea are not objectively locatable 'things', literally present as recoverable properties of the music considered neutrally, as an analytical object. On the contrary, such meanings are contingent, socially conditioned, the results of understood agreements between composer and listener – a willingness on both sides to 'play the game', to hear certain kinds of ideas and certain kinds of musical topics and traditions as alluding to larger facets of human experience.[8]

Enriching an idea's vertical meanings from a differing axis are its horizontal meanings. These are the functional and relational meanings that accrue additionally to a musical module by its placement within the linear context of the work at hand. ('*This* module also suggests *that* because it is situated *here* as opposed to *there*.') These meanings are dynamic, relational, and dependent upon contextual placement. Horizontal connotations arise from an idea's position and structural treatment within a musical discourse in dialogue with generic norms, from its use and specific role within a larger formal plan. It is short-sighted to consider a musical idea's potential content as limited only to its abstract vertical connotations or properties plucked out of context. Any idea takes on additional, more telling implications when we

[8] Normally – considered solely on its own terms – an instrumental idea is underdetermined with regard to the explicitness of its representational intent, apart from clues provided by composers and their circles, allusions to past precedents, and the like. On these fundamental features of programme music with or without explicit programmatic titles or paratexts, see Hepokoski, 'Fiery-Pulsed Libertine or Domestic Hero? Strauss's *Don Juan* Reinvestigated', in Bryan Gilliam (ed.), *Richard Strauss: New Perspectives on the Composer and His Work* (Durham NC: Duke University Press, 1992), pp. 135–41; and Hepokoski, 'Beethoven Reception', pp. 434–7.

regard it as something situated at a certain moment within a musical discourse elapsing in time and participating in a generic field of formal tradition and expectation. To access such potential meanings one must grasp the role that the composer has assigned it to play within an ongoing formal structure. This implicates the idea's relation to all that has happened within the piece leading up to that moment as well as to the norms and expected procedures of the genre and tradition in which the piece participates. Vertical meanings – products of the intense, ephemeral moment – are doubtless more immediate, more accessible to general audiences and non-specialists. Horizontal meanings are dependent on one's knowledge of the relevant tradition, one's musical expertise and experience, and one's ability to process a piece as a continuously unfolding entity of interrelated parts. Section 2 below takes up issues of vertical meaning in the Welsh Tune of *Introduction and Allegro*; section 3 proceeds into horizontal meaning, providing also a reading of the form and content of the piece as a whole.

2

From the vertical point of view, what might the central melody from *Introduction and Allegro* (Ex. 5.1, 2:6ff./bb. 18ff.) mean as an isolated idea? Most of the discussion of the theme has focused on this issue. Its 'Welsh' connotations stem from remarks made by the composer himself in programme notes for the 1905 premiere. And here is where the interpretive complications begin. Some three or four years earlier, in mid-August 1901, Rosa Burley had coaxed a 'melancholy' post-*Gerontius* Elgar ('in one of his black moods of depression', she later reported) to take a restorative holiday in Llangranog, Cardiganshire: sea coasts, nearby cliffs, and the spectacular views from the island of Ynys Lochtyn.[9]

Elgar's 1901 holiday was apparently a pleasant one, and upon his return, by mid-November, he was jotting down ideas not only for what would become *The Apostles* and *The Kingdom* but also for the central theme of what would later become *Introduction and Allegro*. At this point, though, the melody's destination was still unclear: one early version is marked 'cor Ang[lais]' and appears in the context of *Apostles* sketches.[10] One tradition

[9] Quoted in *Letters to Nimrod: Edward Elgar to August Jaeger, 1897–1908*, ed. Percy M. Young (London: Dennis Dobson, 1965), p. 140; cf. the similar account in Rosa Burley and Frank C. Carruthers, *Edward Elgar*, p. 155 ('in one of his moods of black depression').
[10] The *Apostles* sketch-page in question is GB-Lbl Add. MS 63153, fo. 13 (see also n. 11 below). A brief description is in Anderson, *Manuscript*, p. 194. Daniel M. Grimley has also suggested that the tune might be associated with what would become the cor anglais, Christ in the wilderness passage of *The Apostles* (' "A Smiling with a Sigh": the Chamber Music and Works for Strings', *Companion*, pp. 120–38, at p. 125).

Ex. 5.1 *Introduction and Allegro*, bb. 15–31

of commentary – probably guided by a remark by Rosa Burley – associates the relevant sketches at this time with a once-planned 'Welsh Overture' (which may eventually have become *Introduction and Allegro*).[11] Other fragmentary evidence – the sketch marked *Pattern for Bag-Poet*, mentioned

[11] Two sketch pages with this melody are identified as belonging to a 'Welsh Overture' in *Letters to Nimrod*, ed. Young, facing pp. 108 and 109. That facing p. 109 is fo. 13^r (the 'Cor Ang' folio; cf. n. 10 above) in a sketchbook dated 'Nov 19, 1901' by Elgar on the first page. Similarly, Young states that the 'independent, quasi folk-song, tune . . . was intended for full orchestra, and for a "Welsh Overture". This tune became the lyrical melody of the *Introduction and Allegro*' (*Elgar*, p. 293). Perhaps following Young, Kennedy suggests en passant that the 1901 tune was first 'planned as part of a "Welsh Overture"'. (*Portrait*, p. 214). Some years after the premiere of *Introduction and Allegro* – presumably long before Young and Kennedy – Rosa Burley also associated this tune with a 'Welsh Overture' (Young, transcribing a document of recollection by Rosa Burley, found a deleted reference to 'the Welsh Overture', immediately corrected to the 'Introduction & Allegro'; he adds by way of commentary: 'That Elgar had a Welsh Overture in mind is indicated by the suggested scoring of the "Welsh" melody in his sketch book [i.e. "Cor Ang"], which is also inscribed "Ynys Llochtryn" [*sic*]' (*Letters to Nimrod*, p. 142). Other accounts of the sketch: 'On the front page of his first sketch book (dated Nov. 19, 1901) Elgar wrote "Ynys Llochtryn" ' (Young, *Elgar*, p. 293); 'On a page headed "Ynys Lochtyn" [*sic*] he set down a number of ideas developing the fall of a minor 3rd which had reached him through the summer atmosphere at Llangranog' (Moore, *Elgar*, p. 361).

more recently by Percy M. Young and Brian Trowell, 'copied out for Alice Elgar' – suggests that the composer might once have considered turning it into a song.[12] In any event, Elgar's original plans for the theme are anything but clear.

By 1905, though, it had found its home in *Introduction and Allegro*, and the composer's programme notes for the premiere centre on an idealized version of the melody's sources. Whether the details are accurate is a matter of conjecture. More important is that Elgar appended the story to the work, framing the music conceptually and lending an otherwise non-programmatic piece an atmosphere of evocatively Welsh local colour and supposedly autobiographical detail. He surely disseminated this story among his friends as well – including his 1901 hostess, Rosa Burley – and it would be repeated by all commentators on the piece. Its central point was that in August 1901 he had been struck by the spontaneous singing that he heard from the Welsh people in and around the seaside villages and islands. Whatever songs he heard, it appears that Elgar, three years or so later, was interpreting them as images of simplicity, purity, and wholeness.

> In Cardiganshire, I thought of writing a brilliant piece for string orchestra. On the cliff, between the blue sea and blue sky, thinking out my theme, there came up to me the sound of singing. The songs were too far away to reach me distinctly, but one point common to all was impressed upon me, and led me to think, perhaps wrongly, that it was a real Welsh idiom – I mean the fall of a third – [here Elgar inserted a musical staff with three crotchets, g^1, e^1, e^{1}].
>
> Fitting the need of the moment, I made the tune which appears in the Introduction (as a link) and in the *Coda* of this work; and so my gaudery became touched with romance. The tune may therefore be called, as is the melody in the overture 'In the South', a *canto popolare*, but the suggesting country is in this case Wales, and not Italy.
>
> The sketch was forgotten until a short time ago, when it was brought to mind by hearing, far down our valley of the Wye, a song similar to that so pleasantly heard on Ynys Lochtyn. The singer of the Wye unknowingly reminded me of my sketch. This I have now completed, and, although there may be (and I hope there is) a Welsh feeling in the one theme – to quote Shakespeare again: 'All the water in the Wye

[12] Percy M. Young, *Alice Elgar: Enigma of a Victorian Lady* (London: Dennis Dobson, 1978), p. 151; Anderson, *Manuscript*, p. 95; Anderson, *Elgar*, p. 373. Compare Brian Trowell: 'Elgar made a little song out of the "Welsh Tune" in the *Introduction and Allegro for Strings* and presented the MS to Alice for texting, with the title "For the Bag Poet" (but no words survive). The term "Bag Poet" is unknown to the *O.E.D.*, but evidently means a poet in one's bag, or household verse-manufacturer. On the title-page of the MS orchestral score of *Sea Pictures*, "C.A.E.", who wrote the text for "In haven", is described in a pencil annotation as "Bag poet". That is not because the text is slightly altered from her earlier "Lute Song" to the same music, but because the "Lute Song" is itself a second attempt to provide words for the tune'. Trowell, 'Elgar's Use of Literature', in Monk, *Literature*, pp. 182–326, at p. 273.

cannot wash the Welsh blood out of its body' – the work is really a tribute to that
sweet borderland where I have made my home.[13]

There is much to consider here. Apart from the presumably Welsh marker
(the falling third) and 1901 holiday connection, one might suspect that in
Elgar's story we are getting an idealized, high-poetic account of all of this. It is
striking, for instance, that the crucial event of overhearing a simple but
authentically 'rooted' melody occurs not merely once but *twice* (the second
time in the Wye valley – close to Wales – presumably around Plas Gwyn,
Hereford, then Elgar's home). Note that Elgar was offering this story four
years after the fact and in the contexts both of 'publicity' and the crafting of a
conceptual context for the reception of the piece. Next, in Elgar's recounting
of these incidents, he was invoking a familiar Romantic trope – aligning
himself with a well-worn aesthetic posture. This was the image of the
melancholy modern artist perched high above the 'natural', non-reflective
world (first on the Welsh cliffs, then on the hills above the Wye valley). From
this detached position the artist is struck by sounds emerging from that
prelapsarian or more naive world from which, with modern consciousness,
he has been effectively exiled. The defining aspects of the image are twofold.
First, we find evocations of artistic 'elevation' or at least the physical separation and distance of the artist from the simpler world of everyday assur-
ances and, more important, from manifestations of a natural beauty
overwhelming in its naivety. Second – because of that separation – what
one hears is only an impression of a blurred, far-away incompleteness. The
conceptual distance that one has travelled in exile from that world has
rendered the integrity of the tunes indistinct: they are intact melodies of
which one is permitted to perceive only hazy images or fading echoes.

The trope could hardly be more familiar. It is a governing idea, for
example, behind Schiller's *Naive and Sentimental Poetry* of 1795–6, an
essay that could serve as a propaedeutic to any sustained inquiry into
Introduction and Allegro. Schiller's naive is that which exists purely, non-
reflectively, in 'simple nature', is at one with it (as with the Welsh voices that
Elgar constructed in his retelling), but it becomes perceptible as such only
when viewed from the perspective of its opposite, the sentimental, a state of
human advancement – and alienated exile – from this originary purity, 'in
the midst of artificial circumstances and situations'. Perceiving the natural as
naive entails the sense 'that nature stand in contrast to art and put it to
shame. As soon as the latter is joined with the former, not before, nature
becomes naive.' Such an awareness of the naive affects us 'particularly

[13] My source is the programme note as
published in Grimley, 'A Smiling with a
Sigh', pp. 124–5. Portions of it had already
appeared in Moore, *Elgar*, pp. 353 and
451–2; Kennedy, *Portrait*, p. 218; and
elsewhere.

powerfully and most universally' when we are confronted with 'such objects as stand in close connection with us, affording a retrospective view of ourselves and revealing more closely the unnatural in us, as, for example, in children and childlike folk'. As for naive objects of all kinds: 'We love in them the tacitly creative life, the serene spontaneity of their activity, existence in accordance with their own laws, the inner necessity, the eternal unity with themselves.' For Schiller, writing from the perspective of the sentimental, the naive can involve the surprise of '*childlikeness where it is no longer expected*', a surprise that can apply 'only insofar as in this moment [a human being is suddenly reminded that] he is no longer pure and innocent nature'. Thus the presumed truth-content of the 'naive of surprise' is dependent on our awareness of 'the contrast between [children's] naturalness and the artificiality in ourselves', an artificiality that is necessarily part of a more philosophically advanced but essentially 'depraved world' within which innocent, natural things and beings are blissfully non-complicit. From the standpoint of the sentimental and its separation from the non-self-reflexive natural, the sudden surprise of encountering naive things or events can stand as both an occasion of admiration and a pang of reproof:

> *They are what we were*; they are what *we should once again become*. We were nature just as they, and our culture, by means of reason and freedom, should lead us back to nature. They are, therefore, not only the representation of our lost childhood, which eternally remains most dear to us, but fill us with a certain melancholy. But they are also representations of our highest fulfilment in the ideal, thus evoking in us a sublime tenderness . . .
>
> What determines their character is precisely what is lacking for the perfection of our own; what distinguishes us from them, is precisely what they themselves lack for divinity. We are free, they are necessary; we change, they remain a unity . . . *In them*, then, we see eternally that which escapes us, but for which we are challenged to strive, and which, even if we never attain to it, we may still hope to approach in endless progress.[14]

Elgar's *Introduction and Allegro* is readily heard under the sign of what Schiller identified as elegy, one of the three registers of the sentimental (along with the satire and the idyll). The elegy is preoccupied with 'sadness at lost joys, at the golden age now disappeared from the world, at happiness departed with youth, with love, and so forth', when 'those states of sensuous

---

[14] Friedrich von Schiller, *Naive and Sentimental Poetry* [*Über naive und sentimentalische Dichtung*, 1795–6] *and On the Sublime; Two Essays*, trans. Julius A. Elias (New York: Ungar, 1966); source for the translation, Schiller, *Säkular-Ausgabe* (ed. Eduard von Hellen, Stuttgart and Berlin: Cotta, 1904–5). P. 83 ('simple nature', 'in the midst of artificial circumstances' [Elias translation, p. 83; Hellen edition p. 161]), p. 84 ('that nature stand' [pp. 161–2]), p. 86 ('particularly powerfully', 'such objects as stand' [p. 164]), p. 85 ('we love in them' [pp. 162–3]), p. 90 ('*childlikeness*'), p. 91 ('only insofar', 'naïve of surprise' [p. 169]), p. 90 ('the contrast between' [p. 168]), p. 93 ('depraved world' [p. 171]), p. 85 ('*They are what we were*', 'What determines' [p. 163]).

satisfaction can also be construed as matters of moral harmony'. Idealizing
the lost past is pivotal: 'The content of poetic lamentation can therefore never
be an external object, it must always be only an ideal, inner one; even if it
grieves over some loss in actuality, it must first be transformed into an ideal
loss.'[15]

The trope runs throughout nineteenth-century literature – the sudden
confrontation with a more guileless world lost to modern poetic consciousness. One can find it, for instance, in Wordsworth's 'The Solitary Reaper'
('Will no one tell me what she sings? – / Perhaps the plaintive numbers flow /
For old, unhappy, far-off things, / And battles long ago: / Or is it some more
humble lay, / Familiar matter of to-day? / Some natural sorrow, loss, or pain, /
That has been, and may be again?' Or in his 'Ode: Intimations of Immortality
from Recollections of Early Childhood' ('Whither is fled the visionary gleam? /
Where is it now, the glory and the dream? . . . Shades of the prison-house
begin to close / Upon the growing Boy, / . . . At length the Man perceives it die
away, / And fade into the light of common day. / . . . Then, sing ye birds, sing,
sing a joyous song! / . . . Though nothing can bring back the hour / Of
splendour in the grass, of glory in the flower'). Or in Keats's 'Ode to a
Nightingale' ('Still wouldst thou sing, and I have ears in vain – / To thy
high requiem become a sod'). Or in Byron's *Manfred*, scene ii, complete with
cliff, mountain, and shepherd's pipe ('Hark! the note, / The natural music
of the mountain reed – / For here the patriarchal days are not / A pastoral
fable . . . / My soul would drink these echoes. Oh, that I were / The viewless
spirit of a lovely sound, / A living voice, a breathing harmony, / A bodiless
enjoyment'). Or in Tennyson's 'Far – Far – Away (For Music)' ('What sound
was dearest in his native dells? / The mellow lin-lan-lone of evening bells /
Far – far – away. / A whisper from his dawn of life? a breath / From some fair
dawn beyond the doors of death / Far – far – away'). Or in dozens of other
such poems[16] – and even in celebrated nineteenth-century musical compositions, such as Berlioz's Byron-grounded *Harold in Italy*.

Some time after the premiere of *Introduction and Allegro* Rosa Burley, in
two separate documents, confirmed Elgar's report in her own descriptions of

[15] pp. 126–7 ('sadness', 'those states' [p. 203]);
p. 127 ('the content' [pp. 203–4], pp. 127–8).
[16] I am grateful to Lawrence Kramer for
suggesting to me, in private communication,
the titles of some famous additional instances
in English poetry of the trope (an 'ideal type
that rarely appears full or intact, but of which
various pieces are periodically found in
combination') or related variants. (Byron's
Manfred was cited by Kramer, en passant, as
'complete with pastoral', a phrase that I have
adapted here.) Related examples brought to
mind by Kramer were: the first episode (ll.
1–61) of Wordsworth's *The Prelude* (1805
version); Tennyson's 'Come Down, O Maid,
from Yonder Mountain Height' (where the
idealized maid is the one occupying the higher
position); Matthew Arnold's 'The Scholar
Gypsy'; and other nineteenth-century
'mediations' or 'readings' of the pastoral
tradition that might well be traceable back to
Virgil's *Eclogues*.

the composer's visit to Wales.[17] Burley's accounts are probably less independent statements than they are well-meaning propagations of an official
line. They were doubtless filtered through Elgar's 1905 retelling of the story.
In any event, they do differ from Elgar's version in a few details. The
composer's elevated position is not insisted upon: if anything it is the singers
(which Burley identified as a choir or choral society) that on one occasion
might occupy the higher ground, 'on the hillside across the bay' from Ynys
Lochtyn ('at that distance no melodic line could be identified but one could
distinguish the very frequent drop of a third, of a minor third, to which
Edward drew my attention as typical of Welsh music'), while on a separate,
additional occasion they are merely 'on the little quay in front of the pub'.
Most important, though, are Burley's descriptions of what must have been
the songs' personal effect on Elgar: 'It was so natural and beautiful' – once
again, the Romantic trope of modern, 'sentimental' distance from the naive,
the lost 'natural and beautiful'.[18]

  Tropes of loss, distance, and yearning lie at the heart of much of Elgar's
music. They resonate with a commonly encountered style of his often
depressive response to the world, manifesting itself in different ways at
different times. Although these are not adequately tabulated on a simple
list, they would include the shattering loss of the innocence and security of an
earlier time to which he would return; the loss of friendships; the loss of an
overarching happiness in life (perhaps even love); the loss of hopes for his art
and his 'outsider' status within it; and, as some documents suggest, the
corroding, if intermittent, loss of religious faith as well. From this perspective
the spatial distance of the only partially heard 'Welsh' or 'Wye' tune – in
Elgar's story – is readily converted into an image of temporal loss as well:
the loss of the once-whole security of the past, both personal and historical.
The valley of the Wye suddenly – metaphorically – becomes the valley of the
irrecoverably lost past.

---

[17] Burley and Carruthers, *Edward Elgar*,
pp. 155–6, and *Letters to Nimrod*, ed. Young,
pp. 140–2.
[18] Quoting Burley: 'A little company of men
used to collect on the little quay in front of the
pub. They used to talk & smoke and then
someone would hum a note and they would all
sing a hymn or song in four part harmony. It
was so natural and beautiful,' in *Letters to
Nimrod*, ed. Young, p. 142. Burley also
mentioned the 'hillside' incident in this
account and credited that as the source for the
'translated … effect' in *Introduction and
Allegro*. Compare Diana McVeagh's
'recreation' of Elgar's experience; she describes

Ynys Lochtyn, 'that tiny but steep-sided islet at
the low north end of the great peninsula.
Unlikely that Elgar could have climbed onto it
without grappling irons, and if he had, the
great bulk of the cliff behind him would have
cut off sounds of singing. So he probably
thought that Ynys Lochtyn was the name of
the whole headland.' McVeagh also speculates,
reporting a discussion with a local choir
director, that 'Elgar might have heard a
neighbouring Sunday School outing, and that
one of the tunes [might have been] the hymn
"Moriah".' McVeagh, ' "Moriah" and the
Introduction and Allegro', *ESJ*, 4/4 (1986),
pp. 23–4.

But the vertical connotations of the Welsh Tune are not exhausted by only one approach, even though that approach seems primary. Other stories about its implications – along with later conjectures, in part based on sketch evidence – have appeared over the years. W. H. Reed wrote in 1936, for instance, that one moment in the piece – the third (*ponticello*) appearance (fig. 15:6–12/bb. 137–43) – captured 'an exact impression' of a breeze-driven Aeolian harp lodged in the window of Elgar's home.[19] Still other conjectures have involved the possible connection with *The Apostles* and Ian Parrott's provocative suggestion about the possibility of underlaying a hand-clasping text of Alice Elgar's poem, 'Reconciliation', under the tune.[20] The 'Welsh' music, in its vertical dimension, is a complex, ad hoc symbol combining aspects of nature, yearning, distance, and spiritual loss that Elgar may have been taking in a personalized sense.

Combining the vertical, Welsh associations of the theme with other generalized aspects of the composition encourages some initial observations about the work as a whole. In response to the London Symphony Orchestra commission Elgar seems to have brought together a number of differing

[19] 'When I first visited Elgar at his home in Hereford, he had an Aeolian harp, of which he was very fond, in the crack of a partly opened window, so that the breeze blowing across the strings set them in vibration. This produced a shimmering musical sound of elfin quality, the strings being tuned to concordant intervals; therefore the effect, when the velocity of the wind varied and swept across the strings, was entrancing . . . In the Introduction and Allegro for Strings, when the *tremolo* in the violins begins against the second subject-tune in the quartet, the *crescendo* and *diminuendo* in the *tremolo* give an exact impression of the minstrelsy of that harp in the window.' William H. Reed, *Elgar as I Knew Him*, pp. 147–8. See also the discussion of Elgar and the Aeolian harp in Matthew Riley, 'Rustling Reeds and Lofty Pines: Elgar and the Music of Nature', *19CM*, 26 (2002), pp. 155–77.

Reed also provided a more 'standard' retelling of the Welsh source of the tune. '[Elgar] would not rave about folk-tunes. I don't think he ever made use of one in his works. He held that the business of a composer is to compose, not to copy. Certainly the second subject in the Introduction and Allegro for Strings has a slight folkish flavour; but that was because he was sitting out on the Cardigan coast one day when some Welsh people were having some sort of gathering a little way off; and, as they always do when they get together, they burst into song. Their music came to him

on the wind as he sat there. Their tunes and phrases were nothing to him; but he seized on the effect with which, whatever they were singing, the interval of a falling minor third seemed to predominate; so he wrote the subject, [four and a half bars of the Welsh Tune, in E♭, with a two-flat signature] etc., which, though entirely his own tune, shows how susceptibly he could extract honey from wild flowers. I suspect that the tune of the *canto popolare* from *In the South* may have come to him on the wind in Italy in the same manner' (*Elgar as I Knew Him*, p. 87).

[20] On the possible connection with *The Apostles*, see Grimley, 'A Smiling with a Sigh', p. 125. Parrott quotes Alice Elgar's lines: 'Come back, and lay thy hand, / As thou wast wont – just so, / Within mine own; then stand / And smile, and whisper "Lo" ', and continues: 'All Elgarians will know the bars which follow my quotation, marked "largamente", "molto espress" and "ff", as an agonized outburst. Like the wringing of hands, what do they mean specifically? Perhaps we need not delve.' Parrott, 'Elgar's Harmonic Language', in Monk, *Studies*, pp. 35–45, at pp. 37–8. Parrott also proposes, rather than McVeagh's suggestion of a 'Moriah' source for the Welsh Tune (see n. 18 above), 'the second half of [the Welsh national anthem], *Hen Wlad fy Nhadau*', as 'the most likely music, with dropping thirds, to have influenced the 'Welsh' theme' (ibid., pp. 36–7).

conceptions in *Introduction and Allegro*. First, the fourteen-minute work would be in overture format – perhaps a recasting of the earlier 'Welsh Overture' plan. If so, it would continue, albeit more abstractly, a series of concert overtures evocative of specific locations (*Cockaigne* and London; *In the South* and Italy). Second, the work would be written not merely for large string orchestra but for strings supplemented by a more intimate string quartet placed in front of the orchestra. Strings plus string quartet would be a textural reference to the distant Baroque past (another valley below), and this texture, in part, would also help to set up the neo-Baroque connotations of the brilliant 'modern fugue'. Third, there was the elaborate fugue itself, initially suggested by Jaeger in October 1904,[21] which occupies the middle section of the sonata form, that is, its developmental space, treated as a dazzling centrepiece. And fourth – somehow apart from the central display-fugue – the larger purpose of the piece was to pivot on the fortunes of the nostalgic Welsh Tune, the evocation of a simpler, whole past, now distant (far below), lost to modern times. This theme was to serve both as the source of intermittent, shadowy side-events in the course of the otherwise mostly shiny-bright piece and, ultimately, as the climactic string apotheosis at its end.

Introduced by the solo viola and supported by *pianissimo* strings in the orchestra, this twelve-bar Welsh Tune (Ex. 5.1), is grounded in a repetitive circularity, conveying a drifting away from linear time through expressive repetitions of a single melodic idea, a dissolving into an idealized, indulgently constructed memory. We have already noticed that the tune is first presented in two cycles (figs. 2:6–3:4/bb. 18–29, figs. 3:5–4:4/bb. 30–41). More to the point, each cycle comprises multiple sub-cycles or inner reiterations of a two-bar idea treated in sequences. As will emerge, it is important to observe that Elgar provides each of the two twelve-bar cycles with a slightly different harmonization: the most prominent variants are found between their fifth and eighth bars. I distinguish these as the 'weaker' (more 'modal' in its central modules) and 'stronger' (more cadentially directed) versions of the tune. While the differences between the two versions might seem relatively innocent, even straightforward, in this first presentation of the tune, in their subsequent appearances throughout the work Elgar differentiates them expressively, and his selection of either the one or the other at crucial

---

[21] Jaeger to Elgar, 28 October 1904. Jaeger initially suggested 'a *brilliant* quick *String Scherzo* . . . a real bring down the House *torrent* of a thing such as Bach could write (Remember that Cologne Brandenburger Concerto!) a five minutes work would do it! . . . You might even write a *modern Fugue* for Strings' (*Publishers*, p. 595). Moore notes that Jaeger was referring to a performance of Bach's Third Brandenburg Concerto 'conducted by Fritz Steinbach at the lower Rhine Festival in May 1904' (Moore, *Elgar*, p. 451, n. 234).

moments becomes a significant factor in assessing the theme's horizontal implications within the larger discourse.

In each version we encounter a short thematic-modular shape led higher and lower through different harmonic colorations – a quintessentially Elgarian procedure, one of his musical thumbprints. In this case the fundamental shape is a six-note contour-module restated on different pitch levels, each of which exerts a different emotional pull on the original idea. These affective colours project a shifting, positive-negative chiaroscuro, dependent on the expressive effects and interplays of sequential ascent (suggesting positive) versus sequential descent (negative) and major harmony (positive) versus minor harmony (negative). The result – again distinctively Elgarian – is that of a single, reiterative, small musical contour being moved up and down through different affective regions, as if inviting us to feel the nuanced moods of each of these harmonic nooks: a more or less stable identity or persona groping its way through a tellingly expressive harmonic field of lights and darks.

What we first hear, then, is the 'weaker' version – that shown in Ex. 5.1. Its first eight bars (bb. 18–25) are built from four statements of this two-bar cell (grouped $(2+2)+(2+2)$ bars or aa') as if trying to capture it, to make its indistinct pastness more fully present through sheer repetition. The first of the four statements (bb. 18–19) brings us the nostalgic, six-note Welsh 'memory-cell' emerging *pianissimo* on the gateway-opening tonic $^6_4$ sonority: the clouds part; the vision begins. These first two bars clarify the new tonic, Eb major, through a descending bass (via a passing V^4_2 in b. 18, beats 3–4) that finally completes the stabilization of Eb with the attaining of the tonic chord in root position in b. 20. The immediate repetition of the Welsh idea, bb. 20–1, settles snugly into the protective comforts of this new Eb major, cradled with the rocking of cosy tonic–dominant oscillation: the passing sensation of a once-glimpsed security. The earlier dactylic supportive rhythms in the string orchestra, bobbing repetitions of dotted crotchet and quaver (bb. 18–19), also broaden out here to dotted minim and crotchet.

The third statement, bb. 22–3, provides us with its intensification one step higher, elevated onto the major subdominant, as if initiating a normative harmonic progression with a strong chordal move. But now the characteristic elements of the 'weaker' version unfold. This *major*-mode subdominant slips down a notch at once, to the *minor* mediant in b. 23 (that is, to the more modally 'antique' or 'remote' iii). To be sure, this moment of wistful, downward slippage away from a 'strong', forward-looking pre-dominant onto a 'weak' mediant may be taken locally as a signifier of a pre-modern, 'Welsh' folk-authenticity. Still, the descent onto iii here leads to a parallel slippage in the next bar as well (the beginning of the next two-bar cell) onto the minor-mode supertonic in b. 24, thereby tracing a threefold set of descending parallel $\frac{5}{3}$ triads (major–minor–minor), with parallel tenths between the melody and the bass (bb. 22–4). These seemingly small harmonic details, these parallel-motion falls away from the brighter, major-mode subdominant, are the primary markers of the 'weaker' version. More than bearers of the merely picturesque or antique, they may be heard also as suggesting a sinking of the heart, an alienated pang of a distance that cannot be bridged. Here in bb. 22–3, instead of the anticipated strong progression, we experience the collapsing chordal succession A♭–g, in which the stark parallels and sudden shift to a *minor*-chord sonority is mediated only by the half-diminished vii $\frac{6}{5}$ in b. 22, beat 4. The 4–3 melodic suspension over iii in b. 23 – a sigh, a mere descent of a second, not of a third, as in the model (b. 19) – is also telling. It reinforces the deflationary, minor-sonority downturn of spirits, suggesting the sense of how distant, how evaporative, this musical vision might be.

While the third statement of the thematic cell had begun more affirmatively, a step *higher* than the original model and on a major chord, the fourth statement, bb. 24–5, begins a step *lower* than that model. And it brings us, in this initially presented 'weaker' version, through two more darkly colorized stages of this downward, quasi-modal disintegration: first, as mentioned above, through parallel $\frac{5}{3}$ slippage onto the supertonic (ii, b. 24); then, starkly – with a sobering plunge of a fourth in the bass onto C, a collapse of the 'merely' descending seconds preceding it, A♭, G, F – onto the sub-mediant (vi, b. 25), both with resigned minor-mode inflections.[22] In sum, in the first eight bars of the theme, Elgar provides us with an up-and-down wave of modular reiterations, moving from a nurturingly secure promise of normative diatonic harmony grounded in major-sonority chords (I–IV) to a 'weak', decaying dissolution onto more remote, modally antique minor-sonority chords (iii–ii–vi).

These bars of decay are responded to with an anguished two-bar continuation, bb. 26–7, surging forth *fortissimo*, *largamente*, and *molto espress[ivo]*. Here the full quartet rushes in with a module enriched by expressive inner-part voice-leading, bold contrary-motion contours between the first violin and the cello (as if the two normally 'outer' lines were straining momentarily to touch or embrace each other, however futilely, at the downbeat of b. 27), and much voice-crossing in the lowest three parts. Is this to be taken as an outpouring of false-hope resistance against the 'weak' deflation of the initially major-mode thematic module down to minor-mode loss? Is it a privately confessional gesture, as Ian Parrott has suggested, 'an agonized

[22] Scoring and register are also central participants in these opening eight bars (along with dynamic swells and receding diminuendos). Notice especially the open-string G and C in the cello, both with spectrally 'hollow', open-string fifths (d, g) directly above them, underpinning the minor-mode iii and vi (bb. 23 and 25).

outburst. Like the wringing of hands?'[23] Or is it, as I suspect, a desperate attempt to keep the vision from fading, a plea for it not to disappear altogether? With its impassioned swerve back into non-modal diatonicism, its function in this 'weaker' version of the theme (in which the defining characteristic is that the minor-mode decay appears in the *second* four bars of the theme, *before* any opportunity for this shoring-up) is that of a forceful reaction ('No!') to the preceding disintegration into minor-sonority quasi-modality, as if seeking to pull the music back to a lost tonal principle, to cling onto what is dissolving away. So much is clear from the underlying current of harmonies. A half-diminished vii$_3^4$ (b. 26 as a whole, beginning, though, as 'f^6' ii^6 on beat 1 before being immediately enriched into a Tristanesque, half-diminished seventh with the leading-note as root)[24] serves as a trigger-chord initiating a descending circle-of-fifths progression that seeks to reinstate and stabilize the tonal E♭ major on which the theme had begun. What follows are iii^7 (b. 27, beats 1 and 2, reclaiming the G minor chord that had marked the moment of modal decay in b. 23), vi (beats 3 and 4), ii^7 (b. 28), and the now fully secure V^7 (B♭^{7}, b. 29; the seventh is provided by the second violins on beat 4). In these final two bars of this portion of the theme (bb. 28–9) the preceding central outburst (bb. 26–7) subsides and yields to a *pianissimo* return of a variant of the basic idea.

It is possible to interpret what we have heard in bb. 18–29 in differing ways. From one angle it may seem to articulate a compound musical idea anticipating a perfect authentic cadence of closure (E♭: PAC) at its end but kept from that PAC by being stopped short on its dominant in b. 29. From another standpoint the dominant arrival at b. 29 invites us to hear it as functioning locally as a half cadence (with passing seventh on beat 4) – a harmonic interruption – and the Welsh Tune recommences in b. 30 with what becomes a harmonically strengthened repetition or second cycle of the theme, launched again with an E♭ chord in $^6_4$ position. By this point, one might suppose, the theme's formal signals seem clear: bb. 18–29 may be construed as a three-limbed, 'weaker' twelve-bar sentential antecedent – ([2 + 2] + [2 + 2]) + (2 + 2) – decaying toward minor chords and a quasi-modality in the middle (that is, the end of the presentation modules in the seventh and eighth bars) but shored up tonally at the end (in the sentence's continuation, beginning in the ninth bar) with a more 'determined' circle-of-fifths descent, producing a 'weak' dominant arrival (the last notch of the circle), which is then to be taken contextually either as a half cadence proper or as a nearly identical substitute for one.[25]

[23] Parrott, 'Elgar's Harmonic Language', p. 38.
[24] The potential for a *Tristan* chord reference at this point was suggested by Patrick McCreless; see also this volume, pp. 8–18.

[25] The terminology and concerns at issue here may need clarification. In many cases a dominant arrival (as in b. 29) following a mere chain of descending fifths might not strike all

As the theme restarts in b. 30 in the full string orchestra (also doubled in the upper two voices of the quartet) with an enriched accompaniment and a texturally enhanced quality of emergence), we notice that a number of other things about it have also been altered (see Ex. 5.2). From its opening through b. 37, for instance, its bass line advances consistently in more self-assured crotchets. Not only do they provide a less tentative initial linear fifth-descent in the bass to the E♭ chord root (B♭–E♭ now in only five beats, bb. 30–31; cf. the slower, nine-beat descent in the "weaker" version, bb. 18–20), but their measured, striding pulses, proceeding with smooth confidence, will eventually provide the bass foundation for the 'English-imperial' apotheosis of the theme in the coda (b. 279). In addition, we also perceive that a crucial portion of the Welsh Tune's melodic contours and harmonic content differs from those of the first cycle. At the moment where the "weaker" version of the theme had lapsed into minor-mode-grounded quasi-modality and the concomitant descent of a *second* (Ex. 5.1, b. 23), here in the 'stronger' version that decay is repaired, fortified, made 'stronger' and more locally confident by impressing the entrenched diatonicism into the service of a more traditionally linear harmonic progression (Ex. 5.2, bb. 34–7: ii^6 in b. 34 leading to varying positions of V^7) and by altering the initial major-second melodic descents in the 'weaker' version to more consistent, more confident thirds (Ex. 5.2, bb. 35 and 37). Such alterations give this version of the theme a differing character. Now the impassioned *largamente* 'response' (Ex. 5.2, bb. 38–9) is not shoring up two preceding bars of 'modal' dissolution (as in the 'weaker' version) but responding to two bars of a confidently growing cadential strength. Notwithstanding the local 'stalling' or slippage onto the half-diminished, Tristanesque vii$^4_3$ expressed by b. 38 as a whole, a broadened drive-to-cadence seems well in hand. Here, more than in the 'weaker' version, we anticipate an E♭:PAC of closure within only a few bars – in which case the 'stronger' version would produce the normative parallel consequent to the antecedent of bb. 18–29. However banal such a cadential conclusion might seem to us in retrospect – knowing the piece as a whole – at least for the moment such a cadence would seal off the theme as a completed formal structure and make this E♭ major vision more 'real', more graspable, by

listeners as bearing the potential of conveying a strong half-cadence effect. At stake is the formal definition of what is required to produce what we should regard as a legitimate half cadence. Still, the metrical and schematic positioning of such a dominant within an ongoing, unmistakably generic theme-type (large antecedent) is also in play here – decisively so, in my view. On the problematics of dominant arrivals versus half cadences, see William E. Caplin in 'The Classical Cadence: Conceptions and Misconceptions', *JAMS*, 57 (2004), pp. 51–117. The issue is revisited further – including some disagreements with Caplin – in Hepokoski and Warren Darcy, *Elements of Sonata Theory: Norms, Types and Deformations in the Late-Eighteenth-Century Sonata* (New York: Oxford University Press, 2006), pp. 24 (nn. 1–2), 27–8 (n. 6), and 31 (n. 11).

Ex. 5.2 *Introduction and Allegro*, bb. 28–49

completing the thought with a sign of closure and attainment.[26] But Elgar does not permit this nostalgic tune to conclude. What one might have predicted would be a 'stronger' consequent, bb. 30–41, is only a fortified version of the antecedent. It ends not with an E♭:PAC but again only with a weak dominant arrival, b. 41, this time an even weaker one that avoids a root-position dominant in the final bar, continuing a diminuendo that is soon choked back to triple *pianissimo*. In short, Elgar brings the 'stronger' version of the theme close to a potential cadence point, then draws back from that cadence with another dominant arrival marked also by a reverential hush that then merges into a hazy appendix prolonging and enhancing the reverie, bb. 42–6.

[26] On the attainment of full closure via a PAC – even at the phrase level – and the concomitant transformation of potential or merely proposed tonics into fully 'real' tonics, see Hepokoski and Darcy, *Elements of Sonata Theory*, pp. 20 and 250–1.

Although brief, the appendix falls even deeper into the still-non-closed dream. Even while the metrical beats of real time continue to tick away – though almost in the background – the compositional time of the piece is put on hold. Intoxicated by what precedes it, the appendix at b. 42 brackets off the outside world, drifts even further away from the forward-vectored 'responsibilities' of a formal musical composition. Beginning at triple *pianissimo*, a six-bar, cradle-rocking prolongation of an E♭ chord unexpectedly drops down a step, in an even more hushed, quadruple *pianissimo* (now 'asleep' to the world, absorbed into a full withdrawal), onto a foreign D♭ chord, b. 43, beat 3 – the magic moment (achingly, 'if only!'), ♭VII of the local E♭, a distant ♭V of the more broadly governing G minor and its responsibilities.

But while the nostalgic Welsh Tune, saturated with Schillerian naivety, may fleetingly trigger a welcome shift of modern consciousness – a vision of escape into a warmly nurturing security – the glimpsed vision cannot last, nor can it ever be fully closed. It is as though Elgar were suggesting metaphorically that the purity of the Welsh Tune, welling up indistinctly from the cleaner valleys of the past, could in fact be fully recovered or 'made real' for us if – *if* – we could rejoin its innocence by managing to bring that distant idea to a real, cadential conclusion: a perfect authentic cadence in the relevant tonic of the theme, in the pursuit of which the 'stronger' version of the theme is an essential constituent. But that closure never happens. And that, surely, is its point. And so in b. 46 the stilled reverie, having settled statically on the distant D♭, is unsettled via a common-tone diminished chord, bolstered by the resolve of a sudden, broad crescendo-swell, in order to re-enter the compositional task at hand, to return to the prosaic duties of the commission, with its *Tempo primo* return to G minor and grim reignition of the piece's opening: b. 47 = b. 1, albeit now more unstably, over the dominant. (Again Wordsworth's Ode: 'Whither is fled the visionary gleam?')

In the Introduction, then, Elgar floats two differing cycles of the Welsh Tune past our awareness – a 'weaker' and a 'stronger' version – but provides neither with a final crystallizing into a perfect authentic cadence. This will also be a decisive feature of this theme in all of its subsequent appearances in the Allegro. Regardless of the version, this musical idea is fated to remain an incomplete hope, unable to bring itself to an end, incapable of fixing itself as a secured reality by means of a cadence. As a result, it takes on the character of a musical mirage, a vision that can never be adequately materialized. To return again to the Romantic trope of the despairing modern artist standing on illusion-shattered ground: in modern times, such cleanness and innocence can never be more than a mirage from the naive past, something that dissolves into vapour when we try to grasp it or make it real. This understanding of the theme resonates with what we know of one facet of Elgar's personality: his intense nostalgia for lost childhood wonder – a common

theme of poignant yearning and regret also prominent in much late
Victorian and Edwardian culture. (One need hardly point out that we find
it also, for instance, in Lewis Carroll and, especially, in such works as J. M.
Barrie's evocation of 'Neverland' in *Peter Pan*, published in 1904, only one
year before *Introduction and Allegro*.)[27]

In sum, there is something 'vertically' in the theme, in each of its appearances, to suggest that it is a poignant fantasy, a glimpse of Neverland, a futile
yearning for a permanently lost wholeness. This aspect of the theme pervades
the entire conception of *Introduction and Allegro*. The work may be interpreted as an aesthetic attempt to make this illusion real, to place it into a
context where it will be able to complete itself with a cadence and become
tangible once again – the past recovered through art, through the structural
processes of music. But this brings us to the *horizontal* implications of the
music: its articulation of loss within the larger structure of the whole.

3

From this horizontal or linear-structural perspective, the three-minute
Introduction may be construed as a sonic image of the social circumstances
of the work to follow – a representation of the plotting-out of the sonata-
form-to-come, all considered in the external context of the London
Symphony Orchestra's request for a substantial and brilliant work. The
Introduction is built from three musical ideas. The composition begins
with a resplendent, stiffly formal G minor exhortation, perhaps suggesting
the seriousness of the task at hand, the commission itself: 'Attention!' or
'Let's build a grand piece – a grand sonata for strings – for this new national
orchestra!' (Ex. 5.3, bb. 1–4). The open-fifth, open-string resonance of the
downbeat precipitates both the archaic flavour of much of what is to follow
and the sonorous richness that this string orchestra is about to provide.
A threefold statement of the self-important, tumbling triplets – 'exhortation'
or 'the commission' – leads to an expectant pause, V of G minor, on the
second half of b. 4, awaiting the action to follow.

Picking up on the cue, a second idea springs forth (Ex. 5.3, bb. 5–6, fig. 1).
Retailored into the major mode and refitted onto different scale-degrees, it
will be used as the main theme at the outset of the Allegro (7:1/b. 59): 'And
this will be our sonata's first subject (primary theme, or P).' (In the manuscript Elgar wrote the words, 'A smiling with a sigh' over this melody, and the

---

[27] The relation of Elgar's 'retrospective
aesthetic' to the work of such writers as these is
explored in Michael Allis, 'Elgar and the Art of
Retrospective Narrative', *Journal of
Musicological Research*, 19/4 (2000),
pp. 289–328.

Ex. 5.3 *Introduction and Allegro*, bb. 1–8

words appeared also in Elgar's programme note for the 1905 premiere.)[28] Additionally, this incipit of the primary-theme-to-come obviously 'pushes toward' the Welsh Tune in its insistent dactylic rhythm. Moreover, it leads at once to another modular fragment to be associated with P, a swelling figure sounded in the bass in bb. 7–8, here inflected towards D minor. Following a gentler restart of the initial, annunciatory idea (b. 9, now on an A major chord, locally heard as V of D minor) and some wistful, parallel-fourth, 'bichordal' arpeggiations (b. 10: the regeneration of the creative impulse? the inflowing of inspiration? a gentle movement of the spirit toward the next theme? the dream that is music?),[29] we hear again a fragment of the 'primary-theme'

---

[28] Grimley, 'A Smiling with a Sigh', p. 124. See also Kennedy, *Portrait*, p. 220. The allusion, provocatively enough, is to Shakespeare's *Cymbeline*, IV.ii, Arviragus's description (outside a cave in the mountains of western Wales, no less) of his impression of Imogen, who is in fact his sister, but has disguised herself as a youth named 'Fidele'. Arviragus and his brother believe she is a boy, and yet she provokes, mysteriously, a strong emotional attraction from them. Upon her exit into the cave: 'How angel-like he sings! . . . Nobly he yokes / A smiling with a sigh, as if the sigh / Was that it was, for not being such a smile; / The smile mocking the sigh, that it would fly /

From so divine a temple, to commix / With winds that sailors rail at.' Shakespeare, *Cymbeline*, Act IV, scene ii, lines 48 and 51–56 (reference from the Arden edition, ed. J. M. Nosworthy (London and New York: Routledge, 1955), p. 120).

[29] On the face of it, the *pianissimo* bichordal arpeggiations in bb. 10–11 would seem to be a more obvious candidate for the representation of Elgar's window-lodged Aeolian harp (though associated by Reed with a later recurrence of the 'Welsh' theme; one wonders whether he might have mistakenly provided the wrong reference. See n. 19 above.

proposals (b. 13, now starting on F but soon returning to G minor, b. 15), and ultimately a drift into the third idea, the two versions of the nostalgic Welsh Tune on E♭ major (Exx. 5.1 and 5.2). In his programme note Elgar called the theme a 'link' – whatever that might mean – but the most likely connotation at the moment is: 'And this will be the sonata's lyrical, "second subject" (S). Can past innocence be recaptured, made real, in this sonata?'

Elgar's Introduction could be understood as composing out the idea of the commission and staging what he might have wanted his listeners to regard, in the manner of a tabular prolepsis (flash-forward), as the most recognizable plan for its two most central structural themes. This reading – by no means the only one possible – construes the Introduction as a projection of the compositional process and the nature of the compositional planning. (This is a self-representational trope historically foreshadowed in late Beethoven, most famously in the finales of the *Hammerklavier* Sonata and the Ninth Symphony.) In its larger formal layout, Elgar's Introduction unfolds as a series of rotations: repeated modular cycles with, in this case, modular accretions as they move toward the exposition. Each cycle starts with the introductory exhortation, which also serves, therefore, as a signal of rotational rebeginning:

start–1:1:4/bb. 1–8	Rotation 1	Exhortation – P-fragment
1:5–4:9/bb. 9–46	Rotation 2	Exhortation – 'bichordal drift' – P-fragment – 'S' (at length)
5:1–6:7/bb. 47–58	Rotation 3	Exhortation – 'pause' and backward glance at 'S'-fragment before proceeding

The third rotation leads most directly into the sonata-to-come. Once again the exhortation pauses (as in Rotation 1) on a strong V^7 chord (V^7 of G minor, fig. 6:1/b. 52, in this case fortified with two preceding string chords): 'Now let the sonata begin!' Indeed, the dominant chord could pass directly into the exposition, fig. 7:1/b. 59. Instead, following a sharp diminuendo, the music drifts off once more, fig. 6:2–7/bb. 53–8, to a reflective, sombre reconfiguration of the dropping thirds of the Welsh Tune dream – again heard here as a 'stepping-out' of the predicted responsibilities of the moment, a stopping of compositional time (although the dropping thirds also gratifyingly lead the top voice d^2 of b. 52 to the d^1 onset of P at the beginning of the exposition): 'Is it possible? *Can* we recapture, if only in music, what is otherwise forever lost?' The third introductory cycle propels us into the Allegro proper, where its interior contents are much expanded with the added material necessary to flesh out a full-scale sonata exposition.[30]

[30] One might notice that Rotations 1 and 2 begin with the succession: exhortation–P. Rotation 2 furnishes an 'expanded' version of Rotation 1 by branching out further into a proposed S: thus Rotation 2 recycles and varies Rotation 1, providing also new

But something strange happens in the G major Allegro. The introduction had seemed to suggest that the incomplete Welsh Tune could serve structurally as its secondary theme – and recall that even though Elgar himself called it only a 'link', it was identified as the piece's 'second subject' by both Rosa Burley and W. H. Reed. Moreover, considered both historically and generically, it would have provided a familiar type of secondary theme – initially recessive, *dolcissimo*, intimate, circular, sensuous, and destined for an apotheosis of triumph at the end, a standard feature of many later nineteenth-century secondary themes, often with 'feminine' or possibly eroticized connotations, as I have proposed elsewhere, from Weber's overtures onward.[31] And yet within this work it does not serve in that secondary-theme capacity at all.

The Allegro launches a cleverly complicated exposition. The G major primary theme – the one proposed in the introduction, 'smiling with a sigh', pressing wistfully towards the Welsh Tune's rhythm – is shaped as a (perhaps-Mendelssohnian) rounded-binary idea, AA'BA'' whose final, much-expanded limb (A'', at fig. 9:1/b. 75), as is often characteristic, begins an energy-gaining transition of the dissolving-reprise type, thus pushing toward what should be the relatively efficient preparation for the secondary theme.[32] But it is clear that at the exposition's centre, just where we might

elements. Rotation 3, on the other hand, provides us with exhortation-S, seeming to 'omit' the second element, P, although this S-fragment (fig. 6:2–7/bb. 53–8) is followed by a more expansive version of P (as an exposition) at fig. 6:8/b. 59. It is possible to construe this expositional P (b. 59) as the more normative *second* element of an ongoing, even larger rotation that had begun at fig. 5:1/b. 47 with the exhortation. (Put another way: a P-*prolepsis* had followed the exhortation in both Rotations 1 and 2; what had been a mere prolepsis in those rotations is now launched in earnest as the first forward-vectored impulse of an exposition.) This would suggest that in any such even more extended 'third' rotation the P-element flowers into a decisively new tempo and into a full exposition proper, finally 'crossing a conceptual line', as it were, between introduction and Allegro. Such a view would have to contend with the 'out-of-place' S-fragment at fig. 6:2–7/bb. 53–8, which might be relegated to the status of a backward-looking, 'non-rotational' (or 'extra-rotational') *interpolation* within Rotation 3 – a rotational 'pause' before proceeding, perhaps a pause that reflects on the expected role that this 'proposed S'

might have to play within the exposition-to-come, perhaps merely marking a reluctance to tear oneself away from the dream in order to plunge into the task at hand. Should one wish to pursue this line of interpretation, one might contend that the now much more expansive Rotation 3 (part of an unfolding series of increasingly complex rotations) would stretch from the 'third' exhortation at fig. 5:1/b. 47 (a return to the duties of 'the commission') through the end of the exposition, probably best regarded, as will be proposed later in this essay, as occurring at fig. 15:1/b. 132, some twelve bars before the start of the fugal development at fig. 15:13/b. 144.

[31] I refer here to the typical S-theme treatment in what I have called the 'Dutchman' expositional model (so named because of its influential deployment in the overture to Wagner's Overture to *Der fliegende Holländer*). See Hepokoski, 'Masculine–Feminine', *MT*, 135 (1994), pp. 494–9, and 'Beethoven Reception' (see n. 3 above).

[32] The guidelines (and classical precedents) for these terms and assessments are laid out in Hepokoski and Darcy, *Elements of Sonata Theory*, Chapters 3–6.

158 James Hepokoski

Ex. 5.4 *Introduction and Allegro*, bb. 85–91

etc.

have expected the Welsh Tune to surface as that secondary theme, what we find instead is an idea that seems more appropriate as a nervous, quasi-transitional cover-up (Ex. 5.4). This is built from nervously chattering semi-quavers on a phrygian-inflected D major at fig. 10:1/b. 85. Moreover – and most problematically – it was this theme that was identified as 'the second subject' in the analytical portion of the 1905 programme notes written by Edgar F. Jacques and F. Gilbert Webb, proofs of which were approved by Elgar.[33] This theme is constructed from a single musical module that regularly elides with slightly varied versions of itself on the downbeat of its fourth bar, sometimes with a sudden harmonic shift at the joining-point. As a result the modular shape is made to chatter away on different pitch levels: on its tonic D (bb. 85–8), on D again, lifting up to the dominant as its last move (bb. 88–91), on the dominant A, returning to D for the next statement (fig. 10:7/bb. 91–4), and finally back to that D, more expansively (11:1ff./bb. 94ff.). As will be seen, this aspect of 'movable', edgy harmonic shifting will play an important role in the recapitulation.

For now, we may be content to observe that this supposed 'second subject' eventually drives to what may be regarded as a rhetorically expansive perfect

---

[33] 'Development ensues, and we then reach the second subject [solo violin 1, bb. 85–7]'. I thank Daniel M. Grimley for providing me with a copy of the 1905 notes. Moore, following the original programme notes, also considered it to be the 'second subject', which he then claimed, somewhat puzzlingly (perhaps on the basis of its notable third?), 'developed the "Welsh" theme in semiquavers' (Moore, *Elgar*, p. 453). This opinion, not self-evident to the present writer, was shared by Michael Hurd: 'A contrasting subject – a bustling semiquaver figure full of nervous energy and subtly based on the general shape of the 'Welsh' tune – appears at fig. 10.' Preface to the score (London: Eulenburg, 1985), p. v.

authentic cadence in D. This is built from a powerfully articulated dominant attained at fig. 11:9/b. 102, which is then hurtled vigorously into an airy emptiness, through which determinedly vectored strings rush and fall toward the inevitable tonic resolution four bars later, landing squarely on the octave Ds on the downbeat of fig. 12:1/b. 106.[34] Under this interpretation b. 106 represents a structural moment of central importance to the exposition: the attaining of the point of essential expositional closure (the EEC) – the generically requisite attaining of the first satisfactory perfect authentic cadence in the secondary key (V:PAC) that goes on to differing material.[35] The immediately ensuing *nobilmente* return to and sumptuous expansion of the introduction's exhortation, bb. 106ff. (with the effect of a celebration: '"the commission" satisfactorily carried out . . . thus far!'), unfurl a broadly generic, richly confident closing theme (C) in V, as expected. The exposition proper comes to a vigorous close at fig. 15:1/b. 132, with strong D major PAC-effect, locally articulated with massive confidence (Ex. 5.5, bb. 129–32).[36] With this resonant, *fortissimo* arrival, the exposition is completed: it has produced its concluding cadence.

[34] At least to this listener the cadence-effect of the 'fall' from the V of fig. 11:9/b. 102 to fig. 12:1/b. 106 seems rhetorically unmistakable. Issues of perfect-authentic-cadence (PAC) definition may be at stake here, however, both because the tonic-downbeat moment is represented only by octave Ds (b. 106), not by a full chord (though that chord, in a manner parallel with b. 1, to whose content it refers, instantly materializes on beat 2) and because of the suddenly produced textural gap from b. 102 to b. 106. As I hear it, the sudden, blunt 'stopping' of the V at b. 102 throws forward the ensuing four bars – like a projectile cast through the air by the momentum of what precedes it – which in turn find their obvious target, and complete the bull's-eye cadential resolution, at the downbeat of b. 106.

What muddies the interpretive situation here is that the sudden halt of most of the orchestra at b. 102 texturally resembles an unusually strenuous articulation of a medial caesura (MC) on V of D, and bb. 102–6 respond by taking on the texture of an expanded caesura-fill. On this reading, which I find less convincing, the MC-effect seems to arrive 'too late' and would prompt one to consider the possibility that Jacques's and Webb's supposed S (fig. 10:1/b. 85) still belongs to a prolonged transition (TR). This reading also entails the relegation of the seemingly V:PAC-effect downbeat at b. 106, seemingly the point of essential expositional closure (the EEC), to a secondary structural event, since caesura-fill, by definition, cannot accomplish such a structurally strong cadential articulation.

[35] On the definition and crucial role of the EEC within expositions, see Hepokoski and Darcy, *Elements of Sonata Theory*, especially pp. 117–49 (Chapter 7, 'The Secondary Theme (S) and Essential Expositional Closure (EEC): Initial Considerations'). As mentioned in the preceding note, though, some generic and cadential ambiguities are present at this important arrival point in Elgar's exposition.

[36] As with b. 106 (n. 35 above), issues of cadential definition may also arise here. The chord immediately preceding the octave Ds in b. 132 (fig. 15) is not in root position, which seems to disallow it as capable of producing a *perfect authentic* cadence on the next beat. On the other hand, the more structural chord-representative involved in this cadence is provided on the downbeat of b. 131, the root-V implications of the octave As, whose implicit sonorities are then fleshed out via a $\hat{5}-\hat{4}-\hat{3}-\hat{2}-\hat{1}$ passing motion in the bass. Whether or not this qualifies strictly as a 'PAC', the effect of bb. 131–2 nonetheless seems that of cadential closure, the articulated sign of a satisfactory expositional completion.

Ex. 5.5 *Introduction and Allegro*, bb. 129–146

At this point – one of the telling structural moments in the piece – the blustery confidence just projected with such string brilliance collapses, both dynamically and registrally, with an entropic, *dim*[*inuendo*] reappearance of the opening exhortation from the introduction. ('What has happened to "the commission"?')[37] With its appearance at b. 132 a gap – a blank, a void, an

[37] It is possible to hear b. 132 (a varied return to the opening, the work's initial spawning impulse) as marking the onset of an even broader *fourth rotation* of materials within the piece. For some of the reasoning involved, see n. 31 above, which considers one way of understanding the possible morphology of the first three rotations, each of which is larger than its predecessors. Those pursuing this line of thought might wonder whether the exhortation-based closing area of the exposition, b. 106, might not itself begin a new

empty space – is opened up after the end of the exposition proper. And into that post-expositional gap, rendered even more brittle in its connotations through the indications *con sordino*, [*sul*] *ponticello*, and *poco a poco rall*[*entando*], enters the 'mirage' of the first part only of the Welsh Tune, on D major. Once again that theme is kept from closure, this time by breaking off, *molto rit*[*ardando*], precisely at the point of its first, heartsick sign of minor-mode decay – the deeply felt, two-bar identifier of the 'weaker' version of the theme (Ex. 5.5, bb. 141–2 of bb. 137–43), here bleakly unable to proceed beyond b. 143 into any subsequent, fortified solace. In short, we discover after the exposition's evident end (b. 132) that no room had been left in it for the once-proposed secondary theme to appear: the Welsh Tune was never integrated into the essential trajectory of the exposition. What we have experienced in the exposition is the virtuosic brilliance of public music serving as an exhilarating mask for a deeper lack. The exposition proper is marked by the absence of this second theme. This may be regarded as a horizontal or linear enriching of the theme's vertical connotations of loss, distance, and non-recoverability. And this is why, between the end of the exposition proper and the development, the tempo and dynamics collapse, and the 'weaker', more remote or antique version of the nostalgic tune-mirage – the first part (only) of the vision, the ghost – suddenly emerges in the string quartet, *pianissimo*, muted, and shot through with glassy *ponticello* textures, cold, shivering tremolos and pizzicatos, music that eventually pauses, incomplete: 'And was there no room to recover lost wholeness in this exposition?'

The bulk of the developmental space is occupied by the vigorous G minor fugue, intensifying and darkening as it proceeds, at least through fig. 20:1/b. 196. Elgar famously described this section as 'no working out part but a devil of a fugue ... with all sorts of japes & counterpoint'.[38] The fugue subject is shown in Ex. 5.5, bb. 144–6. The overall effect of the developmental

rotation (since the exhortation proper, as we have construed it here, is typically a sign of restarting a rotation). This seems unlikely, since there can be no question that bb. 106–32 are deployed in still-viable expositional space. One line of the sonata tradition was the frequent basing of an exposition's closing thematic material (C) on music from earlier in the work – on TR, on P, or, in this case, on the opening of the introduction (Hepokoski and Darcy, *Elements of Sonata Theory*, Chapter 7, 'The Closing Zone (C)', pp. 180–94.) Instead of beginning something rotationally new, b. 106 ends – and rounds – the rotation currently in play. By contrast, as will be suggested above, the rapidly collapsing exhortation at b. 132 (fig. 15), as marked especially by its horizontal placement immediately following the closing

cadence of the exposition, may be heard as seeking, however unsuccessfully, to restart another structural rotation.

[38] Elgar to Jaeger, 26 January 1905 (*Publishers*, pp. 607–8). The potentially diabolical connotations of the particulars of this extraordinary fugue have been explored in Julian Rushton, 'A Devil of a Fugue: Berlioz, Elgar, and *Introduction and Allegro*', in *ESJ*, 11/5 (July 2000), pp. 276–87, which includes a look at precedents in a brief demon-fugato passage in *The Dream of Gerontius* as well as in earlier passages and commentaries associating fugues with demons. These latter include especially fast-tempo fugues 'with angular subjects articulated staccato'; 'most are in flat minor keys' (p. 281).

space – probably self-consciously, albeit with softened contours – is not unlike that of the storm-representation in Beethoven's *Pastoral* Symphony, from the initially light-staccato raindrop patter, through a darkening swell and extended *fortissimo* precipitation, to the eventual receding of the storm and the cleansed, fresh-air return of sunshine. Here we find an invigorating display of brilliant counterpoint and string writing, as Jaeger's original proposal from the preceding year had suggested. Notwithstanding its contrapuntal energy, the unexpected abstraction and academic historicism of its contents set off the developmental space from the largely complementary exposition and recapitulation on either side. In this sonata context the sudden shift to the abstraction of a fugue – with an essentially 'new' theme – can also be understood as a changing of the subject, a cover-up of expositional loss through the strategy of sheer energy and compositional display.[39]

This is not to say that the fugal material is entirely unrelatable to that which has preceded it.[40] The fugue is tracked in the minor tonic, G minor, for instance (Elgar: 'G major & the sd. divvel in G minor')[41] – the key of the introduction – which suggests that we might be invited to hear it as a nervously alert writing-over of the opening G minor exhortation, now reinterpreted to suggest 'what "the commission" demands'. That the fugue is overlaid several times with the swelling-figure fragment from P (fig. 17:1–5/bb. 161–5 and fig. 18:5–14/bb. 176–85), a fragment also important in the first, brief rotation of the introduction (bb. 7–8 of Ex. 5.3), bolsters this reading. On this line of interpretation the suddenly fresh, livelier impulse of the fugue subject at its first appearance is a corrective reigniting of a new, more expansive structural rotation, whose initial attempt to appear on its own terms at fig. 15:1/b. 132 had melted away at once, had slipped out of the piece proper to turn to a memory-image of the lost mirage, the Welsh Tune.[42]

[39] While fugato passages within developments were anything but uncommon in sonata-form compositions, it was more unusual to occupy the bulk of a development with a fugue. Predecessors for Elgar include Spohr's Overture to *Faust* and the first movement, 'Jeu de sons', of Tchaikovsky's Suite no. 2 in C for Orchestra, op. 53. Cf. Rushton: 'A major source of tension in late 19th and early 20th-century music is what to do about sonata form. It is a way of imposing control upon rhapsody, but because of the elements of symmetry and repetition, it may actually be a straitjacket: there is often too much control. Recognition of this, I think, led Elgar to dispense with working out and use fugue instead. The devil of a fugue avoids the problem of developing themes that don't need it, by using a musical texture which is intrinsically developmental' ('A Devil of a Fugue', p. 285).

[40] 'No doubt with some ingenuity one could discover a relation between the subject and earlier themes, but it certainly *sounds* new, at least until we recognise that this sinister element is integral to the trajectory of the work. Recognition comes with a new countersubject, which is the first solo entry in the fugue [fig. 17:1/b. 161, touching on material from Ex. 3, bb. 7–8]' (Rushton, 'A Devil of a Fugue', p. 285).

[41] Elgar to Jaeger, 26 January 1905, after which he transcribed the first three bars of the fugue (*Publishers*, pp. 607–8).

[42] It is doubtless significant that fig. 15:1/b. 132 provides the last appearance of any version of the exhortation-module that could conceivably serve as the opening gesture of a

The chattering semiquavers pervading the fugue might be additionally relatable to those that dominate what the original programme notes reported was the 'second subject' of the exposition (Ex. 5.4; notice also the telling string figuration within the closing material at fig. 14:1–4/bb. 122–25).[43] From this perspective, the fugue, whatever its relationship with the introductory exhortation might be, also establishes a rhythmic connection with that area of the exposition where the apparently 'originally planned' S, the Welsh Tune, had been elbowed out or at least had failed to appear. Allusions to that semiquaver-driven 'second subject' recur more explicitly at the end of the developmental space, as a finally brightened transition out of the fugue (fig. 21:1/b. 202), whose dark storm-swell has by now subsided over a dominant exit-pedal (V of G minor) and given way, at a *pianissimo* dynamic, to the first ray of a clarifying G major at b. 202.

Beginning at fig. 22:1/b. 209, the recapitulation proceeds more or less regularly up until the point of the chattering 'second subject', whose generic task, as with all such passages within recapitulations, is one of tonal resolution – that of producing the moment of essential structural closure (ESC): attaining a secondary-theme-space perfect authentic cadence (PAC or workable substitute) in the tonic.[44] The 'second subject' begins normatively, transposed into the tonic G major, at fig. 25:1/b. 231, up a fourth from the exposition. Instead of allowing it to proceed as a strict transposition of the exposition, however, midway through the theme Elgar takes advantage of the theme's fidgety harmonic shifts to move it unexpectedly to the subdominant, the 'wrong-key' C major. The theme's original harmonic levels in the exposition, at three-bar intervals – D, D, A, and D – are twisted here into G, G (altered in the second half of b. 236), C (!), and C again, all the while maintaining a rhetorical sense of bar-for-bar correspondence measures with the expositional model (figs. 25:1–27:1/bb. 231–52 = figs. 10:1–12:1/bb. 85–106). The result is that the strong PAC-effect is produced in C (IV), not in the tonic G. This 'wrong-key' downbeat is incapable of closing the recapitulation tonally: it does not provide us with the expected ESC, which by generic definition must be in the tonic. The tonal demands of the sonata are left open, spilling into what was C-space in the exposition (fig. 27:1/b. 252 = fig. 12:1/b. 106, only now in IV).

rotation. The triplet-tumbling exhortation-idea will of course reappear as a closing idea in the recapitulation, fig. 27:1/b. 252, but this appearance, as in the exposition, will be a celebratory concluding gesture, not the onset of a new rotation. See n. 38 above.

[43] Moore states bluntly: 'The fugue subject in G minor derived from a figure of semiquavers at the exposition climax [probably bb. 122–25?]; counter-subjects were similarly derived from exposition material [cf. Rushton, n. 40 above]; and all worked to a fine climax. But the *Allegro* primary subject never appeared, and the secondary subject [appeared – i.e., bb. 68ff] only when the fugue wound down toward recapitulation' (Moore, *Elgar*, p. 454).

[44] Note 38 provides some of the ingredients for an interpretation along these lines.

The burden of recapitulatory tonal resolution is thus transferred onto the *nobilmente*, exhortation theme – the exposition's closing theme – which shifts with full confidence to the proper G major at fig. 27:6/b. 257. All seems prepared for a brilliantly executed PAC-effect in the tonic, which soon, via correspondence measures with the exposition, is now aimed directly at the downbeat of fig. 30:1/b. 279 (= the final bar of the exposition, fig. 15:1/ b. 132). But instead of closing forcefully on the tonic, this thematic zone, rushing frantically toward its conclusion, is stopped short at the penultimate chord, on V$_3^4$ of G (fig. 29:6/b. 278, beat 4), a maximally expectant domi-nant, blocked by two fermatas and a decisive double-bar (Ex. 5.6), 29:3–6/bb. 275–8). At the corresponding 'final-gesture' moment of the exposition, one recalls (Ex. 5.5), the music had proceeded unimpeded into its resolution (b. 132) and had been followed by a rapidly dissolving variant of the opening exhortation (bb. 132–6), soon dying away into the spectral, incomplete vision of the 'weaker' version of the Welsh Tune (bb. 137–43). Here what had been a decisive, resolving phrase in the exposition is converted into a broad, spring-loaded anacrusis (b. 278), interrupted with a tense, dramatic pause. What it releases on the other side of the double-bar (b. 279) – the grand moment of the piece – is the long-suppressed Welsh Tune in a tonic apoth-eosis, *fortissimo* and *molto sostenuto*.[45] Significantly, this is the 'stronger' version of the theme, securely underpinned by the noblest and most sturdy of 'English-imperial'-Handelian striding basses (Ex. 5.6, bb. 279ff.).

With the cadential interruption at the end of b. 278 the tonal resolution of the recapitulation (including the generically obligatory tonic-cadence ESC) is once again frustrated. The requisite I:PAC (G:PAC) has remained unsounded, and the closing zone left behind is still tonally open. Thus the entire recapitulatory span, bb. 209–78, should be regarded as a non-resolving recapitulation – one that is staged as failing to accomplish that tonal-generic norm.[46] In turn, the tonic-cadential burden that had been deferred into closing space with the subdominant ('wrong-key') PAC-effect at fig. 27:1/ b. 252 is thrust forward once again, onto the shoulders of the next thematic module in line. Here (and this is surely the point) this is the Welsh Tune, relaunched *fortissimo* at fig. 30:1/b. 279. What is 'horizontally' predicted (or hoped) with this do-or-die apotheosis appearance is that the theme and all that it stands for will finally be made fully present and granted the honour of closing the entire structure with its own PAC. But with the tune's entrance, the cadential situation-to-come is anything but secure. In all of its past appear-ances, the Welsh Tune, sounded in the elegiac register of the Schillerian naive,

[45] On S-apotheosis models within the tradition see n. 31 above.
[46] This deformational strategy and its hermeneutic implications are discussed in
Hepokoski, 'Back and Forth from *Egmont*: Beethoven, Mozart, and the Nonresolving Recapitulation', *19CM*, 25 (2002), pp. 127–54.

Ex. 5.6 *Introduction and Allegro*, bb. 270–82

had been represented as a distant vision of loss and non-recoverability. Most important, one of its central features is that it had never been able to attain closure with a perfect authentic cadence: the mirage had never been able to be precipitated into a closed reality; the vision of the theme had always broken off or dissolved into non-cadential mist. What we are invited to hope, then – 'one

Ex. 5.6 (cont.)

last time!' – is that the theme will now find in itself the resources of a noble or heroic strength that will push it all the way to the long-delayed perfect authentic cadence in the G major tonic. Will it be able to do this or will it not? Those are the stakes governing this apotheosis moment.

Before addressing this matter directly, we need to consider one more issue of form. Is this apotheosis in fact a coda, as Elgar described it in his 1905 programme notes? It occupies a more complex position than that quick description suggests. The recapitulation had been left unclosed with the abrupt stop on the dominant (V_3^4) at the end of 29:6/b. 278. Here the apotheosis coda, if coda it is, is given the task of cadential closure, which the composer had denied to the recapitulation's closing zone proper. From that point of view, the 'coda' makes a strong bid for inclusion within the confines of sonata-space. Moreover, it does so with the apotheosis of the idea

Ex. 5.6 (cont.)

Ex. 5.6 (cont.)

that Elgar had staged, in the introduction, as having been the 'originally planned' secondary theme – the Welsh Tune – which had been notable in its absence from the exposition proper, having been ejected into a cold, post-expositional space of trembling loss and regret (see Ex. 5.5). Still, one way to include such an afterthought-space within the sonata proper is to remove the quasi-cadential gesture that had originally set it apart as such a space. This is just what Elgar does at the double-bar seam joining bb. 278 and 279. That the first four pitches of the striding bass, b. 279, replicate the pitches of the bass line of b. 278, with some octave adjustments, also suggests that the opening of the theme backs up to interlock with its preceding measure: another gesture of inclusion into sonata-space. Both coda and eleventh-hour sonata functions seem conceptually in play. Rather than declaring on behalf of either the one or the other, we seem invited instead to savour the formally ambiguous placement of this now richly sonorous Welsh Tune passage, as we had also done with its earlier sounding after what we had regarded as the end of the exposition.

The larger point, though, remains the attainment of that cadence of closure that had been smothered off at the end of b. 278. Here, finally, the Welsh Tune is not sounded quietly, as in its three prior appearances, but in a richly warm, all-embracing *fortissimo*. More than that, pushing toward that needed I:PAC, it also sets forth as if trying to recapture, and then fortify further, the theme's 'stronger' version. Ex. 5.7 provides a much-simplified melodic reminder of the crucial details upon which the fortunes of the entire piece and the conception of the Welsh Tune hang. Fig. 30:1–10/bb. 279–88 correspond to figs. 3:5–4:2/bb. 30–39, the second, 'stronger' cycle of the tune. Let us again recall the differences between the two versions. The 'weaker' version is identified by the minor-mode, quasi-modal decay-bars in its fifth to eighth bars (IV–iii–ii–vi: Ex. 5.1, bb. 22–5) – a four-bar sense of slippage and loss, a melancholy collapse away from a strong, linear progression toward a cadence. We might construe those four bars as a 'negative' block, characterized also by descending-*second* suspensions in the upper voice (bb. 23 and 25). By contrast, in the 'stronger' version this four-bar block is replaced by a more 'positive', stronger-progression mod-ule (Ex. 5.2, bb. 35 and 37), marked by an increasing harmonic drive and a retention of more confident descending *thirds* in the upper voice. In the 'stronger' version the two *largamente* bars (Ex. 5.2, bb. 38–9) produce an added fortification of this drive, suggesting more robustly the imminence of a cadence; they also reappear here in the apotheosis (Ex. 5.7, bb. 287–8), ecstatically enriched, *sul G* in the violins. Spurred onward by the presence of all these musical signals, a PAC-to-come might seem virtually secure. 'Ah!' we might think. 'At last! Here the mirage will finally turn real – strong, solid, and clear. Here past memories will be recaptured. Here, surely, the

Ex. 5.7 *Introduction and Allegro*, bb. 279–310

fortissimo dynamics will remain stable, and here, surely, the theme will be brought to a magnificent completion, to a cadential completion that will also close the entire piece tonally.'

   But at this crucial point, so close to cadence, agents of dissolution intrude once again, undermining even this resonant version of the theme, turning it once again, and forever, into an ungraspable mirage. Bar 289 essentially replicates its model bar (Ex. 5.2, b. 40), but this turns out to be a fatal step. That was the bar in which decay had begun to take hold in the model: within only one more bar (b. 41) the 'stronger' version would also be kept from its anticipated PAC. To follow that model is to follow it inevitably into non-resolution, which is just what this music, in its intensity, is trying to over-come. Grasping this – and understanding the passionate desire finally to bring the Welsh Tune apotheosis to its own I:PAC – provides the basis for an interpretation of all the details that now follow. The 'fatal-step' bar, b. 289, triggers the slippage of a *stringendo* (comparable to the fleeting *accel* [*erando*] of Ex. 5.2, b. 40). Bar 290 is a disturbing bar of sudden realization, of panic, of scrambling ('No! It can't be lost to us!'). In bb. 291–2 (fig. 31) the music is backed up, heartrendingly, to an intensified, *con fuoco*, version of the *largamente* bb. 287–8, as if trying to reverse the slippage of time or to stop it altogether in a last embrace (*'Verweile doch! du bist so schön!* – But stay! So beautiful thou art!').[47]

Coextensive with the elapsing of time, however, is the principle of brute reality, which will not permit such mirages to be anything more than unattainable visions of the naive. All the remaining signs of the Welsh Tune apotheosis will be ones of decay and non-resolution. Though entered ecstatically, b. 292 is dynamically gutted by a rapid diminuendo. In bb. 293–6 the curtains part to reveal the unalterable content of this theme: the 'negative' block is brought back with its tear-flooded descending seconds (bb. 294 and 296) and its harmonic decay into minor-inflected quasi-modality (IV–iii–ii–vi), the defining features of the 'weaker' version of the theme ('Lost ... lost forever!'). Triple *fortissimo*, that sentence of inescapable dissolution and non-resolution is acknowledged, wailed out one last time, in 30:7–10/bb. 297–300. The various appearances of the Welsh Tune have persistently held out visions of the naive, the pure, the whole that we can no longer attain, even through the fictive processes of art. Such dreams are phantoms that flow through our hands like water. They can only be lamented in their loss; held up as a critique ('if only!') of the prosaic reality that actually is. And that, at the end, is the central message staged so richly, and with so many extraordinary musical details, in *Introduction and Allegro*.

The sober reality principle drives this piece to its final ten bars. Drawing the curtains on the non-realizable mirage of the 'Welsh' theme, Elgar bids the dissolved illusion a brusque farewell and returns stoically to the formal demands of ending the piece. One still has one's duty. Soldier on. Major mode. *Il faut d'abord durer.* The piece concludes in a ten-bar rush of publicly 'official' music, based on primary-theme material – the commission fulfilled.

---

[47] Goethe, *Faust. Eine Tragödie. Erster Teil*, line
1,701; *Zweiter Teil*, line 11,612.

6 Elgar's deconstruction of the *belle époque*: interlace structures and the Second Symphony

J. P. E. Harper-Scott

1. Autobiographical, intertextual, and socio-political content

Elgar's Second Symphony, first performed in 1911, has invited strongly extramusical interpretations.[1] A poetic epigraph from Shelley ('Rarely, rarely comest thou, Spirit of Delight!'), a loyal dedication to 'the Memory of His late Majesty King Edward VII', and two place-names at the end of the score ('Venice–Tintagel') are all signs which seem to point to meanings that reach beyond mere syntactic connections between notes. Authors have been inventive in exploring the implications of these broad hints, and their different hermeneutic interpretations may be arranged into three classes which correspond to what Lawrence Kramer calls 'hermeneutic windows'.[2] Taken together they amount to a range of interpretations whose breadth speaks to the symphony's trenchant expressiveness.

The simplest of Kramer's hermeneutic windows is the 'textual inclusion', which means for instance 'texts set to music, titles, epigrams, programs, notes to the score'. A 'less explicit version of the first' window is what Kramer calls 'citational inclusions', which includes 'titles that link a work of music with a literary work, visual image, place, or historical moment', as well as intertextual reference to other compositions, whether as direct quotation, more indirect allusion, or even parody or pastiche. The third, and for Kramer most complex, kind of hermeneutic window is opened up by 'structural tropes', by which is meant 'a structural procedure, capable of various practical realizations, that also functions as a typical expressive act within a certain cultural/historical framework'.[3] An example of this would be the musical topic of the march, which has musical characteristics that can be defined, and as a whole invites the listener to make broader social connections – for instance to ask if it is signifying something regal, military,

---

[1] I am grateful to Daniel M. Grimley, Patrick McCreless, Charles Edward McGuire, Bernard Porter, and Matthew Riley for suggesting improvements to this essay.

[2] Lawrence Kramer, *Music as Cultural Practice, 1800–1900* (Berkeley, CA and London: University of California Press, 1990).

[3] All quotations from Kramer, *Music as Cultural Practice*, pp. 9–10.

imperial, or funereal.[4] By opening a fourth, 'mimetic window', using Martin Heidegger's analysis of the temporality of human existence to make connections between music's temporality and certain existential issues, it is possible to open up a still more complex view of the rich meaning of the symphony. An outline of the necessary philosophical ideas is given in section 4 and applied to interpretation of the symphony in section 11.[5]

First among the interpretative strands of existing commentary on the Second Symphony there is the view that the autobiographical element in the work is strongest. This springs most straightforwardly from Elgar's reference to Venice and Tintagel in the score, and from the fact that in letters to his (almost certainly non-physical) lover, the 'Windflower' Alice Stuart-Wortley, he called it *her* symphony.[6] Both of these are textual inclusions. Exemplifying this hermeneutic approach to the symphony, Christopher Kent and Michael Kennedy look beyond the dedication to Edward VII to a deeper and more personal dedication of the symphony to the woman he loved best. Kennedy even delicately suggests that the symphony's biggest climax, the crisis of the Rondo, might convey something of the pain of Elgar's suppressed passion for the woman.[7]

Analysis of citational inclusions has naturally led writers to speculate on the significance of the Shelley poem with which Elgar enigmatically linked the symphony. Most agree that, as the full poem indicates, Delight is a flighty state not easily retained, and that the symphony does not long maintain the Delightful countenance of its opening bars. In his reading of the work, Brian Trowell largely dismisses the Shelley association as a red herring and suggests instead that lines from Tennyson's *Maud*, which Elgar associated in a letter with the Rondo climax, could mean that the work carries a remembrance of the composer's earlier suicidal thoughts.[8] Allen Gimbel, meanwhile, in a daringly imaginative essay, links the work with the *Preislied* from *Die Meistersinger*. This merely strengthens the view that the

[4] On the semiotics of 'topics', see V. Kofi Agawu, *Playing with Signs: a Semiotic Interpretation of Classic Music* (Princeton, NJ: Princeton University Press, 1991).
[5] My own particular conception of music as a mimesis of human temporality is developed in my *Edward Elgar, Modernist* (Cambridge: Cambridge University Press, 2006).
[6] The relevant quotation is this, from a short note to Alice Stuart-Wortley, then at Tintagel, dated 24 March 1911: 'I have asked Alice [Lady Elgar] to send you . . . the sketches of the (your) symphony.' *Windflower*, p. 82. See Christopher Kent, 'A View of Elgar's Methods

of Composition through the Sketches of the Symphony no. 2 in E♭ (op. 63)', *Proceedings of the Royal Musical Association*, 103 (1976–7), p. 41–60, at p. 41. The 'Windflower' was the daughter of the painter Sir John Everett Millais, and her mother had previously been the wife of John Ruskin.
[7] See Christopher Kent, 'A View of Elgar's Methods of Composition', and Michael Kennedy, *Elgar Orchestral Music* (London: BBC, 1970), p. 62.
[8] Brian Trowell, 'Elgar's Use of Literature', in Monk, *Literature*, pp. 182–326, at 256–7.

symphony was 'a love-letter to Mrs. Stuart-Wortley' – a conclusion which, it would appear from other interpretations, doesn't require intertextual support.[9]

On the broader issue of the structural tropes in the symphony, attention has been fixed by Jerrold Northrop Moore and James Hepokoski on what can broadly be defined the socio-political aspect of the symphony, something hinted at by its official dedication, by the martial stamp of much of the first movement, and by the state-funeral solemnity of the Larghetto. Moore attributes a short-range political dimension to the symphony, hearing it as a reaction to the Liberal Party's war against the Lords.[10] This is a charming hypothesis, but it seems unlikely that any composer, however strong his ambition to become a peer, could be moved to create a substantial master-piece out of a feeling of concern at the tabling of the first Parliament Act.[11] The need to open a wider socio-political view seems indicated. Hepokoski does so intriguingly by suggesting that the motivic teleology of the work, directed (he argues) towards the theme representing 'Hans [Richter] him-self!' in the finale (first given at fig. 139), gives the whole work an 'encyclo-pedic quality' that summarizes and bids farewell to the 'institution of the public concert' itself.[12]

2. Elgar's unimperialism

Any interpretation that places Elgar's music in a broader social or historical context must inevitably examine the composer's place in the history of the British empire. Imperialism (used as a watchword rather than a concretely defined concept) is of profound significance in the Second Symphony, but not at all in the way that might be supposed. A pile of accumulated critical

[9] Allen Gimbel, 'Elgar's Prize Song: Quotation and Allusion in the Second Symphony', 19CM, 12 (1989), pp. 231–40, at p. 239.
[10] Moore, Elgar, p. 597.
[11] The Act emasculated the Lords who were opposed to the Liberals' equalizing legislation for selfish reasons: landowners, represented by Tory peers, would be hit strongly by the Liberals' economic policies. In an early moment of glory, the then Liberal cabinet minister, a waspish Winston Churchill, was behind some of these important reforms intended to share the nation's wealth more equably. See H. C. G. Matthew, 'The Liberal Age (1851–1914)', in Kenneth O. Morgan (ed.), The Oxford History of Britain, updated edition (Oxford: Oxford University Press, 2001), pp. 518–81, at pp. 574–6.

[12] Elgar labelled the theme 'Hans himself!' in the sketches. See James Hepokoski, 'Elgar', in D. Kern Holomon (ed.), The Nineteenth-Century Symphony (New York: Schirmer, 1997), pp. 327–44, at p. 339. A countervailing breath of gentle mockery animates Robert Meikle's reading of the symphony's closing movement. 'There is something about its placid, unruffled, even slightly self-satisfied air, that imparts the unmistakeable atmosphere of a Sunday bandstand in the park. The band is out of sight – probably just beyond the rhododendrons – and so we cannot hear all the instruments; but the lower ones come over quite well, and the occasional chirp from flutes, clarinets, and oboes is carried by the afternoon breeze.' Robert Meikle, '"The True Foundation": the Symphonies', in Monk, Literature, pp. 45–71, at p. 55.

baggage must be dealt with before the nature and role of Elgar's imperialism is clarified.[13]

There have been various reactions to the critical responsibility of analysing Elgar's historical situation. One, represented by Moore, is to transmute the imperial issue into a concern with pastoralism.[14] Michael Kennedy's approach in *Portrait of Elgar* is (to put it crudely) to claim that Elgar rejected the imperialism of his age.[15] Repudiating Kennedy, Jeffrey Richards has argued that although Elgar was 'steeped' in imperialism, it was of a benevolent kind, and therefore one we can happily embrace without experiencing post-colonial guilt.[16] Standing back a little from this position, Corissa Gould and Charles McGuire prefer to say that though definitely influenced by what they regard as the 'dominant ideology' of the age, Elgar's imperialism is clearly neither extreme nor wicked, and can be properly understood as merely an inevitable product of this part of our shared history.[17]

The marmoreal presumption uniting all these differing arguments is that Elgar's age, in every part of British society, was rank with imperialism. If Elgar lived between 1857 and 1934, the thought runs, he *must* have been an imperialist: it stands to reason that anyone whose skin was even slightly porous to the 'dominant ideology' of that time must have been infected by the airborne disease. But if this presumption is wrong, or a tendentious distortion of the historical record, then the entire question must be rethought from first principles.

Bernard Porter made a first tentative attempt at this in an article on Elgar's imperialism.[18] His argument hinges on two principal claims. First, that Elgar's background as a middle-class boy from Worcester cannot have made him an imperialist. (There is no documentary or musical evidence of an interest in empire before he met Alice.) Second, that the combination of the effects of fervid late-imperialist propaganda and the exigencies of marriage to his thoroughly imperial wife made him *assume* an imperial countenance. His conclusion is that

[13] I am indebted to Bernard Porter, whose comments on a draft of this essay helped me clarify my thoughts on Elgar's imperialism.

[14] See his *Elgar* and *Elgar: Child of Dreams* (London: Faber and Faber, 2004).

[15] Kennedy, *Portrait*. He is less defensive in his *The Life of Elgar* (Cambridge: Cambridge University Press, 2004).

[16] Jeffrey Richards, *Imperialism and Music: Britain 1876–1953* (Manchester and New York: Manchester University Press, 2001), p. 45.

[17] Corissa Gould, 'Edward Elgar, *The Crown of India*, and the image of empire', *ESJ*, 13

(2003), pp. 25–35, and Charles Edward McGuire, 'Functional Music: Imperialism, the Great War, and Elgar as Popular Composer', in *Companion*, pp. 214–24. My breakdown of the critical fortunes of Elgar's imperialism mirrors that in McGuire's essay.

[18] Bernard Porter, 'Edward Elgar and Empire', *The Journal of Imperial and Commonwealth History*, 29 (2001), pp. 1–34, reprinted as 'Elgar and Empire: Music, Nationalism and the War', in Lewis Foreman (ed.), *'Oh, My Horses!': Elgar and the Great War* (Rickmansworth: Elgar Editions, 2001), pp. 133–73.

[I]f Elgar was an imperialist – and that is not a thing that matters greatly, being more a question of semantics or, at most, degree than of fact – he was not a 'natural' one; or a very deep or fierce one; or an 'inevitable' one because of the dominant imperial ethos of his time. He came to imperialism accidentally, through his marriage, and in order to find some sort of *social* space for composing, in the stifling social and artistic environment of his day.[19]

Daniel M. Grimley airs legitimate concerns that the context for Porter's discussion is not sufficiently widely drawn;[20] but this criticism has since been met in Porter's book-length study of imperialism in nineteenth- and early twentieth-century Britain, *The Absent-Minded Imperialists*.[21] Space here allows for only the most superficial assemblage of evidence from this deeply impressive (and, for the Saidists, unsettling) study.[22]

In a nutshell, the claim, prevalent in post-colonial studies, that imperialism was the 'dominant ideology' of British society in the nineteenth century is untenable because during that period there was no such thing as a single British society. The Industrial Revolution and the potential for political revolution (like that seen on the European continent) exacerbated divisions in the country which were already complex and profound. 'Britain in the nineteenth century, and for some way beyond, comprised not one but a number of "societies", each with its own value system and characteristic "discourse"; the differences between which are far more important in relation to the impact of the empire on Britain (and vice versa) than any features that might have been common to them all.'[23]

The classes, then, must be viewed separately in a history of imperialism in Britain; and the only truly imperial section of British society until the last decade or so of the nineteenth century was that containing the upper and upper-middle classes. These provided the colonial governments and civil servants who administrated the empire. Through most of the nineteenth century the middle and lower classes were inessential to the running and expansion of the empire, and as a rule the upper and upper-middle classes were happy to keep these – in the absence of universal suffrage – 'politically irrelevant'[24] groups at a distance.

Elgar was raised in the lower-middle class, and what is more, in the provinces. As Porter notes simply, 'imperialism was not an issue in

[19] Porter, 'Edward Elgar and Empire', p. 26.
[20] Daniel M. Grimley, review of '*Oh, My Horses!*': *Elgar and the Great War*, *ML*, 85 (2004), pp. 325–9, at p. 326.
[21] Bernard Porter, *The Absent-Minded Imperialists: Empire, Society, and Culture in Britain* (New York: Oxford University Press, 2004).

[22] 'Saidist' is the mischievous term coined for a follower of Edward Said in John MacKenzie, *Orientalism: History, Theory and the Arts* (Manchester: Manchester University Press, 1995), p. 5.
[23] Porter, *The Absent-Minded Imperialists*, pp. 22–3.
[24] Ibid., p. 133.

Worcester in the 1860s and 1870s'.[25] The middle and lower classes did not
have to think about it. Non-human imports from the empire, such as
clothing and food, were domesticated and anglicized; only the bric-a-brac
brought back by ex-colonials (such as Alice Elgar's father) was an exception
to this rule, in being genuine. Elgar had a room devoted to such bibelots at
Severn House, but we should note that the house *was* called 'Severn House',
recalling provincial Worcester, and not 'Pondicherry Lodge' or some other
imperialist name,[26] and that after Alice's death Elgar handed the entire
collection over to the Victoria and Albert Museum.[27] This is not the behaviour of a natural or fervent imperialist.

   And there is no obvious reason why he should have been one; nothing at
home or school could mould him that way. Provincials weren't naturally
disposed to care about empire, and even the famous red maps showing the
extent of empire 'cannot have appeared [in schools] before the 1880s',[28] long
after Elgar removed his last pair of short trousers. Indeed geography, insofar as
it was taught at all in middle-class schools during Elgar's schooldays, concentrated largely on maps of the Holy Land: the colonies didn't get a look in.[29]

   The familiar *fin-de-siècle* propaganda was necessary precisely because a
generation of middle-class children had been raised either to have a mild
distaste for empire or else to be almost completely ignorant of it; Sir John
Seeley's famous suggestion that Britain acquired its empire 'in a fit of absence
of mind' was a reaction from a pro-imperialist against a nescience among the
general population which, he believed, threatened the continued existence of
the empire.[30] The new urgency in imperial thought at the close of the
nineteenth century sprang from the competition between several empires
for what would later be called *Lebensraum*, living space; 'securing it in this
environment [of heightened competition among European empires] would
require far more effort, and consequently more commitment, than before'.[31]
Although socialism was still a middle-class politics and the Labour movement was young, the working classes were gaining in political strength, and
were no longer irrelevant. With growing social challenges for the ruling elite
the need to bind society together, to maintain the status quo, became
important, and uniting the whole nation behind the imperial effort seemed
like a solution to all manner of political problems. In short, an attempt was
made to use imperialism as a 'social adhesive'.[32]

[25] Bernard Porter, 'Edward Elgar and
Empire', *Journal of Imperial and
Commonwealth History*, 29 (2001), pp. 1–34,
at p. 5.
[26] The specific county-association of the
house's name seems to have been significant to
Elgar. The house had a Somerset name,
Kelston, when the Elgars moved in, but Elgar

changed it. See Robert Anderson, *Elgar*
(London: Dent, 1993), p. 104.
[27] Anderson, *Elgar and Chivalry*, p. 313.
[28] Porter, *The Absent-Minded Imperialists*, p. 66.
[29] Ibid.
[30] Ibid., p. 169.
[31] Ibid., p. 165.
[32] Ibid., p. 168.

But to bring the majority of the population on board, the propagandists had to make the imperial project appealing to all, not just the upper classes who found imperial rule either diverting or self-aggrandizing. Hence the picture-painting of the 'mystical imperialism' of truth, right, and freedom, with which Jeffrey Richards associates Elgar's imperialist traits. 'The moralism of it is sometimes cloying, and can arouse suspicions of hypocrisy, but it was probably this that enabled the middle classes to stomach the empire at all.'[33]

So Elgar's imperialism came late, and was, according to Richards, of a 'mystical' sort. It follows from the evidence that Elgar's entire interest in empire was adopted as a result of the Roberts family's adverse reaction to Alice's choice of husband, one from the lower middle classes, whose interest (as a class) in empire was spread out on a scale between complete ignorance and manifest disinterestedness. What was used as social adhesive for the rest of Britain was probably used by Elgar as a marital adhesive. It seems very likely that he felt the need to prove to Alice, if not to her imperially steeped family, that he was recognizably 'of the right sort'. A chance remark by Elgar's daughter Carice at a tea party given to celebrate the awarding of Elgar's knighthood offers an insight into this aspect of the Elgars' marriage. 'I am so glad for Mother's sake that Father has been knighted', Carice said. 'You see – it puts her back where she was.'[34] How many thirteen-year-olds, uninspired by a mother's private grumbles, would be capable of such vicarious self-ishness? The atmosphere in the Elgarian home is tangible even now.

Elgar appears to have copied Alice's imperial demeanour with a certain vim; but there is no evidence in his music or writing to suggest that he had a serious or informed understanding of empire. In fact all the evidence sug-gests that he had only the vaguest notion of what empire was. Unlike Kipling's, Elgar's was not an imperialism of experience; it was an imperialism of artefact and third-hand memory (communicated through Alice from her father and brother). Had he married his near-exact contemporary Emmeline Pankhurst instead of Alice Roberts, Elgar might have adopted revolutionary ideas in a similarly shallow manner. As it was, having made his bed with the daughter of an officer in the Indian Mutiny, he wrapped himself in an imperial aura which – because it exuded originally from domesticated artefacts redolent of a past when he had sat 'in the reeds by Severn side with a sheet of paper trying to fix the sounds & longing for something very great'[35] – could act as another portal to his precious, strength-giving youth. Judging purely (as one should, to avoid presumption) from the limited amount he wrote for empire, and the notable lack of a masterpiece among

[33] Ibid., p. 242.
[34] Rosa Burley and Frank C. Carruthers, *Edward Elgar: The Record of a* *Friendship* (London: Barrie and Jenkins, 1972), p. 174.
[35] Anderson, *Elgar*, p. 151.

that music, it is difficult to agree with Richards that his was even a 'mystical' imperialism of the sort that pro-imperial propaganda could bring on. Elgar was not sufficiently optimistic to hope that a little island had the power (or political will) to spread truth, right, and freedom around a benighted world. So more than being 'mystical', Elgar's imperialism was romanticized and nostalgic – maybe not so very different from the imperialism of present-day conservatives who keep pink-bespeckled world maps in their vestibules or sing along heart-on-sleeve to 'Land of Hope and Glory' at the Proms.

The psychological need not to disappoint his wife was a powerful urge for Elgar, and given the circumstances of his upbringing and class position, and the general state of British society or societies in the nineteenth century, it provides today the strongest – probably the only strong – explanation for Elgar's late-assumed 'imperialism'. The traditional interpretation of Alice's role in Elgar's musical achievement is not entirely wrongheaded, simplistic and romantic as it is; but while his creative spark was definitely not extinguished when Alice died (as in the orthodox theory), one thing her passing definitely did almost entirely kill off was his uxorious imperialism: and it was only ever tweed-deep anyway.[36]

So, in considering the nature of the imperial impulse in this symphony – an aspect of its 'meaning' that should be gauged alongside the autobiographical and socio-political interpretations summarized above – we must bear in mind two essential facts: first that it was superficial, nostalgic, and romantic, and second that it was 'unnatural' and assumed relatively late in life, as a response to his marital situation. It was a nervous, class- (and in-laws-) conscious psychological tic. A solid interpretation of the meaning of the imperial element in the Second Symphony depends on holding this problematic context in mind. The importance of this will become clear in the final section of this essay.

3. Interlace structures

Elgar's music, in the Second Symphony as much as anywhere, communicates meaning through the dialectical interweaving of discordant threads: public and private, optimistic and pessimistic, conservative and modern, among others. To understand the music, an analysis must illuminate the germination and expansion of these threads on the levels of intramusical process and activity on

---

[36] More imperialist music was written after Alice's death for Wembley in 1924, but it is rather bloodless and carries none of the conviction of parts of *Caractacus* or *The Crown of India*.

the one hand and extramusical signification on the other.[37] On the purely musical level, such analysis must account for Elgar's technique of charting two parallel temporal courses, rooted in and given heft by a struggle between opposed tonalities – not a classical polarity between tonic and dominant, but a more radical opposition of tonalities whose presentation amounts to a crisis of hegemony, as each tonal focus vies for control of the whole structure. On the level of extramusical signification, of broader 'meaning', it means accounting for the 'narrative' effects of an elaborate interlace structure. And in this context it may be appropriate to bring the ancient poem *Beowulf* into the discussion.

The idea of structural interlace has been a commonplace in *Beowulf* criticism since 1967, when John Leyerle first codified it.[38] It is drawn from that feature of seventh- and eighth-century Anglo-Saxon art, but in fact common to most peoples through history (with its ultimate roots, perhaps, in prehistoric Mesopotamia), whereby bands are 'plaited together to form a braid or rope pattern'.[39] Its effects, some of them spectacular, are familiar from stone sculptures, jewellery, and monastic copies of sacred texts (with their elaborate 'carpet pages') from the period.[40] Frequently zoomorphic, the 'heads' of each plait sometimes bite into their own tails and so create a sense of infinite movement. Retaining the animal element in the dragon motif, *Beowulf* employs a literary form of the lacertine interlace – the so-called *entrelacement* which was an essential part of medieval Continental literature, although *Beowulf* appears to be a rare use of the design in England.[41]

> The device is self-conscious and the poets describe their technique with the phrases *fingera serta* and *texere serta*, 'to fashion or weave intertwinings'. *Serta* (related to Sanscrit *sarat*, 'thread' and to Greek σειρο, 'rope') is from the participle of *serere*, 'to interweave, entwine, or interlace'. The past participle of *texere*, 'to weave, braid, interlace', is *textus*, the etymon of our words text and textile. The connection is so obvious that no one thinks of it. In basic meaning, then, a poetic text is a weaving of words to form, in effect, a verbal carpet page.[42]

The stylistic connection across art forms is plain enough. But it is the interlace's effect on the narrative which is of chief concern to Leyerle, and is of most interest to a critic of Elgar's Second Symphony. The interlace structure allows the author to bring different temporal strands into meaningful interaction, as if they overlap as threads before continuing on their

---

[37] Agawu calls the twin pillars of this dialectical approach 'introversive semiosis' and 'extroversive semiosis' respectively. See Agawu, *Playing with Signs*.

[38] John Leyerle, 'The Interlace Structure of *Beowulf*', *University of Toronto Quarterly*, 37 (1967), pp. 1–17. Reprinted in *Beowulf: a Verse Translation*, trans. Seamus Heaney, ed. Daniel Donoghue (New York: Norton, 2002), pp. 130–52. Page references are to the reprint.

[39] Leyerle, 'The Interlace Structure of *Beowulf*', p. 131.

[40] They are also seen in the currently popular, and superhumanly tasteless, modern 'Celtic jewellery'.

[41] See T. A. Shippey, *The Road to Middle-earth* (London: HarperCollins, 1982), pp. 144–50.

[42] Leyerle, 'The Interlace Structure of *Beowulf*', pp. 139–40.

separate courses. In the structure of *Beowulf*, two threads, utterly separate temporally, interact in this way. The first thread follows Beowulf's story, the principal interest of the poem; the second recounts certain significant events from a different narrative time, involving Beowulf's king Hygelac. The *Beowulf*-poet splits the two temporal threads into episodes and weaves them around one another 'to achieve juxtapositions impossible in a linear narrative'.[43] In each case, the interweaving of temporal strands has an explicit narrative purpose. Before embarking on his expeditions, Beowulf recalls how similar actions had led to his own king's downfall. The positioning of these temporal interweavings is, on one level, easily understood: juxtaposition of a scene of hope with a baleful prophecy signifies that Beowulf's deeds will lead eventually to his unravelling, and the destruction of his people. But the device bears a structural burden just as great as its narrative one.

> The four Hygelac episodes, like all the narrative elements in the poem, have positional significance; unravel the threads and the whole fabric falls apart. An episode cannot be taken out of context – may I remind you again of the etymology of the word – without impairing the interwoven design. This design reveals the meaning of coincidence, the recurrence of human behaviour, and the circularity of time, partly through the coincidence, recurrence, and circularity of the medium itself – the interlace structure. It allows for the intersection of narrative events without regard for their distance in chronological time and shows the interrelated significances of episodes without the need for any explicit comment by the poet. The significance of the connections is left for the audience to work out for itself. Understatement is thus inherent in interlace structure, a characteristic that fits the heroic temper of the north.[44]

The emotionally red-hot surface of much of Elgar's music, the Second Symphony not least, might seem incommodious to understatement. But while the dialectic of the public and private, life-affirming and depressive Elgar seems obvious enough from the surface of the music and the opposition of moods such as the ebullience of the work's opening and the deep meditative sadness of the Larghetto, the subtlest dialectic is reserved for the level of structure. Here juxtaposition is more difficult to spot, more cunning

---

[43] Ibid., p. 145.
[44] Ibid., pp. 145–6. The 'understatement' characteristic of the 'heroic temper of the north' is what J. R. R. Tolkien called the Northern 'theory of courage' ('*Beowulf*: the Monsters and the Critics', in Christopher Tolkien (ed.), *The Monsters and the Critics, and Other Essays* (London: Allen and Unwin, 1983), pp. 5–48, at p. 20), and W. P. Ker identified in the belief in *Ragnarök*, the Twilight of the Gods, as 'absolute resistance, perfect because without hope' (W. P. Ker, *The Dark Ages* (Edinburgh: Blackwood, 1904),

p. 57). In the face of the certain annihilation of *Ragnarök* no individual, however heroic, can hope for ultimate triumph; and pure, unambitious courage for courage's sake is therefore 'the great contribution of early Northern literature' (Tolkien, '*Beowulf*: the Monsters and the Critics', p. 20). It is very likely what W. B. Yeats had in mind when he referred to Elgar's 'heroic melancholy' in a letter to Elgar, 23 March 1902, in *The Collected Letters of W. B. Yeats*, ed. John Kelly, 3 vols. (Oxford: Oxford University Press, 1986–97), vol. III, p. 163. See also ch. 8 of this volume.

and understated in its arrangement. But the exact positioning of certain broad structural gestures – the relations unfolding between two jostling tonal centres – is just as essential to the form of the work and its 'meaning' as the interlace structure is to *Beowulf*, its use perhaps as self-conscious as the poet's use of *entrelacement*.[45] In the interweaving of two tonal threads – two temporal identities tracing their own courses but necessarily overlapping in the musical time which is common to both – Elgar tells the greater part of his tale. To miss it is to risk failing to appreciate the total hermeneutic significance of the way the fabric of the symphony is woven.

4. Existential responsibility

I must outline one more structure before offering an analysis of the symphony, this time an existential rather than an artistic one. The philosopher Martin Heidegger gives the name 'falling' (*Verfallen*) to an existential structure of Dasein (Heidegger's term for the human way of being). It is a counterpart of Dasein's 'thrownness' (*Geworfenheit*), the state of its being thrown into an existence already rich in cultural and historical data which suggest (and limit) possibilities for future ways of being. The sense of 'thrownness' might be grasped by considering the situation in which Gregor Samsa finds himself when, in Kafka's *Metamorphosis*, he awakes one morning transformed into a giant bug, asking himself who, what, where, and when he is, and what is to be made of the situation now and in the future. All Dasein is thrown, by birth, into a situation, if rarely one so peculiar, and it is Dasein's responsibility to itself to work with the available possibilities allowed by its situation in space and time and form, to carry out the lifetime's project of constructing a self which is 'authentic' because responsive to personal development as an individual being, rather than the sheepish ('inauthentic') mimicry of other Daseins. In the 'moment of vision', the *Augenblick*, Dasein sees its own 'authentic' future and decides to work towards it resolutely by making a series of choices which, being responsive to its history and situation, will bring it into being. In the *Augenblick* Dasein chooses itself and begins the process of creating itself *as itself*, not merely as a copybook version of something which the mass of popular opinion offers as a possibility.[46]

[45] The structure is definitely as self-conscious in the case of Elgar's First Symphony, written as the result of a bet that he couldn't compose a symphony in two keys at once. See Kennedy, *Elgar Orchestral Music*, p. 54.
[46] Insofar as the unfolding of music in time is a mimesis of the temporality of human existence – a claim that cannot be justified here – it is appropriate to say that music has *Augenblicke* too, moments that define its 'authentic' form and identity, even when this means flying in the face of generic or structural expectations raised by a musical tradition. The musical *Augenblick* is discussed in detail in my *Edward Elgar, Modernist*, and it will be invoked again briefly towards the end of this study.

Heidegger calls this complete set of Daseins (of which every Dasein is also logically a member) 'the They' or 'the One' (*das Man*) – the 'they' or 'one' in such sentences as 'I'm becoming a coal miner because that's what *they* expect me to do', or 'I leave my bottom waistcoat button undone because that's what *one* does.' Although no Dasein could ever responsibly be wholly oblivious to 'the they' – we write in English or wear shoes on our feet because 'one does' – nevertheless it is possible, realizing one's ownmost character as an individual existent, to freely and authentically choose to live out a script which 'they' provide. One's own marriage is not necessarily untrue to oneself simply because in every age of modern human history 'one tends to get married'. The nature of one's interpretation of the script of marriage might be very personal. So inauthenticity does not snuff out being; it is merely a specific mode of being in response to one's thrownness.

'Falling' gives a firmer definition to inauthenticity. 'The term does not express any negative evaluation' (especially not a theological one), 'but is used to signify that Dasein is proximally and for the most part *alongside* the "world" of its concern.'[47] This is a natural response to thrownness. If we wake up as a bug, or indeed as anything else, we must concern ourselves with the arrangements of our 'world' (in the sense of a network of interrelating objects, persons, and responsibilities, rather than in the sense of a planet) in order to make sense of what choices are available for us to make in future life. It is unhelpful to ourselves not to conduct such an examination. But, crucially, 'in falling, Dasein *itself* as factical Being-in-the-world [i.e. as an existent with a specific historical and spatial location within a social and geographical situation], is something *from* which it has already fallen away'.[48] That is to say that it is an inbuilt risk of falling that it can lead Dasein away from its primary concern, which is the need to assess and understand its status as an individual, and to make choices which will advance its personal existential project, its '*own*' life' (as opposed to a life that others might envisage for it).

So generally, and this is pertinent to an examination of the meaning of Elgar's Second Symphony, Dasein 'falls' into a concern with other people, 'the they'. This is comforting because, in trying to understand one's place in the world, it is useful to have companions who have already, collectively, gone some way towards reaching an understanding of what it means to be a Dasein. But unfortunately convention and 'the way things have been publicly interpreted' obtrude on all discourse with 'them', and discussion with other Daseins naturally descends into 'idle talk' (*Gerede*), a 'tranquillizing' gossip

[47] Martin Heidegger, *Being and Time*, 7th edn, trans. John Macquarrie and Edward Robinson (Oxford: Blackwell, 1962; orig. edn 1927), p. 220.
[48] Ibid.

which offers pre-packaged answers to basic questions ('What am I to do with my life?'; 'Can a man like me be a politician?'; 'Would marriage be the right way for me to seek happiness?') but does not, perhaps, rise to the level of insight. Nevertheless, it is *tempting* to accept the common wisdom of the masses on basic life questions, not least because if one toes the line it is likely that support will be given to fulfil the requirements of the imposed script. 'Idle talk and ambiguity ['ambiguity' means the difficulty of telling whether a public conception is a genuine understanding or not], having seen everything, having understood everything, develop the supposition that ... [they] can guarantee to Dasein that all the possibilities of its Being will be secure, genuine, and full.'[49]

But what is the nature of the support that 'the they' gives Dasein in its task of responding to its thrownness? First, it is conditional: misstep or abandon the script and 'they' will most likely say that one is making a dreadful mistake or (depending on how wide of the mark one steps) bringing shame on the community. Second, and more important, it is patronizing, even if one accepts its beneficent aid willingly. It pays no respect to the individual potential of a Dasein to say 'You really must get a degree rather than pursue vocational training', even if what motivates the suggestion is genuine concern for the well-being of the individual ('I'm only saying this because if you don't get a degree the government will punish you'). Every Dasein must be allowed to self-define.

Even in a bare-bones presentation like this, Heidegger's notions of falling, idle talk, and the *Augenblick*, when taken together, can offer a sophisticated means of understanding motivation and responsibility which links the personal and historically situated to the social and transhistorical. If it all still seems very abstract so far, the flesh put onto the bones in the concluding section of this essay will show that however abstruse they may be, these observations are never empty or unimportant. They can translate music's gestures into comprehensible meanings.

5. The first thread

The Second Symphony, like the First, opens with non-thematic material whose function is principally to act as a call to attention. The First Symphony opens with a drum-roll on the initial tonic, A♭, the Second with a *largamente* throb on a three-octave B♭, leaping to a two-octave G (Ex. 6.1, which shows only part of the texture). Not inappropriately, a similar gesture heralds the opening of *Beowulf*, whose first word is 'hwæt'. This word has been variously

[49] Heidegger, *Being and Time*, p. 222.

Ex. 6.1 Symphony no. 2, *Hwaet*-gesture and opening theme (string parts only)

Allegro vivace e nobilmente

rendered in translation as 'Listen!', 'Hear me!', 'Attend!', and 'So',[50] but the best idiomatic English-English translation is probably 'Right'.[51] Expressing the function of these openings in terms of J. L. Austin's philosophical linguistics, one could say that the locutionary force of each (i.e. the sense of the utterance) is practically nil, its illocutionary force (what the 'speaker' is doing with it) is merely to draw the listener's attention to the fact that a discourse is about to begin, and the perlocutionary force (the effect it has on the hearer) is to encourage the listener to stop shuffling about or gossiping, and turn his or her attention entirely to the art-work.[52] It is worth mentioning this because during the course of the first movement, the symphony's *hwæt*-gesture gains locutionary force – as it were, finds that it has something to say about the event it is introducing – and this impacts upon the 'narrative'.

As in *Beowulf*, the monochrome simplicity of the *hwæt*-gesture allows Elgar to seize the listener's wandering pre-symphonic attention and snap it directly to the first real object of interest, in this case the work's first melodic

[50] The sources are *Beowulf: A New Verse Translation*, trans. Roy M. Liuzza (Peterborough, Canada: Broadview Press, 2000); *Beowulf: a New Translation with an Introduction*, trans. Burton Raffel (New York: New American Library, 1963); *Beowulf: A Verse Translation*, trans. Michael Alexander, 2nd edn (London: Penguin, 1995); and

Beowulf, trans. Seamus Heaney (London: Faber and Faber, 1999).
[51] *Beowulf: A Student's Edition*, trans. E. L. Risden (Troy, NY: The Whitston Publishing Company, 1994).
[52] See J. L. Austin, *How to Do Things with Words* (Oxford: Clarendon Press, 1962); revised edn by J. O. Urmson and M. Sbisà (Oxford: Clarendon Press, 1975).

material, which Elgar associated with Shelley's 'Spirit of Delight'. Its steady march-like tread – thirty-three of the first forty-five bars have strong bass notes on each of the four beats of the bar – will inevitably link the familiar musical topic in the listener's mind with symbols of empire. Of course the British empire is not the only thing in human history that has marched: American schools and universities do it too, and quite often to Elgar's music (perhaps the first time was when Elgar was awarded an honorary doctorate at Yale),[53] but the musical signs are suggestive enough, even without the dedication to the late Emperor of India, to justify the instinctive association in this symphony.

Fig. 6.1, which is not intended to be comprehensive, tabulates some of the most important motives in the symphony, of which the principal melodic signifier of 'Delight', appearing in three movements, is motive 2. The combined effect of the *hwæt*-gesture and the exposition of motives 1–2 is, in structural terms, to give the movement's *Kopfton*, g^2, supported by the root of the tonic, E♭, a strong gestural spotlighting. So Elgar opens one of his most conventional symphonic formal sections. Ex. 6.2, a middleground Schenkerian reading of the exposition, demonstrates the relative orthodoxy of the voice-leading design, and Fig. 6.2 gives a formal summary of the movement.[54]

In the P-section, where the primary thematic material is exposed, $\hat{3}$ is prolonged by simple neighbouring motion and a third-descent from b♭^{2} to g^2 (motive 3, fig. 1:1–4). This third-descent is enlarged into a first-order progression (containing an octave transfer) that stretches from figs. 5 to 17:4, ultimately prolonging the *Kopfton*, which is regained at that point.[55] In the first transitional section, TR1, the first step of the third-progression, b♭^{1}, is prolonged between figs. 5 and 6 by a quick rising fifth-progression moving in tenths with the bass (motive 5, with its lower-fifth-reinforced, compulsive chromatic rising movement),[56] and after the eruption of motive 6 at fig. 7, bass and melody fall back, still together in a linear intervallic pattern of

[53] Moore, *Elgar*, p. 462.

[54] In this formal summary and the commentary that accompanies it, abbreviations are used for primary, secondary, transitional, or closing thematic sections or materials ('P', 'S', 'TR', and 'C'-sections or - materials, respectively).

[55] It is typical of Elgar to extend a middleground progression across a sonata form's internal subdivisions (here from TR1, through S1, to TR2). The rhetorical weight in his sonata plans is often thrown onto the second S-section, where a secondary thematic idea which is stated first in a gentle form reappears in a substantially more forceful guise. The First Symphony has an almost identical treatment of the S-materials in its

first movement (cf. 11:5–10 and 17:1–16), and in *Falstaff*, the secondary theme associated with Prince Hal (first given at fig. 4) undergoes a series of transformations which, viewed whole, carries a weighty hermeneutic burden. (See my *Edward Elgar, Modernist*.) The first-movement secondary materials of the Violin Concerto are treated in a similar fashion, although not purely within the confines of the exposition.

[56] The rising fifth progression, with bass and soprano moving with each other in tenths, is a favourite Elgarian middleground formation. It is used in the S1 section of the First Symphony's first movement, and again in that work's finale. See my *Edward Elgar, Modernist*, Chapter 3.

Fig. 6.1 Symphony no. 2, motives

consecutive tenths, to prepare the entry of the melodic b♮^{1} which, in S1, will act as a chromatic neighbour to b♭^{1}.

The first section containing secondary materials does not, in Elgar's hands, always establish the secondary key area, and in a sense this is not unusual.

Fig. 6.1 (cont.)

Ex. 6.2 Symphony no. 2, middleground graph of first-movement exposition

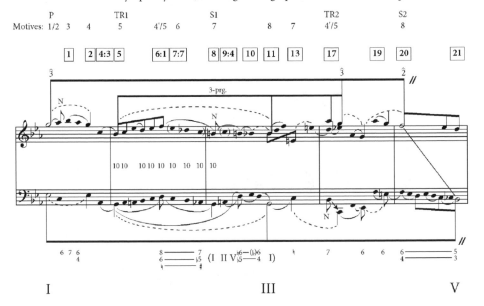

James Hepokoski considers the drive towards an exposition's 'essential expositional closure' (EEC), a strong and well-prepared perfect cadence in a sonata's second key, rather than the straightforward arrival of a second key at the beginning of the S-section, where the S-materials are introduced, to be

Exposition	Introduction	Bar 1
	P	0:2–4:4
	TR^1	5:1–7:7
	S^1	8:1–14:6
	TR^2	15:1–19:4
	S^2	20:1–21:6
	C	21:7–23:4
Development	E	24:1–34:7
	P	35:1–38:4
	TR	38:5–40:3
Recapitulation	Introduction	41:1–6
	P	42:1–44:4
	TR^1	45:1–7
	S^1	46:1–51:7
	TR^2	52:1–58:4
	S^2	59:1–60:5
	C	61:1–62:4

Fig. 6.2 Symphony no. 2, formal outline of first movement

the more essential structural function of the S-section in all sonata forms.[57] Elgar's characteristic practice is to split the S-section in two, interposing a second transitional section between the two halves, and to establish the secondary key only at the end of the S2 section. The effect is to transform the philosophical meaning of the arrival of the 'expected' alternative key of a sonata design. The secondary key is not arrived at by virtue of what Adorno, writing about Mahler, characterizes as the sonata form's overweening, 'Idealist' control of musical materials, but rather as a culmination reached through a wholly free and individual impulse.[58] In the first S-section of this movement, Elgar mixes the mode of the bass arpeggiation which is cementing the tonic E♭. Motive 7 gives the major-mode colour at fig. 8, motive 8 the minor colour at fig. 11. But the minor mode is not firmly established as the secondary key: the S1 section is, structurally, a 'failed', or at least (and to use a more dispassionate word) an 'open' one. When its miniature ternary form is rounded by the return of the A section (motive 7) at fig. 13, the key is not G but C, a key that will grow in importance later.

[57] James Hepokoski, 'Beyond the Sonata Principle', *JAMS*, 55 (2002), pp. 91–154.
[58] Theodor W. Adorno, *Mahler: a Musical Physiognomy*, trans. Edmund Jephcott (Chicago and London: University of Chicago Press, 1992; orig. edn 1960).

Ex. 6.3 Symphony no. 2, arrival of the structural dominant, first movement

Structurally this C that functions as VI/E♭ is a preparation for the arrival of the real secondary key of the exposition, B♭. TR2 prolongs VI, changing its mode, and builds tension breathlessly with the aid of the rising, yearning motive 5 (figs. 18–20), before discharging it all on the arrival of S2, the goal of the exposition, with motive 8 and its supporting bass movement grinding out the eventual and massive arrival on V/E♭ which comes in two waves. First the melodic $\hat{2}$ which brings about an interruption in the *Ursatz* arrives at fig. 20:1 (over a bass F, V of the eventual V/E♭). Then the bass B♭ arrives twice: first at fig. 21:2 (*fff*, and with a local V–I cadence provided by the timpani) and then again, when a chromatically rising motion in brass and woodwind reaches that far, at 21:3 (Ex. 6.3). Once attained, the music comes to a rest, almost seeming to tread water for eleven bars, on the dominant.

Both the formal ordering of the parts of this exposition and the voice-leading structure of its middleground levels are quite orthodox by early modernist standards. Certainly there is none of the First Symphony's obvious surface conflict between 'immuring' and 'immured' tonalities (A♭ and A minor in that symphony's first movement): although E♭ plays a relatively small role in the structure of the exposition, the keys that take up most of the music – G major/minor, C major/minor, and B♭ – can all be interpreted as falling within in an orderly I–III–(VI–)V bass arpeggiation supporting the movement's tonic. The melodic 'thread' signifying the 'Spirit of Delight' (especially motive 2) is never reined in, and although the tone of the S2 section jars against the vivacity of the bulk of the exposition, on a first hearing this will probably not concern most listeners. In short, the symphony appears to open in an untroubled, life-affirming spirit one could fairly, and without pressing parallels with Shelley too far, call 'delight'.

6. The second thread

But the situation changes abruptly as the development opens (fig. 24). Here is a quite different mood, which within the space of sixteen bars develops into what Elgar called 'the *most extraordinary* passage I have ever heard – a sort of malign influence wandering thro' the summer night in the garden'.[59] If the delight of the exposition section can be considered a kind of Elgarian arcadia (he was too politically conservative to countenance utopia), then the garden could be Eden, and the malign influence to which it is the unwitting host would be a serpent. It might also be heard, especially given the (perhaps)

[59] Letter to Alice Stuart-Wortley, 29 January 1911, *Windflower*, p. 75; quoted in Kennedy, *Portrait*, p. 246.

imperial redolence of the march-like bass, as a musical symbol of the 'age of empire',[60] into whose idyll would enter the 'vampire of Europe's wasted will' – German-sparked annihilation, in the image Elgar would set to music four years later in *Spirit of England*. At any rate, even if no hermeneutics should yet make such bold associations, the metaphor of the serpent will serve well to get across the point that the opening of the development introduces the second thread in the work's lacertine interlace, which I shall call (for reasons which will gradually become clear) the Spirit of Decay.

In his original plan for the symphony, this passage was to return between figs. 62 and 64 in the first movement (during the closing section of the recapitulation) as a relentless pounding statement – horns, timpani, side drum, tambourine, cymbals, bass drum, harps, violas, cellos, and double-basses all with the same thumping ♫ ♫ ♫ rhythm, intended to drown out the rest of the orchestra – which, in rehearsal, Elgar compared evocatively to the feeling experienced by 'a man in a high fever . . . That dreadful beating in the brain – it seems to drive out every coherent thought'.[61] But although the sketches held in the Elgar Birthplace Museum make it clear that this climax was originally intended for the first movement, at some stage – probably while scoring the Allegro – Elgar decided to transplant it to a late stage of the third movement.[62]

The precise dates of the sketches for the Second Symphony are unusually well documented. At the time of composition Elgar had just bought a set of date stamps, and he enthusiastically thumped his manuscripts with them as often as possible, sometimes several times on a single page. Unfortunately, no date was stamped on a remarkable continuity sketch Elgar produced for the third movement,[63] but it could only have been produced after the decision was taken to implant there the climax first meant for the Allegro's coda, i.e. some time during or after January 1911.

It is important to understand the general order of events, because when the first-movement development section was first sketched, there was no hint of the cello countermelody which would provide the main melodic weight of both the development section and the (now) much later climax, and the reason for its inclusion in the final version of the symphony could be hermeneutically significant. In its first guise, when sketched at the same time as the work's opening ideas, the opening of the development relied heavily on motive 1 (see Ex. 6.4). Diana McVeagh suggests plausibly that the

[60] The title of Eric Hobsbawm, *The Age of Empire: 1875–1914* (London: Weidenfeld and Nicholson, 1987).
[61] Bernard Shore, *The Orchestra Speaks* (London: Longmans, 1938), p. 135.

[62] See Kent, 'A View of Elgar's Methods of Composition', p. 57, on the original plans for this passage: Elgar also seems at some stage to have considered it for the finale.
[63] Transcribed by Kent, in 'A View of Elgar's Methods of Composition', p. 53.

Ex. 6.4 Symphony no. 2, opening of first-movement development section, first sketch

1st sketch of Symphony No. 2 - Ghost.

Ex. 6.5 Symphony no. 2, motivic connections with 'Spirit of Decay'

version of the theme eventually presented at fig. 28 was probably derived from the prominent $f\sharp^2$ (the only accidental) in the opening bars: 'the augmented triad of the first subject made in passing by a purely decorative melodic chromaticism, an F$\sharp$ for an instant over B$\flat$ and D, is in the development isolated, seen as a harmonic, not melodic factor, and as such generates a great new tune.'[64] Yet even more striking than this is a neighbour-decorated, descending fourth-progression at the surface of the theme (marked *x* in Ex. 6.5) which both typifies the Spirit of Decay (shown there in the form it takes at figs. 24 and 33) and ties it in with the opening themes of the third

---

[64] McVeagh, *Elgar*, p. 165.

Ex. 6.6 Symphony no. 2, middleground graph of first-movement development

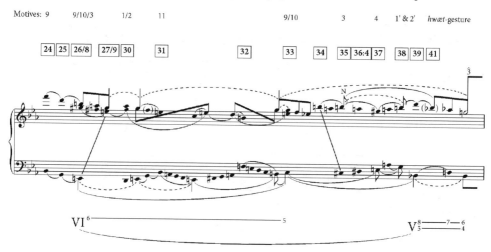

and fourth movements.[65] I suggest that if the F♯ which stands out in the Spirit of Delight is the first seed of the Spirit of Decay, then through the course of the symphony that seed gradually enables a morbid outgrowth to develop (as it were) on the face of the Spirit of Delight, which is still present between figs. 28 and 33, before being banished, significantly, at the point of the arrival of root-position C major at fig. 33. It was a decision of the greatest moment when Elgar added this cello countermelody to the beginning of the development section.

   The voice-leading structure of the development section is uncomplicated (see Ex. 6.6). Its opening bars descend by thirds to an early bass plateau on E♮, a semitone distant from the tonic root of the movement. Above this pedal (reached at fig. 26) the Spirit of Decay makes its first appearance (fig. 28). At first E♮ supports an E major chord, but a descending third progression overarching the Spirit of Decay (and recalling the long third-progression of the exposition) pulls the melodic line down to the *Kopfton* g^2 and the harmonies to C major. Elgar often 'puns' on the *Kopfton*, sharing it between two keys in this manner, and demonstrating the evenness of the match between his opposed tonalities. By doing so here he creates a new identifying mark for his two 'threads', a voice-leading one. Both threads have a focus (so far) on a melodic G, but for Delight that is $\hat{3}$ /E♭, for Decay $\hat{5}$ /C. Throughout the symphony, $\hat{3}$-lines will be associated with Delight, $\hat{5}$-lines with Decay, adding a subtle new constituent to the associative matrix

[65] Anderson also notices the important similarity between the Spirit of Decay and the Rondo's opening theme: 'The thirds and octave leaps of the Presto theme recall at once the first movement's "ghost" and its semitones hint at the strange cantilena of the night' (*Elgar*, p. 337).

which already involves themes and keys – and timbres too, since so far themes of Delight have been given strong orchestration with heavy brass scoring, while themes of Decay have had softer orchestration and lower dynamic levels.[66]

The new key's root is reached at fig. 33 by means of a rising sixth motion in the bass – its last note decorated by descending motion from F♮ – and the ternary 'episode' based on the new thread, the Spirit of Decay, gives way to the development's second section (fig. 35). Based on the P-materials, this section recalls the melodic b♮^{2} from the opening of the development and, in another gesture towards a process of the exposition, falls to b♭^{2} at fig. 41, the moment that corresponds to the *hwæt*-gesture that opened the symphony. This in turn precipitates another third-descent to the *Kopfton* which, at fig. 42, corresponds exactly with the beginning of the recapitulation of the P-materials. At the same time, the root of C major is (again as in the exposition) interpreted after the event as VI/E♭, and treated as an upper neighbour to the dominant.

Two critical observations can now be made. First, the main voice-leading structures of the exposition are simply recalled in the development; the only innovation here is a pair of unfoldings, accompanied by a new cadential idea, motive 11, acting to reinforce the I^6–V^6–I cadence into C major. Second, the section grants fifty-one of its seventy-six bars to exposition of new material (and because of the slower tempo of the first part, it accounts for four fifths of the development's temporal span); the twenty-five-bar rump provides only a very perfunctory 'symphonic development' of the P-materials – and even sounds almost like a false recapitulation. In the light of these observations, the development space can be regarded less *as* a development, and more as a second, and thematically contradictory, exposition. Indeed its main tonal focus, C major, receives stronger support than the exposition's E♭: both rise to their dominant, but only C major receives a firm V–I cadence (at fig. 33). For these thematic and voice-leading reasons, the development's C major might be regarded as a tonality with equal claim on the movement's (and, we shall see, the symphony's) hegemony – one 'immured' by an 'immuring' tonality which begins and ends the movement (and the symphony). One need hardly note that it is in the nature of things which are immured to attempt to break free, or that a strong beast caged is not always safe to approach.

Considered together, then, the exposition and development function as parallel sections of exposition: one each for the two main threads of the work,

---

[66] I am grateful to John Pickard for suggesting that timbre could have an associative use in this symphony.

the Spirit of Delight and the Spirit of Decay. Both are associated with themes (motive 2 for Delight, motive 10 for Decay), keys (E♭ for Delight, C for Decay), and timbres (strong Delight, soft Decay). As the symphony progresses, its narrative, insofar as we can grasp it, will be played out on the thematic, tonal, and timbral levels.

7. The first synthesis

But the first step towards regaining the Delight of the opening, and to picking off and discarding the signs of its decay – that is, towards forging a synthesis from the thesis and antithesis of the preceding formal sections – is not a promising one, because in the first-movement recapitulation Elgar unveils one of his most astonishing sectional structures (see Ex. 6.7).

The first point of interest concerns the *hwæt*-gesture that heralds the recapitulation. This has a radically different character from the one that preceded the exposition: what was at first merely a jabbing three-octave B♭ is now a gigantically orchestrated and greatly extended passage which has become clouded by a melodic B♮ (sometimes spelt C♭) left hanging over from both the profile of motive 9 (which is the overlay to the Spirit of Decay) and an important voice-leading component of the development space (see Ex. 6.8). The moments of this strong conflict between B♭ and B♮ are on the third beat of fig. 41:2 (B♮/C♭ on flute II, clarinet II, bassoon I, trombone II, violin II, and cello, set against B♭s on both oboes, cor anglais,

Ex. 6.7 Symphony no. 2, middleground graph of first-movement recapitulation

Ex. 6.8 Symphony no. 2, *Hwaet*-gesture, opening of recapitulation

four horns, and trombone I), on the third beat of fig. 41:5 (a similar distribution of instruments), and again from the first to third beats of fig. 41:6, this time exacerbated by false relations either within parts or across families of instruments (e.g. bassoon I, and the top three string parts). The monochrome, suggestible B♭ of the original version has become rather troubled. And what functions on one level as a simple third-descent to regain the *Kopfton* (see Ex. 6.6) operates on another as an almost baleful warning to the Spirit of Delight, which is about to reignite. The tale will not be the same the second time round.

If the symphony's metaphorical reciter begins the exposition's tale with a confident 'Right!', then upon his return to the same material at the recapitulation, although the *hwæt*-gesture's illocutionary force is still to direct the attention forward to the 'main material', the fact that the gesture has itself gained locutionary force – narrative import, indeed, from the imposition of Decay-thread material onto the reintroduction of the Delight-thread – means that its perlocutionary force is rather different. The listener still prepares to hear what is to follow, but now with a set of prejudices built in. In short, the listener wants the 'main material' to substantiate its claim to the tonal throne. And the recapitulation finds this a cumbersome responsibility.

After the grand preparation of the dominant leading up to fig. 39, progress towards firm resolution in the newly resumed tonic area is remarkably slow. In the first bar of P-material recapitulation, actually marked *Lento*, motive 1 is supported by a B♭ in the bass which descends to A♭ and G in the second and third bars, as motive 2 drives an *accelerando* to the main tempo. But once G, supporting I^6, has been reached, the bass motion stalls. There is a descent to E♭ in fig. 42:3, but it is heard in context as a local dominant to A♭, and not as the tonic root; and the E♭ on the first beat of fig. 42:7 is heard as the second step on an arpeggiation of a C minor chord. Structurally there is no imme-diate descent from G.

The arrival of motive 3 at fig. 43 introduces a neighbouring $a♭^2$ (as the goal of a descending fifth progression) which will be prolonged through the bulk of the recapitulation. At the restatement of motive 4 at fig. 44, the bass begins a rise which will take it to C by fig. 45:4, and thence to F for the start of the first section of secondary materials at fig. 46, at which point the neighbouring $a♭^2$, transferred down an octave, receives its own chromatic neighbour, $a♮^1$. The II–V–I motion towards F, begun once the bass descent stalls on G, is repeated during the S1 section so that with the arrival of motive 8 in its gentle form at fig. 50, the second degree scale has been reached firmly.

The tonic root is now only one step away, but we are already well into a recapitulation whose primary materials, originally taking up forty-five bars of exposition, have been squashed into just twenty-four bars. The seventy-two bars of S-material recapitulation almost precisely equal the seventy-five bars of S-material exposition, but since the E♭ root is not reached until the end of the recapitulation, with the same weighty S2-version of motive 8 that had cemented the arrival of the dominant in the exposition, $\overset{\wedge}{2}$ has an unusually long prolongation in the bass. In fact a G–F–E♭ motion which could have been accomplished within the space of two bars (if the pace of descent in the opening bars of the recapitulation were continued) takes ninety-one bars instead. The first strong E♭ root of the recapitulation coincides with the return after its long neighbour-note prolongation of the *Kopfton*, g^2 – and in a sense the recapitulation's achievement is merely to work its way towards a *starting* point. Had the shattering climax based on the Spirit of Decay been given in its original position, between figs. 62 and 64, the movement could not even be said to have accomplished that. As it is, the *Urlinie* does not descend further from this point, and the last melodic note of the movement is a G. Elgar had been composing structures with static *Kopftöne* at least since the Variations, op. 36,[67] and their effect in his symphonic works is, very subtly, to imply a structural (if not a temporal) *attacca*, a conceptual bridge to the next movement. Hermeneutically, the structure seems to imply that, however the burden of the movement is to be understood in the final analysis, for the moment no conclusion can be reached.

8. The threads interweave

The key signatures of the two middle movements suggest a focus on C (minor and major modes respectively), but the deeper structures of each call such hasty judgement into question. Having established joint melodic/ motivic, tonal, and timbral associations for the threads signifying Delight and Decay, Elgar explores possibilities of interaction between the keys of E♭ and C and the themes and timbres with which they have so far broadly been conjoined. Astonishing processes evolve.

The funereal Larghetto is in a simple sonata form without development (see Fig. 6.3) – what Charles Rosen identified as 'slow movement sonata form' and James Hepokoski and Warren Darcy call a 'Type 1 sonata'.[68] As in the first movement, the secondary materials are presented in two separate sections, S1 and S2, and taken together they once again effect the principal

[67] The technique is probably Elgar's own invention. See my *Edward Elgar, Modernist*, Chapters 1 and 2.
[68] See Charles Rosen, *Sonata Forms*, 2nd edn (New York and London: Norton, 1988), pp. 106–12, and Hepokoski, 'Beyond the Sonata Principle'. See also a substantial study by James Hepokoski and Warren Darcy, *Elements of Sonata Theory: Norms, Types and Deformations in the Late Eighteenth-Century Sonata* (New York and Oxford: Oxford University Press, 2006).

Exposition	Intro	−67:1
	P	67:1–68:12
	TR¹	69:1–70:4
	S¹	71:1–73:6
	TR²	74:1–75:6
	S²	76:1–77:8
	C	78:1–7
Recapitulation	P	79:1–80:8
	S¹	81:1–82:12
	TR	83:1–84:6
	S²	85:1–86:10
	C	87:1–88:2
Coda		88:3–89:5

Fig. 6.3 Symphony no. 2, formal outline of second movement

Ex. 6.9 Symphony no. 2, middleground sketch of second-movement exposition

articulation of the movement's deep structure. The primary materials, motives 13 and 14 (motive 12 performs an introductory function), quite quickly take the music away from the opening C minor. By fig. 68:10 motive 13 has begun tentatively to project F minor as an interior focus of the first formal section (see Ex. 6.9). The first transitional section expands on this promise by arpeggiating up from F to f in the bass, motive 15 providing elegant neighbouring-note decoration of the Ab en route (figs. 69:3–70:4).

The first section of secondary materials (beginning at fig. 71) introduces a Mahlerian theme of slightly uncertain tonal identity (motive 16) which nevertheless implies F minor quite strongly;[69] and as the second transitional section gradually brings a melodic B♭ (given in two octaves) into focus as a seventh over V/f, the grand new theme at the beginning of S2 (fig. 76) can utilize the slow fifth-descent to the root which had generated the form of the first movement's recapitulation to solidify F (now in the major mode) as the central key of the movement so far. Motive 19 itself can be regarded as a compression of the first three bars of the symphony, a new melodic form of the Spirit of Delight: the prominent rising sixth of its first bar and the strong descending contour of its second bar could be a skeletal reinterpretation of the original form of the theme; the strong brass peals also bring the Delightful timbre into the movement. In voice-leading terms the *Kopfton* which had begun as the putative $\hat{8}$ of an $\hat{8}$-line in C can better be conceptualized as $\hat{5}$/F, and the descent to the consonance of a♮^{1} in the melody and F in the bass – although not the perfect consonance of the traditional $\frac{\hat{1}}{I}$ contrapuntal close – lends further structural gravity to the immured F tonality.

A two-bar transition leads back to C minor and the recapitulation. Despite a considerably elaborated texture, the course of this section quite closely follows that of the exposition, but its divergences are important. Again a quick move is made away from C minor towards an immured tonality; really this movement spends very little time on its ostensible tonic.[70] But before the progress of establishing the second immured tonality is properly begun, this key (E♭) is treated to a lush upper-third decoration with motive 14 supplying a brief, unforgettable moment which some might hear as (misplaced?) confidence, others as a continuation of the unsettling weirdness of the beginning of the recapitulation (fig. 80), before the secondary materials enter at fig. 81. The key is E♭, and it can be regarded on one level as chord III in a bass arpeggiation of the C minor triad (as indicated by the broken extension of its stem in Ex. 6.10), but because of the curiously offhand way the tonic is treated in this movement it makes more sense – and in any case corresponds better with the impression the music makes when heard – to regard it as a tonal focus in its own right. It is, furthermore, the key associated with the Spirit of Delight.

The working of C (major or minor) and E♭ into a duotonal structure is characteristic of some of Elgar's strongest music. In the second part of *The Dream of Gerontius* the pairing is still being used in a traditional late nineteenth-century manner as a more or less stable but complex tonic

[69] Tovey says this moves 'in broad lines and with free rhythm, as if Bruckner had become a master of phrasing'. Donald Francis Tovey, 'Elgar: Symphony in E flat, no. 2, op. 63', in *Essays in* *Musical Analysis*, vol. II (London: Oxford University Press, 1935), pp. 114–21, at p. 118.
[70] In this characteristic at least it is like the first movement of the First Symphony.

Ex. 6.10 Symphony no. 2, middleground graph of second-movement recapitulation

reference point.[71] Soon after the completion of the Second Symphony the structure would be given its most probing examination in *Falstaff*, where C is associated with Falstaff and E♭ with Prince Hal/King Henry V.[72] Within the Second Symphony, the keys are used in a manner not dissimilar to the way A♭ and D are used across the four movements of the First Symphony, which is to say essentially in a combative manner, each vying for position. That they are more closely related than the tritonally divided keys of the earlier symphony allows Elgar's play with them to be more nicely ambiguous.

As in the Larghetto's exposition, motives 16–19 perform the task of building up to a I–V–I cadence into the immured tonic. Because the recapitulation picks up melodically on g^1, and rises to $\hat{5}$/E♭ by fig. 79:4 on its way towards the immured tonic, there is the potential for something singular to happen: full contrapuntal closure in a single key. From fig. 81 to fig. 86 progress is solid, and $\hat{2}$, supported by chord V, is reached during the glorious restatement of the 'new Spirit of Delight', motive 19. But this time the by-now familiar bass slide to the root doesn't reach completion. At the point when melodic resolution to $\hat{1}$ over I/E♭ would have led to an even stronger contrapuntal affirmation of the immured tonality than in the exposition, the

[71] See Christopher Orlo Lewis, *Tonal Coherence in Mahler's Ninth Symphony* (Ann Arbor, MI: UMI Research Press, 1984) and essays in William Kinderman and Harald Krebs (eds.), *The Second Practice of Nineteenth-Century Tonality* (Lincoln: University of Nebraska Press, 1996) for discussions of the way these tonic complexes can be understood.

[72] See my *Edward Elgar, Modernist* for analysis of the significance of this tonal pair in that work.

expected melodic pitch is modified to e♮^{1}, and the bass rises to G (instead of falling to the expected E♭), which then functions as V/C.

This moment, highlighted in Ex. 6.10, comes as quite a surprise. The work's firmest closure so far has been prepared for the key of the Spirit of Delight (albeit with the $\overset{\wedge}{5}$-*Kopfton* of Decay) and using a new melodic form of the original theme, but all of this is peremptorily swung into a strong affirmation of the key of the Spirit of Decay, C. And the return of this C major coincides exactly with the thematic recall of motives 1–2 from the beginning of the symphony, which together compose the theme originally associated with the Spirit of Delight – now, for the first time, clothed in the softer timbre of Decay, which gives the Spirit of Delight an entirely new countenance. One might have expected this theme to add dignity and security to the perfect consummation of contrapuntal tension in the key of Delight, and to create a sense of teleological arrival on account of its motivic relation to the main secondary key of the movement; but it is instead shunted away, and full closure in the key of Decay (and with its $\overset{\wedge}{5}$-*Kopfton*) is effected by the Larghetto's principal motive, 13. In the closing gestures the *Kopfton* of the first movement, g^2, is restored to prominence as a reminder that the biggest question still facing the symphony is how reliable the Delight it introduced at the outset actually is.

By testing the strength of the connection between the themes and the key of the Spirit of Delight Elgar foreshadows the moment in the Rondo which is, perhaps, the key to the meaning of the symphony. The slow movement's failure to connect tonal resolution with thematic return is of an importance magnified to the monumental in the Rondo. And, as is the case when the threads in *Beowulf* intersect, the precise coincidence of the return of the first theme of the Spirit of Delight and the point when its tonal resolution is refused is narratively critical. An essential part of the symphony – it may be associated with Edward VII, the last connection with the Victorian age – dies here. Its significance will be explored in the final section.

9. The threads fray

The form of the movement Elgar designates 'Rondo' is a cause of concern for Robert Meikle, the writer who has given it most attention, most fundamentally because 'its dimensions as a rondo are far from clear'.[73] He proposes three readings of the form: two of them rondos, the other a scherzo and trio (although he notes that this latter is a formal category 'with which Elgar quite deliberately chose not to label the movement').[74] His second rondo reading is

[73] Meikle, 'The True Foundation', p. 53.   [74] Ibid., p. 55.

Scherzo	A	−92:12
	B	93:1–97:13
	A	98:1–99:11
	C	100:1–101:16
	A	102:1–105:20
Trio	D (a)	106:1–115:12
Scherzo	A	116:1–16
	Episode: Decay	117:1–122:2
	B	122:3–125:20
	A	126:1–128:8
	C	129:1–131:16
	A	132:1–135:16

Fig. 6.4 Symphony no. 2, formal outline of third movement

his most persuasive mapping of the movement, and it comes close to my own formal outline, presented in Fig. 6.4, which combines scherzo and rondo elements.[75] Ex. 6.11, a middleground graph of the movement, marks the formal sections on both views.

For our reading of the work as a whole, the crucial section is the climax that was originally planned for the coda of the first movement but moved to the Rondo at the full-score stage, and in voice-leading terms it is the first really remarkable passage in the movement. The first theme, motive 20, which is related to the Decay theme (see Ex. 6.5), picks up the *Kopfton* of the preceding movement and begins to establish the major mode of the Decay-key, C. The entry of motive 21 and the first rondo episode at fig. 93 switches to the minor mode, and the combination of the first will-o'-the-wispish return of the A section at fig. 98 and the C section beginning at fig. 100 move the music, via a secondary dominant, to V/C. This is prolonged thereafter until the end of the trio, section D, where it ends on a second inversion that denies the scherzo return at fig. 116 any strong gestural emphasis. Progress is then swift towards the (relatively) long episode which must figure prominently in any reading of the symphony.

Writing before the premiere, Ernest Newman thought that 'altogether this strange and powerful episode, occurring as it does in the middle of a Rondo seemingly given up to the pure joy of motion, will give us something to think

[75] Meikle's placing of the beginning of the trio, or the D section of the rondo, at fig. 107 instead of fig. 106 is puzzling (unless motivated by the mere fact of a change of key signature), since the material introduced at fig. 106 (motive 23) is definitely trio/D-section material. But Elgar does create a sense of continuity that cunningly dovetails the sections at fig. 106, and perhaps it is this that leads Meikle to his decision.

Ex. 6.11 Symphony no. 2, middleground graph of third movement

about when we hear it. We shall probably not understand it all at first.'[76] Among writers on the symphony there is certainly no consensus on the 'meaning' of this moment, or even (setting aside the larger hermeneutic questions) on the immediate effect it makes. One problem facing the interpreter is the sense that the episode seems almost spliced into the general scheme of the work – a feeling perhaps reinforced by the knowledge that its placement here was not part of Elgar's original intention. There is also a strictly formal reason why the interruption seems peculiar, namely that for the rondo design to be (for all practical purposes) symmetrical, section B, and not this new episode, should return at fig. 117. Furthermore, on a rhetorical level, what actually occurs in the episode – a colossal mechanistic hammering and grinding, as close as Elgar comes to a topic of dystopia in his music – seems to have virtually no effect on what immediately follows it. There is no awed holding back of the tempo or augmentation of the intervals beginning the B section (motive 21) which might indicate the form's sensitivity to its content. With the arrival of the sectional boundary the form trots out the theme of the B section as if all that was at stake in the movement was the chance to create a copybook rondo design.

The only signal event at the formal join, easily missed, is an allusion to *Tristan*.[77] As shown in Ex. 6.12, Elgar prepares the C minor in which section

[76] Ernest Newman, 'Elgar's Second Symphony', *MT*, 52 (1911), pp. 295–300, at 299.

[77] I am grateful to Patrick McCreless for drawing my attention to this. See this volume, pp. 15–16.

Ex. 6.12 Symphony no. 2, allusion to *Tristan*: (a) Elgar Symphony no. 2, third movement; (b) Wagner, *Tristan* Prelude

(a) Elgar, Symphony No. 2, third movement

(b) Wagner, *Tristan* Prelude

B will return by alluding to the closing bars of the *Tristan* prelude, where V^7/c is tonicized in a notably similar fashion. Elgar's treatment of Wagner's pre-cadential motion here may be significant. Elgar gives the *Tristan* chord at fig. 122.1 (with E♭ on top) and resolves it a bar later to the same dominant minor ninth Wagner gives at b.100 and b.103. Wagner finally resolves his lingering A♭ to G to form V^7/c at b.106, but Elgar leaves his A♭ unresolved. Not only is the similarity in the spacing of the chords at the end of Ex. 6.12 (a) and (b) remarkable, but there is not much to differentiate their orchestration: clar-inet, bass clarinet, bassoons, timpani, and low strings for Wagner; the same but with horns substituting for clarinets in Elgar. (The retention of the portentous drum roll is perhaps the clinching touch.) It is what follows in each case that marks these moments out. In the context of the opera, the Sailor's song very quickly moves to a strong cadence in E♭. If Elgar had followed Wagner, that would strongly affirm the key of Delight. But instead Elgar makes good on the potential resolution that Wagner decides against, by discharging his V^9/c directly into a return to C minor – the key of Decay. There is an inevitability about this progression and Elgar's rejection of E♭, even within an allusive context which seems to offer a precedent for a confirmation of Delight's associated key, that we could be foolish to disregard.

Critics have viewed this moment in different ways. Meikle baulks at it. 'After the "hammering" music ... the momentum of B returns and the movement ... inexplicably carries on as if nothing had happened, as if the intervening tumult had changed nothing.'[78] Tovey, by contrast, and with period charm, considers the move back into the B section extremely elegant.

> It is always an interesting problem in aesthetics how, when a lively movement has mounted on to a sublime pedestal, it can come off it again. Elgar's solution of this dangerous problem is Schumannesque and classical. Without any preaching or tub-thumping, the music resumes the first episode ... quietly, as Schumann's Florestan, or any other nice young undergraduate, might relight his pipe after he had allowed it to go out during an outburst of enthusiasm.[79]

This reading is too tidy, not to say too picturesque. A balanced view lies somewhere between this and Meikle's imputation of amateurishness. The music between figs. 118 and 122:3 is a crisis, ear-splitting and palpitating with fever. Decay has taken on the timbre of Delight, and uses it to assault the listener. If the nice young undergraduate relights his pipe, he does so after airing the kind of view that drowns conversation in stricken silence. The burden of his comment is unclear as yet – as Newman says, we shall have to think about it – but the voice-leading of the crisis gives some indication of what has occurred.

The episode, which recalls the first-movement theme signifying the Spirit of *Decay* (motive 10), is rooted on E♭, the key of *Delight*. Indeed it very nearly composes-out a first-order contrapuntal closure there. While $\hat{5}$/E♭ descends to $\hat{1}$, the bass all but completes a I–V–I supporting motion (albeit with the wrong harmonies: the B♭ at fig. 121:7 supports chord I, not the cadential chord V), with a descending fifth progression cut short by the entry of G at fig. 122:2. So the most powerful structural motion yet in the *Delight-* key is composed-out by the *Decay*-theme. This is the second, and the most definitive, rupture of the association between keys and themes that has been so carefully upheld by the symphony as a whole, and it amounts to a fraying of one of the two principal threads of the work. The strong, and this time complete and properly cadential, first-order close in C, during the repeat of the C episode between figs. 129 and 131, suggests that it is the *Decay*-thread that is holding up better under the strain. Viewed retrospectively, both the instrumental strengthening of the Decay material – it has the most powerful orchestration of the entire symphony, making the work's opening seem limp-wristed by comparison – and Elgar's decision on how to deal structurally with the *Tristan* allusion seem to confirm that impression. (This resolution is, furthermore, an echo of the closing section of the Larghetto, reminding the listener of the strong Decay-key there.)

Although the movement ends once again with a static *Kopfton* (see Ex. 6.13) – the g^2 that has lingered since the second bar of the symphony – and a wailing chthonic plunge (fig. 135:2–9), both the key and latest thematic

---

[78] Meikle, 'The True Foundation', p. 54.   [79] Tovey, 'Elgar: Symphony in E flat', p. 119.

Ex. 6.13 Symphony no. 2, foreground sketch, fig. 134 to end of Rondo

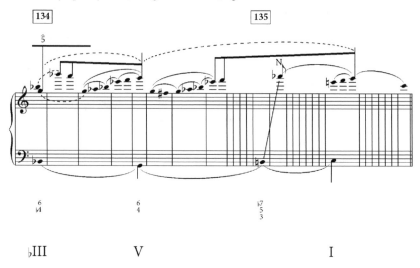

indicator of the Spirit of Decay wrap up the penultimate movement with a convincing display of structural unity and coherence. There is no sense yet (if there ever will be) that the Decay-key and -theme(s) are losing sight of their ultimate structural objective, which is a definitive closure of the symphony in C. The friction caused by the interweaving of the work's two threads appears to result in wear and tear only on the Delight-thread, and by the final pages of the rondo, the clear aims, claims, and argumentative processes of the first movement's exposition themes and tonality (i.e. ultimate closure in E♭, and with the Delight-theme) seem to have disintegrated. The confusion – it might be too much to say schizophrenia – wrought in the Spirit of Delight by the closing stages of the slow movement has come to its logical conclusion: raggedly twitching uncertainty. That is not to say that the situation at the end of the Rondo is a hopeless one for the Spirit of Delight, but there are difficult questions to answer, and if conventional closure is to be achieved the finale is required not only to provide a new synthesis of the opposed forces but also to *reconstruct* the Delight-thread.

If Elgar had put this crisis into the place he originally intended, between figs. 62 and 64 at the end of the first movement, none of this would be an issue: the symphony would have three more movements in which Delight could transcend Decay. But he deliberately moved it to the closing pages of the penultimate movement, and so greatly expanded its reach. Although the Second Symphony's third movement ends in a very different way from that of the First Symphony, the position going into the finale is remarkably similar. The 'immured' tonality, ostensibly structurally inferior, finds its strength waxing while that of the 'immuring' tonality wanes. New themes and strong middleground hints towards ultimate closure confirm its ascent, and if Delight is to triumph, the finale has the work of an entire symphony to perform.

10. The plot sewn up

Commentators have generally remarked that the finale of the Second Symphony is one of Elgar's most straightforward and satisfying sonata-form designs,[80] and in many ways it is (see Fig. 6.5). The P-materials, motives 25 and 26, open the movement in E♭. The main theme is given first by bass instruments, and an initial ascent to the *Kopfton* begins only once the theme is transferred to higher strings at fig. 138 (see Ex. 6.14; the preceding rising third from g¹ is a covering progression formed by the chirruping violin and woodwind accompaniment to the bass theme). The two sets of secondary materials – here, unusually for Elgar, not separated by transitional material – lead the music on conventionally via chord IV (fig. 139, motive 27 – the so-called 'Hans himself' theme, which James Hepokoski considers the work's *telos*; see above) to chord V (fig. 142, motives 28 and 29).[81]

The main theme has motivic links with the Spirit of Decay (see Ex. 6.5), but few ears will spot this and the effect of the new tune is quite different. If the signal of Decay is being repeated here, it is in an unthreatening way. Nothing disturbs the late-summer, Sunday-afternoon tranquillity of the P-section, and while the S-materials are, viewed in terms of their voice-leading, probably more insistent than strong (both stick tenaciously to their principal melodic pitches: respectively a♭¹ and f¹), the structure of the first formal section is satisfyingly conventional. The *Kopfton* $\hat{3}$ that has been in evidence in every movement of the symphony is in the lower octave as g¹, and for the first time since the first-movement exposition, it descends in ortho-dox manner to $\hat{2}$ for the interruption to the *Ursatz*. All seems well. The development section projects a local incident onto the middleground by

---

[80] See, for example, Christopher Mark, 'The Later Orchestral Music (1910–34), in *Companion*, pp. 154–70, at pp. 159–60; McVeagh, *Elgar*, p. 166; and Meikle, 'The True Foundation', pp. 55–6.

[81] The P- and S-materials break down into three subsections apiece. A small ternary design sandwiching motive 26 between two statements of motive 25 fills out the P-section (with the second and third subsections beginning at figs. 137 and 138 respectively). Section S1 has three smaller modules – 139:1–12; 140:1–9; and 140:10–141:11 – which

compose a little I–V–I progression within the movement's subdominant, A♭. The subdivisions of S2 are 142:1–12, 143:1–6, and 143:7–14. The proportions are varied in the recapitulation, notably in the third part of S1, which increases the sense of anticipation leading up to the structurally crucial S2 there. In the recapitulation the materials are distributed in the following manner: P¹ (157:1–8), P² (158:1–10), P³ (159:1–9); S¹·¹ (160:1–11), S¹·² (160:12–161:6), S¹·³ (161:7–162:10); and S²·¹ (163:1–8), S²·² (164:5–165:7), S²·³ (165:8–166:4).

Exposition	P	−138:8
	S1	139:1–141:11
	S2	142:1–143:14
	C	144:1–8
Development	I	145:1–148:5
	II	149:1–151:8
	III	152:1–156:11
Recapitulation	P	157:1–159:9
	S1	160:1–162:10
	S2	163:1–166:4
	C	166:5–167:7
Coda	I	168:1–170:6
	II	170:7–171:10

Fig. 6.5 Symphony no. 2, formal outline of finale

Ex. 6.14 Symphony no. 2, middleground graph of finale, to point of recapitulation

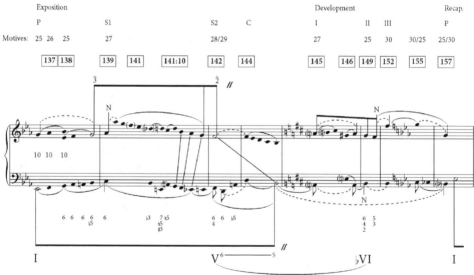

making a structural feature of the five bars of B major which had added a gleam to S2 at fig. 142:8–12. Transferred to the minor mode, and with its own theme (motive 30, given in the third part of the development, at fig. 152), this ♭VI functions unproblematically as a chromatic neighbour to the dominant.

The recapitulation opens with more confidence than was shown at the equivalent point in the first movement. Because the main component of the P-material is a bass theme strongly affirming the pitch E♭, the symphony's

Ex. 6.15 Symphony no. 2, middleground graph of finale, recapitulation and coda

last recapitulation can begin with the tonic in root position, after only one bar of the dominant (Ex. 6.15). But the absence of any strong preparatory rhetoric in the bars preceding this assured point of recapitulation (compare the ulcerous eruption within the recapitulatory *hwæt*-gesture in the first movement) gives a sense – which confirms a feeling that has grown through the movement so far – that however secure all this music may be, it is not very vital or energetic. And given the symphony's conduct so far in interweaving its two threads, perhaps this material, this orthodox form, this potential conclusive composing-out of an orthodox descent from an orthodox $\hat{3}$-*Kopfton*, could never ultimately ring true, because it would be too simplistic an outcome, too hidebound to a tradition that at the time of composition had lost the historical justification for its ubiquity.

So it is that as the recapitulation unfolds, although E♭ is confirmed by strong middleground preparations for its rhetorical restatement at structural points (I–III–V–I closing into S1 at fig. 160; I–IV–V–I closing into S2 at fig. 163), Elgar introduces a mild but hermeneutically eloquent structural side-step. The melodically insistent materials of S2 arrive heftily in E♭ – the tonic of the movement and the symphony, the key of Delight, and with its original brassy timbre – but now their mighty insistence prolongs a new *Kopfton*, b♭[1], the starting point within E♭-Delight for a $\hat{5}$-line *Urlinie* of Decay. The symphony will compose-out an *Ursatz* at last, but not in unambiguous terms. A classic heroic resolution to $\hat{1}$, with the *Urlinie*'s stepwise descent from the *Kopfton* given contrapuntal support by a I–V–I bass arpeggiation, is forgone, and an option that has presented itself twice in the course of the

Ex. 6.16 Symphony no. 2, middleground graph

Allegro   Larghetto   Rondo   Moderato

20 42 60 71 79 81   87   89 118   123   132 142 157 163   171

symphony so far will serve as denouement in its stead: a $\hat{5}$–$\hat{1}$ descent in
E♭ throughout section S2 (beginning fig. 163). Is what is stated thrice, as the
Snark-hunting Bellman asserts, to be taken as true?[82] And what does it mean
if it is?

The descent from B♭, which now appears for the third time at a crucial
point in the symphony, has never had a function that can be assigned to its
movement's broader goals, if those are defined in terms of Schenkerian
Ursätze. Ex. 6.16 summarizes the middleground processes of the entire
symphony, which few if any listeners could be expected to hear, but which
demonstrate the complexity and originality of Elgar's handling of the symphonic tonal form, and clarify the workings of the interlace structure.[83]

Of the two partial closures of the *Ursatz* in the Larghetto, the first in F
major has the secondary function of steering the *Urlinie* down from the
movement's opening $\hat{8}$ to the $\hat{5}$ which will provide the starting point for the
close at its end. But the $\hat{5}$–$\hat{1}$ descent in E♭ after fig. 81 serves no such broader
structural purpose. Its initial B♭ is reached by a consonant skip from the
newly established $\hat{5}$, and the miniature *Ursatz* follows its own counsel,
weaving the middleground syntax of Decay into Delight. In strikingly similar
fashion to the Rondo, while the first-order descent in C after fig. 123 is a
direct prolongation of the movement's *Kopfton*, the first descent in E♭ is
reached by another consonant skip and operates on a different structural
plane from the rest of the movement.

---

[82] The reference is to Lewis Carroll's poem, *The Hunting of the Snark*.

[83] Bar lines show the breaks between movements, and the rehearsal figures that follow indicate the first important structural moment *after* each movement's opening. The conceptual continuity between the two middle-movement *Ursätze* is symbolized by the broken beam in the bass and the dotted slur between *Urlinien*.

This latter incident coincides with the definitive breaking of the connection between the themes, key, and *Urlinie* signifying Delight. It is the symphony's moment of truth – its *Augenblick*, indeed, to revert to Heidegger's terminology (as adapted for musical application). In hindsight one can see that that moment brings into focus the authentic future of the symphony, and its ownmost form, which it can choose to bring about. The symphony runs ahead to its own 'death', i.e. conclusion, and assesses in the light of that knowledge the options open to it. Just as I know that in the years left to me, and given my current situation, my becoming an internationally renowned cosmologist is not within the realm of practical politics, so also it becomes clear at this moment in the symphony's progress that the orthodox closure which the symphonic tradition seems to be urging in one ear is not actually possible. The climb from here is too steep. But what also becomes clear is that a *different* conclusion can be reached, and if not one so magisterial and awesome that it could reconcile the two threads and tonalities of the work, then at least one that is in its more modest way at least sturdy, believable – and above all, authentic. The symphony can, and in composing-out an authentic structural closure does, enact a $\hat{5}-\hat{1}$ *Urlinie* descent, terminating in a powerful, but not omnipotent, closure into E♭ at the end of the work.

This middleground motion is thoroughly implicated in the rupture of the link between keys and themes in the Delight-thread, and some will consider the qualified nature of the resolution it brings, and the reminder of the 'falseness' of the close provided by the *Kopfton* on which the work ends as it had begun, to be characteristic of the musically modern conception of closure. The fact that the closure in the Decay-key in the Larghetto was much stronger (because it more strictly conforms to traditional tonal unfolding, and composes out a complete $\hat{8}$-line) could diminish the accomplishments of the finale's affirmation of Delight still further. But to demand full Beethovenian satisfaction from a modernist work might seem naive, and on the other hand to imagine that one that diverges from the straight path is somehow effecting an easily pigeonholed critique of the tradition might seem too glib.[84] But to all reflective listeners, the symphony's decision to close in this manner, after the surprising option had been identified in its own situation (i.e. both within the tradition and as an evolving entity on its own), will demand assessment.

The urgent question for the hermeneuticist is whether the alternative ending compellingly resolves the tensions of the work. Is it significant that

[84] Daniel M. Grimley reflects sensitively on this issue in another work that ends in E♭ in 'Modernism and Closure: Nielsen's Fifth Symphony', *The Musical Quarterly*, 86 (2002), pp. 149–73, and Arnold Whittall's cautioning against unambiguous readings of modern-classical closure in Sibelius is also pertinent. See Whittall, 'The Later Symphonies', in Daniel M. Grimley (ed.), *The Cambridge Companion to Sibelius* (Cambridge: Cambridge University Press, 2004), pp. 49–65.

the secondary material of the finale wraps up the plot, and that the Spirit of Delight re-enters only within the structural and formal coda (fig. 168), once closure has been accomplished? Once back in the musical present it can't even reiterate the recent closure from b♭^{1}: it stalls at $\overset{\wedge}{2}$ and ends ambiguously with a strong recall of the *Kopfton* G in harp, brass, and woodwind, but with unequivocal E♭s on strings. It is in some ways a difficult conclusion to assimilate. And the answer to the question of meaning in the work can only be answered by a consideration of the interweaving of two threads which led to this perplexing final situation.

11. Falling and hermeneutics: our *Beowulf*-poet of music

In the final third of *Beowulf*, the hero kills the dragon but in so doing is mortally wounded. The closing lines tell of the funeral for the 'lord far-famed and beloved', the construction of his memorial barrow, and the lament of his people, the Geats, at his passing. 'They said that of all the kings upon the earth / he was the man most gracious and fair-minded, / kindest to his people and keenest to win fame.'[85] But woven into this, a solitary figure standing by the funeral pyre has a baleful vision.

> A Geat woman too sang out in grief;
> with hair bound up, she unburdened herself
> of her worst fears, a wild litany
> of nightmare and lament: her nation invaded,
> enemies on the rampage, bodies in piles,
> slavery and abasement. Heaven swallowed the smoke.[86]

Beowulf's death offers more to his people than the opportunity to reflect on the great achievements of his life – among which the establishing of political security ranks high. The end of an age, symbolized by the death of a king, is jointly a cause of regret at its passing and fear for the future.

Elgar's Second Symphony is dedicated to the memory of a king who had ruled over the end of a period in which England had never seemed more comfortable, powerful, or secure. Whatever its private associations for Elgar, the most public meaning of the Larghetto's funereal overtones is grief at the passing of an age-defining monarch – and by extension this also means the long-reigning queen to whose rule Edward VII's was but the guinea stamp.[87] Twinned with political revolution in England (the expansion of the franchise, even to women, and the subordination of the House of Lords to the

---

[85] *Beowulf*, trans. Seamus Heaney (London: Faber and Faber, 1999), ll. 3142 and 3180–2.
[86] *Beowulf*, trans. Heaney, ll. 3149–55.

[87] I have already noted that the fracturing of the join between Delight's theme and key comes as that king, the last link with the Victorian age, is laid to rest.

democratically elected House of Commons), it is natural that in this historical moment a conservatively minded composer should look back fondly on a recent past he had loved, and regard both the politically convulsive present and the coming future with vague but consuming unease. The gentle nostalgia of the bulk of the finale and the sunset glory of its Delight-infused coda have always suggested this most obvious of readings to listeners and commentators. However much they are nuanced, interpretations must boil down somehow to this general theme, or risk seeming irrelevant to experience of the music. Yet the symphony is more satisfying than that simple outline suggests, and that must be because there are deeper issues at work in it.

One of these is the nostalgic dimension. And to the extent that Elgar's understanding of it was wrapped up with regret at the loss of his youth and an ill-defined sense of the glittering splendour of that time of his life, the question of nostalgia brings with it Elgar's idiomatic imperialism. Altogether, the mid-nineteenth century he remembered, however rosily, was to his mind animated by a Spirit of Delight; and that allows for an immediate negative, and Beowulfian, reading of the valedictory closing pages.

Elgar's late-flowering imperialism was a romantic and mythic imperialism of heroes like St George – a character who features prominently, indeed crucially, in almost all his texted imperialist works.[88] If, for the purpose of argument, one stretches his almost certainly superficial interest in empire to the very limits of plausibility, one could say that Elgar might have felt that the imperial British, like the Geats in *Beowulf*, saw it as their mission to establish peace and a bourgeois material comfort on as broad a global scale as human beings could manage. In this case, the passing of a king, and the slow decay of the age he and his mother had represented, would not merely augur the end of a time of relative (but by no means untroubled) material happiness, but could actually signify the end of the idealistic dreams of imperial Europe, and perhaps even of the noblest hopes of humanity. But as we have seen, it is extremely unlikely, given the nature of his understanding of empire, that Elgar ever subscribed to those hopes in the first place.

Although war was felt to be inevitable, not everyone in 1911 could have foreseen that, broadly speaking, the attempted annihilation of a large part of the human race was to become the principal project of the twentieth century. Yet Elgar could not fail to see the utopianism of the leftist revolution sparking all round him, and that that could bring problems of its own. There is always a sense in political ideologies directed towards utopia that the struggle to bring material comfort and political security (in this case, to

---

[88] *Caractacus* is the exception, but of course it has its own mythic hero.

the workers) *guarantees* a bad outcome, for the simple reason that it deals in absolute goods which can never be achieved, and must end either in failure or – worse, and this would become a twentieth-century speciality – the bloody desperation of rulers who feel history slipping from their fingers and slaughter millions in an attempt to save face and delay the inevitable. Small things point this way, such as the scene in *Beowulf* when the hero readies himself for battle with the dragon (the ultimate threat to security and happiness). Even as he prepares to end the anguish of his people and for a moment bring on their finest hour, he knows that the victory will be Pyrrhic, his own end and the end of his back-broken people likewise assured. Tolkien is eloquent on this moment. 'Disaster is foreboded. Defeat is the theme. Triumph over the foes of man's precarious fortress is over, and we approach slowly and reluctantly the inevitable victory of death.'[89]

Like the *Beowulf*-poet, in his Second Symphony Elgar recounts the glories of the (Victorian) age which had been laid waste by 'enemies on the rampage'[90] and mourns the rulers who had brought and to a certain extent sustained it. In a god-making tribute, Alice Stuart-Wortley said Elgar was 'our Shakespeare of music';[91] but in this context it is perhaps even more suggestive to say that he was our *Beowulf*-poet of music. Like the end of the first great poem in English, the closing pages of the Second Symphony and to an extent the whole last movement, are deeply pained, however much that pain is hidden behind a smile. But what causes this pain – the mere passing of the time of his youth and the romantic past of the Oriental Room at Severn House? Not quite. There is the meaning of the Rondo crisis to consider.

Derridians would call that moment an 'aporia', a perplexing hermeneutic problem the resolution of which is postponed till later. Adapting Heidegger, I call it the symphony's *Augenblick*, the (as it were existential) moment when its available options come into focus with immaculate clarity. We have observed that structurally its effect is to light up an alternative means of closing the form, but in hermeneutic terms it has something of the character of the Geat woman's wailing. To pride, nostalgia, and gracious farewell it adds the final Beowulfian element: sharp, searing terror. Elgar's narrative is told just as vividly through its interlace structure as *Beowulf*'s is; 'unravel the threads and the whole fabric falls apart'.[92] It might disambiguate an interpretation to forget that the ultimate closure in Eb is fundamentally related to the Decay-thread, but to make that analytical choice means taking the risk of misconstruing the meaning of the symphony.

[89] Tolkien, '*Beowulf*: the Monsters and the Critics', p. 30.
[90] *Beowulf*, trans. Heaney, l. 3154.
[91] In a letter to Carice just after Elgar's death. *Windflower*, p. 339.
[92] Leyerle, 'The Interlace Structure of *Beowulf*', p. 145.

The finale denies the ambiguous outcome, an equal poise of hope and fear, which the ruminations of the first three movements seem to postulate as the only 'true' one – that is, a tentative compromise between the keys of Delight and Decay – and in the end we might not have been given enough information to be able to decide whether Elgar's Beowulf has killed the dragon. In Heidegger's hermeneutic terms we can say that the finale seems to simplify things down to what is comfortable, down to what 'they' consider right and proper. The material of the music proposes a form which the closing argument refuses to allow to come into being, and that is, potentially, its tragedy. But on closer inspection it becomes clear that Elgar does not actually give 'them' what 'they' want. Partly this is because there are two 'theys'.

First, the 'beautiful they' of the *belle époque*, the decadent bourgeoisie. To suggest that the (rose-tinted) Victorian element of the age would endure (passively) despite the powerful destructive urges at the heart of Western capitalism – of which Marconi-style financial irregularities and the tensions fomented by the antagonism between the 'Triple Entente' and 'Triple Alliance' were just two of the most prominent[93] – is one thing. To suggest that the defining feature of the age, its self-destructive energy, could be nullified (actively) by the 'beautiful' parts of the epoch is another, and more demanding claim. In musical terms this suppression of the inner enemy would result in a finale that functionally accommodates C, signifying Decay, into a firm closure in E♭, signifying the youthful, Victorian Spirit of Delight. But that would be an inauthentic conclusion to a symphony which has so far followed unorthodox structural processes, and Elgar rejects it while simultaneously appearing to bow under pressure from the other 'they' – the 'they' of social revolution and (because this was part of the age's Decay too) of war. This second 'they' would require firm closure in C and the concomitant rejection of beautiful, Victorian E♭.[94]

In mediating between these conflicting 'theys', Elgar provides a unique solution: an E♭ resolution without the subordination of C, and then only by employing a voice-leading structure that disobeys traditional rules and follows its own authentic course. Yet by seeming to give what the 'beautiful they' require of him, and at the same time demonstrating why it would be artistically unacceptable to follow it through, he takes apart and analyses – for short (but not in a strict Derridian sense), 'deconstructs' – the meaning of the demand.

In Elgar's deconstruction of it, the *belle époque* is seen as a period when existentially inauthentic gossipy statements (or the centralized form of these,

[93] See Hobsbawm, *The Age of Empire*, Chapter 13.
[94] The heroic associations of that key in works by Beethoven and Strauss, for instance, not to mention in Elgar's own *In the South*, might have weighed on the choice of key for Delight.

i.e. propaganda) are taken to be reasoned argument; when prejudice and convention are elevated over engaged thought and change; and above all, an epoch that dreamt that no matter how hard the foundations were shaken, the *status* would always remain *quo ante*. It could have seemed that way until Archduke Franz Ferdinand was shot, three years after the Second Symphony's premiere, and the world ended for ever; but the end was almost certain long before then, as Eric Hobsbawm writes:

> What is peculiar about the long nineteenth century is that the titanic and revolutionary forces of this period which changed the world out of recognition were transported on a specific, and historically peculiar and fragile vehicle ... [As the *belle époque* drew on] it became clear that the society and civilization created by and for the western bourgeoisie represented not the permanent form of the modern industrial world, but only one phase of its early development.[95]

The end approached with relentless steps, and Elgar's play with form does not muffle its tread. Indeed it is in his handling of form that Elgar reveals himself unequivocally in this symphony as a modernist.

Adorno regarded the use of sonata form in modernist music as a totalitarianizing tendency which straitjackets the individual impulse of a musical work.[96] Switching from socio-political to Heideggerian existential critique, one can say that the acceptance of closure – either bringing C within an E♭ ambit, or closing in C – is tantamount to 'falling' into the comforting inauthenticity of obedience to 'the they'. It entails giving in to accepted wisdom, whether conservative or revolutionary.

On one level, 'falling' into 'idle talk', into an uncritical closeness to the immediate concerns of the environment in which we find ourselves, is not necessarily bad. We are bound up to a point to accept that the general state of our world and its history are as 'they' (the media, the academy, the mouthpieces of government) tell us they are. We have to take many things on trust – for instance that King Edward VII actually existed – without digging up every old bone to reassure ourselves on every point. But on occasion, one hopes, the essay-writer or symphonic composer will emerge from his or her ivory tower and engage with the world, even just one small part of that world, and may on occasion even be brave enough resolutely to say something uncomfortable about it.

The problem with the state of 'fallenness' is that no such resolutely pursued discomfiture is a natural consequence of the mood. It is far more convenient and natural to 'flee in the face of death', as Heidegger puts it, or in this case to ignore the complex and unsettling outcome proposed by the first

[95] Hobsbawm, *The Age of Empire*, p. 11.
[96] See, for instance, his dialectical reflections on sonata form as the 'totality that sanctions for its own glory the destruction of the individual' in Mahler's Sixth Symphony, in Adorno, *Mahler*, p. 97.

three movements of the Second Symphony. And to retreat from 'authentic' disclosure of the reality of, say, an intricate network of interrelationships such as the *belle époque*, into a comfortable but 'inauthentic' *Gerede* or (propaganda-fuelled) chatter about it, reinforces Dasein's tendency, in fall-enness, to accept (for instance) the view of the zealots like Kipling as truth rather than (what it really is) mere assertion, and to assent to an argument without attempting to understand it. Elgar does not 'fall', but on the other hand the symphony's most revolutionary possibility is not chosen. The work ends authentically with a close in E♭ that is appropriate to its own materials, but not with an alternative authentic closure in C which would unambiguously kill Delight. Perhaps Elgar did not choose to end with Decay because to promote the destruction of the way of life he had pulled himself up to would have been a kind of suicide.

The Second Symphony's concluding movement could be read in at least two diametrically opposed ways. Its calm assurance will palliate those who are succoured by the past or the comfortable predictability of the status quo; but it will clang like the Geat woman's lament at Beowulf's funeral for those who are anxious in the face of the future and free society's fate in it. Tovey said that 'the symphony ends in solemn calm',[97] but failed to mention that one can be as calmly certain of a bad as of a good end. These calmly solemn closing pages could either be a reaffirmation of a promise whispered by the spirit of an age, or the dying puff of a dream that's banished by the cold, raised finger of the dawn.

---

[97] Tovey, 'Elgar: Symphony in E flat', p. 121.

7 'Music in the midst of desolation': structures of mourning in Elgar's *The Spirit of England*[1]

Daniel M. Grimley

The impact of the First World War on Elgar's career, and on his critical reception, has been widely acknowledged and extensively documented.[2] But Elgar's creative response to the conflict nevertheless remains an ambiguous episode in his life. Many critics, especially following the promotion since the late 1960s of a revisionist image of Elgar as an inward melancholic rather than a red-blooded supporter of Empire, have considered the war to be a crucial testing ground, where Elgar's supposedly patriotic sentiments are ultimately believed to have betrayed him. According to this line of thought, his war works are either regarded as hollow propaganda, or dismissed as incidental pieces that fail to live up to the inspiration of his pre-war symphonic music, and which lack the 'autumnal' depth and gravity of the Brinkwells chamber music and the Cello Concerto.[3] Certainly, the most significant products of Elgar's war years, the Kipling song cycle *Fringes of the Fleet*, the incidental music to *The Starlight Express*, and *The Spirit of England*, do not enjoy the permanent place in the concert repertoire occupied by Elgar's other major works. But other critics have made strong claims for Elgar's war music, seeing it rather as an essential and valuable part of his compositional achievement. For these writers, such as Jerrold Northrop Moore, Elgar's war music offers privileged access into his musical character at a time when issues of community and national identity were under their greatest strain. The war music therefore points to an acute problem in Elgar's

---

[1] A preliminary version of this paper was read at the Elgar Conference hosted by the University of Birmingham at the Shakespeare Institute, Stratford-upon-Avon, on 1 July 2005. I am grateful to the conference convenor, Matthew Riley, and to Byron Adams and the editors of this volume for their thoughts and comments on earlier drafts of this work.

[2] Elgar's war music has been the subject of a recent collection of essays edited by Lewis Foreman, *'Oh My Horses': Elgar and the Great War* (Rickmansworth: Elgar Editions, 2001), as well as one of the topics in a chapter by Charles Edward McGuire, 'Functional Music:

Imperialism, the Great War, and Elgar as Popular Composer' in *Companion*, pp. 214–24.

[3] The chief exponent of this view is Michael Kennedy, for whom the war works mark the beginning of a creative decline; see *Portrait* (1987 third edn, pp. 265ff.). Bernard Porter passes a similarly damning view on much of the 'rousing' music Elgar wrote during the war, including *The Roll Call* and *Fight for Right*, but makes a notable exception for *The Spirit of England* ('Elgar and Empire: Music, Nationalism and the War', in *'Oh My Horses'*, pp. 133–73, at pp. 146–9).

critical reception, focusing upon the meaning and significance of his work and its broader historical context.

The reception of *The Spirit of England* is a case in point. The work was vigorously promoted by Novello during the war itself, and was initially acclaimed by audiences and critics alike. For example, Ernest Newman claimed in the *Musical Times* that 'here in truth is the very voice of England, moved to the centre of her being in the war as she has probably never been moved before in all her history'.[4] For Newman, Elgar's musical achievement served an inherently moral purpose that in turn provided political justification for the conflict. He compared the tone of Elgar's work with that of the celebrated young poet Rupert Brooke, who had recently died on active service in the Dardanelles: 'It is love and gratitude and pride and sorrow for these children of England and their self-sacrifice, – a sacrifice of which Rupert Brooke, in the eyes of lovers of art, will be for ever the shining symbol, – that Elgar *sings* in such noble accents in the third of these new works of his' (my emphasis).[5] Newman later proposed an open-air performance of the piece 'with a thousand or more of singers and players, and with the solo part sung by some twenty or fifty sopranos'. Under such conditions, presumably following a glorious Allied victory, Newman believed that 'the people would realise that Elgar has expressed the enduring emotions of the war better than anyone else has done or can hope to do either in music or in poetry'.[6] More recent commentators have resisted Newman's exuberantly nationalist rhetoric, but continue to hold the work in high regard. Moore, for example, has described the work as Elgar's finest music since the Second Symphony, a verdict that implicitly places it above *Falstaff*, not to mention *The Music Makers*; Binyon's poetry had 'given an ultimate subject for Edward's nostalgia'.[7] Similarly, John Norris has claimed that 'it is not until *The Spirit of England* that we finally see Elgar's true personality fully revealed',[8] thereby locating it at the very heart of Elgar's output alongside such overtly autobiographical works as the 'Enigma' Variations.

Yet *The Spirit of England* remains a problem, too closely tied to its immediate historical surroundings to have maintained a lasting place in the concert repertory. Furthermore, it is hard to escape the sense of jingoism that surrounds the work. Elgar's use of the demons' chorus from *The Dream of Gerontius* to depict the supposed barbarism of the Hun in the first movement, 'The Fourth of August' – a parallel that was particularly obvious

---

[4] '"The Spirit of England": Edward Elgar's New Choral Work', *MT*, 57 (May 1916), pp. 235–9, at p. 239.
[5] Ibid., p. 235.
[6] *MT*, 58 (November 1917), p. 506 (reproducing a review first printed in *The Birmingham Post*, 5 October 1917).
[7] Moore, *Elgar*, p. 682.
[8] John Norris, 'The Spirit of Elgar: Crucible of Remembrance', in *'Oh My Horses!'*, pp. 237–61, at p. 259.

since the two pieces were frequently programmed alongside each other – retrospectively reflects the worst kind of war-inspired xenophobia. It does little to advance the case for a general reappraisal of his war works. The decision not to use Elgar's music for the unveiling of Edwin Lutyens's Cenotaph in Whitehall on 20 November 1919, as originally planned, fore-shadowed the work's subsequent fate.[9] It remains effectively a lost landmark, praised by connoisseurs but more often the victim of its perceived association with the political institutions that have since been regarded as responsible for the carnage and bloodshed of the war itself.

The Spirit of England demands recontextualization, in that it can be understood as part of wider cultural discourse about the war in which images of mourning are of central importance. As Jay Winter has observed:

> [T]he backward gaze of so many writers, artists, politicians, soldiers and everyday families in this period reflected the universality of grief and mourning in Europe from 1914. A complex traditional vocabulary of mourning, derived from classical, romantic, or religious forms, flourished, largely because it helped mediate bereavement.[10]

For Winter, this process of mediation explains the immediate purpose of war memorials, those 'sites of memory', he suggests, which, like Walter Benjamin's Angel of History, 'faced the past, not the future'. Elgar's music arguably enacts a similar process, and betrays a more ambivalent response to aspects of Binyon's text than its immediate historical reception might appear to suggest. The work's rhetoric is ultimately distanced from the mood of confident certainty and collective optimism that its title evokes. Borrowing from the work of Judith Butler in the latter part of my discussion, I shall consider the structure of mourning in Elgar's music, the way in which processes of mourning become part of the music's discourse. The ultimate impression in *The Spirit of England*, I conclude, is of an intense sense of hollowness or loss, an expression of private grief that the outward spirit of public restraint cannot wholly conceal.

The sense of ambivalence identified by Winter was in fact widespread at the outbreak of hostilities on 4 August 1914. On 2 September, a group

---

[9] For a summary of Elgar's correspondence surrounding the unveiling ceremony at the Cenotaph, see the editorial foreword to *The Music Makers, Spirit of England, With proud Thanksgiving, ECE*, vol. X, ed. Anderson and Moore (London: Novello, 1986), pp. x–xi. Henry Clayton from Novello came to Severn House to discuss the idea in January 1920, which resulted in the reworking of 'For the Fallen' under the title *With Proud Thanksgiving*. This was published in May, though it was not used for the November ceremony in Whitehall. An orchestral version was premiered in the Royal Albert Hall on 7 May 1921. On the design and symbolism of Lutyens's monument, see Alex King, *Memorials of the Great War in Britain; the Symbolism and Politics of Remembrance* (Oxford: Berg, 1998), pp. 143–7.

[10] Jay Winter, *Sites of Memory, Sites of Mourning: the Great War in European Cultural History* (Cambridge: Cambridge University Press, 1995), p. 223.

of prominent literary figures met at the Department of Information, Wellington House, to consider ways in which their work could contribute to the war effort by inspiring a heightened sense of patriotism, duty, and national pride. Members of the group included a number of writers with previous or prospective Elgarian connections, including A. C. Benson (author of the words to 'Land of Hope and Glory', which gained particular popular appeal during the conflict) and Rudyard Kipling, as well as Thomas Hardy, Sir Arthur Conan Doyle, the Poet Laureate Robert Bridges, and his eventual successor as Laureate, John Masefield.[11] Masefield's immediate response to the conflict was the poem 'August, 1914', published in the September 1914 issue of the prominent literary periodical *The English Review*, which Elgar read and admired. In a letter to Ivor Atkins dated 26 October 1914, Elgar wrote excitedly: 'Have you read Masefield's poem in the *English Review*? That is the best thing written yet.'[12] Alice Elgar's diary the following year recorded, 'Glorious glowing red wheat fields & Cotswolds in distance. One feels the summer glow & the spirit of Masefield's August.'[13] What apparently attracted the Elgars in Masefield's poem was its sense of pastoral epiphany, a nationalist vision of England conceived in ideological terms as a lost rural idyll. It is simultaneously a lament for the young men killed in conflict. Though its best-known passage is perhaps the opening line ('How still this quiet cornfield is tonight!'), the true crux of the poem is located in the fifteenth verse:

> Surely above these fields a spirit broods
> A sense of many watchers muttering near
> Of the lone Downland with the forlorn woods
> Loved to the death, inestimably dear.

As Samuel Hynes has suggested, the primary emphases in Masefield's poem are on themes of continuity and permanence.[14] The image of moonlight 'upon the ancient way' in the final stanza is juxtaposed with a sudden sense of rupture ('The breaking off of ties, the loss of friends'), which in turn becomes part of a universal cycle of destruction and renewal. This sense of continuity is concerned also with the preservation of a particular kind of literary discourse. Hynes has described it as 'an elegy for the lost peace of the English countryside, and for men who would leave it to die in the war. It is

---

[11] The meeting is discussed in Samuel Hynes, *A War Imagined: The First World War and English Culture* (London: Bodley Head, 1990), p. 26.
[12] *Lifetime*, p. 284.
[13] Diary entry dated 25 March 1915, quoted in Andrew Neill, 'Elgar's War: From the Diaries of Lady Elgar, 1914–1918', in *'Oh My Horses!'*, pp. 3–69, at p. 23.
[14] Hynes, *A War Imagined*, p. 31.

also an elegy for a kind of poetry.'[15] Masefield himself described 'August, 1914' as the end of his verse-writing during the conflict (he temporarily gave up poetry and served as a Red Cross volunteer on the Western Front), intensifying the poem's imminent sense of closure.[16] But interpreting poems such as 'August, 1914' solely as backward-looking, historically redundant and outmoded attempts to preserve a literary tradition that had been shattered by the war reinforces an established cultural-historical myth of the conflict in which the war marked the birth (or coming of age) of a particular kind of modernism whose roots lay in the Edwardian period. Rather the poem points to a series of discursive strategies that, as Winter has argued, served to deal with the immediate processes of grief induced by the war: 'the Great War brought the search for an appropriate language of loss to the centre of cultural and political life. In this search, older motifs took on new meanings and new forms.' Hence, '"Seeing" the war meant more a return to older patterns and themes than the creation of new ones. Among the most powerful was the reformulation of the sacred, as an exploration of apocalyptic themes in prose, or as a poetic language of communication about and with the dead.'[17] Masefield's poem can therefore be read as an attempt to address both the personal experience of loss and bereavement and a collective sense of purpose or belonging, by *ritualizing* the conflict, reinvesting meaning and value in a conventionalized set of poetic images (England as pastoral Arcadia) with a vivid contemporary awareness of the proximity of death as a means of allegorizing the suffering caused by war.

Even though Elgar never attempted a setting of Masefield's poem, there are striking parallels between 'August, 1914' and the work of Laurence Binyon, from whose collection *The Winnowing Fan* Elgar selected the texts for *The Spirit of England*. Like Masefield's work, Binyon's poetry often dwells on a symbolic set of metaphors in which descriptions of war and conflict are ritualized. In a poem entitled 'Thunder on the Downs' written in 1911, for example, Binyon closely anticipated the mood and imagery of Masefield's later work. Whereas Masefield's woods are dark and forlorn, however, for Binyon they still retained a sense of freshness and innocence:

> And this is England! June's undarkened green
> Gleams on far woods; and in the vales between
> Gray hamlets, older than the trees that shade
> Their ripening meadows, are in quiet laid
> Themselves a part of the warm, fruitful ground.
> The little hills of England rise around;

---

[15] Ibid., p. 33.
[16] Masefield in the introduction to an American edition of his poetry and plays, published in New York, 1918, quoted in Hynes, ibid., p. 32.
[17] Winter, *Sites of Memory, Sites of Mourning*, p. 7.

The little streams that wander from them shine
And with their names remembered names entwine
Of old renown and honour, fields of blood
High causes fought on, stubborn hardihood
For freedom spent, and songs, our noblest pride,
That in the heart of England never died
And, burning still, make splendour of our tongue.
Glories enacted, spoken, suffered, sung![18]

The sense of stillness, as in Masefield's poem, nevertheless seems strained or unearthly, the image of 'fields of blood' both a reference to an established historical geography of English conflict (from Agincourt onwards) and perhaps also an uncanny premonition of future events. Binyon himself subsequently wrote of 'a kind of fever, an almost exasperated craving for the violent, the elemental, the barbaric, for energy and self-assertion at all costs' that permeated poetry in the years leading up to the war.[19] In a later poem, 'For the Fallen', which became the third movement of *The Spirit of England*, military struggle is presented as a form of solemn service or sacrifice, a duty to the nation as motherland that stresses the supposedly organic relationship between community and nation state: 'England mourns for her dead across the sea / Flesh of her flesh they were, spirit of her spirit.'

The idea of setting Binyon's text had first been suggested to Elgar by Sidney Colvin, who wrote on 10 January 1915, 'Why don't you do a wonderful Requiem for the slain – something in the spirit of Binyon's "For the Fallen"?',[20] already hinting at the work's quasi-liturgical context. As Elgar scholars have noted, two substantial interruptions delayed the work's completion.[21] The first was the discovery that another composer, Cyril Rootham, was already engaged on a setting of 'For the Fallen', and had been contracted by Elgar's own publisher, Novello. Though Elgar initially offered to withdraw, he was persuaded to continue with his setting following the direct intervention of both Colvin and the poet himself. The second, more substantial interruption took place during the composition of the first number, 'The Fourth of August'. Though the second and third movements were premiered in Leeds on 3 May 1916, the full work was not heard in its entirety until the following year, when it was premiered in Birmingham by Appleby

---

[18] Reproduced in the section entitled 'Poems of England and the War' from *A Laurence Binyon Anthology* (London: William Collins, 1927), pp. 37–42, at p. 38. Binyon's work clearly draws on a set of images promulgated especially by the work of A. E. Housman. Compare, for example, Housman's 'On the idle hill of Summer' from *A Shropshire Lad* (1896).

[19] *Tradition and Reaction in Modern Poetry*. The English Association. Pamphlet no. 63 (April 1926), p. 6.
[20] Quoted in Moore, *Elgar*, p. 674.
[21] See the editorial foreword in *ECE*, vol. X, pp. ix–x, and Moore, *Elgar*, pp. 674–6.

Matthews and the New Zealand soprano Rosina Buckman on 4 October.[22] Elgar himself offered a reason for the delay in a letter to Ernest Newman dated 17 June 1917:

> Do not dwell upon the demons part; – two years ago I held over that section hoping that some trace of manly spirit would shew itself in the direction of German affairs: that hope is gone forever & the Hun is branded as less than a beast for very many generations: so I wd not invent anything low & bestial enough to illustrate the one stanza; the Cardinal [Newman] invented (*invented* as far as I know) the particular hell in Gerontius where the great intellects gibber & snarl *knowing they have fallen*:
>
> This is exactly the case with the Germans now; – the music was to hand & I have sparingly used it. A lunatic asylum is, after the first shock, not entirely sad; so few of the patients are aware of the strangeness of their situation; most of them are placid & foolishly calm; but the horror of the fallen intellect – *knowing* what it once was & *knowing* what it has become – is beyond words frightful.[23]

Commentators have usually taken Elgar entirely at his word, and believed that the reason for holding back the first movement was purely due to the problematic sixth strophe. But Elgar's reasoning is surely open to other interpretations. He casually invokes a common idea promulgated widely during the early part of the conflict: the notion that the enemy suffered from a lack of 'manly spirit', and hence that the war was a result of the perceived degeneracy of contemporary German culture. Elgar's earlier works readily reveal, however, that his relationship with the idea of the chivalrous hero is not as straightforward as his letter suggests.[24] Furthermore, the idea of a fallen intellect (not least in Elgar's own mind) cannot have been limited solely to the German side of the conflict. This potentially adds a new dimension to the dedication in the title of the final number, 'For the Fallen'.[25] Like Masefield's poem therefore, the work becomes a more universal tragedy, not just for combatants, but also for a particular world view: in essence, the hierarchical social structure that Elgar felt he properly belonged to and towards which he aspired.

---

[22] Brian Trowell has pondered the significance of this event, and Elgar's apparent absence though he was staying with his sister at Stoke Prior nearby, in his essay 'The Road to Brinkwells: The Late Chamber Music', in *Oh, My Horses!*, pp. 346–85, especially pp. 360–1. For Trowell, the participation of a soloist from New Zealand is a poignant detail, following the death in action of Lt. Kenneth Munro, a member of the Wellington Infantry Regiment and son of Helen Munro (née Weaver), Elgar's former fiancée from Worcester. Trowell lays great weight on Munro's death as one of the primary reasons for Elgar's creative breakdown in 1916, but the evidence he presents is circumstantial (pp. 355–60).

[23] Quoted by Anderson and Moore in *ECE*, vol. X, p. x.

[24] See, for example, James Hepokoski's discussion of the symphonies in D. Kern Holoman (ed.), *The Nineteenth-Century Symphony* (New York: Schirmer, 1997), pp. 327–44.

[25] Elgar in fact wrote at the head of the published score: 'My portion of this work I dedicate to the memory of our glorious men, with a special thought for the WORCESTERS', but this localized emphasis on his native regiment arguably serves to heighten the work's universality.

Elgar's letter also points to an underlying musical insecurity. Closer examination suggests that the confident opening lines of Binyon's text ('Now in thy splendour go before us, / Spirit of England, ardent-eyed') were not easily realizable in musical terms. The opening bars characteristically avoid articulating a root-position tonic triad, leaning more heavily on the relative minor and the supertonic (Ex. 7.1). They therefore suggest harmonic instability, a lack of resolution or hopeful expectation as yet unfulfilled, rather than the breezy confidence of earlier ceremonial pieces such as the opening of the *Coronation Ode*. The pointed reminiscence of this opening gesture at the words 'but not to fail!' in the second movement 'To Women', in a chromatically remote key (A♭ major) that brings to mind the 'ideal call' of the First Symphony, only serves to heighten the sense of anxiety (Ex. 7.2). The rounded binary strophic structure of the first movement reinforces this sense of formal emptiness: the climactic return of the opening material is expanded and enlarged by a false reprise at the start of the seventh stanza ('Endure, o Earth!', fig. 13), whose harmonic function is subsequently undercut by a highly chromaticised interpolation for *a capella* chorus ('O wronged, untameable, unshaken Soul) at fig. 14. Though the reprise proper regains a more confident dynamic level (and is marked *nobilmente e grandioso*, fig. 16) as the first stanza is repeated, there is no genuinely clinching point of apotheosis before the movement ends.

The conclusion represents not so much a failure to respond adequately to the text as a structural reflection of the music's prevailing harmonic syntax. In many senses, this is of course a general characteristic of Elgar's mature works, and not exclusive to *The Spirit of England*. As James Hepokoski has observed, in Elgar's music 'the magnificent, *fortissimo* moments of attainment and affirmation seem simultaneously to be melting away, and Elgar often shores up such moments with rises and underswells in unexpected places, as if he were trying to sustain an illusion forever slipping away from his grasp'. Hepokoski concludes that 'in such an environment of dissolution, diminuendos and simple descending sequences can take on enormous expressive significance'.[26] But such gestures surely assume a special significance in *The Spirit of England*. The abruptness of the final bars of 'The Fourth of August', for example, captures a feeling of *Realpolitik*, a realization that war was no longer simply noble nor uplifting, but brutal, bloody, and violent. Elgar's apparent inability in 1916 to progress with the composition of the first movement may not have been motivated solely by doubts regarding the setting of the sixth verse, therefore, but more deeply by a sense of philosophical and aesthetic bleakness.

---

[26] Hepokoski, 'Elgar', p. 329.

Ex. 7.1 'The Fourth of August', opening (reduction)

Ex. 7.2 Quotation of opening gesture, 'To Women' (fig. 10)

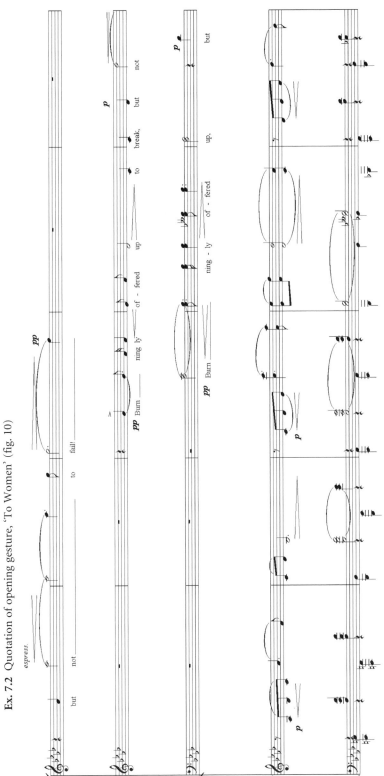

There is a further irony that, though commentators have focused on the literal quotation in the sixth strophe from the demons' chorus in *The Dream of Gerontius*, they have ignored the wider allusions to other parts of the oratorio in *The Spirit of England*, particularly the *mistico* orchestral introduction, the portrayal of Gerontius's soul in purgatory, and the chromaticism of the Angel of the Agony's lament. These allusions suggest that Elgar imagined the work as a form of sacred ritual. Indeed, it can be heard as a communion rite (inspired in part by the imagery of Binyon's text), organised as a musical triptych in three ascending semitone steps (G major, A♭ major/minor and A minor) whose rising tonal contour might suggest striving towards a higher spiritual goal.[27] Reference to *Gerontius* also allowed Elgar to re-engage with the musical text and iconography of an even earlier work concerned with notions of sacred duty and sacrifice, Wagner's *Parsifal*.[28] Though references to *Parsifal* are not new in Elgar's work, as Aidan Thomson and Byron Adams have shown, they seem to serve a particular purpose at the start of the third movement, 'For the Fallen'.[29] The initial bars, marked *solenne*, suggest a ritual procession or cortège (Ex. 7.3). Harmonically, they articulate a series of unresolved imperfect phrases (corresponding gesturally to the lack of tonic articulation at the start of the first movement), creating a sense of forward movement or restless expectation. The opening phrase (bb. 1–4) itself contains two significant components which direct the subsequent structural progress of the movement: the symmetrical pitch structure E–A–D, which recalls the bell motive from the *Verwandlungen* (transformation sequences) in Acts I and III of *Parsifal*, and the problematic chromatic pitch elements e/f♮ and c/c♯.[30] Texturally the music also suggests bell sounds: the rich low scoring for strings, harp and doubling bassoon

---

[27] Notice particularly how the mixed modality of the middle movement further serves to mediate this large-scale tonal plan. Indeed, the subtle blending of major and minor modes in 'To Women' is a technical characteristic of the movement that analysts and Elgar commentators have apparently overlooked; see, for example, the careful juxtaposition of C♭ and C♮ in the opening phrase (bb. 6–8), to which the closing bars specifically refer.

[28] For a richly contextualized reading of *The Dream of Gerontius* that draws attention to its preoccupation with ideas of loss, mourning, suffering and redemption, see Byron Adams, 'Elgar's Later Oratorios: Roman Catholicism, Decadence, and the Wagnerian Dialectic of Shame and Grace', in *Companion*, pp. 81–105. One of the central contentions in my current

essay is that *The Spirit of England* draws upon this earlier decadent aesthetic as part of its search for a communal musical language.

[29] Aidan Thomson, 'Elgar and Chivalry', *19CM*, 28/3 (Spring 2005), pp. 254–75, especially pp. 256–67. Thomson shows how *Parsifal* influenced Elgar's construction of chivalry both in his earlier oratorios, particularly *The Black Knight*, and the First Symphony. See also Adams, 'Elgar's Later Oratorios', p. 91.

[30] For discussion of a similar recurrence of symmetrical bell-motives from *Parsifal* in a later symphonic context, see Nicholas Baragwanath, '*Fin-de-siècle* Wagner: *Parsifal* Analysed through Berg's Programme to Mahler's Ninth Symphony', *Music Analysis*, 23/1 (March 2004), pp. 27–56.

Ex. 7.3 'For the Fallen', opening

adds a particularly resonant 'tolling' quality to the opening bars. The tonal ramifications of this gesture are the polarization of flat-side versus sharp-side harmonic fields, a tension that Elgar negotiates through a series of enharmonic transformations, not least the sequential 'jolt' at fig. 1.

After the choir has intoned a solemn statement of the opening couplet, the next significant event is the setting of the final two lines of the first verse ('Flesh of her flesh they were, spirit of her spirit, / Fallen in the cause of the free', figs. 4–5; Ex. 7.4). This moment of heightened melodic expressiveness is a characteristic Elgarian gesture. Comparable examples include the 'Welsh tune' in the *Introduction and Allegro*, and the appearance of the poignant 'Failings and Desires' theme at fig. 146 very near the end of *Falstaff*. Such passages are set off from the main body of the work in some way, either by textural means (such as a reduction from full scoring to soloist plus small accompanying ensemble), or by abrupt dynamic or registral change. Here, the *espressivo* direction, the sopranos' use of their upper tessitura and the canonic imitation (contrasting with the homophony of the initial entry) means that the passage can be heard as representing a celestial voice or song. Indeed, such moments in Elgar's music often seem to serve a special expressive purpose, or possess an unearthly or spiritualized quality. They try to capture in physical form the supernatural, noumenal quality of what Carolyn Abbate identifies as the narrative voice

Ex. 7.4 'For the Fallen', fig. 4

in music.[31] In other words, their textural and/or dynamic presentation often seems spatially or temporally distanced. The melodic material often appears unmotivated by its local context, although in most cases (as here) it can be motivically derived from previous music. Furthermore, such passages commonly articulate an archetypal musical shape: often a simple rising or falling contour. At the same time, their harmonic support carefully avoids strong root-position triads, so that, though their immediate environment might seem to be diatonic, their ultimate effect is dissonant and unsettling.

Fig. 4 is arguably the most structurally significant passage in the setting. After an altered restatement of the opening material at the beginning of the second verse, including a supercharged C major setting of the phrase 'Death, august and royal' that Moore hears as a macabre coronation march,[32] the earlier song passage returns in a *fortissimo* apotheosis. As in the first movement, Elgar's setting suggests that Binyon's words ('there is music in the midst of desolation') are more hopeful than affirmative. The other striking feature of this passage, which becomes even more apparent on rehearing, is

[31] Abbate, *Unsung Voices: Opera and Musical Narrative in Nineteenth-Century Music* (Princeton: Princeton University Press, 1991), pp. 5–29. It is significant in the context of the present discussion that Abbate opens her book with a discussion of the 'Bell Song' from Delibes's opera *Lakmé*: bells acquire particular narrative significance as sounding objects within late nineteenth-century music, a topic that Elgar draws upon at the opening of 'For the Fallen'.

[32] Moore, *Elgar*, p. 680.

its sequential character. The music not only resists diatonic containment, but evades harmonic closure. Elgar's immediate response to this structural rest-lessness is an invigorated further restatement of the opening music, but this merely results in two contrasting subsidiary episodes at the centre of the movement (verses 3–4 and 5–6, figs. 10–18 and 19–24) which ultimately reinforce the pattern of cyclic sequential behaviour. The first episode is a jaunty marching song, which Elgar described to Newman as 'a sort of idealized (perhaps) Quick March, – the sort of thing which ran in my mind when the dear lads were swinging past so many, many times'.[33] Once again, the idea of singing, the marked articulation of a performative musical voice, is brought to the foreground.[34] Though the upbeat tempo and major mode suggest a more positive frame of musical mind, the music's fragile outward optimism is undermined by the angular profile of the orchestral refrain and the chromaticism of the inner parts (which make much use of the c♮-d♭/c♯ semitone cell from the opening phrase). And, despite the music's momentary urgency, the passage eventually seems circular and undirected. The second episode is a setting of what later became the most famous quatrain in Binyon's poem, beginning 'They shall not grow old, as we that are left grow old'. As Moore notes, this is the only point at which the metre changes to 3/4, suggesting at least some sense of positive structural pro-gress.[35] The harmonic circularity, however, is even more pronounced than in the earlier sequential 'song' passages. The mood of Binyon's text, not least through its later association with the Cenotaph ceremony, might have been expected to have prompted a hymn-like setting from Elgar. Indeed, this is what he provided for the revised version of 'For the Fallen', titled 'With Proud Thanksgiving', which was initially commissioned for the unveiling. But in the original version, the second episode is the most chromaticized sequential music in the whole work. The setting becomes saturated in the oscillating chromatic semitone figure from the opening four bars, culminat-ing in the soprano soloist's poignant emphasis on the e"–f" cell in her *lento* cadential phrase at the end of each verse (Ex. 7.5). Elgar's music therefore suggests a state of musical, as well as spiritual, purgatory. In Elgar's setting, Binyon's words 'At the going down of the sun and in the morning / We will remember them' become an anguished expression of longing for closure or

[33] Letter dated 15 April 1916, quoted in the preface to *ECE*, vol. X, p. viii.
[34] Songs, and more particularly the *sound* of singing voices, appear to have been a recurrent theme in much poetry written during the war. Compare, for example, poems as diverse as 'All the Hills and Vales Along' by Charles Hamilton Sorley, 'Song of the Dark Ages' by Francis Brett Young, and the opening lines of Wilfred Owen's 'The Send-Off' ('Down the close, darkening lanes they sang their way / To the siding shed, / And lined the train with faces grimly gay'). The prominence of the sound of singing voices both refers to the importance of marching songs as recruitment propaganda, as Elgar's letter suggests, and also serves as a symbol of youth and creativity.
[35] Moore, *Elgar*, p. 681.

Ex. 7.5 'For the Fallen', fifth strophe (fig. 19)

death, and not merely a patriotic act of remembrance. Far from being a moment of consolation, it is the most troubled music in the whole work.

This reading of 'For the Fallen' again suggests *Parsifal*: not simply the communal sense of chivalric purpose celebrated by the knights of the grail (a means of ennobling conflict through appeal to a higher moral purpose), but the ritual transformation of suffering into redemption. Elgar's interpretation points to a deeper engagement with the psychological process of mourning itself. For Judith Butler, mourning is essentially a performative act, an acknowledgement of vulnerability (often resisted), that willingly accepts the possibility of emotional exchange, danger, and violence. It is through such openness that we become aware of ourselves as social beings, part of a community and not just isolated individuals: 'each of us is constituted politically in part by virtue of the social vulnerability of our bodies – as a site of desire and physical vulnerability, as a site of a publicity at once asserted and exposed'.[36] Hence, Butler claims that

> mourning has to do with agreeing to undergo a transformation (perhaps one should say *submitting* to a transformation) the full result of which one cannot know in advance. There is losing, as we know, but there is also the transformative effect of loss, and this latter cannot be charted or planned. One can try to choose it, but it may be that this experience of transformation deconstitutes choice at some level. I do not think, for instance, that one can invoke the Protestant ethic when it comes to loss.

[36] Judith Butler, *Precarious Life: the Powers of Mourning and Violence* (London: Verso, 2003), p. 20.

> One cannot say: 'Oh, I'll go through loss this way, and that will be the result, and I'll
> apply myself to this task, and I'll endeavour to achieve the resolution of grief that is
> before me'. I think one is hit by waves, and that one starts out the day with an aim, a
> project, a plan, and finds oneself foiled. *One finds oneself fallen.*[37]

The sense of longing for harmonic closure that Elgar creates in the fifth and
sixth verses of his setting is akin to this process of transformation. It is only
through a repetitive process of ritualistic transformation, via the sequential
music indebted to *Parsifal*, that any sense of emotional or musical release can
eventually be attained. The lack of a fixed musical goal at this point, an
immediate resolution of the chromatic sequential behaviour that underpins
the second episode, corresponds to the state of unknowingness that Butler
identifies as crucial to the mourning process:

> when one loses, one is also faced with something enigmatic: something is hiding in
> the loss, something is lost within the recesses of loss. If mourning involves knowing
> what one has lost (and melancholia originally meant, to a certain extent, not
> knowing), then mourning would be maintained by its enigmatic dimension, by the
> experience of not knowing incited by losing what we cannot fully fathom.[38]

In 'For the Fallen', Elgar suggests a heightened state of self-consciousness, an
act of letting go, through the gradual return to the music of the opening
verse. The first stage in this process is a significant change of texture and
affect: the *quasi recit.* entry of the soprano soloist at fig. 25, which suggests a
momentary sense of 'present tense' or awakening. The words themselves
support this reading by invoking a greater mood of anticipation than hitherto, speaking of 'where our desires are and our hopes profound', by implication looking forward beyond the immediate sense of tragedy towards
a more positive future prospect. The recapitulation of the opening music
at fig. 27 subsequently becomes almost incidental, a local event subsumed
within a longer-range process of enharmonic sequential change similar to
that which prefigures the return of the Adagio theme at the end of the finale
of the Cello Concerto (from the soloist's *con passione* entry at fig. 69, to the
actual return of the slow movement at four bars after fig. 71, likewise a
moment of intensified expectation). The circular harmonic tendencies of the
earlier passages in the movement at last seem more directional, even if the
music's ultimate goal or destination characteristically remains elusive until
the last minute. Unlike the Cello Concerto, in that sense, there is no moment
of nostalgic or sentimental reflection. Rather, the movement's eventual high
point, appropriately, is a dynamic and registral expansion of the sequential
'song' passage from fig. 4, marked *grandioso* ('Moving in marches upon the
heavenly plain'). The raised dynamic level reinforces this more immediate
feeling of presence, as though the solemn procession distantly heard in the

---

[37] Ibid., p. 21.   [38] Ibid., pp. 21–2.

Ex. 7.6 'For the Fallen', conclusion

opening bars has finally arrived in the musical foreground. The process of transformation is only complete, however, once the music has achieved a more permanent sense of rest (Ex. 7.6). Elgar's setting of Binyon's emphatic final lines (fig. 32, 'To the end, to the end, they remain') returns to the music of the opening, which is now heard in a renewed light. Though the music retains its sense of ritualistic circularity until virtually the final bar, the restless process of sequential modulation is eventually stilled. The ascending bass steps in the penultimate bars and the shifting *morendo* chords summarize and resolve the problematic chromatic elements from the opening four bars as the music recedes slowly into the distance. The final chord itself represents no triumphant victory or apotheosis, but merely a state of consolation or compassion. It is also an act of self-identification, akin to the moment at the close of Wagner's opera when Parsifal touches Amfortas with the tip of his spear. This identification with suffering is the key to resolution of the mourning process. As Butler concludes, 'The disorientation of grief – "Who have I become?" or, indeed, "What is left of me?" "What is it in the Other that I have lost?" – posits the "I" in the mode of unknowingness.'[39]

Elgar's invocation of a ritualistic framework, and the references to two earlier musical works, his own *Dream of Gerontius* and Wagner's *Parsifal*, suggest a strong mood of retrospection rather than looking forward beyond the end of the conflict to a new musical world. Perhaps this was one of the reasons why, when he was approached to set a further Binyon poem after an Allied victory had become virtually assured, he wrote 'I do not feel drawn to

[39] Ibid., p. 30.

peace music somehow.'[40] Interpreting *The Spirit of England* purely as a reactionary work, however, misses the powerful way in which it engages with the process of mourning itself. Elgar was not alone in adopting this strategy.

> Is it fanciful [Jay Winter asks] to suggest that rituals at war memorials, and in particular the reading of the names of the fallen, and the touching of those statues or those names, were means of avoiding crushing melancholia, of passing through mourning, of separating from the dead and beginning to live again? Ritual here is a means of forgetting, as much as of commemoration, and war memorials, with their material representation of names and losses, are there to help in the necessary art of forgetting.[41]

By locating *The Spirit of England* as a musical memorial within this broader discourse of loss, grief and mourning, we can gain a clearer sense of both its immediate historical context and its universality. By foregrounding particularly heightened moments of musical expression associated with the idea (and sound) of the singing voice, such as the *quasi recit.* entry at fig. 25 in 'For the Fallen', *The Spirit of England* suggests that it is through the redemptive power of ritual, and the transformation of suffering, that music is ultimately able to heal. In words taken from Masefield's poem, Elgar's work is moved by the sense of something 'loved to the death, inestimably dear'.

---

[40] Letter to Binyon, dated 5 November 1918. Quoted in Andrew Neill, 'Elgar's War', p. 64.   [41] Winter, *Sites of Memory, Sites of Mourning,* p. 115.

8   Japing-up the Cello Concerto: the first draft examined

John Pickard

In addition to the tireless protection and encouragement of her husband's talent, perhaps Alice Elgar's greatest gift to posterity was the careful preservation of the sketches and drafts of most of his major compositions. These offer the musically literate enthusiast an almost unparalleled insight into the working methods of one of the great late Romantic composers, an insight significantly enhanced by the unusual clarity and explicit self-criticism that the sketches consistently display. Particularly promising ideas are often noted as 'good', like a teacher assessing a pupil's work: 'will do' pronounces Professor Elgar over one connective passage in the first symphony; 'I hate this diminished 7th', he chides above an abortive draft for the terrified Gerontius's deathbed visions.

Elgar's readiness to give away sketch pages as mementos to friends implies a certain ambivalence on his part: he was simultaneously uncaring of their dispersal and evidently conscious of their potential value. Following Alice's death in 1920, the uncaring view appears to have won out: not only were sketch pages often given away but a good deal of working material for newer pieces seems to have been destroyed by Elgar himself. In a diary entry Elgar's daughter noted: 'Very busy day – turning out stationery cupboard – Father went through all his sketches, M.S.S. etc. sad work. Destroyed much & got all in order. At it all day.'[1]

The main motivation for the clear-out was Elgar's decision to sell his imposing Hampstead home, Severn House, and move to a service flat, though it is inconceivable that the action was not in some way triggered by the desolation that consumed him following Alice's death. Along with manuscript material, many corrected proofs seem to have been destroyed, an especially grievous loss to the would-be editor, since, as well as correcting errors, Elgar was in the habit of making significant textual changes at proof stage.

Elgar's destructive spree probably had serious implications for the sketch pages of the Cello Concerto, a work less than two years old at the time. Little preparatory material now survives, making documentation of the compositional

[1] Carice Elgar-Blake's Diary, 2 July 1921.

process especially elusive for this work. Furthermore, very few references to the work appear in any letters or diaries until June 1919, by which time composition had already reached an advanced stage. Robert Anderson has summarized what remains of the manuscript sources.

> A sketch for the thirty-eight bars of the first movement Moderato from cue 1 was perhaps written when Elgar was in hospital for an operation on his tonsils in March 1918 . . . The sketch was transcribed later for piano as a gift to Lady Stuart of Wortley. A full score version of the Concerto's last 24 bars, with various amendments to the solo part and dated July 1919, was sent to Elgar's friend, Edward Speyer. Otherwise there have survived only two drafts of the piano score and a fair copy of the solo part in the British Library and the MS full score at the Royal College of Music in London.[2]

Though not quite complete, this brief list makes a stark contrast with the plethora of extant materials for the Violin Concerto, first performed in 1910. Here, the profusion of sketches is such that 'every stage of its composition can be minutely plotted'.[3] These principally comprise a complete draft, devised from separate sketches according to Elgar's usual working habit, a violin and piano arrangement, and a full score. Corrected proofs of the piano arrangement are preserved in the Memorial Library of Music at Stanford University, and a set of orchestral proofs is held at the British Library.

Elgar was fond of playing new compositions through to friends while he was working on them, but even by his standards the Violin Concerto's genesis was unusually public. Numerous accounts survive of Elgar playing passages to, for instance, Alice Stuart-Wortley; of Elgar and W. H. Reed working through sketches while Ivor Atkins played the piano part; of sessions in a locked room (though with witnesses present) where Elgar and Fritz Kreisler thrashed out technical matters; and of two semi-public pre-premiere performances (first with Reed, then with Kreisler) during the 1910 Three Choirs Festival, both with Elgar filling in the orchestral part at the piano.[4] Both the printed violin and piano arrangement and the miniature full score were available for sale in advance of the concerto's first performance. Indeed, when writing the full score, Elgar was able to save himself time and effort by pasting proof copies of the solo part into the manuscript instead of copying it all out by hand. However, the process of refining the music continued well into the proof stages; the manuscripts of both piano arrangement and full score contain numerous deviations from the final published version, with

---

[2] Anderson, Robert, 'Toward a Flawless Work', *Affetti musicologici: Book of Essays in honour of Professor Zygmunt Marian Szweykowski in* [sic] *his 70th birthday,* ed. Piotr Poźniak (Kraków, 1999), pp. 433–9, at p. 436.
[3] Ibid., p. 434.
[4] *ECE*, vol. XXXII, pp. vi–xi.

Ex. 8.1 Violin Concerto, first movement, fig. 11:8

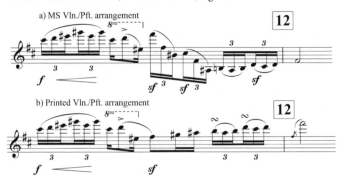

some of the changes sketched out in pencil on the verso pages of the piano arrangement (Ex. 8.1).

Taken as a whole, the preparatory materials for the Violin Concerto reinforce anecdotal accounts of its composition and paint a vivid picture of a successful composer at the height of his creative powers, working under pressure with the committed support of family, friends, and professional associates. The Cello Concerto had a very different start in life. Its first mention in Alice's diary comes as late as 2 June 1919 ('E. played some of the Concerto to Lan[don Ronald] who loved it at once'), implying that the composition was well advanced at this time. Three days later: 'Felix Salmond came up after dinner to try Cello Concerto, sounded beautiful. F. S. most delighted & enthusiastic.' Salmond was to be the soloist at the first perform-ance on 27 October 1919, and he fulfilled the same role in the Cello Concerto's preparation as Kreisler and Reed had with the Violin Concerto nine years earlier. This time, however, most of the discussions and alterations took place in the seclusion and privacy of the Elgars' Sussex retreat, Brinkwells, with a private run-through reserved for a few friends at Severn House on 5 July. The full score was completed on or around 8 August, the day Alice took it to the post office.

Attempts to trace the concerto's emergence are therefore frustrated by a relative lack of documentary and anecdotal evidence. A significant and tantalizing exception is offered by Reed, whose account suggests that work on the concerto was under way during the later months of 1918.

> After the signing of the Armistice, Sir Edward returned to Brinkwells until the end of the year, working at the details of the [string] quartet and [piano] quintet, which we frequently played in the studio. We also played over something he had sketched while he was on one of his London visits and which he said was to be a 'cello concerto. The sketch is interesting because it is covered with his comments as usual, but they are inscribed with a typewriter instead of in his own handwriting. This was a new toy, and had to be used. The instrument did not lend itself to variations except

in its black and red ribbon. The original jumps from one colour to the other in the most erratic manner.[5]

No trace remains of this strange-looking document and one must assume that it too was a casualty in the purge of July 1921. The remaining major sources confirm Anderson's small inventory of manuscript materials. The lack of a compositional draft derived from the sketch material has been a particularly serious loss, for it would have been here that the major compositional decisions, the 'forging' (as Sibelius might have described it) of the whole work from diffuse jottings, would have taken place.

Anthony Payne has outlined Elgar's normal practice when composing an extended work:

> The composer had an extraordinary way of working, jumping from movement to movement as the spirit took him. It was as if he was shaping the various pieces of the jigsaw, before fitting them all together. Ideas sometimes came to him outside the context of a tempo, for instance, and one, clearly marked 'scherzo', eventually ended up in the [Third Symphony's] slow movement.[6]

Thus a long period of apparently aimless sketching, often reworking the same passage, and sometimes without any clear context, would suddenly be brought into focus by the gathering together of the sketch pages and their sorting into something resembling a continuous short score. This would then form the basis for the final fair copy or full orchestral score. With the Violin Concerto, Reed witnessed the process in action:

> I found E. striding about with a lot of loose sheets of music paper, arranging them in different parts of the room. Some were already pinned on the backs of chairs or stuck up on the mantelpiece ready for me to play . . . He had got the main ideas written out, and, as he put it, 'japed them up' to make a coherent piece.[7]

In the case of the Cello Concerto, there exist not one but two complete drafts, both in ink, of the composer's own cello and piano arrangement. The latter forms the basis of the printed score which, in telling contrast with the Violin Concerto, was issued by Novello a month *after* the first performance. The printed full orchestral score had to wait a further fifteen months for publication and the miniature score did not appear until 1937, three years after Elgar's death.[8] It is apparent that Elgar was writing the second draft, a 'fair copy', at the same time that he was preparing the orchestration, for on 23 July he wrote to Alice Stuart-Wortley: 'I am arranging the accpt for piano and writing it out fair – which I detest.'[9] This slightly misleading remark may account for the relative lack of attention afforded the two drafts by most

[5] Reed, *Elgar as I Knew Him* (London: Gollancz, 1936), p. 64.
[6] Elgar, Edward, *The Sketches for Symphony No. 3, Elaborated by Anthony Payne* (London: Boosey and Hawkes., 1998), p. [v].
[7] Reed, *Elgar as I Knew Him*, pp. 23–4.
[8] Anderson, 'Elgar and his Publishers', in *Companion*, pp. 24–31, at p. 29.
[9] *Windflower*, p. 228.

Elgar scholars. It implies that Elgar was creating his piano arrangement by
reducing it from the full orchestral score to a rough draft, and then copying it
out neatly. This is reinforced by the catalogue citations for the two scores at
the British Library where they are designated 'Arrangement for 'cello and
piano. First draft' and 'Final draft'.[10] Furthermore, a note at the head of the
first draft of the Finale reads 'NB for corrected Solo part see other pft arrgt',
implying that this first draft is also an 'arrangement'.

Taken at face value, the descriptions suggest an anomalous compositional
practice for a composer whose inspiration may sometimes have been capri-
cious, but whose working methods were characterized by professionalism
and a high degree of organization. It would be uncharacteristic of Elgar to
have made a piano reduction from his orchestral score in the first place, let
alone go to the trouble of writing it out twice. More likely, the first draft was
written before the orchestral score and then used as the basis of the cello and
piano arrangement. In other words, the first draft is not merely a draft of the
arrangement, but, at least in part, the missing compositional draft that Elgar
then went on to orchestrate.

Most of Elgar's major orchestral works were issued in solo piano versions
more or less concurrently with their premieres. The purely orchestral
works, the symphonies and overtures, usually arranged by others, range
in ambition and accomplishment from the workmanlike arrangement of
In the South, attributed to Adolf Schmid, to Sigfrid Karg-Elert's monumental, and truly inspired, transcriptions of the symphonies. In the
days before the gramophone these arrangements were a vital means by
which the public could become familiar with music outside the concert
hall, and the production of arrangements could be a lucrative exercise for
publishers and (if they were fortunate enough to negotiate a royalty) for
composers. But the piano reductions of the choral works and the concertos
had an additional function. They would be used in rehearsals, and the
rehearsal piano score had to be issued in print many weeks before the first
performance, so that choirs and soloists could prepare. With his habitually
close-to-the-deadline working methods, Elgar often completed the full
orchestral score of a new work a matter of days before the first rehearsal,
far too late for anyone else to produce an arrangement. So the piano
arrangement had to be prepared by Elgar himself at an earlier stage, usually
between the first continuous 'short score' draft of the music and its
orchestration.

Awareness of this practical necessity certainly affected Elgar's approach to
the compositional process and it is clear that he frequently used the 'short

[10] GB-Lbl Loan 69.4 (fair copy and solo
part), GB-Lbl Loan 69.5 (first draft)

[these citations have been erroneously
transposed in the BL catalogue].

Ex. 8.2 *The Dream of Gerontius*, Part I, figs. 58:2–59/bb. 521–6: sketch showing already highly developed piano part

score' notation of his sketches for the choral works as the basis of the published piano reduction. For example, many passages from the sketch pages of *The Dream of Gerontius* form the basis of the piano textures of Elgar's final vocal score; rarely do the sketches suggest anything more complex than what can be achieved by ten reasonably practised fingers on one keyboard (Ex. 8.2).

The Violin Concerto also shows clear signs of having been conceived in terms of a solo line plus piano accompaniment. Though fragmentary, the working sketches are often remarkable for the polished quality of their piano writing, complete in almost every detail of texture and articulation, ready, even at this early stage, to be carried intact to the complete draft piano score (Ex. 8.3). By contrast, the sketches for the purely orchestral works, which were unlikely to have further practical function after their orchestration, tend to be more elaborate, frequently extending well beyond anything effectively performable by one pianist and clearly not conceived with an eventual piano reduction in mind (Ex. 8.4).

Despite this, Elgar's approach to the orchestra is no less adventurous or colourful in the choral works or the concertos than in the symphonies and overtures. Indeed, the mature choral works, particularly *The Apostles*, contain some of the most complex and elaborate orchestral textures Elgar ever attempted. There is no question of the first sketches being conceived as piano

Ex. 8.3 Violin Concerto, second movement, opening: sketch showing already highly developed piano part

music, with the orchestration 'grafted on' at a later stage. However, it is possible to detect a distinct difference in working method, based on the pragmatic realization that the sketch would have a practical function after the completion of the full orchestral score, and that time and effort could be saved further down the line if the early drafts were already notated in pianistic terms.

Other features suggest that the first draft of the Cello Concerto was in fact a compositional draft predating the orchestral score. A pencilled set of page numbers appears intermittently throughout the first three movements, beginning with '2' placed to the left of the first system (the full score begins on page 2) and continuing to '14'. Apart from the numbers 14 and 20 (corresponding to the pagination of the fair copy for cello and piano) at fig. 21:4/b. 32 and fig. 29:3/b. 98, the only marks in the second movement refer to the last two pages (66–67) of the autograph full score, while only the

Ex. 8.4 Symphony no. 1, first movement, fig. 12:1–5/bb. 114–18: sketch on four staves

first page of the slow movement (70) is indicated (incorrectly as it turns out).[11] Pagination marks in both pencil and green ink are almost continuously present during the finale, running consecutively from 78 to 134. Only 110 and 111 are missing from their expected position on p. 35 of the MS, obscured by a pasted-over sheet. The marks correspond with both the numbering and the page breaks of the autograph full score now held at the Royal College of Music Library. This suggests that the draft was used as the basis of the full score, with Elgar marking out the pagination which Lady Elgar, who often assisted her husband by laying out the bar lines and instrument names, could then follow when drawing up the full-score pages.

Perhaps the most compelling evidence is simply the 'look' of the MS. Compared with the 'final draft' of the cello and piano arrangement it is inevitably more untidy, with innumerable alterations, additions, and removals. However, its provisional nature extends beyond relatively simple decisions concerning how best to represent an orchestral texture in

---

[11] The autograph full score of the slow movement begins on p. 68. This mysterious anomaly leads one to wonder whether an additional draft full score of this movement (perhaps even the whole work) may once have existed (see note 15 below).

keyboard terms (the Cello Concerto tends to be texturally simpler than most of Elgar's earlier orchestral music) to actual compositional decisions affecting the substance of the music. The autograph full score finds many of the alterations already incorporated, suggesting that these had already been resolved at short-score stage. However, some details, such as the cello line during the finale's *Allegro molto* coda, were evidently revisited at the orchestration stage (see below), while others, particularly details of the cello part in the finale, only crystallized after the full score had been prepared, probably during rehearsal, necessitating alterations to the autograph score.

In view of the paucity of sketch material, a detailed examination of the first draft probably affords the clearest glimpse we are now likely to have of how the concerto came to life. The draft of the finale, onto which falls the concerto's main structural and emotional weight, is particularly revealing. Not only is the reworking of passages far more explicit than elsewhere, but even the handwriting reveals something of the emotional excitement under which the music was written (and is thus inevitably more difficult to decipher). As part of the ongoing process of revision, the 'painting' as Lady Elgar called it, the composer liberally employed red and green inks. Red appears to have been most commonly used for tempo indications and dynamic markings, though the alternation of the two colours generally seems arbitrary. It would certainly be quite wrong to think they represent two separate phases of revision; a crossing-through in one colour is often overlaid by a modification in the other, the two colours alternating quite freely. Further revisions are frequently made in pencil (and often subsequently overwritten in one of the coloured inks). Again, it is unlikely that these represent just one 'sweep' of revision but, like the multi-coloured changes, were part of a continuous process of re-evaluation and refinement that continued well into the rehearsal stages.

First movement

The first page of the MS draft (the first thirteen bars of the work) is written on a separate sheet pasted over an already existing page (just enough of which is visible to show Elgar using the page to experiment with green ink, inscribing the word 'green' a couple of times along the side of the page). From the very opening the draft reveals two striking deviations from the final version. The single low E, with which the orchestral cellos and basses reinforce the solo cello's first two chords, moves down to a C to double the soloist's lowest note at the beginning of b. 2. This is then crossed through, to leave the solo cello unaccompanied throughout b. 2 (Ex. 8.5).

Ex. 8.5 Cello Concerto, first movement, opening, first draft

In the final version the solo cello's opening statement extends to five recitative-like bars, one bar fewer than the draft, where the penultimate B is extended across an extra bar before resolving to the E in b. 6. The dominant chord in the low orchestral strings on the fourth beat of b. 4 is crossed through and transferred to the third beat of the next bar. In the published version, Elgar removed the fifth bar entirely, reinstating the orchestral chord in its original position (albeit as a quaver and silent pause). All MS sources, including the autograph solo cello part and the autograph full score, show signs of adjustment to include this alteration, suggesting that the change was made at a very late stage.

In common with Elgar's other short scores for works likely to need a piano reduction, the orchestral part then proceeds on two staves almost exactly as it eventually appears in the fair copy (and ultimately the published score) of the cello and piano arrangement. Various pencilled alterations redistribute some chords between the hands, change the clef for ease of reading or, in the case of the climax at fig. 16:1–5/bb. 92–6, reinforce the piano texture. These were probably added immediately before the preparation of the fair copy of the arrangement. However, two significant elaborations do not appear at all in the draft: the IV$^{\natural 7}$–V progression of fig. 10:4/b. 66 (Ex. 8.6 (a)) and fig. 12:4/b. 74 (Ex. 8.6 (b)) and the rustling viola, flute, and violin scales of fig. 14:3–5/bb. 82–4. (Ex. 8.7). The alterations shown in Ex. 8.6 replace the original, much plainer, progression from chord IV (without the seventh) to a rather stark octave B. These were quite a late afterthought, for the fair copy conforms to the draft with the alterations clearly added at a later stage. The scales of fig. 14:3–5/bb. 82–4 were evidently not envisaged at the draft stage, where Elgar took the trouble to add full bars of rests in the upper staff of the accompaniment. In their absence, the original intention was to have

Ex. 8.6a Cello Concerto, first movement, fig. 10:4/b. 66

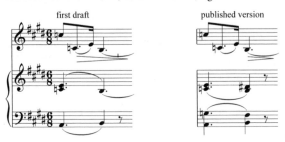

Ex. 8.6b Cello Concerto, first movement, fig. 12:4/b. 74

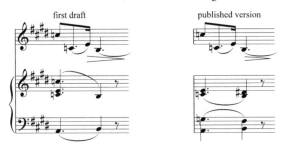

Ex. 8.7 Cello Concerto, first movement, fig. 14:2–5/bb. 81–4, first draft

the solo cello playing entirely alone through fig. 14:4/b. 83 after the first crotchet beat.

Second movement

Together with an equivalent passage in the finale, the short cadenza near the beginning of the second movement (fig. 19:3–4/bb. 11–12) was thoroughly

Ex. 8.8 Cello Concerto, second movement, fig. 19:4/b. 12, first draft

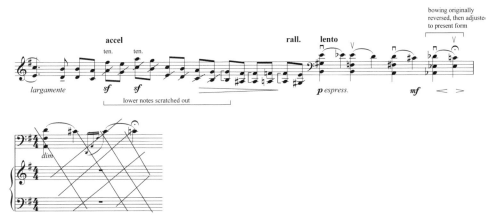

revised in the first draft. In both cases the revisions were written on separate sheets pasted into the score and were then subjected to further modification. Without resorting to X-ray analysis, it is possible to discern something of what Elgar was attempting to achieve in his revisions.

The paste-over of the second-movement cadenza consists of a single system. The first attempt, which it now obscures, originally ran on to the beginning of the next system for four crotchet beats, which were later heavily double-hatched out, making them difficult to decipher (Ex. 8.8). However, it is just possible to discern that the harmony of the final two beats (a 4–3 progression on a Neapolitan A♭ in the finished score) was originally intended as a dominant chord whose added sharpened seventh descended chromatically to a rather lame dominant seventh cadence. Anxious to avoid the 'commonplace' (always a strong term of Elgarian disapproval), the composer substituted the more oblique approach to a G major tonic which, at this early stage in the movement, has yet to be fully established, remaining in the shadow of the previous movement's E (relative) minor until fig. 20.

This small piece of evidence implies the possibility that the pasted-over cadenza revisions included other matters of harmonic or melodic substance. Reworkings of the Violin Concerto's cadenza show Elgar adjusting the notation of bar lines in order to achieve a greater sense of flexibility and it is possible that similar changes were made to the Cello Concerto's cadenzas for the same reason. Playability was also a factor. Elgar was an accomplished violinist, but not a cellist; the first draft finds him becoming slightly over-ambitious, writing a long sequence of double-stopped sixths at the top of the instrument's range, before thinking better of it and scratching out most of the lower notes.

The draft as a whole contains few indications of instrumentation. The first two pages of the second movement are therefore unusual in specifying 'cor' for the single sustained notes in bars 4, 6 and 8 (an anomaly that made it into

Ex. 8.9 Cello Concerto, second movement, fig. 21:7–8/bb. 35–6, first draft

the fair copy and even into the printed edition of the arrangement),[12] 'wind' (in faint pencil) for the chords at fig. 20/b. 16, and 'clar' at fig. 20:10/b. 25.

The harmony of fig. 20:6–9/bb. 21–4 (repeated at fig. 23:3–6/bb. 50–3) is based on an alternation of chords a tritone apart (E♭ and A), and a pencilled sketch on page 12 of the draft (bottom right) finds Elgar experimenting with the voice-leading of this exotic progression in four-part harmony. Whether this was made during the composition of the first draft or at a later stage is impossible to determine, as this particular type of voice-leading is not to be found in any of the autographs. Throughout this passage, and at fig. 21:7/b. 35 (Ex. 8.9), Elgar can be seen to be continually refining the texture to arrive at the gossamer-light touch achieved in the definitive version.

Elsewhere, the draft reveals minor differences from the final score, some of them highly revealing of Elgar's super-refined feeling for the relationship between harmony and instrumental balance. A fine example occurs at fig. 22:1/b. 40, where the original chords accompanying the solo cello's broad theme are redistributed to achieve the open spacing and the mid-range clash that lend the final version its pungent character (Ex. 8.10). Much of the effect of this movement derives from the solo cello's almost continuous confinement to the tenor and treble regions. At fig. 30:6–7/bb. 109–10 Elgar's original intention was to extend the downward leap of the broad theme to a full two octaves. However, the draft shows that the plan was soon modified (in a combination of red and green ink) to produce the now-familiar descending seventh (Ex. 8.11). The final bars include a further interesting modification: the solo cello's descending four-note scale at fig. 33:2/b. 127 (three bars from the close and leading into the final *pizzicato* flourish) turns out to have been an afterthought, inserted in green ink to replace the original, rather mundane, continuation of the rest of the bar's repeated-note semiquavers (Ex. 8.12).

[12] Deleted in the new Novello edition
published in 2004.

Ex. 8.10 Cello Concerto, second movement, fig. 22:1–2/bb. 40–1

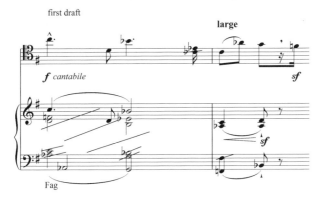

first draft

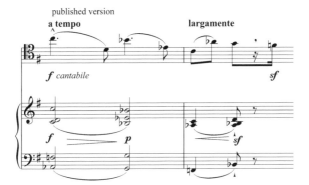

Ex. 8.11 Cello Concerto, second movement, fig. 30:6–7/bb.109–10, first draft(Crossed through clefs apply to notes with downward-pointing stems.)

Ex. 8.12 Cello Concerto, second movement, fig. 33:1–4/bb. 126–9, first draft

Ex. 8.13 Cello Concerto, third movement, fig. 41:1–8/bb. 53–61, published version

(B♭ major: I - II^{13} - V)

(F major: IV -V^{13} - I)

Third movement

Apart from a few small details (for example, the syncopated inner parts of fig. 35:1/b. 8 and fig. 37:4/b. 29 which respectively begin one and two bars later in the original draft and a *stringendo molto* at 37:6/b. 31 which seems to have originally begun on the second quaver beat of the following bar), the most significantly different detail of the first draft of the slow movement comes in its closing bars.

Because the movement ends on the dominant, Harold Brooke of Novello enquired whether another ending would be required for occasions when it was performed on its own. On 12 August 1919, Elgar replied: 'I fear I cannot think of an[othe]r. ending for the slow movement – it will do as it is if played separately.'[13] The slow movement closes with a reprise of the opening eight bars, which moves from the tonic B♭ major to its dominant via a I^6–II^{13}–V cadence (Ex. 8.13). However, the pull to G minor at fig. 41:5–6/bb. 57–8 is sufficiently strong to undermine the B♭ tonic and allow the equally effective interpretation of this cadence as one moving IV^6–V^{13}–I in F major, while nevertheless still retaining enough of a residual B♭ major association to form a natural link with the B♭ minor-ish opening of the finale.

The final page of the slow movement's draft shows Elgar experimenting with the suggested full close. A barely legible snatch of figured bass, in faint pencil (possibly VI^7–$^{\sharp 4}_{2}$) is followed by a hastily written, and crossed-out, pencil sketch for an alternative ending, cadencing on the tonic (Ex. 8.14). It is highly revealing that Elgar rejected this banal ending in favour of the unorthodox and exquisitely judged original. The suppression testifies eloquently to his powers of instinctive discrimination overriding 'commonplace' invention, when convention seemed to suggest otherwise.

[13] *Publishers*, p. 809.

Ex. 8.14 Cello Concerto, third movement, fig. 41:1–8/bb. 53–61, first draft, with Elgar's sketch for 'full close' in B♭ major

The original draft emphasizes further the implicit link between slow movement and finale with the direction 'segue IV' at the end of the slow movement. However, the direction is absent in both fair copy and full score (the link between the first two movements, marked 'attacca' in the draft, is similarly absent in the later manuscripts, but clearly indicated by the lack of a final bar line at the end of the first movement and the tied note in the lower strings). This clearly suggests that Elgar finally, and quite deliberately, decided *not* to join the third and fourth movements. Yet this happens almost automatically in many performances of the work, where the tonal link between the movements appears to justify the curious (and regrettable) convention of breaking whatever atmosphere has been created in the concerto's slow movement by attacking the finale without a pause.[14]

Fourth movement

From the start of the finale, the character and appearance of the first draft changes dramatically. Where the first three movements, though obviously carefully amended and refined through several stages of revision, remain clearly ordered and generally quite legible, the finale is much more chaotic, provisional, and uncertain. Legibility becomes a major problem on many pages and interpretation of Elgar's working process is not always possible. However, it is clear that Elgar originally planned the *Allegro* introduction in 4/4, not 2/4 time and presumably at a pulse double the present speed. He then changed the marking to 2/2 (probably a simple clerical error when he

---

[14] In this respect, the recordings of the work conducted by Elgar offer no clue to his final intentions, due to the inevitable side changes between movements.

Ex. 8.15 Cello Concerto, fourth movement, fig. 45:5–10/bb. 32–7, first draft with discarded additional bars

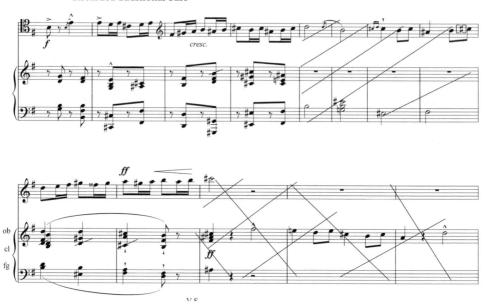

really intended 2/4) and adjusted all the notes to half their original time value.

The movement is the longest of the four and contains the greatest proportion of traditional 'development', its first half almost Schumannesque in its obsessive working of the opening motif. The draft shows evidence of considerable revision, both of melodic profile and harmonic direction, with the relationship between soloist and orchestra constantly under review. The forceful orchestral tutti at fig. 46 extends for just four bars in the original draft before the re-entry of the soloist for a further four bars. The solo part is crossed through in the draft and the material transferred to the orchestra. Alternative possibilities for development are sometimes stopped in their tracks. A particularly intriguing example occurs between figs. 45 and 46 (Ex. 8.15), where the first draft threatens to broaden the pulse, as well as to invert the head of the motif at fig. 45:9/b. 36 and to cadence in F♯ major at fig. 46:1/b. 38 instead of the now-familiar F♯ minor.

The compositional method is somewhat less consistent in the finale than elsewhere in the concerto. The previous movements' harmonic textures are, on the whole, fully and confidently realized in the draft – the solo part, for all its many modifications and improvements of detail, remaining basically compatible with the final version of the score. The finale is a different matter: fully realized passages constantly give way to areas where a basic skeleton, often just solo part and bass line, is clearly outlined in ink with internal details and counterpoints hastily sketched out in pencil (see the discussion of the *Adagio* interlude below). This working practice is consistent with the approach described by Christopher Kent in a reference to the draft of the famous 'Enigma' theme: 'a clear instance of Elgar's *basso continuo* thinking where in the first six bars the melody and bass are in black ink, and the "realized" harmonies in between are in pencil'.[15]

Kent rightly characterizes Elgar's working method as the creation of a musical 'mosaic', and the draft of an extended episode in the finale demonstrates Elgar's willingness to manipulate pre-formed blocks of material, chipping away at their contours to fit the new context. The passage occurs at the start of the first phase of the central 'development' section and runs from fig. 49:7/b. 79 to fig. 52:5/b. 116. Elgar initially pasted three systems of revised music over a passage running from fig. 49:8/b. 80 to fig. 52:1/b. 112, leaving the final system of the original attempt (fig. 52 itself) intact at the bottom of the page (see Fig. 8.1). The final bar of this paste-over is crossed through, perhaps because Elgar disliked the rather abrupt harmonic jolt from F major to F♯ minor to E♭ major in successive bars (Ex. 8.16), or perhaps because the rejected bar was unacceptable for the extension he now considered to be necessary before rejoining fig. 52. That extension, a thirteen-bar passage running from fig. 50:16/b. 99 to fig. 51:12/b. 111 of the final version, is written out on a separate unnumbered sheet, with a *dal segno* symbol after the final bar, indicating the need to turn back to the previous page and join up with its bottom system (see Fig. 8.2). The join itself is then subject to modification as Elgar altered the profile of the solo line (Ex. 8.17).

The passage described above is part of a larger paragraph, from fig. 50:1/b. 84 to fig. 52:14/b. 125, whose *moto perpetuo* character involves the cello in forty-two bars of unbroken semiquaver activity. Much of it is extended sequentially and the draft's numerous alterations to the solo line show Elgar alert to the risk of tedium. The passage from fig. 52:1/b. 112 to fig. 52:6/b. 117 involves three sequential repetitions, each a whole tone higher than the last, of the same two-bar phrase whose second bar is itself a repetition of the first. By fig. 52:7/b. 118, already skating on perilously thin sequential ice, Elgar attempted another repetition, transposed up yet another whole tone. Happily, the critical instinct asserted itself; Elgar saved the day by scribbling out the fourth repetition and sketching a much more interesting alternative in the top stave of the 'piano/orchestra' part (see Ex. 8.18).

The transitional passage between figs. 53 and 54, originally six bars long, connects the two main phases of the 'development'. Elgar decided to extend

---

[15] Kent, 'Magic by Mosaic: Some Aspects of Elgar's Compositional Methods', in *Companion*, pp. 32–49, at p. 36.

Fig. 8.1 Cello Concerto, fourth movement, sketch showing the paste-over from figs. 49:8–52:1/bb. 80–112

it to eleven bars by writing out the additional music on a separate piece of manuscript paper and pasting it into the score along its left-hand edge only, thus creating a hinge that could be pulled aside to reveal the beginning of fig. 54. Eight bars later, and once again aware of the potential for monotony,

Ex. 8.16 Cello Concerto, fourth movement, figs. 51:11–52:1, first draft

Elgar made a four-bar cut of what appears to have been a full orchestral anticipation of the four-bar phrase from fig. 54:9/b. 145 to fig. 54:12/b. 148. Further sequential pruning occurs between figs. 55 and 56, with the removal of two bars from the last of three sequential repetitions of a four-bar phrase (fig. 55:1–4/bb. 149–52). As the phrase itself divides into more or less identical two-bar phrases, this disruption of regularity is particularly welcome, the asymmetry of the resulting paragraph (ten bars instead of the original twelve) offering necessary lubrication in an otherwise routine passage. The same deletion is found during a similar passage between figs. 57 and 58.

Tonally, the entire 'development' section is unusually wide-ranging, a feature already anticipated in the finale's orchestral introduction, which dramatically approaches the tonic E minor from the most oblique angle possible, B♭ minor, a tritone away (see Ex. 8.19). For the 'recapitulation' (fig. 59), Elgar presumably wished to re-establish the tonic with some force, and achieved this by grafting a reprise of the introduction onto the end of the development (fig. 58:9–16/bb. 189–96). This magnificent stroke seems to have been achieved with considerable effort, with a revision of fig. 58:1–12/ bb. 181–92 pasted over the original draft. Its continuation through to fig. 59, initiated the most bizarre looking page of the entire draft (see Fig. 8.3). Here, no fewer than three separate paste-overs conceal yet another paste-over, with only three bars of the original page surviving intact (the first three bars of the bottom system). Of the three visible paste-overs, the middle one (systems 4 and 5) was evidently the first to be made. A significant alteration to these bars affects the fanfare-like repeated semiquavers at fig. 61:11–12/bb. 227–8. These originally conformed to the prevailing dactylic figuration but were modified later in pencil to provide welcome rhythmic variety. Although the fair copy of the cello and piano arrangement incorporates this change without any signs of physical adjustment, the autograph full score originally did not, and shows signs of modification at a later date. This is one of many such anomalies throughout the work, underlining the fluidity of Elgar's movement between draft, cello and piano fair copy, and full score. In this case the

Fig. 8.2 Cello Concerto, fourth movement, sketch of figs. 50:16–52:1/bb. 99–112 (see Ex. 8.17)

Ex. 8.17 Cello Concerto, fourth movement, fig. 51:1–12/bb. 100–11, first draft (see Fig. 8.2)

Ex. 8.18 Cello Concerto, fourth movement, fig. 52:5–10/bb. 116–21, first draft

Ex. 8.19 Cello Concerto, fourth movement, opening

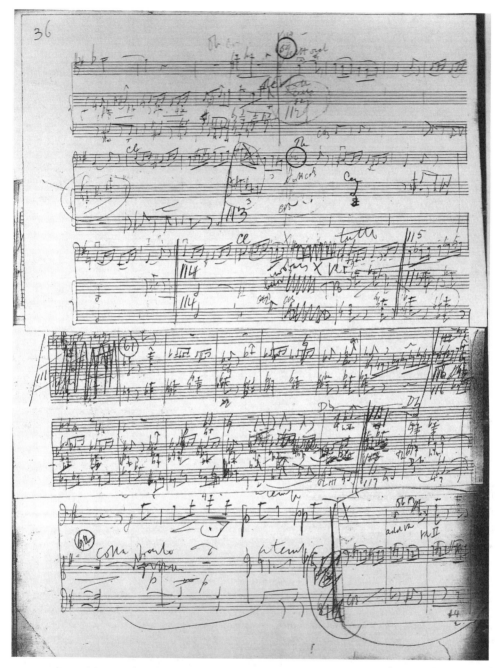

Fig. 8.3 Cello Concerto, sketch for the fourth movement, figs. 58:13–63:3/bb. 193–235 (the final three bars are fig. 60:8–10/bb. 212–14, to be inserted at 'X' on the third system)

orchestral scoring appears to have occurred before the cello and piano fair copy was made.

The upper half of the page seems likely to have been the next paste-over to be added, because it slightly overlaps the middle one. It contains another

Ex. 8.20 Cello Concerto, fourth movement, fig. 59:8/b. 204

rhythmic variant from the ubiquitous dactyls: the first beat of fig. 59:8/b. 204 is modified to a triplet metre, a detail whose striking effect in performance is out of all proportion to its size (see Ex. 8.20). A single bar of connective tissue beginning at fig. 60:8/b. 212 is then extended by an additional two bars, the whole three-bar passage appearing at the bottom of the page as the third and last of the legible paste-overs.

The first system of p. 37 presents something of a puzzle. It consists of five crossed-through bars that appear to duplicate fig. 61:14–62:3/bb. 230–4 from the bottom of the previous page. There the continuation of the passage was apparently rejected and is now concealed by the third of that page's paste-overs. It is therefore impossible to deduce exactly how Elgar originally intended the passage to connect to the top of the next page, though it does seem that he envisaged some sort of repetition of the preceding bars. Instead, the passage was excised, the lower stave of the piano part doing service for a small alteration to an originally treacherous run in the solo part on the next system. The bottom system of the page was also subjected to considerable modification and, quite possibly, extension, as it consists of a seven bar paste-over (fig. 63:6–12/bb. 246–52) on a page whose other systems are either five or six bars in length.

Although most multiple additions, crossings-out and reworkings in the first draft eventually arrive at a fairly definitive version, some details were fixed only at fair copy/full score stage. The solo cello's double-stops at fig. 63:9/b. 249 and fig. 63:11/b. 251 were evidently the result of some experimentation, the first (a perfect fifth) added to the draft as a modification, the second (a more technically demanding augmented fourth) not appearing in the draft, but as a modification to the fair copy and the autograph full score. The solo part between figs. 65 and 66 went through at least three revisions, only two of which appear in the first draft. The first four bars, though featuring variants of phrasing and articulation, remain largely unchanged. However, fig. 65:5–6/bb. 270–1 began life as yet another continuation of the dactylic figure, only to be crossed through and replaced by regular crotchets doubling the upper voice in the orchestra (Ex. 8.21). But the second draft, the fair copy, includes a scrap of paper pinned to the page, containing the

Ex. 8.21(a) Cello Concerto, fourth movement, fig. 65:1–7/bb. 266–72, first draft

Ex. 8.21(b) Cello Concerto, fourth movement, fig. 65:1–7/bb. 266–72, published version

definitive rising semiquaver passage that carries the solo line into treble register. Even here the high cantilena of fig. 65:7–14/bb. 272–9, so crucial to this important transitional passage, appears an octave lower in both scores (and also in the autograph solo part). The *8va* sign is to be found in the autograph full score, hastily scribbled in pencil (possibly during orchestral rehearsals) and the line is adjusted to incorporate the other changes outlined on the pinned sheet.

The extended slow interlude from figs. 66 to 72 is sketchily presented in the first draft, with numerous crossings out and alterations in red and green ink as well as in pencil. At first glance these appear to show intensive revision, but on closer inspection turn out to be mainly revoicings of chords and second thoughts about octave displacements in the solo part. For example, the solo part at fig. 67:8–9/bb. 295–6 is written first in tenor clef, in the version familiar from the published score, then crossed through and replaced by the same passage an octave lower in bass clef (by the time the fair copy was written it reverted to its original octave). The only paste-over occurs on the third system of page 39 (fig. 67:4–68:1/bb. 291–7) and even here four of its seven bars comprise a literal repeat in the orchestra of figs. 66:5–67:1/bb. 285–8, so Elgar only wrote out the top line and left the rest of the piano part blank.

These draft pages have a distinctly fraught appearance, as though hastily dashed off in a bout of intense creativity. The many *fortissimo* and *sforzando* markings of the solo part are all present, even at this draft stage, along with quite a number of additional ones which were later excised (fig. 70:5/b. 318 and fig. 70:6/b. 319 are marked *fff*, later toned down to *ff*). All of this suggests that the passage, the concerto's emotional high point, was conceived in a state of great excitement and that these pages are in fact the scene of its conception and not simply the 'japing-up' of an earlier, now vanished, sketch.

The coda, from fig. 72 to the end, gave Elgar considerable trouble. From a surviving full-score draft of the final seventeen bars, given by Elgar to Edward Speyer in July 1919, it is clear that the cello line of the concluding *Allegro molto* was only finalized at the orchestration stage.[16] The first draft of fig. 72, the dramatic return of the concerto's opening, finds the orchestral cellos and basses once again reinforcing the bottom C of the soloist's third chord, just as they originally had done in b. 2 of the first movement (Ex. 8.5), but this time with a *crescendo* from their sustained E leading to a preparatory anacrusis on the C followed by a *sforzando* downbeat. The effect is undeniably dramatic, even melodramatic, which is perhaps why Elgar removed it.

The last page of the first draft is taken up with several attempts at the final *a tempo* (the nine bars from fig. 74 to the end). At least six reworkings are identifiable. The first is broadly similar to the first seven bars of the final version, though in this case the solo cello is absent until the last sustained chord and the final cadence is curtailed to an abrupt I–V⁷–I progression. Elgar was evidently confident about this conclusion at the time it was written, for he drew a double bar line after it and added the marking *Fine* (Ex. 8.22 (a)). However, this is immediately followed by a pencilled addendum which extends the cadence through a series of descending chords, landing on a C major triad (i.e. chord VI in the tonic E minor) before closing on a sustained unison E (Ex. 8.22 (b)). This first version and its extension occupy the first two of the page's four systems. The third system, again in pencil, attempts to sustain the C major triad across three and a half bars (the chord includes a crescendo and an almost illegible marking – possibly 'brass') before cadencing, again on a unison E (Ex. 8.22 (c)).

All three attempts are heavily crossed through and a more nearly definitive version appears on the final system, identical in most respects to the published version, with the exception of the soloist's arpeggiated upbeats (fig. 74:5–6/bb. 348–9), which were originally intended to be played by the orchestra (indeed, they appeared in the Speyer copy of the full score, only to be scratched out), and the final chord which is now filled out to a full E minor triad but simply held for a whole bar with added caesura (Ex. 8.22 (d)). The final bar is then crossed through and, with little room left on the page for further changes, Elgar filled up a small space at the end of the third system (connecting it with an arrow) to create for the first time the concerto's final three bars. These were initially intended to include the solo cello sustaining a

---

[16] A facsimile of one of these pages appears in *ECE*, vol. XXXII, p. xix; see also the commentary, p. xxxiii.

Ex. 8.22(a) Cello Concerto, fourth movement, original ending

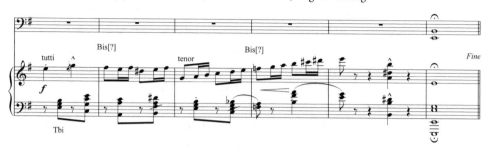

Ex. 8.22(b) Cello Concerto, fourth movement, extension of original ending

Ex. 8.22(c) Cello Concerto, fourth movement, alternative extension of original ending

Ex. 8.22(d) Cello Concerto, fourth movement, rejected final cadence

Ex. 8.22(e) Cello Concerto, fourth movement, toward a definitive final cadence

tenor register e[1] over an E minor triad in the orchestra (both written in red ink), but the superfluous notes are scribbled out and 'e only' is added in pencil above the piano part with 'chord' above the final bar (although the sustained triad is in fact retained in the trombones in the full orchestral score). The solo cello's final four-note chord does not achieve its definitive version in the first draft (Ex. 8.22 (e)).

The fair copy and the autograph solo part

The provisional nature of the first draft and its many problems of legibility clearly made a fair copy for rehearsal purposes an absolute necessity. This is certainly the copy to which Elgar was referring in his letter to Alice Stuart-Wortley (quoted above). Elgar also copied out a solo cello part for Felix Salmond's use and both scores are inscribed to him, the piano score simply bearing Salmond's name in Elgar's hand, the solo part inscribed to 'Felix Salmond with best regards from Edward Elgar Oct 1919', suggesting that it may have been given to him on the occasion of the first performance (27 October).

The piano score forms the basis of the published cello and piano arrangement and Elgar takes great care on the first page to ensure the correct wording of the title: '(Title) / Concerto / in E minor / for / Violoncello & Orchestra / composed by / Edward Elgar Op.85 / Arrangement for Violoncello & Piano / by the composer'. The score includes some further refinements in addition to those mentioned earlier. For example, the solo line at fig. 12:3/b. 73 only achieves its definitive state as a modification to this particular score (Ex. 8.23). Elsewhere, a supplementary half-sheet offers an alternative to the solo part of figs. 25:3–27:2/bb. 69–79 with the query 'Is this too difficult for the repetition[?]'. The amendment was largely incorporated into the final version.

Elgar took great pains over the notation of the piano part throughout the score, particularly the distribution of notes between the hands, and between figs. 53 and 54 in the finale a small additional page is pinned to the score providing an alternative distribution. The piano score is marked up by the printer with the pagination of the published version, but it is clearly the separate autograph part that formed the basis for the printing of the solo

Ex. 8.23 Cello Concerto, first movement, fig. 12:3/b. 73, fair copy

cello line. Here one finds abundant evidence of the close working relationship between Elgar and Salmond in the preparation of the first performance.
The fingerings, probably by Salmond, are relatively few in number and
mainly confined to high-lying passages on the A-string as well as some of
the finale's more intricate passage-work. The bowings may be a combination
of Elgar's own and Salmond's, and therefore have a particular authenticity.
Robert Anderson remarks:

> As a sometime violinist of distinction, and Hans Richter's successor as conductor of
> the London Symphony Orchestra, Elgar's assessment of Salmond's suggestions
> would have been decisive and clear.[17]

The MS also contains a query from the engraver: 'Copy bowing marks into
Full Score & *make phrasing there agree with this*', to which Elgar replies 'Yes',
and a further note from the engraver, 'Omit *fingering* at *present*', suggests that
at some stage there was discussion about including it in the printed part
(though in the event this never materialized).

The details of the autograph solo part and the cello and piano arrangement
do not always correspond with the full score. It is assumed that the discrepancies occurred at proof stage, but as the proofs are lost, it is impossible to tell
which score is the more authoritative. A list of the major discrepancies can be
found in the new Novello edition of the piano arrangement and solo part,
where the bowings agreed by Salmond and Elgar can also be consulted.[18]

The autograph full score of the concerto's last twenty-four bars given by
Elgar to Edward Speyer adds a further layer of mystery to the work's genesis.
Clearly predating the final autograph full score, it is also written on a different type of manuscript paper, with the instrument names ready-printed.
Why only the last four pages? Is it possible that, in addition to the two piano
scores, Elgar wrote a complete full-score draft for this movement (if not the
whole concerto) and subsequently destroyed all but its last four pages? Given
its greater textural complexity and its sketchy first draft, the idea of a rough
orchestral draft for the finale is a real possibility.

The autograph fair copy for cello and piano includes three supplementary
sheets of sketches. The first contains a single line of music: the definitive
version of the troublesome cello part at fig. 73. It is marked 'on p17', referring
to the relevant page of the autograph solo part where the revision has been
neatly pasted in. It seems reasonable to assume that the change was made in
the course of rehearsals with Salmond and jotted down here for the first time.
The second sheet consists of two sides of sketches for the opening of the

---

[17] 'Toward a Flawless Work' p. 438.

[18] Elgar, *Concerto for Violoncello and
Orchestra Op. 85*. Arrangement for violoncello
and piano by the composer, ed. Robert
Anderson and John Pickard (London:
Novello, 2004).

Ex. 8.24(a) Cello Concerto, sketch for third movement

Ex. 8.24(b) Cello Concerto, sketch for third movement

Piano Quintet, op. 84 (whose composition overlapped with that of the Cello Concerto, as well as the String Quartet, op. 83 and the Violin Sonata, op. 82). It is dated 'Sep 8 1918' (during which period Elgar is known to have been completing the Violin Sonata) and inscribed 'to Felix Salmond / in remembrance of / Dec 14 1919 Ed. Elgar'. According to Alice's diary, on this day the quintet was privately performed at Salmond's home (Alice, with just four months to live, was too ill to attend):

> Mr. Reed to dine & went with E. to the Salmonds. A. *could not* go – Rapturous reception of E'.s music, especially the 5tet people were wildly excited & mad over it – A.S. of W. & Charlie, Frank, Robert Nicholls especially enraptured, Newmans, &c &c –

The final supplementary sheet, torn off at the bottom, includes on one side a sketch for the link to the recapitulation in the first movement of the String Quartet. The reverse contains one of the few remaining sketches for the Cello Concerto: a rough draft of the opening of the slow movement. Dated 1919 and inscribed 'Felix Salmond from Edward Elgar', the draft reveals that the movement was initially conceived a whole tone lower, in A♭ major. The page also contains two ideas that were not used in the final version, the latter a particularly haunting phrase whose chromatically rising sequence is more appropriate to the finale's harmonically adventurous slow interlude (Ex. 8.24).

Ex. 8.25 Cello Concerto, sketch for third movement, figs. 37:1–40:4/bb. 26–52, solo line only

Interestingly, a further sketch for the slow movement is preserved within the autograph full score. It is found on the verso of a substitute sheet for the opening of the second movement and runs from fig. 37:1/b. 26 to fig. 40:4/b. 52. Though lacking a key-signature, and with harmonic indications both flimsy and illegible, the music is clearly intended to be in B♭ major, suggesting that this sketch is later than the one presented to Salmond (Ex. 8.25). The sketch is especially fascinating, showing the earliest (and extremely raw) unfolding of what would eventually become one of Elgar's finest harmonic sequences.

Elgar's gift of these pages to Salmond appears carefully calculated, for they are all works of which he gave the premiere.[19] This gesture, together with the gift of the autograph fair copy, indicates the high esteem in which Elgar appears to have held Salmond. It is unfortunate that Salmond never recorded the works for the gramophone and perhaps inevitable that the concerto should have become more closely associated in the early years with Beatrice Harrison, who did. Elgar and Salmond's collaboration on the late works, especially the concerto, is less well documented than Elgar's work with W. H. Reed, or even with Kreisler in the case of the Violin Concerto. Yet these manuscript pages testify to a professional collaboration burgeoning into warm friendship, as Alice's diary entries during 1919 and early 1920 confirm.

---

[19] The Quartet and Quintet were first performed at the Wigmore Hall, London on 21 May 1919. The string players were Albert Sammons and W. H. Reed (violins), Raymond Jeremy (viola) and Felix Salmond (cello). The pianist in the quintet was William Murdoch.

The presentation to Salmond of these few sketch pages probably saved them from the destruction of July 1921, when it seems almost certain that materials for the Cello Concerto and the chamber works were either thrown out or burned. Quite how extensive those sketches originally were is now impossible to determine. Perhaps it is significant that the surviving sketches do not relate to the finale, but that the first draft of that movement contains relatively extensive cutting and pasting directly into the score of what appear to be portions of sketch pages. While it is reasonable to assume that the first three movements were quite thoroughly 'japed-up' prior to the creation of the surviving draft, the finale appears to have developed in a different way. It is possible that a fair proportion of it may well have been more through-composed than was Elgar's custom. The rather chaotic nature of some of its pages may have resulted from an unusually concentrated burst of creative activity in which the music sprang to life more fully formed than usual.

An alternative possibility presents itself: perhaps Elgar created, and later discarded, an even earlier draft for the first three movements along the same lines as the patchwork draft for the finale, then prepared a more legible version (the preserved first draft), but for some reason decided not to do the same for the longer and more complex finale.

Whether this is the true picture or not, it is undeniable that the identification and study of the concerto's first draft brings us significantly closer to the creative decisions behind one of Elgar's greatest works. The composer no doubt took his own famous assertion that 'there is music in the air ... and you simply – simply take as much as you require'[20] quite seriously, but he undoubtedly recognized this to be only part of the truth. Inspiration is one thing; shaping and ordering it into a coherent whole is another matter entirely, and is a process requiring reflection, ruthless self-criticism, and sheer hard work. The first draft of the Cello Concerto, Elgar's final completed masterpiece, reveals the consummate craftsman, still at the height of his powers in the summer of 1919, still struggling to give form and substance to the 'Spirit of Delight' that, within a few short months, would so cruelly desert him.

---

[20] Buckley, Robert J., *Sir Edward Elgar*
(London: John Lane, The Bodley Head, 1904),
p. 32.

9 Lost love and unwritten songs. Elgar's Parker cycle, op. 59

Julian Rushton

In 1908, Elgar received from its author a volume of poems, newly published and significantly entitled *Embers*.[1] Sir Gilbert Parker (1860–1932), an acquaintance of the Elgars through the Stuart-Wortleys, first made a name as a 'popular' novelist; many of his sentimental and heroic adventures were linked to his native Canada.[2] Marrying an American heiress, he settled in Britain and became Conservative MP for Gravesend. Later he was responsible for wartime propaganda, intended to influence the USA to join the Allies; he became a Privy Counsellor, and was created baronet in 1915. His second volume of poems, however, was deliberately disconnected from his busy public persona, being 'printed for the author's personal friends only; they [the verses] ask no public consideration, they struggle for no place'.[3] His first volume of poetry, *A Lover's Diary: Songs in Sequence*, had been published in 1894.[4] It consists entirely of sonnets forming a slender narrative thread, whereas the poems in *Embers* range widely in length and metrical structure, and in genre they include the heroic and folkloric as well as love poems. When republished in the 'Imperial Edition' of Parker's works, the poems were offered with a renewed apology, *Embers* being described as 'merely a book of youth and memory and impressionism in verse'.[5]

Stephen Banfield is surely correct to suggest a match of personality between Parker and Elgar, a conflict between 'the outer love of invigorating, sometimes vulgar spectacle and bombast ... and the inner, private hypersensitivity'.[6] But when Elgar marked eight poems for possible setting, he

---

[1] Gilbert Parker, *Embers. Being a Book of Verses (for private circulation only)*. The copy in the British Library is dated 1908, but Parker wrote inside '1886/G.P./1909'.

[2] Parker's imaginative prose started with short stories (*Pierre and his People*, 1892), and continued in a considerable series of novels. See Damian Atkinson, 'Parker, Sir (Horatio) Gilbert George, baronet (1860–1932)', *Oxford Dictionary of National Biography* (Oxford: Oxford University Press, 2004; online edn, May 2006).

[3] Parker, Foreword to *Embers*, p. v.

[4] Parker, *A Lover's Diary: Songs in Sequence* (Cambridge, MA, and Chicago: Stone and Kimball; London: Methuen, 1894).

[5] Parker, foreword to vol. XVII of the 'Imperial Edition' (London: Macmillan, 1913), p. v. For this edition, he cut about one fifth of the sonnets from *A Lover's Diary*, and added a few poems to *Embers*.

[6] Stephen Banfield, *Sensibility and English Song* (Cambridge: Cambridge University Press, 1985), p. 18. Another resemblance to Elgar

lighted only on those of a hypersensitive nature.[7] At some point he narrowed down the selection to six, and then completed settings of only three. The selection does not adhere to the ordering of verses in Parker's vanity publication, and two of the three completed songs do not set the whole of the chosen poem. Parker seems to have raised no objection to this, nor to have asked for payment; on the contrary, he claimed that having 'the Master of English Music enshrine my words' was reward enough. Although other composers set some of his verses, the tally is not large, certainly if one compares it to contemporaries such as Housman.[8]

Elgar's songs have had an uneven reception, and his choice of poetry may sometimes appear unaccountable. Op. 59 is hardly to be excluded from that stricture, but Parker's occasional stumbles should not cause us to underrate the intensity of feeling embodied in the music. Indeed, critical opinion has tended to favour these songs relative to others, and the words undoubtedly served Elgar's apparent purpose at the time. Diana McVeagh singles out op. 59 as 'the most poignant' of his songs.[9] Michael Kennedy, who once rather oddly associated the first two songs of op. 59 with Elgar's 'happiest vein of fantasy and romance', recently offered a more considered view, characterizing the set as 'nostalgic and intensely romantic, telling of unrequited love'.[10] Nostalgia is also remarked on by Robert Anderson in his fuller discussion of the set.[11] Banfield comments that, in song, 'Elgar's feelings seem to retreat into the poem that expresses them ... The work in which one most regrets this snail-shell retreat is the Gilbert Parker cycle.'[12] Brian Trowell, in his definitive essay on Elgar and literature, discusses all six poems, although without tracing any narrative pattern in Elgar's selection, or any cyclic tendencies in the music.[13] Anderson, however, hints at the latter when he

---

was that Parker was heartbroken at the death of his wife in 1925, but he had already abandoned creative writing; he died in 1932.

[7] The poems (pages in *Embers*) were 'Proem' (p. xi); 'At Sea' (5); 'Was it Some Golden Star' (12); 'There is an Orchard' (69); 'The Waking' (98); 'Aloes and Myrrh' (100); 'The Twilight of Love' (112); and 'The Last Dream' (117). A ninth poem, 'Inside the Bar' (123), was not selected at this time, but was added to *The Fringes of the Fleet*. See Brian Trowell, 'Elgar's Use of Literature', in Monk, *Literature*, pp. 250–3.

[8] Moore, *Publishers*, p. 726. In the foreword to the Imperial Edition, Parker notes that 'Sir Edward Elgar ... has made a song-cycle of several' of the poems, adding that others had been set by 'Sir Alexander Mackenzie, Mr. Arthur Foote, Mrs. Amy Woodforde-Finden, Robert [*recte* Reginald] Somerville

and others' (Arthur Somerville's setting, 'Will You Come Back Home', appears to be later, being published in 1922; one of the Woodforde-Finden settings, however, is dated 1897 in the British Library catalogue, suggesting that some of the poems must have been in circulation prior to publication of *Embers*.

[9] Diana McVeagh, 'Elgar, Edward', in *New Grove 2*, vol. VIII, p. 127.

[10] Kennedy, *Portrait*, p. 230, also drawing attention to a connection of mood between the third song and the Violin Concerto (which is in the same key); Kennedy, *Life*, p. 114.

[11] Robert Anderson, *Elgar*, p. 293: 'the words [*sic*] are instinct with Elgarian nostalgia'.

[12] Banfield, *Sensibility and English Song*, p. 18.

[13] Trowell, in Monk, *Literature*, pp. 251–3.

identifies 'the intervals contained within a descending fourth' as 'an obvious hallmark of the completed songs'.[14]

Late in 1909, when Elgar seems to have contemplated a cycle of six Parker settings, he was more preoccupied with the Violin Concerto. The three he finished were orchestrated – exquisitely – in time for performance by Muriel Foster at the memorial concert for August Jaeger (24 January 1910).[15] The completed songs were to be the third, fifth (or fourth) and sixth of the cycle, and were eventually published as numbers 3, 5, and 6 within Elgar's op. 59; these numbers will be used in the ensuing discussion. The publication of the three completed songs with piano accompaniment suggests that Elgar, in orchestrating them, had not yet abandoned his project of setting more of the poems, and indeed at least two more settings were cursorily sketched.[16] Jerrold Northrop Moore suggests that it was characteristic of Elgar to begin in the middle of a project.[17] The sketches of op. 59 neither confirm nor disprove that this was the case here. There is no knowing why Elgar failed to complete the set, but to leave a work or group of shorter works incomplete was by no means uncommon with him, and perhaps no complicated reasoning is needed to account for it. He turned instead to the 'Pietro d'Alba' songs op. 60, the bassoon Romance, and of course the Violin Concerto.

Viewed as a cycle of six songs, op. 59 lacks its inception (the intended song 1) and part of its development (the intended songs 2 and 4); Moore, therefore, opines that 'the surviving songs must stand individually'.[18] One purpose of this essay is to register dissent from this view. What Elgar left us does form a coherent sequence, and the three songs benefit from being linked by performance.

The order of the planned cycle of six songs is presumed to have been as follows:

1. 'Proem'
2. 'There is an Orchard'
3. 'At Sea' (Elgar's title is 'Oh, Soft was the Song in my Soul'; op. 59, no. 3)[19]
4. 'The Waking'

[14] Anderson, *Elgar*, p. 292, mentioning 'no. 3' but clearly alluding to op. 59, no. 6.

[15] The printed piano accompaniments (London: Novello, 1910, reprinted in *An Elgar Song Album*, 1984) include a few small notes taken over from the orchestral score, which at the time of writing is unpublished. The MS full score is GB-Lbl Add. MS 58025, although listed by Christopher Kent as a sketch (*Guide*, p. 252).

[16] The sketches are in GB-Lbl Add. MS 63157. The MS piano scores of the completed songs,

which preceded orchestration, are in the Elgar Birthplace, Mss 107–9. I am grateful to the staff at the Birthplace for their prompt response, during a period of closure, to my request for copies.

[17] Jerrold Northrop Moore, 'Introduction', in *An Elgar Song Album* (London and Sevenoaks: Novello, c. 1984), p. [iii].

[18] Moore, 'Introduction', p. [iv].

[19] The published version reduces the title to 'Oh, Soft Was the Song'.

5. 'Was it Some Golden Star' (op. 59, no. 5)

6. 'The Twilight of Love' (Elgar's title is 'Twilight'; op. 59, no. 6).[20]

A reading of the sketches shows that the cyclic nature of the project emerged gradually, and may never have been finalized, even as an intention. Elgar may not have worked through his sketchbooks systematically from the first page to the last, but assuming for the purposes of discussion that he did so on this occasion, the first reference to the Parker cycle in Add. MS 63157, on fo. 14, gives the page number of 'The Waking'. The music beneath this, however, has no words, unlike the other sketches, and appears instrumental in character; it may not be for the song at all. The first clearly musical reference is on fos. 19–20, and is a sketch of no. 6, containing the essence of the song in outline. Then came concentrated work on fos. 42–5. On fo. 42^v the opening accompaniment figure of no. 3, 'Oh, Soft was the Song', is marked for flute, the only suggestion of orchestration in all the sketches. The melody that follows, in 3/2 time, was quickly abandoned. Elgar then turned to 'Proem', sketching a setting of about half the poem (fos. 43^v–44). The music is in a stern E minor, but curiously is headed 'after E♭ (or C ?minor)', rendering uncertain its status as no. 1 in the cycle. A sketch for 'There is an Orchard' (fo. 44^r) is perfunctory; the leaf also contains some contrapuntal material which may be a first idea for no. 5 ('Was it Some Golden Star?'), of which a full sketch follows on fo. 44^v, in B minor. Finally there is a near-complete sketch for no. 3, in E♭, starting on fo. 45 and doubling back for a few bars onto the preceding verso; this would have been enough for Elgar to proceed to a voice and piano score.

'Proem' precedes the normal pagination of *Embers* and implies that Parker may have conceived his collection as more than the sum of its parts. It is a metrically free dialogue between a man and an angel, proposing a philosophy of memory and nostalgia in the man's response: 'Who am I that I should hope? / Out of all my life I have been granted one / sheaf of memory ... / Of all else I was robbed by the way, / but Memory was hidden safely / in my heart – the world found it not.' One can imagine Elgar applying this to himself, but he abandoned the setting before reaching these lines, perhaps because it was difficult to find musical ideas more interesting than a form of recitative. Thus, apart from a hint that the 'Man' might sing more lyrically than the angel, and make some use of the major mode, the sketch remains somewhat barren.

---

[20] Trowell, in Monk, *Literature*, pp. 251–2, although he notes that 'The Waking' might have changed places with 'Was it Some Golden Star'; the latter bears the roman IV in the piano MS and, like no. 3 (III), has a note from the composer to the publisher: 'NB Do not engrave the large numerals'. Kent, *Guide*, p. 252, lists 'The Waking' as no. 2 and 'There is an Orchard' as no. 4 or no. 5. Trowell's ordering reflects better what may have been Elgar's intended poetic narrative.

The intended no. 2, 'The Orchard', is a simple love lyric in the present tense: 'There is an orchard beyond the sea . . . / O warm is the nest that is built for me – / In my true love's heart I bide!'[21] Otherwise the linking theme for the songs chosen by Elgar is memory: memory of a love that has ended. We may thus assume 'Proem' to be a preamble, as it is in *Embers*, 'The Orchard' to represent an unsullied memory of contentment in love, and the remainder to trace the broken relationship. Some of Parker's poems apostrophize a dead woman, but in those Elgar chose she seems to be alive, but to have abandoned the poet, who loves her still. In no. 3 ('Oh, Soft was the Song') the poet recalls love-making 'at sea'. Elgar suppressed half the poem and used the first words he set as a title. The first stanza, hardly sensational half a century after *Les Fleurs du mal*, perhaps contained too explicit an allusion to nudity ('And love brooding low, and the warm white glory of thee').[22] An interesting feature is the lack of any main verb in the first stanza; only with the second, which Elgar did set, does it become clear from the past tense that the poem is an erotic memory: 'Oh, soft was the song in my soul, and soft beyond thought were thy lips, / And thou wert mine own, and Eden reconquered was mine.' Elgar constructs a musical form at variance with the poem: he forms two parallel strophes from pairs of the long lines, overlapping at b. 11, and a third strophe (from b. 24) is formed by repeating words in a new combination, the melody punctuated by tender arched phrases from the clarinet. Nevertheless the song is marked 'Allegro' and could easily be interpreted, on its own, as reflection of a love still alive.

'The Waking' begins 'To be young is to dream, and I dreamed no more', but otherwise seems alien in mood. It is in the eventual No. 5, 'Was it Some Golden Star?', that the unhappy outcome of the affair becomes manifest. This poem is a fantasy born of desperation, taking the form of wished-for metempsychosis: 'Once in another land, / Ages ago, / You were a queen, and I / loved you so.' The poet cannot locate his fantasy precisely: 'Was it in Malabar, / Italy, France? / Did we know Charlemagne, / Dido, perchance?'; Elgar here marks the voice *scherzando*, as if trying to raise a smile from some shared memory, but the musical character, governed by an ostinato (see below), does not essentially change. The poet tries to impose retrospective order on his dream: 'I fought for you', he claims, to be rewarded with love. But then (after a pause in the music) he risks the question: 'Have you forgotten it?' Were this poem patterned on Verlaine's *Colloque sentimental* the answer, undoubtedly, would be 'yes'.[23] In *pp*, the lover claims to

[21] 'Proem' and 'The Orchard' are quoted in full in Trowell, in Monk, *Literature*, p. 252.
[22] Trowell considers the first stanza was omitted out of regard for 'propriety' (ibid., p. 251).

[23] In Verlaine's poem, set by Debussy in *Fêtes galantes* (second set, 1904), the ardent lover's 'Do you remember?' is answered by a reiterated 'No', until, in a cynical concession, the last response is 'Perhaps'.

remember it all and ends: 'Whisper the word of life, – "Love is not dead".' There is no reply, other than no. 6, 'Twilight', with its reiterated 'Adieu'. The lover wishfully imagines, thanks to his memories, 'Some time shall the veil between / The things that are, and that might have been, / Be folded back for our eyes to see, / And the meaning of all be clear to me.' But the discrepancy between the lover and the object of his love remains: 'our eyes' may see, presumably in the after-life, but the meaning will be clear only 'to me'.[24]

The three completed songs can be experienced as a short cycle on poetic and musical levels. Their mood may be more homogeneous than would have been the case had Elgar set the other poems. The chosen verses explore increasingly dysphoric memories, leaving little place for goal-directed musical integration, with its proclivity for climax and exhilaration, as in Fauré's *La bonne chanson*, or, indeed, in *Sea Pictures*. There is insufficient space for complex tonal architecture, but Elgar's final choice of keys, in the orchestral version, could suggest a cyclic intention, even though he orchestrated them (and they were first performed) in the 'wrong' order (nos. 5, 3, 6).[25]

In the order established for publication, Elgar started in E major (no. 3), going to its relative C♯ minor (no. 5), then ending in B minor for the 'Adieu' (no. 6).[26] This involved transposing all the songs from the pitch levels of the sketches, respectively E♭, B minor, and C minor. Indeed, in the piano version, the first two were composed in E♭ ('Oh, Soft was the Song') and C minor ('Was it Some Golden Star'); Elgar then changed the key signature and wrote in the necessary changes of accidentals.[27] The MS of no. 6 ('Twilight'), however, is all in its final key of B minor. At what point Elgar abandoned flat keys is uncertain; the chromaticism of 'Twilight' might have made on the spot repairs of accidentals more difficult than with the other songs, and a preliminary complete version in the sketch key, C minor, may have been begun, or completed, and discarded. It is also possible that the choice of keys,

---

[24] Elgar omitted the third stanza of four: 'Adieu! where the mountains afar are dim / 'Neath the tremulous tread of the seraphim, / Shall not our querulous hearts prevail, / That have prayed for the peace of the Holy Grail?' Trowell (in Monk, *Literature*, p. 251) considers it inferior poetry. But Elgar could have omitted it because it suggested a different kind of music.

[25] GB-Lbl Add. MS 58025 begins with no. 5, not no. 3, as listed in Kent, *Guide*, 252. It is perhaps significant that all of no. 5 is in Elgar's hand, whereas, presumably to save him time, the voice part and poem were written out by

Lady Elgar for the other two songs. On the order of performance and reception see Moore, *Lifetime*, p. 217, quoting Lady Elgar's diary; 'Oh Soft was the Song' was encored.
[26] No. 3 was also published in D. Novello's plate number – 13306 – is not adjacent to those of the E major version (13170) and the other completed songs (13172 and 13173).
[27] The manuscripts (Birthplace, Mss 107–9) were used as printer's copy, and contain a few bars pasted over, which I have not been in a position to evaluate from a photocopy, and a number of revisions rewritten for the benefit of the printer on convenient adjacent spaces.

Ex. 9.1 'O Soft was the Song', opening

higher than the sketches in two cases, resulted from consideration of the likely singer, Muriel Foster (although the poetic persona is clearly male). The final keys do at least make a sequence sensitive to the properties of the verse. If going from E major to its relative minor (no. 3 to no. 5) is the simplest of dysphoric steps, C♯ minor to B minor for no. 6 is hardly radical. But it is still affective, implying depression in spirits, which surely mattered more than any theoretical connection (such as Elgar himself had recently drawn) between a key and its iv of iv.[28]

The nostalgia already implicit in no. 3 is subtly conveyed by the ruthless treatment of the instrumental idea with which it opens. Within the conventions of romantic song, the brief semiquaver figure (Ex. 9.1) implies an accompanimental continuum. Qualified in b. 2 by a sustained tonic, thinned to single attacks in b. 3, and reduced to a triplet in b. 5, it vanishes like a

---

[28] Elgar justified the move from A♭ major to F♯ minor in the First Symphony, his most recent large work, by calling the latter subdominant of the subdominant. *Publishers*, p. 710.

Ex. 9.2 'O Soft was the Song', conclusion

memory of the breeze from Eden, to reappear in the penultimate bar.[29] The texture is mainly homophonic, and devoted to the motive exposed by the voice in the second and third bars. After two near-identical stanzas, the third is carefully reharmonized to dilate upon inflections towards the subdominant (F♯ minor, A major), intimated as early as b. 5. The dominant is hardly used, unless deemed to be latent in a short passage on its relative, G♯ minor (bb. 15–16). The last stanza completes what the first (see Ex. 9.1) left open, but at the conclusion subdominant inflections are scarcely neutralized and a flattened sixth, three bars from the end, grinds against the bass's attempt at a normal cadence (Ex. 9.2).

No. 5 ('Was it Some Golden Star?') is marked 'Fantastico' for the piano (or orchestra), but the voice is merely 'mezza voce'. The modality is marked as Aeolian, for the flattened seventh predominates over the true leading-note, yet promises no convincing move to the relative major. As well as b. 1, every even-numbered bar begins on C♯, with the main melodic idea played or sung, untransposed ('A' in Ex. 9.3; the *ossia* reminds us of Elgar's attention to detail). As in no. 3, the opening gesture, this time a severe perfect fourth, is swiftly and progressively eliminated: it covers four beats (b. 1), two beats (b. 3), one beat (b. 5), then disappears until the end. Most of the song is based on the workings of a contrapuntal combination. The main idea ('A') is set successively against two counterpoints ('B' and 'C') that always lie above it, 'B' characterizing the second stanza, 'C' the third (Ex. 9.4). The fourth and final stanza (b. 20) begins with a texturally thickened 'B', but the spare textures so characteristic of this song, and generally untypical of romantic songs, are resumed at b. 24, at which point the triple counterpoint is used at last, with some sense of inevitability, none of climax (it is *più lento*, and *pp*).

[29]The semiquavers in bb. 9 and 19, underlying the euphoric words 'Eden' and 'Life', constitute textural reinforcement, as does the timpani roll (in the piano version, demisemiquaver tremolo, bb. 28–31), and not a reversion to the opening figure.

Ex. 9.3 'Was it Some Golden Star', opening

Ex. 9.4 'Was it Some Golden Star', counterpoint

Texture also articulates the rise and fall of the poet's hopes. The third stanza is more homophonic, the poet evoking his own remembered virility without displacing the obsessive recurrence of 'A' every second bar. At the climactic 'more than all men!' Elgar quotes the main melodic shape of no. 3, the more clearly in the orchestral version through making the violins leap-frog over the woodwind (Ex. 9.5; the *ossia* shows the first violin part). This is one of few passages to offer a glimpse of the relative major (tonic of No. 3).[30] The remembered kiss is, naturally, *dolce*, and this passage extends

---

[30] In the sketch, the figure that appears first in b. 3 always descends: thus the second beat of b. 5 would be e[1], not g♯[1], in this key. The shape resulting from this change produces another reminiscence of no. 3, bb. 33–4, where the flute plays the identical pitches – a[1], g♯[1], f♯[1], g♯[1].

Ex. 9.5 'Was it Some Golden Star', bb. 14–19

the vocal range as high as e². Confidence quickly drains away in an uncomfortable return to the tonic, in first inversion, to end the stanza (the difference between b. 19 and the relatively secure moment of III in b. 7 is small but significant: see the *ossia* staves in the last bar of Ex. 9.5). The final stanza, after

Ex. 9.6 'Was it Some Golden Star', conclusion

the pianissimo triple counterpoint, has a brief coda in which the rough bass fourths return, surmounted by a metrically displaced version of the principal motive, and a metrically weak ending (Ex. 9.6).

Love certainly is dead, as the last song makes clear.[31] 'Twilight' is constructed in three stanzas, with ostinato characteristics that resemble a kind of intermittent passacaglia. The 'passacaglia' theme is a stepwise descent over a fourth, usually in the treble, with a harmonic model clearly implied in the sketch. In the eventual composition, there is harmonic variation towards the middle of the song, which then returns to the original. Bars 1 to 3 follow the implication of the passacaglia theme by harmonies proceeding from I to V. The first harmonic variation is to remove the pedal in b. 4, leading to different chords in the second half of the bar (a substitute V on the third beat, an inverted major tonic on the fourth: Ex. 9.7)). This kind of harmonic incompleteness characterizes the whole song, but b. 5, starting from VI, restores the V and resolves into b. 6. The stanza concludes with the first interruption to the passacaglia, coinciding with a notated change from compound to simple metre.[32] This second idea (from b. 6) begins with implications of the relative, D, but is twisted back in b. 7 when A moves up to A♯. The harmony becomes acutely dissonant on the second and third beats before winding down on the dominant (the sharply characterized seventh chord on the second beat is one of the few harmonies filled out in the sketch).

The second stanza is nearly identical. The reharmonization moves further in b. 13, but the B♭, considered as a promise of D, proves illusory. Each of the three stanzas is lengthened by one bar, as Anderson notes.[33]

[31] Anderson (*Elgar*, p. 293) concludes 'The mood [of no. 5] is playful, the technique masterly'; I agree with the second sentiment, but find the first incomprehensible, particularly in the orchestral version where the pizzicato and timpani reiteration of the tonic evoke the tread of a dead march.

[32] Although the music is only notated in 4/4 from b. 8, bb. 6–7 could be in 4/4 time and in the later stanzas (bb. 14–15 and 24–5) this is how they are notated. Elgar entered a 4/4 time-signature for b. 7 in the piano version and for some reason crossed it through; he seems not to have tried to bring the other verses into line.
[33] Anderson, *Elgar*, p. 293.

Ex. 9.7 'Twilight', opening

Bars 15 and 17 correspond to the first stanza's 7–8; the interloper, b. 16, transposes the passacaglia up a fourth, an idea that intervenes assertively at the start of the third stanza (b. 21). The syncopations give this bar the rhythm of a slow barcarolle of uncompromising harshness, especially

Ex. 9.8 'Twilight', conclusion

in b. 21.[34] The last such intervention, b. 29, is *pp* and reverts to the original pitch and harmony, with added syncopations.

The second stanza settles to the previous music, marked each time by woodwind, at 'And the old days never will come again'.[35] The third stanza restores the deep octave, a shadow over the forlorn hope of enlightenment (bb. 27–8). There are other telling variations in this final stanza, such as the second-beat pause that varies b. 23, otherwise a copy of the model. Another pause on 'our' (b. 25) implies no enlightened lovers' reunion, but serves to distinguish the perceptions of the poet-lover, bereft of hope, from those attributed to the object of his passion. The passacaglia's inexorable tread resumes in a six-bar coda that includes the final 'Adieu'. True, the song ends with a 'tierce de Picardie'. But the last chords (Ex. 9.8), although they partly reverse the harmonic model of the passacaglia, are radical enough to question the entire 'PAC' culture of cadential closure.[36] B major followed by A minor might suggest resolution to E; but A minor to F minor is worthy of *Parsifal*.[37] Metrical progress is stifled by a pause – in the piano version,

[34] This syncopation, not used earlier in the piano version, occurs in the orchestral cellos as early as b. 5.

[35] Elgar's attention to detail appears when he raises the bass one octave at this point (piano version); in stanzas 1 and 3 the cellos, using open C as B♯, are in unison with the double basses, but are an octave higher in stanza 2.

[36] On 'PAC', see Patrick McCreless, ch. 1 in this volume. Anderson comments, 'The final

cadence devises a strange harmonic question out of the descending fourth' – but the progression itself is innocent of that element. *Elgar*, p. 293.

[37] Similar progressions are discussed by Richard Cohn, 'Uncanny Resemblances: Tonal Signification in the Freudian Age', *JAMS*, 57 (2004), pp. 285–323. Cohn cites authorities who characterize such progressions as 'weird', 'supernatural',

superfluously, over the whole-bar G chord, but in the orchestral MS on the fourth-beat F minor chord (the version shown in Ex. 9.8). E minor, F minor, and G major might imply C as an outcome, but essentially tonal direction is lost, and the short final B major chord is like the drop of the curtain on an unresolved tragedy. It is one of Elgar's bleakest moments.

Speculation about any biographical significance for the poems themselves, and then for such remarkable musical thoughts, is tempting but may not lead very far. This is not the place to attempt any psychological interpretation of Parker, although an inference, which may be germane, could be drawn of a lost love, from a period before he met the woman he eventually married. Elgar's songs have been associated with Alice Stuart-Wortley, Elgar's 'Windflower' muse in the period of the Violin Concerto, and with Jaeger.[38] But Jaeger's recent death has no direct analogy to the situation of the poems, and the connection with 'Windflower' was continuing, and soon to bear its finest artistic fruit. Many years before, Elgar had lost his 'Braut' – Helen Weaver – to illness, religious difference, and ultimately to another hemisphere and another man. There is no hint in Parker's verses of a rival in love, and none was involved, as far as is known, in the breaking of Elgar's first engagement. But op. 59 is not *Die Schöne Müllerin* or *Winterreise*; it contains no events, only memories, and in any case this lucid, sentimental poetry might have touched chords in Elgar even if he had not experienced that loss. Nothing in Mozart's life corresponds to Pamina's 'Ach, ich fühl's'.

It seems likely that Elgar failed to finish the cycle not because it moved him too deeply – he had after all completed his settings of the most heart-churning poems – but because he had rapidly brought three songs to completion and fulfilment in performance at the Jaeger concert before accomplishing much work on the others. At this point he moved on to two of his greatest orchestral compositions, the Violin Concerto and the Second Symphony, leaving these melancholy songs by the wayside: embers of a dying fire.

'occluding daylight', and 'tonal death'. Literal death, by explosive mines, is certainly signified when Elgar uses the progression D major to B♭ minor in the fourth song of *Fringes of the Fleet*.
[38] With 'Windflower', Trowell, in Monk, *Literature*, p. 250; with Jaeger, Banfield, *Sensibility and English Song*, p. 18; but 'Nimrod' was commemorated on 24 January 1910 by a performance of the 'Enigma' Variations, and it is more likely Elgar presented the songs because he wanted to offer something new and he could get them ready in time.

10   Heroic melancholy: Elgar's inflected diatonicism

Matthew Riley

'Heroic melancholy' (W. B. Yeats), 'noble resignation' (Anthony Payne), 'crippled grandeur' (Peter J. Pirie), 'smiling with a sigh' and 'stately sorrow' (Elgar himself, the first after Shakespeare): such poetic near-oxymorons seem to gather around Elgar's music and capture something salient about the way people have come to hear his peculiar expressive idiom.[1] They form part of a broader discourse, familiar to anyone conversant with literature on Elgar in the later twentieth century, according to which his music intones 'the funeral march of a civilisation', sounds 'a note of recessional', captures a 'sunset quality', or conveys the equivalent of Edward Grey's famous apothegm: 'the lamps are going out all over Europe; we shall not see them lit again in our lifetime'.[2] To some degree these associations are doubtless shaped by an influential strand within the Victorian cult of chivalry (epitomized by Tennyson's *Idylls of the King*), according to which practically all knights are melancholy, all noble ideals doomed, Arthur's passage to Avalon inevitable.[3] And, although some listeners voiced such reactions while the music was still new, it was not until the 1960s and its political winds of change that this way of hearing Elgar's music became commonplace in post-colonial Britain. Yet, despite the host of cultural factors that mediate the music and condition our subjective responses to it, the strangely double-edged emotional vocabulary employed by Elgar's listeners invites an analysis of the musical object – the identification of parameters that enable such patterns of consciousness to project themselves onto Elgar's music with such ease.

---

[1] W. B. Yeats, letter to Elgar, 23 March 1902, in *The Collected Letters of W. B. Yeats*, ed. John Kelly, 3 vols. (Oxford: Oxford University Press, 1986–97), vol. III, p. 163; Anthony Payne, 'A New Look at Elgar', *The Listener*, 72 (29 October 1964), p. 694; programme note to the first performance of *Introduction and Allegro*, cited in Daniel M. Grimley, '"A Smiling with a Sigh": the Chamber Music and Works for Strings', in *Companion*, pp. 120–38, at p. 124; Ernest Newman, 'Stately Sorrow', in Felix Aprahamian (ed.), *Essays on Music: An Anthology from 'The Listener'*

(London: Cassell, 1967), pp. 101–6; Peter J. Pirie, 'Crippled Splendour: Elgar and Mahler', *MT*, 97 (1956), pp. 70–1. See also David Cairns, 'Heroic Melancholy: Elgar Revalued', in *Responses: Musical Essays and Reviews* (London: Secker and Warburg, 1973), pp. 219–23.

[2] Viscount Grey of Fallodon, *Twenty-Five Years, 1892–1916*, 2 vols. (London: Hodder and Stoughton, 1925), vol. II, p. 20.

[3] For evidence of how these themes chime with those in *Beowulf*, see J. P. E. Harper-Scott, ch. 6 in this volume.

This essay examines certain aspects of Elgar's diatonic writing, in particular the characteristic musical fingerprints that arise from his extension of the expressive resources available in the diatonic system through the use of a specific element – the diatonic augmented fourth. In this way it attempts to flesh out our intuitions about the pathos-inflected nobility that seems so quintessentially Elgarian.

Diatonicism vs. chromaticism

In Elgar's music, stretches of 'pure' diatonic writing often participate in semantic oppositions, the other side being associated with an 'advanced' language of chromaticism and the two being juxtaposed, indeed played off against each other, in the course of a work. In such cases, diatonic passages almost always signify something desirable, chromatic passages something undesirable.[4] The desirable objects or states might be youth, innocence, 'old-time' values or past times themselves, nobility, and even benediction. Most of this vocabulary is familiar – not just from Elgar but from late Wagner and numerous late Romantic composers – and need not be rehearsed here in detail. In summary, though, the use of diatonicism to suggest youth or innocence is found in many parts of the *Wand of Youth* suites and *Starlight Express* music, and in the 'Woodland Interlude' from *Caractacus*; and it can be detected in music with neither text nor overt programme, such as the symphonies. The representation of nobility through diatonicism is evinced by most of the slow tunes in Elgar's orchestral marches, in 'Nimrod', and in the slow movements of the symphonies. 'Archaic diatonicism' is usually achieved by means of an Aeolian minor scale, as in 'Tame Bear' from the second *Wand of Youth* suite and part of the second 'Dream Interlude' from *Falstaff*; this scale can also be found in the main theme of the first movement of the Cello Concerto. Meanwhile, the oratorios deploy diatonicism to represent states of spiritual peace or grace. In most cases, the presence of chromaticism as part of Elgar's musical vocabulary is essential for the full significance of these associations to be grasped. Chromatic passages may frame diatonic ones, creating the sense of an idyll, or they may alternate with them, yielding a 'plot' suggestive of heroic romance (a subject's epic confrontation with and overcoming of antagonistic forces). Jerrold Northrop Moore is one writer who has drawn on these oppositions to interpret Elgar's symphonies and the composer's attitude to the modern world itself.[5]

---

[4] But see some exceptions to this general characterization in Patrick McCreless's discussion, this volume, ch. 1.

[5] See Moore, *Elgar*, pp. 516, 521, 536, 601, 606, 609; also McCreless's discussion of chromaticism, this volume, ch. 1.

Inflected diatonicism

This account of semantic oppositions and sharp dichotomies does not tell the whole story about Elgar's diatonicism. His art contains a crucial 'middle level', as it were: a diatonicism that emphasizes a chromatic – or rather, seemingly chromatic – interval. That interval is the augmented fourth occurring between $\hat{4}$ and $\hat{7}$ of a major scale, or $\hat{6}$ and $\hat{2}$ of a minor. (In what follows the interval will often be referred to as a tritone, but it usually functions as a kind of fourth.) Music theory does not possess a vocabulary for speaking about this particular modal/harmonic complex, yet it contributes decisively to shaping the characteristic, ambivalent Elgarian sound-world.

   In most tonal music, the interval of the tritone performs two sharply contrasted functions. Modern harmonic theory since Rameau has recognized that, as part of the dominant seventh chord, the tritone plays a role in unambiguously affirming, or even defining, a tonic. On the other hand, during the nineteenth century, as a component of ambivalent chromatic harmonies such as the diminished seventh and half-diminished seventh chords, the interval increasingly served to undermine 'Classical' tonality. However, in Elgar's 'inflected diatonicism', the tritone assumes neither of these functions. Its use remains indisputably diatonic, but it is not associated with dominant harmonies or key-defining formulae such as falling fifth progressions in the bass. Instead, the tritone tends to appear when the bass reaches scale degrees such as $\hat{2}$, $\hat{4}$ and $\hat{6}$, and especially when it approaches and leaves them by step rather than by leap. Thus the tritone generally occurs in the course of extended stepwise bass progressions *between* or *around* structural harmonies, often involving sequential patterns in the upper parts. What is at stake above all in Elgar's 'tritone events' is the fact that the augmented fourth reflects a translational asymmetry, as it were, within the diatonic system. Consider a descending chain of $^6_3$ chords – an ubiquitous voice-leading pattern in Elgar (Ex. 10.1). All but one of the chords have perfect fourths between their two upper parts. Only the chord on $\hat{2}$ (if the passage is read in the major) has an augmented fourth. Elgar's music thrives on this type of asymmetry. Sometimes a succession of $^6_3$s will conclude with the chord that has the augmented fourth; alternatively, that chord may be highlighted by means of dynamics, instrumentation, the spacing of the parts, or other techniques. In the vocabulary of post-Schenkerian theory, these

Ex. 10.1 Chain of $^6_3$ chords

points can be expressed in terms of a distinction between 'structure' and 'design'.[6] A feature of voice-leading structure – the contrast between the perfect and augmented fourths – is articulated by certain aspects of design (the term here referring loosely to all musical parameters that do not involve harmonic or contrapuntal relationships). In Elgar's inflected diatonicism, the latent tension and chromatic implications of the augmented fourth are harnessed to full expressive effect.

Few composers have been as sensitive as Elgar to this seemingly innocuous wrinkle in the diatonic system, still less seen fit to draw on it as an affective resource. To be sure, much of Elgar's diatonic writing can be situated in a tradition of nineteenth-century British music by composers such as S. S. Wesley and Parry which deployed textures rich in suspensions and appoggiaturas that Jeremy Dibble has dubbed 'English diatonic dissonance'.[7] For Parry this enriched diatonicism came to be attached to certain moral values; in works such as *Blest Pair of Sirens* (greatly admired by Elgar), he laid the ground for Elgar's 'noble' style and fashioned an idiom in British music that we still commonly hear as 'uplifting'. Some of the typical textures and melodic gestures of Elgar's diatonic writing have obvious antecedents in Parry,[8] yet Parry would surely have baulked at the prominence of the diatonic augmented fourth in some of Elgar's music, had it been drawn to his attention. In his book *Style in Musical Art* (1911), Parry pointed out that the tritone 'was considered especially offensive from the eleventh century until the middle of the nineteenth! . . . even little children were taught to evade [it] by recognised methods in the days when Erasmus was a choir boy at Utrecht!'; he warned against its careless use in modern music.[9] There is, then, a subtle but crucial difference between the two composers' voicing of their shared style. Elgar's 'noble' vein often hints at a yearning quality that is less characteristic of Parry.

Of the sections that follow, the first presents a rough typology of the voice-leading patterns underlying most of the tritone events and indicates some historical antecedents for each type. (These are fairly heterogeneous, but if anything that fact serves to confirm the strength of Elgar's synthesis.) The next section gives examples of each type of event, indicating the ways in

---

[6] See for instance John Rothgeb, 'Design as a Key to Structure in Tonal Music', in Maury Yeston (ed.), *Readings in Schenker Analysis and Other Approaches* (New Haven: Yale University Press, 1977), pp. 72–93.
[7] Jeremy Dibble, 'Hubert Parry and English Diatonic Dissonance', *Journal of the British Musical Society*, 5 (1983), pp. 58–71. See also Dibble, 'Parry, Stanford and Vaughan Williams: The Creation of Tradition', in Lewis Foreman (ed.), *Vaughan Williams in Perspective: Studies of an English Composer* (Ilminster: Albion Music Ltd, 1998), pp. 25–47.
[8] See Jeremy Dibble, 'Parry and Elgar: A New Perspective', *MT*, 125 (1984), pp. 639–43.
[9] C. Hubert H. Parry, *Style in Musical Art* (London: Macmillan, 1911), p. 118.

Ex. 10.2 Models for tritone events: (a) upper-tritone events; (b) lower-tritone events

(a)

(b)

which design articulates structure. The following two sections examine inflected diatonicism in connection with the themes of mystery and angels respectively. The essay ends with some reflections on inflected diatonicism as an art of allusion.

Tritone events

Ex. 10.2 divides tritone events into two main types, to be referred to as 'upper tritone' (UT) and 'lower tritone' (LT) respectively. This distinction reflects whether the tritone occurs among the upper or lower voices of a texture, as well as differences in the voice-leading patterns, in particular the way in which the tritone is resolved. Upper-tritone events (Ex. 10.2 (a)) can be broadly subdivided into two types. The first will be called the 'open sonority': a $^6_3$ chord on $\hat{2}$ in major or $\hat{4}$ in the minor (sometimes involving a $\hat{7}$–$\hat{6}$ appoggiatura or suspension), with the voices arranged in a characteristic manner. An octave or tenth separates the two lower voices, and there are tritones among the upper voices. The sixth of the $^6_3$ chord is in the highest voice. The second type of upper-tritone event is a melodic motive outlining a descending augmented fourth. This interval is often complemented by one, or more usually two, contiguous semitones, yielding a three- or four-note descending motive, which will be referred to as *A* (for 'augmented'). The motive is frequently preceded and/or followed by a similar motive involving a perfect fourth and two whole tones, called *P* (for 'perfect'). Both motives fit snugly into a succession of descending $^6_3$s.

Ex. 10.3 (a) Parry, *Blest Pair of Sirens*, 'O may we again renew that song'; (b) *The Kingdom*, Part II ('At the beautiful gate'), opening; (c) Extract from unidentified popular song cited by Parry

There are clear antecedents in Parry for Elgar's 'open sonorities', as the comparison in Ex. 10.3 (a) and 10.3 (b) shows.[10] But despite the similarities in harmony, melodic outline, and arrangement of voices, Parry's version involves a sustained seventh chord, with the second note of the melody, D♮, relegated to the status of passing note. Elgar's version, by contrast, highlights a diatonic $^6_3$ chord with a tritone by means of texture and dynamics, helping to strike the note of 'joyousness mingled with pity' that A. J. Jaeger recorded in his 'Analytical Notes' on *The Kingdom*.[11]

The motive *A* has obvious antecedents in Baroque music, especially in the awkward chromatic leaps known as 'saltus duriusculus' that were used in pieces intended to express sorrowful or supplicatory affections (for instance, the *Kyrie* and *Crucifixus* of Bach's B minor Mass).[12] But by Elgar's day, the stressing of the tritone as a melodic interval had also become common in what Peter van der Meerwe has called the nineteenth-century 'parlour modes' employed in Viennese popular music, the lighter pieces of

---

[10] This comparison has already been drawn by Jeremy Dibble; 'Parry and Elgar', p. 643.
[11] *The Kingdom: Book of Words with Analytical and Descriptive Notes by A. J. Jaeger* (London: Novello, 1906), p. 14.
[12] John Butt, *Bach: Mass in B Minor* (Cambridge: Cambridge University Press, 1991), p. 85.

Ex. 10.4 Possibilities for 'tritone events' in major and minor

Schubert, Chopin, Grieg, and others, and, later, music-hall numbers.[13] For Parry, these were horrifying developments. To his mind, the 'vulgar' practice of quitting the leading note with a downward leap was bad enough, but 'to tack [the tritone] on to a cavalier treatment of the leading note would seem to be an almost superfluous stroke of mischief. Yet it has been achieved, and evidently affords delight to the perverted sense of the uninitiated.'[14] He cites a popular tune of the day (Ex. 10.3 (c)). Elgar's inflected diatonicism, by contrast, thrives on precisely this technique.

Lower-tritone events (Ex. 10.2 (b)) occur when one of the lower voices in a texture moves from $\hat{6}$ through $\hat{7}$ to $\hat{8}$, with $\hat{4}$ beneath descending to $\hat{3}$. In the uppermost voice, $\hat{6}$ descends to $\hat{5}$. Thus the intermediate formation – what might be termed the 'passing sonority' – involves a tritone below, and a minor seventh above, the ascending middle voice. There are several common variants; in particular, the top voice often includes a suspension. Lower-tritone events probably stem from the decorated plagal cadences and 'Amens' that abound in certain nineteenth-century composers' attempts to invoke a *stile antico* suitable for religious music. A survey of Victorian hymn settings by composers such as S. S. Wesley, Sullivan, and Stainer reveals an abundance of almost all the variants from Ex. 10.2 (b).[15] Elgar makes a significant innovation, however: as will become clear, he often highlights in some way the passing sonority containing the augmented fourth. At times it starts to sound like a chord in its own right – a diatonic half-diminished seventh.

At first sight, upper- and lower-tritone events seem rather distinct. Not only are there obvious textural contrasts, but the augmented fourth is resolved differently in each case. (In lower-tritone events the parts resolve outwards to a minor sixth, whereas there is no such restriction in upper-tritone events. Thus, in the latter, the augmented fourth seldom has a passing function.) Nevertheless, in Elgar's music, both types of event are similarly articulated by design features, and both arise from stepwise bass progressions from scale degrees that do not belong to the tonic triad ($\hat{2}$, $\hat{4}$, and $\hat{6}$; see Ex. 10.4). Only very occasionally do the two types of tritone event seem to merge.

[13] Peter van der Merwe, *Origins of the Popular Style: The Antecedents of Twentieth-Century Popular Music* (Oxford: Clarendon Press, 1989), pp. 223–42.

[14] Parry, *Style in Musical Art*, p. 118.

[15] See for instance Wesley's 'Hereford', 'Colchester' and 'Gweedore'.

Ex. 10.5 Upper-tritone 'open sonority': *Caractacus*, scene iii, (a) fig. 1; (b) fig. 11:2

Examples of 'tritone events'

Ex. 10.5 shows two instances of the upper-tritone 'open sonority' without a
$\hat{7}$–$\hat{6}$ suspension. (All tritone events are labelled with asterisks and, where
necessary, brackets.) In each case, dynamic markings precisely highlight the
open sonority. Ex. 10.6 shows instances of the open sonority including $\hat{7}$–$\hat{6}$
suspensions or appoggiaturas. Ex. 10.6 (a–c) illustrates a very common
procedure in Elgar's music: the principal melodic motive of a period or
piece in the highest voice begins on or rises to $\hat{1}$; the bass then rises from $\hat{1}$ (or
at least an implied $\hat{1}$) to $\hat{2}$, and the melody begins its descent with a $\hat{7}$–$\hat{6}$
suspension or appoggiatura. This moment is initially presented in a relatively
reticent fashion. It is only at the final appearance of the motive – usually at
the climax of the period or piece – that the open sonority, in harness with
other expressive devices, is employed. In each case, the second version of the
motive acquires a dynamic swell, as in Ex. 10.5.[16] The procedure can give the
impression of hidden emotional depths revealed in something apparently
mundane, perhaps by means of reflection or recollection.

Sometimes the open sonority seems to be used self-consciously, almost
like a musical signature. In Ex. 10.6 (d), one of the earliest examples in Elgar's
oeuvre, the open sonority interrupts an otherwise banal, elementary violin
exercise, usurping the role of a cadence at the end of the fourth bar. Again,
dynamic markings reinforce the tritone event.

Ex. 10.7 illustrates techniques of melodic articulation of the upper tritone.
Ex. 10.7 (a–b) shows the way a succession of melodic descending perfect

---

[16] See also the similar passages in *Chanson de
matin* and *Carissima*.

Ex. 10.6 Upper-tritone 'open sonority' with 7–6 suspension appoggiatura: (a) *Serenade for Strings*, second movement; (b) *Dream Children*, no. 2; (c) 'Enigma' Variations, no. 6, 'Ysobel'; (d) *Very Easy Exercises in the First Position*, op. 22 (1892), no. 1

Ex. 10.7 Upper-tritone melodic articulation: (a) *Chanson de matin*; (b) *Rosemary*; (c) *In the South*; (d) *The Dream of Gerontius*, Part I ('Be merciful'); (e) Violin Concerto, first movement; (f) *In Smyrna*; (g) Psalm 29 ('Give unto the Lord'); (h) *The Dream of Gerontius*, Part I ('Be merciful')

Ex. 10.7 (cont.)

(g)

(h)

fourths will often end with an augmented fourth. In Ex. 10.7 (a), a crescendo is marked just before the occurrence of the augmented fourth; in Ex. 10.7 (b) the tempo is relaxed instead. The rest of Ex. 10.7 illustrates the melodic articulation of the upper tritone with the motive *A*. In each case, any appearances of the complementary motive *P* are indicated. Each of Ex. 10.7 (c–e) is based on a succession of sixth chords, with the melodic tritone descent coinciding with a $^6_3$ that has an augmented fourth. A similar, though slightly decorated, version of the pattern underlies Ex. 10.7 (f). Ex. 10.7 (h) illustrates a characteristic Elgarian technique: when *P* changes to *A*, various musical parameters combine to evoke a more sombre mood. The statement of *P* is sung by tenors in the middle of their register, whereas the answering *A*, sung by altos at the bottom of theirs and accompanied by clarinets, has a darker colour.[17] (In Ex. 10.7 (h), the final notes of the respective motives seem to be missing, but in fact they occur an octave higher at the start of the next phrases, on 'be gracious'; compare Ex. 10.7 (d), the complete motive.)

Ex. 10.8 shows lower-tritone events; each can be correlated with one or other of the variants in Ex. 10.2 (b). Ex. 10.8 (a–b) confirm the strong religious associations of the pattern. The remaining parts show instances of articulated lower tritones. Ex. 10.8 (c–d) show a typical function of lower-tritone events: to underpin the climax of a musical paragraph, especially one based on sequences or motivic repetition. (This is another common way in which Elgar's music articulates asymmetrical aspects of the diatonic system; further instances are to be found in the second of the *Three Bavarian Dances*

---

[17] For further instances of *A*, see *The Black Knight*, opening of scene, 'Serenade' from the   first *Wand of Youth* suite, and the central section of *Chanson de matin*.

Ex. 10.8 Lower tritone events: (a) Chant for Psalm 68; (b) *The Dream of Gerontius*, Part I ('Go forth'); (c) Symphony no. 1, first movement; (d) *Introduction and Allegro*; (e–h) *The Music Makers*: (e) fig. 2:8; (f) fig. 88:7 ('[renew] our world as of yore; You shall teach us'); (g) fig. 50:6 ('[the] land to which they are [going]); (h) fig. 39 ('a breath of our inspiration')

Ex. 10.8 (cont.)

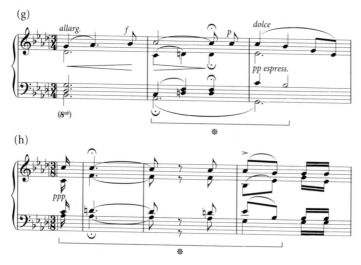

(g)

(h)

and the second movement of the *Sonatina* for piano (1932).) Both instances, in their different ways, have a strong yearning character – the first serene, the second impetuous. Ex. 10.8 (e–h) – four variants of the same idea – again show the lower-tritone progression occurring at climaxes, and reveal an abundance of techniques for highlighting the 'passing sonority' containing the augmented fourth. Ex. 10.8 (e) employs accents and a dynamic swell; 10.8 (f) combines these with a pronounced reduction in tempo; 10.8 (g) combines a pause on the passing sonority with further dynamic and tempo directions; while 10.8 (h) – a remarkable conception – lingers on the passing sonority at *ppp* and then falls into complete silence before effecting the necessary resolution.[18] In the latter case, the passing sonority is almost – but not quite – emancipated from a contrapuntal function and treated as pure 'sonority'.

How do the two main types of tritone event relate to each other? Ex. 10.7 (f–g) show that when the motives *A* and *P* are used in conjunction, *P* may coincide with a lower-tritone event. Yet this merely emphasizes the distinctness of the two types. Ex. 10.9 shows some more significant connections. In Ex. 10.9 (a) a single motive is supported first by an upper- then a lower-tritone event. In Ex. 10.9 (b), the two types of event seem almost to be superimposed. In the penultimate bar, the upper parts suggest an open sonority, whereas the lower parts execute the ascending passing motion characteristic of the lower-tritone model. The presence of the many F♯s in

---

[18] The passing sonority is a *Tristan* chord; see the discussion of Elgar's use of this chord by Patrick McCreless in this volume, ch. 1.

Ex. 10.9 Upper and lower tritones in combination: (a) *The Apostles*, Part I, fig. 40:2; (b) *The Kingdom*, Part I, fig. 34:5–8

the preceding bars enhances the effect of the F♮s, which, when they come, seem all the flatter, and the fourths that they make with the B♮s all the more augmented. Those outward-pressing fourths, heard against a plagal cadence, yield a rich and characteristically Elgarian sound.

Mysterious tritones

Elgar seems to have had a special fondness for the key of G minor, especially when used for sombre or mysterious effects. He liked to combine music in that key with contrasting passages in G major which, in comparison, sound bright, fresh, or idyllic. Jerrold Northrop Moore has pointed out that Elgar returned to the G minor/major complex on a roughly three-year cycle: in 1893 *The Black Knight* (begun three years earlier in 1890); in 1896 the Organ Sonata (as well as the Introduction to *Scenes from the Saga of King Olaf*); in 1899 the 'Enigma' Variations; in 1902 *Dream Children*; and in 1905 in the *Introduction and Allegro* (plus *In Smyrna*). As shown by Ex. 10.6 (b) and 10.7 (f), diatonic tritones occasionally feature prominently in the G major episodes in this music; however, they are more common in the sombre passages in minor, and contribute tellingly to the characteristic mood of these episodes.

The second bar of the 'Enigma' theme contains a fleeting diatonic tritone between first and second violins, although a more distinctive instance occurs in the third bar. The latter is a lower-tritone pattern, albeit with the two upper parts covered by a single voice – a moment of compound melody which is the source of most of the falling sevenths in the 'Enigma' Variations.

(The resolution, however, is relatively unusual in Elgar's practice: instead of proceeding to chord III in first inversion, the next harmony is an applied dominant to chord IV, supporting another falling seventh in the melody.) The tritone event occurs at the melodic apex of the theme's six-bar opening period, and it continues to underpin melodic apexes throughout the work, for instance in Variations IX and XII. Ex. 10.10 (a) shows part of the return of the opening material in the final part of the theme's overall ternary form, the middle section having been a lyrical interlude in G major. Now the mood is still darker and the tritone complex is intensified. Elgar adds a counter-subject in the tenor register played by one of his favourite instrumental

Ex. 10.10 Mysterious tritones: (a) 'Enigma' Variations, theme; (b) *Dream Children*, no. 1; (c) 'The Prince of Sleep'

combinations: violins *sul G* doubled in unison by cellos and clarinets. The countersubject reaches down to an A, making a tritone with the Eb in the bass. It then rises a seventh, exchanging places with the melody of the theme, which falls to the A. Two bars later the countersubject falls by an augmented fourth and then a semitone, imitating the contour of motive A (although the harmony at this point is admittedly chromatic). This wonderfully scored passage – the first violins divided in octaves to produce a more transparent sonority for the theme itself; the dynamic contours of the two lines carefully staggered; wind instruments introduced sparingly to add flecks of colour at melodic apexes or for significant harmonies – is another of those moments in Elgar where hidden depths are unexpectedly revealed.

In *Dream Children* – two short pieces inspired by a ghostly story by Charles Lamb – the expressive role of the diatonic tritone is even more pronounced. The first of the two pieces, like the 'Enigma' theme, is in ternary form, the outer sections being in G minor, the inner section this time in Eb major. The tritone event in question occurs in the final bar of the first section, at the approach to the final cadence of that section (Ex. 10.10 (b)). To this point the music has been hushed: strings are muted while clarinets play a melody in thirds at *ppp*. Now the strings drop out of the texture, leaving only clarinets and bassoons to cadence on the tonic. When, one bar later, the strings re-enter, they form a texture sharply contrasted to that of their previous music. Both first and second violins are divided in octaves, with fourths and fifths between adjacent parts (sometimes augmented fourths and diminished fifths), and they move in contrary motion against the violas and cellos, leaving wide open spaces throughout the textures (at one point a major tenth between second violins and violas). The dynamic level swells suddenly to *forte* before dying away again. The tritone event occurs near the start of the swell: an open sonority on the second quaver of the bar. No fewer than four tritones are piled on top of one another, with none of the 'gaps' between them filled in. Although marked *molto lento*, b. 8 gives the impression of a sudden surge of gloomy emotion which subsides almost as quickly as it had arisen.

Elgar's late part-song 'The Prince of Sleep' (1925), to words by Walter de le Mare, recaptures the G minor tritone complex. This piece has all the virtues of the best examples of the part-song genre: understated but finely crafted, with a subtlety of expression. The first verse of the poem (Ex. 10.10 (c)) is suitably mysterious, and Elgar repeats it, with the same words and music, at the end of the song. He uses diatonic half-diminished seventh chords at bb. 1, 2, 4, 5, and 6 (marked with asterisks), with the tritone between the outer parts. In b. 7, scale degree 2 is lowered, producing Neapolitan harmony and eliminating the diatonic tritones; however, as in Ex. 10.9 (b) this alteration makes the final diatonic tritone event all the more striking when it finally comes. A series of chromatic tritones follows (C♯–G and C–F♯ in b. 8 and D–A♭ in b. 9), before the period finally cadences by means of an upper-tritone open sonority. In the last phrase, marked *pp* and *rit.*, sopranos and second basses fall to their lowest pitches in the song. As in *Dream Children* (and several other G minor pieces, such as the Introduction to *King Olaf*), the upper part leaps to $\hat{5}$ at the cadence. The text at this point – 'Lovely in a lonely place' – is another instance of the ambivalent or paradoxical phrases that point to Elgar's characteristic idiom. He exploits a further ambivalence in the very sound of the word 'lonely'; the open sonority appears precisely when the warm 'əʊ' is replaced by the colder 'i'. Indeed, the whole song evinces a heightened sensitivity to the contrast between 'open' and 'closed' textures – that contrast being a vital technical resource for the composer of unaccompanied part-songs for amateur choirs. Elgar's experience of part-song writing may help to account for his general awareness of the expressive possibilities of open sonorities.

Heavenly tritones

At first glance *The Dream of Gerontius* seems to draw deeply on the absolute semantic oppositions of diatonicism and chromaticism that were outlined early in this chapter. In Part I alone, the motives that A. J. Jaeger labelled 'Fear', 'Despair', and 'Death' are conspicuously chromatic, whereas 'Christ's Peace' and the music for words such as 'Kyrie eleison', 'Rescue him', and 'Novissima hora est' are diatonic.[19] Indeed Part I charts an overall course from agonized chromaticism to radiant diatonicism as the anxious prayers of the dying man and the assistants are replaced by the magisterial intervention of the Priest, banishing the fevered bedside atmosphere in a blaze of pure D major. As for Part II, the music of the rapt opening section, representing the experience of the newly disembodied Soul, does not introduce an accidental until its eighteenth bar, whereas in the Demons' Chorus, the Angel of the Agony's solo and the chords at and immediately prior to the moment of judgement, chromaticism is rampant. From this perspective, the oppositions of good and evil, peace and turbulence, fear and consolation, could hardly be more starkly etched.

But first impressions may mislead. After all, the subject-matter of Newman's poem does not rely primarily on a conflict of antagonistic forces – not, at least, outside the individual soul. The Demons may be raucous and

---

[19] *The Dream of Gerontius: Book of Words, with Analytical and Descriptive Notes by*   A. J. Jaeger (London: Novello, 1901, reprinted 1974), pp. 4–5, 8.

insulting, but by the time they are encountered in Part II they are powerless to influence the Soul of Gerontius. 'I see not those false spirits', he observes, and, in a passage of the text Elgar omitted: 'How impotent they are! and yet on earth / They have repute for wondrous power and skill.' Instead the poem, despite its strong narrative thread, ultimately revolves around a philosophical 'story' concerning the soul's own inner development and consciousness. That story relates the transformation of one mode of 'agony' into another and the eventual release from the second state: the physical agony of death becomes the spiritual agony of Judgement, after which the Soul accepts its place in Purgatory.[20] The events that take place in the poem serve this higher purpose, for they show the Soul learning the mysteries of the spiritual world and the nature of its own fate from a combination of quasi-sensory impressions, the explanations of the Guardian Angel, and, finally, the very sight of God. The Angel describes the effect of the glimpse of the Divine countenance by means of paradoxes: 'that sight of the Most Fair / Will gladden thee, but it will pierce thee too'; 'Learn that the flame of the Everlasting Love / Doth burn ere it transform'; 'the face of the Incarnate God / Shall smite thee with that keen and subtle pain; / And yet the memory which it leaves will be / A sovereign febrifuge to heal the wound; / And yet withal it will the wound provoke, / And aggravate and widen it the more.' These paradoxes explain why the Soul will in due course embrace the flames of Purgatory voluntarily. Indeed, the opposing impulses of love and shame in one sense themselves constitute the purifying flame: 'And these two pains, so counter and so keen, – / The longing for Him, when thou seest Him not; / The shame of self at thought of seeing Him, – / Will be thy veriest, sharpest purgatory.' What Byron Adams refers to as the 'Wagnerian dialectic of shame and grace' in Elgar's mature oratorios is here raised to its highest tension.[21] The sight of God does not effect anything so obvious as a redemption from sin or a triumph over evil, but instead raises the Soul's consciousness of its own imperfection to a new level, so that it willingly accepts its destiny.

In this light it might be expected that a straightforward deployment of the musical opposition of diatonicism and chromaticism could not alone do justice to the philosophical subtleties of Newman's poem. And, sure enough, a closer inspection of Part II of Elgar's composition reveals that, as the poem's philosophy becomes more sophisticated, instances of 'inflected diatonicism' become common. Part I, aside from 'Be merciful' and a few hints in

---

[20] See Michael Wheeler, *Death and the Future Life in Victorian Literature and Theology* (Cambridge: Cambridge University Press, 1990), ch. 7, 'Newman, *The Dream of Gerontius*'.

[21] Byron Adams, 'Elgar's Later Oratorios: Roman Catholicism, Decadence and the Wagnerian Dialectic of Shame and Grace', in *Companion*, pp. 81–105.

the Priest's music, is almost free of them. They are also absent from the diatonic Introduction to Part II, which is altogether too serene to admit such ambivalence. Instead, the expressive effect of diatonic tritones is reserved for the music of beings that possess a clear philosophical understanding of the Soul's destiny – in other words, for the music of angels. The point admittedly does not apply to the Angel of the Agony, for his plea on behalf of the Soul is uttered in a language of the ripest late Romantic chromaticism. Rather, it refers to the Guardian Angel and the choirs of angels who sing the chorus 'Praise to the Holiest'. The calm, poised melancholy of much of their music matches their insight into veiled truths which the Soul itself as yet perceives only dimly.

The first tritone event in the angels' music occurs, appropriately, just as the Soul gains its first intimation of the experience that awaits at its judgement: 'And the deep rest, so soothing and so sweet, / Hath something too of sternness and of pain.' On the word 'pain', the music later to be associated with the Guardian Angel makes its first appearance (Ex. 10.11 (a)) – a lower-tritone progression which is left incomplete, the 'passing sonority' with the augmented fourth receiving no immediate resolution (just as in the 'Enigma' theme, a single part here fleetingly takes on the roles of two different voices). The resolution is withheld until fourteen bars later, following several further incomplete statements of the progression. Appropriately it occurs just before the soul's exclamation, 'Oh what a heart-subduing melody!' In the song that follows, the Guardian Angel sings this complete version of the progression twice; the second occasion carries special force as it coincides with the words 'This child of clay / To me was giv'n, / To rear and train / By sorrow and pain.' In this case the word 'sorrow' is sung to a descending perfect fourth, an interval which makes its own significant contribution to the mood of the angelic music, as will become clear.

The next few tritone events occur during the first chorus of angels in 'Praise to the Holiest' (the 'Angelicals'). The main theme or 'refrain' of the chorus – the material to which the words 'Praise to the Holiest' are set – begins with a five-bar antecedent phrase that sinks through a seventh from Eb to F. After a pause, the melody gains impetus at the start of the five-bar consequent phrase, with an energetic rising sixth marked with a crescendo over a lower-tritone progression (Ex. 10.11 (b)). The descending perfect fourth is again present – at the end of the bar. A little later a tritone event marks another upsurge in energy (this one resembles a lower-tritone event, although the model is significantly deformed). After two hushed phrases, there is a loud outburst on 'To serve as champion in the field / Of elemental war'. Here the diatonic half-diminished seventh chord containing its tritone on 'field' is combined with another descending perfect fourth in the melody. A further tritone occurs in the accompaniment at the end of the phrase, an

Ex. 10.11 Heavenly tritones: *The Dream of Gerontius*, Part II: (a) fig. 9:2 (the Angel); (b) fig. 11 ('Oh what a heart-subduing melody'); (c) fig. 61:5 ('Praise to the Holiest', refrain); (d) fig. 80:5 ('O gen'rous love!'), chorus parts only

example of a diatonic chain of descending fourths in which the final fourth is augmented.

The most sustained use of diatonic tritones in the angels' music occurs when the theologically most significant verses of the chorus are reached, in the section that lies between the two grand statements of the 'Praise' refrain. This section reproduces on a large scale the contour of the two phrases of the refrain itself, for it consists of a great diminuendo leading to a hushed, sombre passage, which leads in turn to a long crescendo into the next statement of the refrain. The hushed passage touches on the keynote of the poem (and the oratorio) – the two forms of agony experienced by the Soul in its passage from death to Judgement:

> O gen'rous love! that He who smote
> In man for man the foe,

> The double agony in man
>   For man should undergo;
> And in the garden secretly,
>   And on the cross on high,
> Should teach His brethren and inspire
>   To suffer and to die.

The setting of the first of these two verses relies largely on just three chords: tonic, subdominant, and supertonic seventh (i.e. diatonic half-diminished seventh). With no dominant chords, the music is conspicuously diatonic (accidentals are required only when the music is transposed to, and repeated in, another key). The harmonies with tritones occur on words such as 'love', 'smote', and 'agony' – a fitting combination for the love that 'doth burn ere it transform'. The first of these coincides with the climax of a dynamic swell (Ex. 10.11 (c)), the second is marked by an accent, and the third is high-lighted by a crescendo through the very word 'agony'. The setting of the second verse draws on a wider harmonic palette, and contains one especially rich harmonic progression, which, though not diatonic, involves a series of tritones in the inner voices. On its repetition it sets the words 'To suffer and to die'.

  'Praise to the Holiest' ends with a triumphant blaze of C major and an emphasis on the diatonic augmented fourth F–B. At fig. 99 there is a series of interlocking rising phrases with $\overset{\wedge}{4} - \overset{\wedge}{3}$ appoggiaturas at the apex of each. The third and final appoggiatura uses the augmented fourth. The concluding cadence that ensues consists of a lower-tritone progression imitating a decorated plagal 'Amen'. The 'passing sonority' becomes the climax of the entire chorus: it is marked with an accent and with *ffz*, while the soprano part leaps up an octave to a top A.

  Diatonic tritones are used sparingly in the remainder of the work, and mainly retrospectively. The Angel's Farewell makes use of the Guardian Angel's tritone event in both its complete and incomplete versions. A notable instance occurs in one of the most beautiful passages in the whole work: that between fig. 132 and 134. Here the music slips from the local tonic, E major, to the flat submediant, C major, for a reminiscence of the first two bars of the 'Praise' refrain, sung by the women's voices. The Guardian Angel's tritone now appears once again and is completed by a resolution to a B major chord. Against these orchestral harmonies the Angel sings the word 'Farewell' to a descending perfect fourth. The consequent phrase of the 'Praise' refrain enters with its lower-tritone patterns as the Angel offers encouragement: 'but not for ever! brother dear'. He continues by echoing the first 'Farewell' with a succession of descending perfect fourths for the words 'Be brave and patient on thy bed of sorrow; / Swiftly shall pass thy night of trial here, / And

I will come and wake thee on the morrow. Farewell.' The melodic contours of the soloist, the chorus and the orchestra all make a series of broad dips, indicating the Soul's gentle descent to Purgatory and its acceptance of its fate. At this point, then, it might be felt that the perfect fourths smooth over the more ambivalent mood of the augmented fourths and lead to the peaceful D major close.

An art of allusion

In Elgar's later works, the profile of tritone events becomes less distinct; they are infiltrated by additional chromatic elements which alter the delicate balance that formerly held between the tritone and its diatonic context. Their expressive quality thus changes too. To the listener experienced in Elgar's style they now function as a form of self-reference or allusion, recalling a familiar Elgarian tone amidst a relatively advanced harmonic language. In 'For the Fallen', the finest of Elgar's compositions from the years of the Great War, a modified lower-tritone pattern is made the basis for a descending chromatic sequence (Ex. 10.12 (a)). The characteristic 6–5 suspension is present, although the passing motion usually found in an inner part is absent, and the bass rises instead of falling. The passage nevertheless mediates between the intense chromaticism of the opening bars of the piece and the relatively diatonic, lyrical melody that follows; in fact the sequence falls away from the climax of the lyrical material and leads back to the opening. When the chorus eventually sings this music, the words strike an appropriate note of heroic melancholy: 'Death august and royal / Sings sorrow up into immortal spheres.'

   Towards the end of the finale of the Cello Concerto a series of modified tritone events occurs during the anguished, highly chromatic music that precedes the coda (Ex. 10.12 (b)). A lower-tritone pattern is twice suggested, albeit beginning with an augmented sixth (and then diminished seventh) sonority rather than a $\frac{5}{3}$ chord, so that the lower parts in fact contain parallel tritones. On the second occasion the pattern resolves with the usual 6–5 suspension to a diatonic $\frac{6}{3}$ chord: a fleeting moment of repose and diatonic clarity. There follows an instance of the motive *A* in the orchestra followed by several melodic tritones for the soloist, again underpinned by chromatic harmony; chromaticism abates only with the subsequent idyllic reminiscence of the slow movement. The expressive significance of these patterns can only be fully appreciated when they are heard against the background of diatonic models in Elgar's earlier music.

   But even in that earlier music Elgar's inflected diatonicism had been developing into a subtle 'art of allusion' in which tritone events are, as it

Ex. 10.12(a) 'For the Fallen' (*The Spirit of England*), fig. 2; (b) Cello Concerto, fourth
movement, bb. 290–300

were, cannily invoked at key moments. The events can be considered to
partake of varying levels of self-conscious reference, partly in accordance
with the degree and manner of their articulation through design parameters.
To quote James Hepokoski, the 'practice of frequent near-quotation or
passing allusion – "intertextuality" – was an essential feature of [Elgar's]
expressive world'.[22] From this perspective, the tritone events take their place
amidst the complex tissue of allusion that marks Elgar's musical aesthetic,
alongside self-quotation, thinly disguised references to other composers'
music, and the recollection of material from one movement of a work in a
later one.[23] They resonate with each other, marking occasions when the

[22] James Hepokoski, 'Elgar', in D. Kern
Holoman (ed.), *The Nineteenth-Century
Symphony* (New York: Schirmer Books, 1997),
pp. 327–44, at p. 328.
[23] Self-quotation is most obvious in *The
Music Makers*, but is already present in *The*

Apostles, where a theme from *The Light of Life*
is recalled. The music for Algernon
Blackwood's play *The Starlight Express*
re-uses material from the *Wand of Youth*
suites, while the *Nursery Suite* (1931)
contains a quotation from the Violin Sonata

musical subject steps 'outside the frame' (to whatever degree) to listen to the characteristic Elgarian idiom.

But in order for Elgar's tritone events to function in this fashion – ranging freely over the space between 'unconscious' personal style and 'deliberate' self-reference – there must be a larger framing context that does *not* employ them. The multitude of examples in this chapter should not create the impression that they saturate his music; in fact, he deploys them relatively sparingly, often keeping them in reserve for decisive moments. This is perhaps the key to the lasting impact of Elgar's diatonic tritone events. If, like the Spirit of Delight, they come but rarely, they come with still more telling effect.

(1918). The most obvious allusion to another composer is a theme in the finale of the First Symphony (fig. 114), which echoes a parallel passage from the finale of Brahms's Third (fig. C). See Aidan Thomson, 'Unmaking *The Music Makers*', this volume, ch. 4; also Allen Gimbel, 'Elgar's Prize Song: Quotation and Allusion in the Second Symphony', *19CM*, 12/3 (1989), pp. 231–40. Recollection of one movement in another is apparent in almost all Elgar's multi-movement orchestral works.

Index